TAMING

THE

POUND

TAMING
THE
POUND

KIM STEPHENSON

Matador
9 Priory Business Park
Kibworth Beauchamp
Leicestershire LE8 0RX, UK
Tel: (+44) 116 279 2299
Fax: (+44) 116 279 2277
Email: books@troubador.co.uk
Web: www.troubador.co.uk/matador

ISBN: 978-1848767-522

British Library Cataloguing in Publication Data.
A catalogue record for this book is available from the British Library.

Typeset in 11pt Adobe Garamond Pro by Troubador Publishing Ltd, Leicester, UK
Printed and bound in the UK by TJ International Ltd, Padstow, Cornwall

Matador is an imprint of Troubador Publishing Ltd

For Douglas Stephenson (1927 – 72) and Margaret Stephenson (nee Milton, 1920 – 1968), I think you would have liked it.

Introduction

This book is about handling money – but most of all it is about you. For fourteen years I was a financial advisor and I made my living from helping people handle their money. For the last thirteen years I've been an Occupational Psychologist and made my living from helping people (in and out of organisations) make the best use of their abilities.

I'm the only person in the world who has done and is qualified to do both those jobs and whatever anybody else tells you, *the important bit about handling money is not the money – **it's you.***

Whether you are reading out of interest, to find some help for yourself, or to help others, it is you that makes the decisions, so **you** are the most important part

But I don't know you personally.

I can give ideas that are proven and use exercises that are established ones used by psychologists and coaches, or things I've devised and tested out in my own coaching and training specifically for handling money. I can try to guide you towards understanding what will work for different types of people, and offer choices of how you *might* do it, but in the end you have to make the decisions as to what sort of person you are and what you *will* do that will work for you.

You'll only get anything from the book if you *do* something aside from reading it. F.E.Smith, a famous barrister, had a wonderful exchange with a judge:

Judge: *Mr Smith, having listened to your case, I find I am no wiser than before.*

Smith: *Possibly not, m'lud, but far better informed.*

You can only get "wiser" if you do something, otherwise you are simply better informed. If you don't do anything other than say, "that book was great, it's really interesting" then, much as I'll be pleased that you enjoyed it, I'll have failed because you won't be any nearer taming your own, personal pound or really understanding how important *you* are.

I've highlighted some things.

Ones like this:

What is money for?

Are exercises to do or questions to ask yourself or to ponder – and preferably to write down your own answers to.

Ones like this

> *So we actually need to understand ourselves rather than the money.* ***You*** *are bigger and more important than money.*

Are points that are particularly important.

And I've put a bullet point summary of key ideas at the end of each chapter.

You can skim it for the key bits, or read it through, but if you want to get the best out of it I'd suggest that you look through the book at least once in order. I've set it out the way I have because I've taught people the material and this order works.

Once you know where things are, by all means dip into the sections that are relevant to your situation at the time. Also, have a look at the website (before, during and/or after) www.tamingthepound.com

Contents

What each chapter is about and books that give more information on that topic.

mistakes we make and have the talents we have. *The Blank Slate* and *How the Mind Works* by Steven Pinker, *The Adapted Mind* by Barkow, Cosmides & Tooby.

What it is useful to teach children about handling money and how do you do it? *The Economic Socialisation of Young People* by Furnham.

Money, money, money - (good God y'all) what is it good for?

The symbols we use for money. What you think about it makes a big difference to whether you use it, or it uses you. The chapter sets out some of the basics and gives you questions to ask yourself about what your symbols are.

What is money for?

Does that sound like a stupid question? Pause a moment.

Imagine that we don't have money. You can't write cheques or hand over a credit card for things, and there is no cash. How do you get food? If you want a Sunday roast, maybe you trade a bushel (whatever that is!) of apples and offer to fix the roof of the person who is trading the roast. Of course, sod's law says he doesn't want his roof fixed, so you have to trade the roof fix job to a woman who will fix this other woman's car who has some coffee that she will trade for the roast. But how do you work out what each job or thing is worth relative to one another, and how do you handle change?

Money is a way to solve those problems. You know how much things cost, in money. The money is easily divisible (you don't have to work out what four fifths of a cow less one third of goat looks like in terms of roof repairs) and everybody accepts the money. Simple. But because it is so simple, people forget what it is for. It used to be a means to an end. Now, for a lot of people, it is an end in itself.

No, keep the change,
they will only bag my pockets.

So what IS money for? It sounds a silly question, but most people don't ask it, they make assumptions based on what we are all told.

We are told, for example:

- Everybody wants more money. So why do we ever give to charity? Do we ever stop to work out what it is we actually want from our money?

- Finance is really complicated and you have to "understand money". But how complicated is money compared to bartering, which is what we used to do? If we can understand barter, why can't we understand money?

- People don't buy pensions because they are too complicated. So how can children of 8 use smart phones, recordable CD players etc? Aren't those complicated? Or do we happily learn complicated things if we want to, but not if we're bored with or scared of them?

- Credit and debit are made too complicated for us, so we need internet sites and experts to help us. But if we know what we want why can't we just buy that and not pay for anything we don't want? Or is it that marketing relies on something more powerful in us than logic, and rather than decide what we want we just buy whatever they are selling?

So we actually need to understand ourselves rather than the money. You are bigger and more important than money.

I want to help you to go from

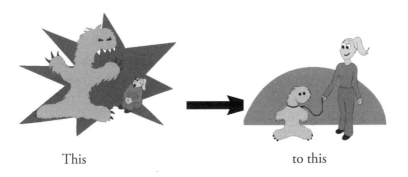

This   to this

I call it **Taming the Pound,**

It is about turning the money from a big, scary monster to a tame beast that does what you want. The aim is that you control the money – not the other way round.

It isn't surprising that you might get confused or scared about money, but the money really isn't complicated. After all, at the end of the day, most people can do £1 + £1 = £2 and get the right answer, even if they need to use their fingers.

That's all money is. You might need to scale it up a bit, but you don't get money suddenly changing identity part of the way through,

£1 is always £1. But people! If you have one person, and add another person, what have you got? You might have a happy couple, a fight, the cure for cancer, a weapon of mass destruction; who knows what you get?

The difficult bit isn't appreciating complex finance, it's understanding a complex person - you. Making the effort to work out what money actually means for you and what you want it to do for you.

That's why the book is about **you**, because nobody knows you better than you do.

As a first step, since you know yourself best, what is it **you** want from your money? To paraphrase JFK –

Ask not what you can do for money; ask what your money can do for you.

When I ask clients, "what is money for?" most people don't really know what I'm getting at. So have a look at some of the answers which I've had to this question: What is money for?

- To spend
- For a rainy day
- Be able to do what I want
- To buy stuff
- Show I've arrived
- Make more money
- To give me a lifestyle
- A way of keeping score
- Give me security

What people want from their money and what they see as its use tends to be a symbol of something, not simply a means to trade for what they want.

> What do you want from your money? What is it for? Think about it. Make a note of the things that you think of.

There are all sorts of ways to categorise what our symbols for money are. One which I find useful is that people often use money to get one of four things:

- Power/Status
- Security
- Love
- Freedom

It can be interesting to see what you think that money is for and see whether it fits into one of those categories. I usually find that it does. You can try putting those "what is money for", answers I gave earlier into the four categories to see where those people come out, or maybe try it out with a friend or partner.

> But whatever you do, try it with your own answer(s) to the question.

It will help you understand what you see in money.

Usually, women and men look for different things from money. Men usually look to money for power and freedom, and women tend to look for love and security. That's a generalisation, obviously, plenty of women like the power they feel at having money and men want the security they see it will provide. It's the same principle as saying "most men are taller and heavier than most women", it doesn't mean that there are no women taller and heavier than most men and no men smaller and lighter than most women. Still, there are reasons for this tendency to have different symbols, which we'll go into in chapter 6.

This drive for power, security etc. is also important in terms of jobs.

In theory a job is just a way to earn money to buy things with, but many of us identify ourselves totally with our jobs. If you meet people for the first time, one of the initial queries is "what do you do", which people are happy to discuss, often at great (and tedious) length!

It's another example of us giving something a meaning that isn't obvious in its intended purpose.

Differences in attitudes aren't purely about gender. Our parents usually have a big influence, either through genes or training, our peers have a big influence too and "society" also tends to mould our attitudes.

As an example of the socially set attitudes to money and incomes, I was once asked to comment on some couples' financial history for a magazine article. The woman of one couple worked for a bank as a senior manager and earned a six-figure salary. In her comments, she said she hadn't revealed her income to her partner for some months after they started seeing one another; she let him think she was quite junior and earned less than him. In fact, the man earned less than his partner and made a point of defending himself from censure, by commenting that he made sure he paid his way and wasn't "living off" his partner.

Hiding her high income was, in my experience, typical of high earning women; but would a man do the same? Being male, and at the risk of sounding crass, I can say that earning lots of money is something I'd be tempted to boast about to attract women, not play down to avoid scaring them off! Similarly, would a woman apologise or be defensive about her partner earning a lot or be tempted to boast about it?

She seemed to be concerned whether money threatened her relationship security; he wondered if people would feel it made him less masculine and have lower status.

It's a social norm, which I suspect we can all understand, but if we think of money only as having the same objective value for all of us and that it doesn't have biological and social values woven in, it doesn't make sense.

There are a couple of other points about social pressures worth bearing in mind.

One is that it is a great taboo.

People seem to be more prepared to talk about several of the taboos of previous eras, like death or sex, than they are about money.

I've had people happily tell me, in a social chat in a pub and not when I'm advising or coaching them, about their father's death or their sex life. I don't think anybody has ever revealed their income. In fact, when I was a financial advisor, it was often like pulling teeth to get an accurate idea of what people earned, even though it was essential to providing the correct advice.

As an experiment, try going to a party and instead of saying what you do for a living say, "I'm a parent, and I give to charity. I like to read mystery novels but I hate reality TV", or something similar. Though this is an interesting experiment, don't expect to be asked back!

On the other hand, if you say, "Funnily enough, I earn exactly the national average wage, £24,908" (that's what it was in April 2008) you definitely won't get another invitation. It is taken to be a social gaffe on a par with extolling oral sex in a Victorian drawing room, or discussing euthanasia with an aged relative. According to at least one study, university students find it easier to talk about the details of having sex after the meal than talk about who will pay for the meal before having sex! So money isn't an easy subject to discuss honestly.

Another illustration of the way we attach symbols to money, rather than it being something with a practical purpose, is the way we see money as being good or bad. That can sound an easy choice. After all, who doesn't want more money, so it must always be a good thing, surely?

But we often talk about "rolling in it", "filthy lucre" and "stinking rich", people "make a pile" and so on, implying that we think it is a bad thing, or at least that it is dirty.

At the same time, we don't have many terms for "good money", and who wants to be "cleaned out"? Similarly "money laundering" is a crime so if you clean it, you're bad! So where are all the "good" words about money that we think that we want so much?

> What "good" words for money can you think of? Is money always "good" if all the words for it are bad?
>
> When Eskimos have 40 words for types of snow, because it is so important to them, how many do we have for good money?

The only one I've come up with is "bread". That's set against all the expressions like "make a killing" or "filthy rich" which have violent or dirty overtones.

Maybe money donated to charity is good, and money used to bribe somebody is bad? The money itself is just money, but we tend to have strong values about what sort of money is good and what is bad, and our values may differ according to personal values.

This also makes the concept of "more money is better", a bit tricky!

You've probably seen the film, Indecent Proposal, but in case you haven't, a young couple are offered a million dollars by a wealthy man if he can spend a night with the wife. If you and your partner (or any significant person, your daughter for example) were faced with a similar decision, what would you do? You can argue that it is different for men, which shows that we have some gender bias if we think that a proposal made to a woman is indecent but it's not if made to a man! But the point is, if more money is always good, why do we have any doubts about it, and why was the film ever made?

A similar point may be that, if you really want more money, why not campaign for child labour laws to be repealed? You could then send your children out to work in sweat shops or cleaning chimneys (as in the mid 19th Century) and your family income would go up. Very few of us would contemplate doing that, not even for a second, so clearly we don't always work on the basis that more money is better, we have values which classify some money as acceptable and some as being too dirty to touch. Moreover, how dirty is "too dirty" will depend on our individual values and our situation.

> What would you do for money? Steal, kill, or perhaps sleep with somebody you don't like? What do you think is "too dirty"? What does that do to your thoughts that, "more money is always better"?

To make our attitudes even more complicated, we can personally think of certain types of money as good or bad and be influenced in those money values by our parents and peers, but we're also influenced by society as a whole. One of those general influences is our political beliefs. Generally, the more "right wing" our economic/political view, the more likely we are to regard money as being a reward for effort and talent, the more "left wing" the more we may be suspicious of the effects of money.

Perhaps a good way to sum up the political/social angle is with a couple of: "I wish I'd said that" items.

First, a quote:

"If you want to know what God thinks of money, look at the people He gives it to."

Joe Moore

If you think that is unfair, perhaps you'll like the story (probably apocryphal) about the reporter who interviews the very rich man. Towards the end of the interview, the reporter says:

"You know sir, if I had as much money as you I'd never work again."
The rich man replies, *"Boy, that is the reason that the Good Lord will see to it that you never have that much money."*

So what does all that add up to?

The way we think, our attitudes, motives, beliefs and all the things that make up our personality influence our concept of whether money is "good or bad" in any situation. The money itself comes a very poor second to what goes on in our heads (and our hearts) when we deal with money.

We all have individual attitudes, shaped by our personal experiences, our parents, our peer group, our gender and biology, the society we live in and our political beliefs. And those attitudes give money a lot more importance for us than just a tool to obtain things. We can see money as the answer to our prayers (or a temptation from something evil), as a symbol of our masculinity or femininity, as something to be hidden away and not talked about, or a thing to be boasted about.

> *So that's why I know **you** are more important than your money!*

And it is why I believe that your thoughts and beliefs are more important to your enjoyment of life than the money you've got, and why 'Taming the Pound' is about understanding **you**, because understanding "you" gives you the key to understand your money.

> *If you aren't aware of what you really think, you can do things that cost you a lot, because in this case, what you don't know **can** hurt you.*

To control your money, rather than have it control you, it helps to be aware of what symbols you're using and how you're thinking.

*But the tree stumps aren't proper chairs, and there aren't any beds. And what **is** this stuff in the bowls, it isn't porridge?*

We're bears, why do we want a house at all? And we mostly eat bugs and tubers, little girl - bear, bear-little girl. Notice any difference?

For example, as a financial advisor years ago I had a new, very wealthy, client. He'd used up all the tax relief available, and as the top rate of tax was then 60%, it made a big difference. His accountant asked me to see if I could find some more savings or investments for this client. When I interviewed him, it turned out that the client had a wife who was born abroad, and they had married after 1st January 1974. You probably think, "OK, so what's that got to do with anything?"

Prior to 1974, the tax laws had a little hangover from the days when women were chattels and Britain had an Empire. It was assumed that "Johnny Foreigner" really wanted to be British (you have to imagine "Land of Hope and Glory" playing in the background here) so if a woman married a British man, she would obviously want to be British and would adopt her husband's "domicile". That means, for certain tax purposes, she was British. After that, the rules changed, women were regarded as independent people, and they retained their original domicile when they married.

This is the sort of thing that makes people think you have to know lots about tax and finance to be successful handling money. I suggested putting more than half of the disposable cash into his wife's name and holding it in the Channel Islands. It would save them 60% of the income from the money invested.

What I said was right, legal and maximised his income. I thought I was jolly clever, knowing these obscure rules, and that the accountant would pass on lots of other clients to me since I was so good.

The client absolutely refused to do it. He kept repeating, "but it is *my* money". The only thing I could think of at the time was that he might believe they were going to split up, but they'd been married about 10 years, and I know that they were still (apparently happily) married for at least three years after that.

At the time, although I was really good on the finance side, I wasn't so clever on understanding values and symbols. He saw it as his money. It was part of his concept of *who* he was, a successful businessman, with a wife he provided for and who didn't need to work. If he moved the money into her name, he'd have cut off a bit of himself. To be honest, I still don't altogether understand it, but I know now that that is just because I put different values on money than he did (and probably still does).

The point is that:

> *In handling and getting control of money, your values and beliefs about yourself and your money are far more relevant to your happiness and success than how "financially astute" you are.*

Remember, the client could afford to hire both his accountant and me to do the technical financial thinking, but what mattered most in the end were his head and his heart, not the financial detail. Spending some time on working out what you really think about money is safer than assuming that "more is automatically better, let's not bother about what I think, let's look at the amount of the money".

And when you've done that, let's have a look at what you really, really want!

Summary:

- Work out what money is for, as far as you are concerned.
- Think what you believe money can, and can't, buy.
- Decide what money is sacred, what is "dirty", what you would do for it and when you wouldn't touch it.
- Always remember that you are more important than the money!

Happiness

People assume that if only they had more money, they'd be happy, despite saying that the "best things in life are free". Don't they want the best things? The chapter is about ways of finding out what will make you really happy, and how you can keep that happiness long term.

What do you want your money to do for you? If it is a "means to an end" and not the end itself, then what is the end you want your money to achieve?

Happiness must be a good place to start looking for what you really want to achieve or to have in life.

> Do you want to be happy? Would you rather be rich and miserable, or be really happy irrespective of money?

Unlike the US, in the UK we don't have a written constitution. If we did, we'd probably all agree that it should, like the US, include the fact that you're entitled to "life, liberty and the pursuit of happiness".

Notice that you are *entitled* to life and liberty, but you only get to *pursue* happiness, it isn't something you just get together with the NHS, habeas corpus and the right to pay taxes.

But wouldn't more money make you happier? What the research says is that:

*Being wealthy won't make you happy, a bit more **might** make you happier – but only in certain circumstances and only if you use the money for some purpose that is related to your particular version of happiness, money by itself won't do it.*

That fits in with accepted wisdom; proverbially money can't buy love (which makes the world go round) the best things in life are free, etc. On the other hand:

*Being poor (not having enough for what you **need**, rather than **want**) is probably going to make you more unhappy more of the time, unless you are an **extremely** rare individual.*

That's pretty simple, so why should we get confused about it?

Perhaps you do make the unconscious assumption that if only you had that bit more money, you would automatically be happier? Lots of people believe it, but in general it isn't true.

Up to a certain level happiness seems to increase pretty steadily with increasing money.

The level is about £50,000 p/a income (in 2009), but it depends on where you are in the country, and particularly on you as a person.

Taking an invented example, it looks as if your household income going up £20,000 annually from, say £80,000 to £100,000 won't make any difference, certainly nothing like as much in terms of happiness as it going up only £10,000, from £40,000 to £50,000 although the proportionate increase is the same and the difference in money is actually bigger.

Beyond that it might seem nice, at least temporarily, but it doesn't actually help that much and it may not help at all.

It seems there are two main reasons for this.

1. If you can't get the basics, like food, shelter etc. in modern society even a bit more money is helpful and takes some of the stress away; the stress that comes from not knowing if the children will eat tonight or whether your possessions are going to be reclaimed by the bailiffs.

Once you get to the point where more money means a five star instead of a four star hotel or a new car every three years instead of five, it doesn't do so much for you. It might feel good for a while, but it doesn't remove stress because you're not really stressed. Of course, you might unconsciously put yourself under stress, because your ideas and emotions are important and you are still being used by your money!

2. As you get more money, you tend to compare yourself with wealthier people.

So for years, you've craved another £10,000 a year, although your car runs well and your house is fine. Finally you get the promotion and a £20,000 raise. You are delighted for a month or so. Then you move to a wealthier neighbourhood, join the golf club and suddenly you need an even better house and car, and you decide that you need *another* £20,000 (or more).

That's what happens when you "move up". A key factor in this is "aspiration" (what you fancy having).

If you constantly aspire to have more "things" than you already possess, you tend to be less happy, if your aspirations match your money, you are likely to be happier

By contrast, you don't adapt as fast going downwards. You want to compare yourself with the brightest, best and wealthiest. So if your income or wealth goes up, you quickly adapt to new "Jones's" to keep up with, but when it goes down, you still try to compete with the first lot of Jones's, the ones who still have what you used to.

> *Most people's aspiration level goes up faster than it comes down, to match changes in wealth. Aspiration is typically relative to other people and what you think they've got, it isn't independent of them and based on what you want. If it was, you'd be happier!*

The speed of adaption is one reason why money doesn't always make lottery winners stay happy for all that long and why many people who have lost a lot of wealth will carry on pretending they can afford things they can no longer reasonably afford. If you've seen the film "The Full Monty" you might remember Gerald the "Company Director" (the part Tom Wilkinson played) who couldn't admit even to his wife that he'd lost his job. Gerald is a perfect example of the common inability to adjust our material sights downwards when things go wrong.

It's not easy, though!

> *It is really useful to try to separate what you **really** want to make you happy from what you aspire to because others have got it, or because it will give you status, security etc.*

Here are some exercises to help you work out what you do really want.

Some people like to enlist the aid of a partner/spouse/significant other, a good friend etc. in order to work through this process. Others prefer to be on their own at least to start with. Whatever you prefer, I'd suggest you sit down with the book, a blank sheet of paper and pen or pencil

Have any notes you made about "What is money for" from the last chapter to hand, but don't worry about them for the moment.

Pick one or more questions or scenarios from those below. It doesn't matter which one(s), choose those that appeal the most, and which stimulate you to think. Make notes on your answers. Be honest about what you really want (this is where sharing with somebody else can be helpful for some people, and inhibiting for others).

- What is your perfect life? Where would you go, what things would you have and what would you spend your time doing? Write down in as much detail as you can what you'd do with your time, how you would live, who you would mix with, where you would go.

- Imagine you're famous and you get to write your own obituary. What are you famous for? What does the Times obituary say about you? What do your favourite actor, your grandchildren, and the friends who knew you say in their eulogies to you at your memorial service at St Paul's?

- How do you want to be remembered – what would be the meaning of your life if you could decide for yourself now? How would you be written up in the history of the period? What would the 9 o'clock news announcement say – "she/he is best remembered for..."

- Imagine you're retired and being interviewed on a TV programme about your life (when I do it, I always imagine Parkinson coming out of retirement especially to interview me!) What do you tell the interviewer? What stories do you tell about your life, the things you are most proud of, memories you recall the most fondly?

- Imagine that you are near the end of your life and have access to a time machine (bear with me!) You get the chance to come back and talk to yourself as you are now. What will you tell yourself? What things were really important? Will you say you should spend more time at work or watching TV or more time with your family and friends? This exercise is your chance to take advantage of the old regret "if only I'd known then, what I know now"!

- Imagine that you have enough money to be totally free of obligations. If money was no object you could have anything you wanted, what would you do, would you still want holiday homes all around the world if you could simply stay in hotels and be waited on all the time, would you buy a football club or an art collection and what would you do with them when you'd got them, what would you have and what would you do with those things?

- Who would you give money to, what charities would you support, what relatives or friends would you help, what businesses or foundations would you start?

- If you knew it was your last, Year, Month, Week or Day, what would you do with your time? What would you spend time on, what would you want to get done?

- What is the very best thing that could happen in your life? What really important thing could happen? What experiences would you have, who would you share them with, what would be one that you'd say was the greatest thing that could happen?

- And lastly – think about what you value and enjoy
  Do you value/enjoy your job?
  Do you value/enjoy your hobbies?
  Do you value/enjoy time with your children/family?
  Do you value/enjoy things to make people jealous?
  Do you value/enjoy your memories of holidays or other experiences?

Do you value/enjoy your computer games, Sky subscription or cigarettes?

What else do you really value/enjoy?

How much time, effort and money do you put into each of these things?

Is the amount of time, effort and money you put into these things proportionate to how much you value/enjoy them?

How many of them feature in your ideal life, "if I had all I wanted I'd...." your ideal obituary etc.?

Many people spend their time, money and effort on things they feel are worthless, and little or no time on the things they say they value and/or enjoy. Is that something that you do?

There is a concept called "opportunity cost" which people often forget. It is the price you pay for making any decision (even deciding not to decide), you could have done something else (or done something instead of nothing). However, you don't get to follow up on the options you didn't choose or to find out what was down the "path you didn't take".

That is the cost to you of the choice you made, the opportunity that you don't take. So part of working out your values is understanding what your opportunity costs are. Another way of putting it is:

One half of knowing what you want is knowing what you must give up before you get it. ~Sidney Howard

One other exercise. It links to the previous one, which you can do separately but if you've already started to think about what you *really* want it is helpful. This is because, if you are like most people, you don't really think about what *you* want, however important it might be.

Imagine that you've won the lottery. You've got £25 million. What are you going to do with it? Make a note of the first 15 things. Try to make it fairly detailed, if you want a house, what sort, how big, what would it have in the way of facilities? If you'd invest the money, what would you want as an income from it and what would you do with that income (and the balance of the money)?

When you've got the list (or the two of you have made it if you're working in a couple) look at it and see where the things on it have come from.

Are these things you want for yourself, or has someone or something pushed your buttons for you? For example, do you feel that if you're a millionaire you have to have a big house to rival somebody you've seen in Hello magazine? Do you want a Ferrari because the annoying bloke at the gym or the pub bought a Porsche? There is an American definition of wealth that says you are rich if you earn $100 a year more than your wife's sister's husband! Are most of the things on the list to compete with your brother-in-law?

Count up the things that come from magazines, the press, the "image" ideas that you hear and see in advertisements. Compare that to the things driven by competition with friends and family, the stuff that "experts" or advisors have told you that you ought to want, the ones you've been sold, the ones that your children want. Then add up the ones that could fulfil your dreams, ones that you (and maybe your partner) would truly value and be happy about long term.

Chances are that if you make a table out of it, you'll get something like this:

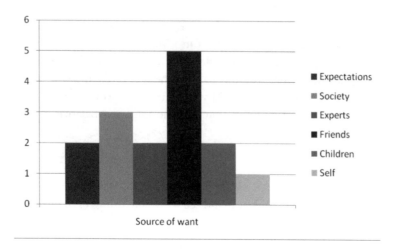

Source of want

When I ask people to make that list of the 15 things, we often get this result, with most having only two or three that are actually ambitions of their own. The others are to prove something to parents, siblings, friends, the bloke in the pub or their children's friends' parents; or possibly to have what a magazine, a celebrity expert or a style programme tells them they *should* want.

Don't get me wrong, there's no problem with having big dreams financially or wanting to be wealthy. There's no harm in big aspirations. If it is really going to make you happy, and it really is for *you*, great. Good luck to you. The point is that if you are going into debt to buy a Lamborghini because the bloke up the road bought a Porsche, or because you think society expects you to have a Lamborghini, I'd say that was not the wisest use of your money. If you've always wanted a Lamborghini, it is your dream and you plan how to afford it, that's fine.

For example, when I was in finance I had a colleague who had always wanted an Aston Martin. He got a promotion, and was relocated from Birmingham down to London, had a huge pay rise, got a good relocation package and so on. So he kept his house in Birmingham, rented it out, moved down to London where he went around the various dealers and finally bought his Aston Martin. It was second hand (he wasn't daft!) so it wasn't going to lose a lot of value, and he worked on it, tuned it, kept it polished and so on. About six months later there was a classic car boom. His Aston Martin tripled in price over the next few months, to the point where by selling the car he could have paid off his mortgage in Birmingham, bought another car and paid off most of his mortgage in London.

But he didn't sell it. He loved that car, he'd wanted one like it nearly all his life. He loved to drive out on a sunny Sunday lunchtime (it wasn't taken out in the rain), feel how well it handled, take his girlfriend to the pub and bask in the glow of his beautiful car. His mates would ask him how it ran and want to have a drive, kids would look at car and say with that awestruck tone, "is it yours mister?" He could feel he'd really achieved something that he'd always wanted. He didn't need to prove it to his dad (who I don't think had been a manager, owned his own house or had a flash car) or anybody else. It was his own dream, and he loved it and was prepared to sacrifice for it.

Also, it isn't only in films that people spend lots of time at work claiming "I'm doing it for the family", to find that in twenty years' time they are divorced and their children estranged because they got their priorities wrong and did well with money and poorly on relationships.

If you're going to pursue money to buy things "for them" (whoever "they" are), make sure you talk to "them" about it first and see what "they" think about it! So if you do these exercises with your significant other(s) you might find you need to reconsider your priorities.

You might decide as a family or a couple that sacrifices in the short term are worth it for later on. You might also decide you'd rather be happy as a family with a bit less money, than be a bit richer, and all thoroughly miserable and maladjusted!

Big financial dreams aren't bad, you just need to make sure that your dreams, visions, values or whatever you want to call them are actually going to lead to you (and those you value) being happy.

You don't want to be constantly stressed about money for the sake of power/status, security etc., because somebody or something else has pressed your buttons, or because you never stopped to think what you really wanted and why.

At the other end of the money scale, if you are tempted to regard money as being the root of all evil, and think your perfect life would involve going back to nature and escaping the rat-race, have a good think about it.

Remember, having too little money can be a significant stress factor, and you have to be realistic.

Going for "the Good Life" or becoming a Buddhist monk, etc. is very rarely a realistic option (and unless you are really dedicated, probably wouldn't make you happy anyway). If you really want it, great, but do remember that if you can't pay the bills and your smallholding is repossessed, it is really not likely to make you or those you love happy!

So master, if I don't drink, I don't smoke or do drugs and I don't cavort with lewd and salacious women, will I live forever?

No, but it will sure, as Hell feel like it!

Compare what you've got on your two lists, the one of what money is for, and the one of what you want from your life.

At this point, there are two main options:

1. If your two lists are much the same, congratulations, you seem to be using your money rather than it using you. You might want to look at the rest of the chapter out of interest, but you could go straight on to chapter 3 about goals right now.
2. If, as happens for many people, your two lists don't bear much resemblance to one another, you definitely want to work on your "happiness plan" a bit longer before moving on. And think about what you want to do with your life. Remember the points about money and "stuff" not magically making you happy.

If you need or want to learn more about happiness, here's a summary of what seems to help. I'll also suggest half a dozen books that you can read up on. There are links to the books on the website (www.tamingthepound.com) as well.

Happiness – the summary

- Seeing some value to your life, the hope of achieving something useful, productive or meaningful to you, and behaving in accordance with that value will almost certainly make you happier.

- Having a meaning to your life that is greater than just yourself, whether you call it spirituality, transcendence or an "extra-personal goal" is likely to make you happier.

- Building relationships and friendships, including helping others less well off than you is very likely to make you happier.

- Becoming mindful of what you are doing, enjoying now, the only time you have, rather than regretting or gloating over the past, or hoping for or fearing the future, is very likely to make you happier.

- Activities that use your strengths or that allow you to engage in "flow" are likely to make you happier.

Un-happiness – the summary

- Chasing money is not a way to happiness. If you live in a peaceful democracy, once you've got enough to eat and have shelter, money is not likely to make you appreciably happier unless you do some of the other things that lead to happiness with it, and most of them you can do with no money anyway.

- Materialistic values are likely to make you unhappier, not happier.

What you do to be and stay happy.

- Focus on the life you want to live, don't get hung up on money and "things"

- Work out what you would really value achieving and act on it.

- Think of ways to "give something back" that have value beyond yourself.

- Look at your relationships – people are more important than things, so invest in what matters, like friends and family.

- Focus on what you have now, thinking "when I get X I'll be happy" wastes time and time *isn't* money, you can get more money, you can't get more time!

- Forget about the destination, life is the journey, so use your money to experience your life while you're living it, not to accumulate things that you can enjoy having on your death-bed.

- And a bonus to all this is that you seem likely not only to be substantially happier, but also live that happy life considerably longer!

Books I'd recommend (and why)

The only common factor in these is that the authors are all world experts on their aspects of happiness and have spent at least a quarter of a century on their subject. They aren't in order of importance – pick the ones that appeal to you.

1. *Man's Search for Meaning, by Victor Frankl*
This book is extraordinarily popular (sold about 10 million copies). Apart from being a Professor of Psychiatry (so he was a Doctor, specially qualified in the mind) Frankl had survived three years in Auschwitz, Dachau and other extermination camps. As a technical expert in people, somebody who had survived horrors that most of us can (fortunately for us) only imagine and who still maintained a purpose and meaning to his life so well that he went on to help millions of others, you've got to figure that what he says about the sources of happiness and meaning is worth hearing.
One thing he says is,
"Man's search for meaning is the primary motivation in his life"
Frankl Page 105

2. *Authentic Happiness by Martin Seligman*
Another concept of being happy is looking at the flip side of being unhappy. About 40 years ago Martin Seligman realised that psychologists and others had thought a lot about depression, illness, things going

wrong. The attitude was that if it wasn't broke (i.e. the person was not clinically ill) don't fix it, ignore it. His enquiry into the positive side of psychology became a massive series of programmes about people's strengths, "flourishing" and happiness. He changed the whole course of a huge section of a science.

He mentions some things that help happiness:

- Live in a wealthy democracy not an impoverished dictatorship
- Get married [basically, have good relationships!]
- Acquire a rich social network [quality, not just quantity]

and some that make little or no difference
- Make more money (money has little or no effect once you are comfortable enough to buy this book and more materialistic people are less happy).

He also showed that using the things you are good at, your strengths, makes you happier than working on covering up your weaknesses. It's a practical "accentuate the positive" attitude and is part of the reason the movement he started is called "positive psychology".

There is also an Authentic Happiness website,

http://www.authentichappiness.sas.upenn.edu/Default.aspx

It has questionnaires that are free at the time of writing, one of them being the Values In Action (VIA) survey, which is a good place to start. You need to log in and confirm that you're happy for the results to be used for research but they don't put your details in the results, they just want data from thousands of people and aren't going to sell you things. This is at:

http://www.authentichappiness.sas.upenn.edu/questionnaires.aspx

There's also, I'm pleased to say, a UK site that gives a lot of resources like articles, research etc. and has some free questionnaires at:

http://positivepsychology.org.uk/pp-online.html

3. Happiness by Ed Diener and Robert Biswas-Diener

Diener is widely regarded as the world's leading authority on the *science* of happiness, so we're not talking about some vague utopian "wouldn't it be nice if being kind to people made you happy and money was not a factor" visions; we're talking about established scientific facts. His son, Biswas-Diener spent several months in "Slumdog Millionaire" territory researching his PhD among some of the poorest people in the world (many of whom are perfectly happy)! Between father and son, they've done immense amounts of research into the facts behind happiness, and some of the conclusions they've come to are that if you want to be happy you should:

- Have values and meaning to your life, and act consistently with those values.
- Build relationships with others,
- Have sufficient money.
- Live as though happiness is a process not a place.

4. The Blue Zones: Lessons for Living Longer from the People Who've Lived the Longest, by Dan Buettner

Not about happiness as such, but about living a longer, more active, and more productive life.

It lists nine elements common to societies around the world that have high proportions of people who don't just live a long life, but are active, happy, productive members of society way past the point where most people in other societies are either dead, grumpy, or basically waiting passively for the end. The elements he lists are:

1. Move: Find ways to stay active
2. Plan de Vida: Discover your purpose in life
3. Downshift: Take a break
4. 80% Rule: Don't overeat

5. Plant Power: Choose greens
6. Red Wine: A glass a day
7. Belong: Stay social
8. Beliefs: Get ritualistic
9. Your Tribe: Family matters

You'll notice that numbers 2, 3, 7, 8 and 9 have already come up. Being sociable, downshifting (in the sense of having your priorities right and lined up with your values), having a purpose, building relationships and having a belief in something beyond yourself are important to life, health and happiness. I'll admit that I haven't found why drinking red wine helps me live longer yet, but I've decided I'm prepared to carry on experimenting with it since I'm sure it makes me happier anyway!

5. *Flow by Mihaly Csikszentmihalhyi*

You might have experienced this in connection with the whole business of "time flying when you're having fun".

If your ability is high and the challenge low, you become bored easily. That applies with mundane jobs, with an opponent that you can beat easily, a puzzle that is too simple or a novice slope if you're a black run skier. If the challenge is high and your ability low, you become stressed. Imagine the new project you don't feel you can handle, the challenge match against the person who always beats you, the insoluble puzzle or the terrifying slope. If the challenge and your ability match, you can find yourself in flow. At that point, your focus is total, you are completely engaged and you don't get distracted, you might not even notice time passing as time is "flying" while you're – well not exactly having "fun" in the usual sense, but totally involved and eventually very fulfilled and happy.

There is also the point that, very often, the flow experience comes from using the strengths you have. There is a You Tube clip with Csikszentmihalhyi discussing flow and how it can connect with the VIA strengths at: http://www.youtube.com/watch?v=GZbUDzmKvus

6. The Mindful Way through Depression: Freeing Yourself from Chronic Unhappiness by Williams, Teasdale, Segal and Kabat-Zinn

This is an unfortunate title! Don't be put off, it isn't really about depression, it is about living your life more fully, so don't worry about not being depressed!

Mindfulness is a way to appreciate that now is the only time we have. Most of us spend so much time gloating over or regretting the past and fearing or anticipating the future that we forget about where we are right now. So we look at a beautiful sunset, and think about previous ones we've seen not what we're seeing now, or we glaze over and anticipate a future event and think about how happy we'll be "when X happens". We never actually see or enjoy that sunset. We sit and wish and worry and a few hours later we are stiff and our shoulders ache and we think, "I must have been tensing up", but we're so involved with our wishes and regrets that we aren't aware of what our bodies are telling us.

7. Happiness, A guide to developing life's most important skill by Matthieu Ricard

The reasons for suggesting this particular book are that it is:

- The best book on living I've ever read.
- The inspiration for me to write this book,
  And
- Ricard is not only a Buddhist monk but a cellular geneticist with a PhD from the Institut Pasteur, whose main thesis advisor was a Nobel Prize winner!

Basically, Ricard is inspiring. He's written several "best sellers" on various subjects with the income from them going to a Foundation that carries out humanitarian and educational projects in Asia. He can simply give that money away and be, by all accounts, one of the happiest and most extraordinary people that you could hope to meet. It is worth reading as a great guide to being happier but also for his personal example of how to achieve something great and lasting, to have a meaningful life, with great relationships, totally engaged in what he is doing for others. And in doing this he is able simply to give away or ignore the money that he could have if it were at all important to him.

Summary:

- Do you want money or happiness (they are not the same)?
- How much money do you need for the things that will really make you happy?
- Remember poor is usually bad but wealthy isn't necessarily good.
- Aspirations change fast going up, slowly going down
- Do the exercises about what you want, including the "first fifteen".
- Sort out who is pushing your buttons, who you wish to impress with "things", yourself and your family, "society" or somebody else.
- Make a list of what you really want from life, what will make you happy
- Don't forget your "significant others" in working out what makes you happy.
- Compare your lists of what you think money is for and what you want from life – and remember that money is supposed to be a means to an end.
- If your lists match – move on (but you might want to read some of the books while you're goal setting).
- If they don't match – then make sure you read at least one of those books and get your priorities sorted out before you set your goals.

Now it is time to work out how you can use your money to achieve your values.

Do you know where you're going to?

Planning for what you want. Lots of people know some system for setting goals, but very few use them at all, especially for finance. But, without a plan for a goal, how are you going to get what you've decided will make you happy?

You have almost certainly heard about setting goals (or targets). You might even have done it, perhaps you were told that all goals are supposed to be SMART (typically Specific, Measurable, Achievable, Realistic, Timed).

The chapter sets out

- what I think a goal is,
- why you need them,
- when you need them
- what you need to remember in setting them,

then we can look at some examples, and ideas for how you might set goals for yourself.

> *A goal is a well-defined objective that:*
> - *Is a practical step on the way to something of personal value in life (it is your goal and it matters to you)*
> - *Has a plan for its completion (it isn't a vague wish)*
> - *Motivates you to take action (or what is the point)*
> - *Allows you to check where you are relative to your personal values (you don't forget about it or get confused as to whether you're heading towards or away from your values)*

Before we get onto the detail beyond my definition, here's a question that is a very good question about most things. **Why bother**?

Lots of people don't bother. They rely on a magazine article, book, "expert" or TV programme to tell them what goals they *should* have. Worse than that, they adopt a "plan" that somebody else designed to fit a different situation, to achieve a goal they haven't set, to reach a value in life they don't believe in or care about.

Why bother, part one.

Imagine you're trying to help a friend whose job is going to be made redundant. Your friend is in his mid-forties, married with two children. He's done the same specialist role for 25 years and doesn't believe he has any other marketable skills. He's going to get about a year and a half's salary tax-free as a lump sum, and will have a pension from age 60. What do you advise?

Then another friend who works for the same company comes to you in apparently an identical position and asks for advice. Do you advise him to do the same, because he is in the same role, earning the same money, with the same prospects and responsibilities?

When this situation happened to me with two clients from a firm I was advising, I had an advantage. It wasn't that we had the contract to give redundancy advice to about 1,300 staff so I knew all the details, or that I was a qualified advisor and knew my stuff (although those obviously helped). The advantage I had was in the two men I saw. Remember, at that point I was a good advisor, but I wasn't a psychologist, I didn't understand anything about values in life, goal setting or personality. What I knew was the technical financial detail, and what the client told me.

To paraphrase, one client said:

"*What am I going to do. I'm 45, I've been an X for 25 years, I don't know how to do anything else. What am I going to do. I've got children, what will I do, my wife doesn't work, she can't keep me, what am I going to do? I'll get a pension eventually but we'll go through the money long before then, what am I going to do?"*

The other said:

"All I'd like you to do, Kim, is tell me about whether to transfer my pension. I've sorted out my redundancy payment. I'm doing an HGV qualification, I'm within the age limit and a mate and I are going to set up a haulage business, my wife's right behind me, she can do the books. It's great, I've been an X for 25 years and never done anything else, I'm so ******** bored with it, this redundancy is the best thing that has ever happened".

So, it did give me a bit of a clue!

Hopefully my point is clear. The second client was easy to advise, because I just had to put in place a plan for his money to fit his goal. He knew what he wanted his life to be like (if I was advising him now, I'd sharpen that up a bit, but he basically knew where he wanted to be).

By contrast, the first client was hard because I had to work out what he wanted to achieve before I could help him plan to achieve it. Even in my state of ignorance, I knew I couldn't advise him what to do until I knew what he wanted. Then, when we knew what he wanted, we'd have to set some goals and plans for him to get there.

> Think about this in terms of my goal definition above, which is the better goal?

So the best goal (and plan to achieve it) depends on what you want to achieve in the end. And if you don't know what you want to achieve, find out (chapter 2) before you start goal setting and planning!

I know it is easy to fall into the trap of starting to organise your money first. Lots of people are told that a family of four "should" be able to live on a certain amount. So, in an attempt to get organised, they try to follow the "rules" and set a "goal" to "live within their means" (although this is not a goal by my definition).

They cut back on spending (leaving in things they don't really need, like subscriptions to magazine they don't read any more) and then find they still struggle, never re-evaluate their life and perhaps end up miserable and still in debt. At best, they might scrape by, but they never get anywhere near their dreams.

They might even start to sort out their real values and the life-style that would make them happy, but because they take somebody else's goals and plans, they never achieve their own values. If they ignored the general purpose "goals", they could find lots of ways to cut back on non-essential (for them) spending to get what they really want. They'd be able to set goals and make plans to fit their values and be happier, while spending a lot less on unnecessary (for them) stuff.

Why bother, part 2.

Because, as we've already said, money tends to be a bit taboo and people get emotional about it, let's use an analogy to think about goals.

Imagine an archer. How likely are they to hit a target? We blindfold them. How likely are they to hit the target now? Now move the target around, to different distances and different directions. How likely? Now take the target away altogether. What about now?

If you try to budget or otherwise plan finances first you end up like that, a blindfold archer shooting at a target that you can't see and that may not even be there. If you don't have a goal (target), then any plan (shot) is going to be lucky to hit, because the goal (target) might not exist and even if it does, you might be shooting in the wrong direction. And it doesn't matter how good an archer you are (how much you know about finance). You'll still be like a boxer against Mohammed Ali, "their fists can't hit what their eyes can't see".

In 2009 the UK took steps to increase "financial capacity" among the population, particularly in schools. This is to make people more financially knowledgeable.

They "should" know all about banks and credit, financial products, pensions and so on, and then the theory is, we won't have a credit crisis again because everybody will be an expert! Of course, the biggest "experts" were the bankers and economists who caused the crash in the first place, but still the argument is that more "capacity", more knowledge of the technical issues is what we all need.

The "make everybody and expert" and increase "financial capacity" argument assumes that people are simple because they are all exactly the same with no personalities, while money is really complicated.

It also assumes that knowing all about money makes you immune to money error, and that the only reason people get it wrong is because they don't know enough technical detail.

Given that the bankers, politicians and economists knew all about money and nothing about people and they messed up more than anybody and the fact that people are far more complicated than money (we invented it, for a start), I'd say this was pretty questionable logic and a massive waste of public money on teaching the wrong things.

Assuming we want to examine the logic of the view that "capacity is the answer to all financial issues, you can ignore what the question is", let's extend the analogy of the archer.

Imagine crowds of people in a field. They represent the public. With them is archery equipment, so there are various bows and arrows in different materials, lots of archery aids, telescopic sights etc. That represents all the financial instruments (pensions, ISAs, bonds etc.). Also there are many expert archers. They represent the Financial

Services Authority (the people who regulate the financial services industry), bankers, financial advisors and so on. The other things in the field, and around it on the surrounding hills, are lots of archery targets, representing the things people want from life.

The "capacity" idea is that we need to teach every man, woman and child archery. They should all know the tensile strengths of materials, understand hysteresis loss and aerodynamics, optics and air friction coefficients. Then they can shoot accurately.

> *I think it would be better just to take off people's blindfolds!*

Sorry, I didn't mention that everybody wears blindfolds, including the expert archers. If we teach everybody how to shoot arrows and leave the blindfolds on, they might become good archers, but will kill one another by accident and won't hit their targets because they don't know what or where they are.

Take off the blindfolds and let people see the targets. Then they might decide that they don't need a bow at all, they can pick up an arrow, walk two paces and stick the arrow in the target. If the target is half a mile away on a hillside, then they need to get the right bow to fire that far, and the expert archers can help them choose and learn to fire the appropriate bow.

So work out your values, what really matters to you. Understand what you currently do with money, which of your buttons get pressed, who presses them, what you try to get from money, who you try to impress and what you use money to try to get. Then, when you are ready you can sort out goals.

Why bother, part 3
Let's think about the archer analogy a bit more and what the goals might look like. I rather liked the fairly recent TV version of Robin Hood, at least for the first couple of series. One reason I liked it was

because it was quite psychologically real (the degree of reality is relative, obviously!). I've never seen a version of the story before where, if I played Robin Hood, I couldn't have sorted out the problem in the first five minutes with a couple of well-placed arrows. Just kill the bad guys, problem solved!

Think about Robin Hood's personal value, what was he trying to achieve in life? He wanted fairness and justice for all. So was that his goal? No, he couldn't impose those standards on the whole country himself.

What did he do? Stole from the rich to give to the poor. Was that his goal or value? No. Stealing from the rich and giving to the poor were parts of a plan to achieve a goal, not the goal itself and certainly not a value.

But he killed the key bad guys (eventually), which is what I would do, so was that his goal or value? No. Because he knew that initially they'd just be replaced by other bad guys. So, not killing particular people (until the right time), was also part of a plan to achieve a goal, not the goal or the value itself.

His value was fairness and justice, but he couldn't impose it.

His goal was to keep things going until King Richard returned, because King Richard could ensure fairness and justice for all.

If you look back at my definition of a goal, that is a reasonably well defined one (it could do with polishing up, but this is only a TV programme!).

Robin had a value of justice, a goal of returning Richard to power and to do that he wanted to keep things going as well as possible. All the "steal from the rich" and "kill the bad guys" were parts of a plan to achieve the goal.

When do you plan and set goals?

People often forget the Robin Hood example. They become obsessive over parts of the plan, let's cut up the cards, let's sell some antiques, let's get a "finance expert" to tell us what we ought to spend and stick to that.

> *That leads to them (metaphorically) killing the wrong people, or stealing from the poor to give to the rich!*

Unfortunately most advice starts by telling you (metaphorically) which arrows to use, the best bow to hit your target and the best way to steal money, before you know what your target is, what obstacles there are to hitting it and how you will know when you have hit it. It is no wonder people have problems with finance and (metaphorically) kill lots of the wrong people and steal and steal and steal and still end up poor, miserable peasants!

What you need to remember when setting goals
It's a shame that SMART, that is so well known, isn't much help!

For a start, usually the A stands for achievable or attainable and the R for realistic or resourced. If a goal is realistic there must be the resources to achieve it and that means it is achievable and attainable. So that is a bit of a waste of a letter, since it is SMAT, not SMART!

Let's look at what a goal should contain. I'm not saying every goal must have every one, I'm just listing some of the things that research indicates are helpful.

A goal may need to be:

- *Congruent with values, value based, intended for long term happiness*
  Goals needs to fit in with whatever your values, life purpose etc. are, or even if you achieve the goal it won't be worth achieving!
- *Clear, specific, defined*
  If you don't know what you're trying to do, it is tricky to plan to do it. This is the S of the conventional SMART goal.

- *Exciting, makes you committed, motivating*
  It needs to get you out of bed – a value based on 20 years time won't usually do that, so an exciting goal probably has to be relatively short term.
- *Timed, time bounded*
  It's handy if your goal has a timescale. However, the point is to get action, so a time set for a short term goal is more important. Having a "time limit" on a life value and a long term goal might just make you stressed over it. If you've got the shorter term goal right, it will be motivating, exciting and get you moving in the right direction towards your longer term goal anyway.
- *Aligned, congruent, internally consistent*
  Between the longer term goal that heads for your values, and the shorter term, exciting goal, you want them pulling in the same direction. Otherwise you'll get all excited about getting further and further from your long term goal and values!
- *Action based, practical*
  It needs to include something that you can work on, not a wish list. The value might be abstract, but the goal needs to contain action steps that you can take, not vague things like "each day try to be a better person".
- *Controllable, effectible, within your scope*
  You want to be able to do it with your own actions. With money, you will not be able to control fund performance so you might have a problem with "my goal is to have a fund worth X", but you can control how much you put into the fund, how balanced it is (see chapter 9) etc.
- *Flexible, adaptable, reviewable*
  If the fund performance, for example, is much better or worse than you anticipated, do you have a "fall-back" position or a plan b? Ideally, your goal can be adapted easily to changing circumstances.

- *Measurable, progress checked.*
  You want to know where you are, the M of the SMART goal. It probably means having particular outcomes, not just processes. With investments it might be, "make some investments" is a process, but "put X amount into a balanced portfolio each month" could be an outcome you can measure success with.

- *Small steps and well planned.*
  Small scale (both in resources and time), simple steps that are properly organised get you to goals. Vague wishes, ones that are left to chance (the money classic being, "if I have some money at the end of the month, I'll save it"), don't achieve anything.

- *Resourced, realistic, stretching but achievable, sustainable.*
  This is where you might need some professional help (chapter 15). Resources can be hard to judge. The stretching part is that you ideally want something that gets you working, that pushes you a bit because a stretch is exciting. Remember "flow", you want a challenge that engages you. But you don't want something that is impossible, because beating your head against a wall is de-motivating!

- *Positively worded.*
  Your mind doesn't work well with negatives. For example, "don't think of elephants", what do you think of? There are different figures given for the difference, but basically if you have a goal that is positively worded ("I want to be comfortably off in retirement"), provided that it is specific enough and so on, you are more likely to achieve it than if the goal is negatively worded, "I don't want to be poor in retirement".

And finally, one there is a huge misconception about:

- *Written goals, recorded.*
  A written goal is probably more likely to be achieved, but any improvement in completion seems to come from reviewing the goal and it being shown to other people or being available (and so increasing commitment because of the embarrassment of not doing

it). Most of the evidence seems to come from New Year Resolutions, and clearly if they are written down they might be reviewed, amended in line with performance, and generally kept as a motivator. If they are just announced drunkenly, to a drunken audience, at 3AM on January the first, they are likely to be forgotten about pretty quickly.

You don't always need all of those. Apply some common sense. Some goals need to be refined, worked on, revised, thought about again and end up with nearly all those points in there somewhere.

Some just need a specific short term goal, a quick check that it is in line with longer term ones, a measure of how you're getting on and how you'll know you've reached it, what actions you'll take and when, and that will do.

If it is all too much for you, you can just use my key points earlier in the chapter. You can use SMART if you really want to (I'd suggest making A stand for "able", meaning you control it) and make sure you've got a series of goals leading to your longer term one.

Running through a longer checklist helps to give you the best chance of achieving your goal, but I'm used to it and what at first looks a lot to remember seems pretty simple to me because it's what I always do. Similarly, my clients have me to help them, and again, if you're just starting off with trying to set goals you might want some help (Chapter 15).

If you want to remember all the points for yourself, so that you can run a check on your goals, the best way is to make up your own mnemonic, a song, make a picture etc. This is because human memory is constructive and if you build it, you'll remember it. If somebody else tells you how to remember it, you'll probably forget it. However, the mnemonic I use is

CHEAP SMART PLAN

When I'm setting a goal with a client, I run through that in my head and check that anything that it makes sense to define and clarify has been defined and clarified (but I don't think I've ever needed to have every single one).

The letters stand for these elements of a person's goal:

Controllable (they control it, they're not at somebody else's mercy as to whether they reach it or not)

Happy (long term it will make them happy)

Exciting (short term it will get them out of bed)

Aligned (the long and the short term are in the same direction)

Positively worded (it aims at a good outcome, rather than starting out to avoid something unpleasant)

Specific (they know what it is, and will know when they've reached it)

Measurable (they know how far they've come and how far they have to go by outcomes)

Adaptable (if things go better or worse than expected, there is somewhere to go with the goal)

Resourced (it is achievable from where they are, but it might be a stretch)

Timed (we know when things, particularly actions are expected to happen)

Planned (it is set out as a plan, not a vague wish that something would happen)

Little steps (this fits with measurement of progress, it doesn't leave yawning gaps)

Action based (it is about doing things, not waiting for stuff to happen)

Noted (it is recorded somewhere, shown to people as a potential source of embarrassment if not done)

The easiest way to work out how you might use this is to look at some examples. Before I set some out, there are a couple of things you need to know about how I work with clients on financial goals.

The way that I look at the technical side of finance is deliberately simple. I spent years trying to explain technical details to people who didn't understand them and wouldn't have cared if they did, and I now spend time avoiding any technical financial details at all. So you can find far more detailed and thorough treatments of how to structure financial data in other books. However, the way I set it out below works for most people, and it is easy to understand.

> *There are two main things that you can do with your money,*
> ***Accumulate*** *it and* ***Reduce*** *it.*

Within accumulating you can save to build up funds, protect what you've got, and generate more.

Within reducing you can spend money on non-essentials, use it to live and you can donate it.

I did say it was simple! You can add complications to each of those if you want, building up funds can be lump sum investments, pensions, tax efficient savings vehicles etc. Protection can be insurance, emergency funds, conservative investing and so on. But the point is, those two categories, and their three divisions each are enough for most purposes, and keep things simple and consistent.

If you want an illustration of how that works, imagine that you follow the common advice of maximising your mortgage to buy a bigger house than you really want as an "investment" (often called leveraging). In my system it is spending on non-essentials, because you're paying for a bigger mortgage than you need to buy a house you won't use fully.

By the time you sell it to realise your profit (assuming it has gone up, which is a potentially big and questionable assumption) you've got used to having all that extra space, the extra convenient shops and schools, the nice location etc. (all the things that made it more expensive than you needed) and you can't bear to part with it (you adapt quickly going up and slowly going down, remember).

And of course everything else has gone up, so you can't get as much profit as you thought, unless you go and live in a tent.

So you thought you were buying an "investment" and you were actually spending on a non-essential. That's fine if that's what you want to do (if the better house is really an essential for happiness), but my system keeps things simple and makes it easier for you to see what you are actually doing, rather than kid yourself that you are doing something sophisticated (rather than silly) by giving what you do lots of fancy labels.

If you want the bigger, better house and that is a value for you and your family, set a goal for it and go get it. If you want to do other things with the money that would go on the bigger mortgage, get a smaller mortgage, set your goals for what you will really value, and go get that instead. If you want an investment to build up money to achieve your values and decide property is the way to go, buy an investment property or fund. Simple!

Look how much I saved, and if you hadn't stopped the credit card I could have got an extra four speakers and saved even more

Back to examples of what I suggest you do. I can only give a few to show the general method. In setting your own goals, you need to adapt the details to your specific situation. I'll take the examples from some real clients (with some details changed to protect the innocent, obviously) that are typical of what are regarded as quite complex financial issues, but the finances are pretty simple, it is the people who are complicated!

Example 1

You are a young couple. You're expecting your second child. With the first, the mother carried on working, you got childcare and everything was fine. Now she's got the longing to spend more time with the children and feels she is missing out on something precious. So the value, the thing that will give meaning needs to be discussed, i.e. what is more important to the couple and their children?

Suppose the decision is that the mother is going to give up work, or reduce hours (of course the father can also give up work to look after the children. That can work just as well, but, as we'll see in chapter 6, the mother is generally more likely to have a stronger drive to be with the children). The longer term goal is then to ensure that this position is sustainable, you don't want to run out of money and be forced to return to work just when the children particularly need attention.

Long-term, the value is to give more time to the children and family and potentially exchange this for some income (and the stimulation of working) and to make sure that you both enjoy what you wanted (time with the children) and can afford to do what you want as a family.

The first goal that might be set is around protecting what you've got. You now have only one income (or one and a bit), and children are quite expensive, so income goes down and spending goes up.

When you had two incomes and no children, you could cope with one of you being ill or dying, it would be sad, but you could cope financially because you both had an income. With only one income, if either one of you dies or falls ill and isn't able to work or care for the children, you've got a huge financial problem. So you decide to check out insurance (see chapter 10 for more details). You set a goal to make sure you're covered.

Look at the CHEAP SMART PLAN mnemonic. Is that a good goal? Without going through every point in detail, I'd say no, and think, it needs to be more specific, how much would we need if one of us was ill or died?

We control the amount of cover, we are looking at something important to us and our short term goal is well in line with our long term, but it isn't measurable until we get to arranging it. So we need action steps.

How about, work out what income or lump sum we'd need in different situations by looking at what we spend now, and researching or asking some professionals for their ideas of what would be suitable and the costs, get together and work out what we want to have, check on the resources to make sure we can afford it, work out how we're going to provide the money (will we earn more, cut down on non-essential spending etc.) then arrange it.

So we'd need a note of who was doing what (so we don't both assume the other person is doing it and it doesn't get done) and some timescales so we don't just let it drift and can make sure that we've got all the details we were each supposed to get when we are due to meet and discuss it.

And finally, I'd want to see if we could build in some adaptability if I could, so that if we changed our minds (the mother got bored of only having children conversations all day and had to get some adult interaction or go mad) we can perhaps vary the terms a bit, perhaps cut down the premiums for a while if they're not needed.

Worked out in that way, the goal is more likely to be reached and you'll be able to have the life you want, even if there is a disaster. And instead of curbing spending or changing energy suppliers or whatever just to "save money", you know what you want to do with the money you save and it provides something you want and need. It takes work, but nothing is terribly difficult and most of the steps don't require any great financial knowledge. They just need you to think through what you would value and a goal to get you towards it, to imagine what you would need in certain circumstances, then get on with organising things and getting the specific financial details and advice that you need.

Example 2

You're in debt. You dread opening the credit card bills, you want to start saving some money but there is always another bill to pay and too much month at the end of the money. You think about cutting up credit cards, consolidation loans, emigration! But all you really want is to be out of debt.

Look at the CHEAP SMART PLAN mnemonic. The first thing I'd notice is that it isn't actually positive, get out of debt. Your mind doesn't do that sort of thing well, remember. You'll work at it for a while, get depressed, rebel, spend some money you haven't got and then beat yourself up for being stupid and end up where you started (but now really depressed).

How about thinking what you actually want, what would your life look like, what would you do if you weren't worrying about money all the time? Go back to your values (chapter 2) and work out what you are trying to achieve. Just being debt free and "getting your life back" is nothing if you don't know what you're going to do with your life when you get it back!

Imagine that you've always wanted a trip round the world, dreamed of the things you'll see, what you'll do, the experiences. All positive, but it's never quite happened because it is expensive, you have to give up your job to do it and you know in your heart that you'll never save enough money, you start saving and then blow the savings (and more) on something.

OK, so the negative "debt free", has become a positive value of taking that trip round the world and a goal of building up enough money to go for it. Think of the mnemonic again. It's not specific enough, so cost out the holiday. Find out what that, plus your debts, totals. That's the amount you're trying to save and which gives you a specific long-term target, you can measure how well you're doing and will know when you get there. It's going to make you happy long term, but it is probably too far away to be exciting. So you need an aligned goal that will take you part of the way there. How about sorting out priorities for tackling debts?

Once you've sorted out your priorities, you know which debt to tackle first to move towards your long term goal as quickly as possible. That gives you a figure that you need to find each week, month or whatever. That's a short term goal, it's clear what it is, it is measurable, it is close enough to drive you on (you'll get satisfaction out of clearing that card, paying off that loan or that bill etc. and knowing that is a positive step towards building up the money for the holiday). You've got some idea of timescale and some action steps (you're finding a given amount of money each period). It is under your control and it can be adapted if there is sudden success or a problem.

That defines the immediate goal fairly well, now you need to plan the steps to find that money to keep living your life while tackling the priority debt, going through each debt or bill in priority order until you are actually building up your holiday fund. That's where the comparison sites, the cheaper shopping advice and so on (look at chapter 4 if spending is a problem for you), will help. But this time, instead of just vaguely trying to save money, you know how much money you're trying to find. If you discover a bigger saving, can eliminate some unnecessary spending or anything similar, you can get to your holiday faster by killing the priority debts quicker. There is more about dealing with debt (including some resources) in chapter 11.

I'll give one more example, but first, you'll have seen in that last example that there is a potential circle around the goal, the time to achieve it, the resources (financial and emotional) you've got available and what you might do to achieve it.

GROW!

This is something that you might want some professional help with, but the help that you get may well use a process that you might use for yourself, called the GROW model. This is used by a lot of coaches and is a relatively simple model to use and teach. I use it to teach financial advisors to use the material in this book.

However, it is something you can use on yourself (it works particularly well if you work as a couple, you can take turns to "coach" one another).

The letters in GROW stand for:

Goal	*What are you aiming for?*
Reality	*What is your real, objective situation now?*
Options	*What could you do to get from where you are to your goal?*
Way ahead	*What are you going to do?*

I won't go through the process in great detail, if my brief description makes sense and works for you, great. If you think it would help, but can't quite work it out then get some professional help.

As in our examples above, you often get to a point where you are looking at resources and options, what level of cover you need, what it costs and how you pay for it, what debts you have, which are priorities and how (and how much) you pay off each month, that sort of thing. They are interdependent, you don't know how much you can pay until you look at ways you can get the money (how much you can economise, how much extra you can earn, etc.). Those in turn will affect the time-scale of the goal. But once you've got the basic goal, look at the *Reality*.

Don't hide your head in the sand. If you're a couple, ask questions of one another, if you're on your own, ask yourself (or get somebody, professional or trusted friend, to question you), but be honest. Don't hide bills, don't assume that "something will turn up" to allow you to keep the second car, pay for day-care, pay for a cleaner etc. Get a clear idea of where you are.

This always interested me as an advisor when talking to people about retirement planning. Clients told me that they "couldn't" find an amount to save for their retirement, they couldn't live on less than 100% of their earnings. I tried to point out that this would mean that when they retired and had about 150% more time to spend the money in, they would be trying to live on about 10% of their earnings, so if they couldn't put away 10-15% and live on 85-90% now, how would they live on 10% in retirement?

But I didn't know how to make that real for them, it was in the distant future and they couldn't see it as a reality. So look at what you really have, what fears you have, what assumptions you make (possibly go over chapters 1 and 2 again, and read chapter 4 to remind yourself of just how well your habits and assumptions fit with what you really want to have in your life).

Once you've got a firm grip on what your *Reality* is relative to your *Goal*, you might need to revise the *Goal* a bit, or you might go on to *Options*.

With *Options*, the more ideas you can generate, the better. Give yourself (or one another) permission to go wild. Can you generate extra income, are there things you can sell, ideas that you can market, small businesses to start from a hobby, overtime to do? What about the subscriptions to things you don't use that you can eliminate, the hobbies or habits that you don't really follow any more so there are things you can sell or give away, the expenditures you don't need or the little luxuries that you don't value? This is where it is very much up to you, there are some ideas in chapter 14 for ways you can use your human habits of thought to your advantage and chapter 4 has ideas for economising, but you know yourself best and you can think of the ideas.

There are lots of useful hints and tips on savings available and this is when they can come in handy. Don't censor the ideas, try to generate as many as you can without thinking "that won't work", or "I can't do that". Jot them down. When you've got every option that you can think of, grab a cup of coffee or whatever your choice of break is, switch off for a few minutes, then go back to it. You'll find some more! When you've got every option you're going to get, look through them and pick the ones that fit best with the goal and the reality. It might be the one that is hard, but generates everything you need, it might be a few easy ones that you are confident that you can do and that don't scare you too much. Incidentally, it is usually more productive to "brainstorm" like this on your own, then to compare notes with a partner or others than it is to try to get ideas in a group first.

You might still have to circle around a bit between the *Goal*, the *Reality* and the *Options* until you find a balance that will get you to the *Goal* bearing in mind the *Reality* and that is an *Option* you can do.

But remember, if the only *Options* to get to the *Goal* from where you are in *Reality* are ones that you don't like much, you've got a choice. You can give up on the *Goal*, or take a deep breath and get on with it.

That's why, often, I spend a lot of time on the *Reality* element with clients, because that is the thing that people don't want to face. It's where you find out whether you want the *Goal* enough, whether it does motivate you enough to do what you need to do to achieve it, (remember the quote from Sidney Howard, "One half of knowing what you want is knowing what you must give up before you get it").

That's also why I spent time talking about having short-term, exciting *Goals*, you generally need something special to overcome your fears, and something small scale and practical to get started on achieving your *Goals* on the way to your values.

Once you've worked out the *Options* that will get you from your

Reality to your *Goal* and defined your *Goal* well enough to include things like resources, alignment, positive wording etc., you get to the *Way Forward*. That is going to be the detailed element of your plan, the small, action steps that will take you to your *Goal*.

Now that final example.

Example 3

You're single, you're well paid but you're bored with your job. You feel vaguely dissatisfied so you look at your values (chapter 2) and you realise that you want to do something more meaningful with your life. So you set a goal to find out what you could do and you find out there is a job you could do that would be perfect. You don't rush into it, you talk to people who do the job, you check it out thoroughly and the more you find out, the more it appeals and the more pointless your current lifestyle seems. But this new job requires training, which you can't afford to do if you give up your current job and even with that training, you'll be competing with people much younger than you for jobs when you qualify.

Now at this point you might just give up, as it's hard to make changes. But if you don't give up, if you stick with the important value to you of having a more meaningful life, what is your goal?

You might try to find another alternative, but if you stick with starting the new job there seem to be two possible immediate goals, to get the qualifications or to make yourself more attractive as a potential employee and work your way in without the qualifications and qualify later.

So let's look at the option of aiming to qualify. Is that a good goal? Think of CHEAP SMART PLAN. It's certainly in line with your values, and quite positive (although you might want to phrase the "qualification" as something more exciting, something that it will allow you to do rather than just being letters after your name). It's quite specific and it is certainly under your control. What you need are some steps, actions, perhaps a timescale and a short term, exciting sub-goal to get you out of bed. Presumably the qualification is made up of different modules or courses, so those break things up for you. You also may have course options to decide upon.

This is where you get to the money element, and the use of GROW in this particular case. Your *Goal* is reasonably clear, but you still need to have a plan and know what action you are going to take first. The *Reality* is, in part, that you don't have enough money at the moment to give up work to study full time. So first, you need to examine whether it is true? Are you saying you don't proceed because you're scared to take a chance? Can you rent out a room, get a part time job, or otherwise increase your income? Can you re-arrange your investments to generate more income, or cut down on your non-essential expenses? Have you got some money (Auntie Gertie's money, chapters 5 and 14) that you are saving for a "special purpose" and what is more special than fulfilling a dream?

You'll have noticed that this look at *Reality* has drifted into *Options*. That often happens, when you're checking out whether the obstacles you see are real or simply come from your own assumptions or self-limiting beliefs.

If it really proves impossible to gain the qualification full-time, what other options do you have? Can you save up for a few years and put the money away, can you do the qualification part-time? Are there colleges that do the course that would let you do distance learning, part time, evenings and weekends, summer schools?

Alternatively, the other option is examine whether there is a way to get into the job by another route, without the qualifications. I said earlier, don't limit yourself, use your imagination. Can you make contact with somebody and talk your way in, do you know anybody who can get you a job in the area? Can you work part time as unskilled labour for a firm while you study, (they get some cheap, reliable and keen help, you get some money and more importantly get practical experience and make contacts, so you become more able to step into a role)?

Then you look again at your *Reality*, and pick out the *Option*, or *Options* that get you to your *Goal*. Then you can work out what you are going to do, which is both the *Way Ahead* (from GROW) and your plan and action steps of your Goal. Whether that is about money or not, and the exact nature of what it is if it does use money (renting a room, saving, economising, seeing what discounts you can get for fee payment etc.) doesn't really matter. The point is that you have a clear idea of what you are trying to do, you know what you need, where you can make economies, where you can get extra income.

And again, note that nearly all of this is about *you*. You generally don't need sophisticated financial knowledge at the start. You only need to find out about finance when you have sorted out what you want to do, and that depends on what you value in life, why you want it, how much you want it. When you know those things, you can sort out goals to achieve what you value, and at some point in that process you might need some specific financial information.

At that point, your priorities are clear, you know how much you want, so it is a lot easier to change your spending habits, make economies and so on, because you understand why you are doing it and have powerful reasons for change. Then whether you need to research the financial details yourself or get professional help, you can clearly specify what you are trying to do, your timescales, your reasoning etc.

Remember my two clients? Who was it easier to advise, the confused one, or the one with a clear purpose and a clear goal?

Hopefully that gives you ideas on how to set your own goals. Ones that fit with *your* values and take account of your personality and habits.

You Tame the Pound by learning about *you* rather than trying to learn about money, because it's you that has the values, sets out the goals and makes the decisions. Think, if you like, of your Tame Pound as being a guide dog for the financially blindfolded!

Summary:

- Remember what a goal is – have you got a goal or a wish list?
- Compare the two clients – your definition of what you will value needs to be like the second one for you to be able to set goals.
- Remember the "archer" analogy,
    - o find out what you want and your real value,
    - o then set your goals for achieving the values,
    - o then make your plans to achieve the goals.
- Remember Robin Hood, take your blindfold off, don't kill the wrong people or steal from the poor to give to the rich!
- Remember Cheap Smart Plan (or whatever mnemonic you want) to make sure your goals work.
- Adapt the examples to your own circumstances.
- Use GROW to think about how this is going to happen.
- Read "Coaching for performance" by John Whitmore

One thing that can help you to do all this is to use your money well, economise to a purpose, set budgets to fit your plans and so on.

But what happens when, despite your best intentions, the money keeps using you?

Spend, spend, spend.

Sometimes we all do odd things with our buying behaviour. This chapter explains some reasons why and, more importantly, what we can do about it if we decide they aren't what we want.

We've talked about the fact that we're often looking at symbols instead of what we need. So we might want money or things to give ourselves power, love and so on.

But we're also doing something else symbolically when we shop, apart from trading for things that we need or want.

When you go shopping, not for the weekly household needs but to buy something for yourself, your partner or family:

- How long do you spend on a shopping trip, on average?
- How often do you go?
- How much planning do you have to do for a trip?
- Do you go on your own (maybe on-line) or with friends/family?
- With whom do you discuss what you're going to buy?
- To whom do you show purchases?
- What proportion of things never comes out of the cupboard or box when you get it home?
- Do you know how much you spend each time (is that accurate, or can you not even guess)?
- How much do you spend, on average, every month?
- Do you tell anybody how much you spend, if so, whom?

Different people may have very different patterns, but they often slot into one of six typical ones. This is not a scientific scale, just a tool I use, but people often seem to treat shopping as being a:

Social event. You might have a "fun day out for all the family". It might be a couple of friends going out for a day to do a bit of bonding, a bit of shopping, a bit of chatting over coffee.

Fantasy. It can be to try bits and pieces on that you aren't going to buy, to look at things on the internet, to have a little daydream about having things that you can't afford, then going back to real life.

Chance to get status, love etc. It isn't something that you actually want or need in reality, you just want to prove something to yourself or to somebody else about who and what you are and you're aiming to do it by symbols.

Chance to buy. You actually feel good spending money (but it is usually on credit rather than cash). The things you buy are actually secondary, you may have a wardrobe full of items you don't ever see again, but the buzz comes from buying, from hunting down the bag to match the shoes, or finding the 7th generation gizmo when your friends only have the 5th generation one.

Chance to own. You get a kick out of having the outfit that was in the style magazine, or the latest mobile phone with personal home cinema and teleport facility. You might never get round to playing with the new item before the next one comes out and don't need to show them to anybody. It is enough to have them and to have (as my wife put it) "the Jimmy Choos sitting on the TV" so you know you've got them.

Chance to show things off. The finding and having are fun, but the real thrill is thinking about showing your purchases off. You'll probably have in mind the person that you want to show it to, and what their reaction will be. In fact, you probably saw the item and before you thought about wearing/using it you imagined the reaction of somebody particular (or a group reaction) to you showing it off.

Of course, if you can just go to buy something that you really need and want, and it will see some use, great!

Similarly, if you just want something and you can afford it, there probably isn't a problem. OK, you know you're not going to like it in a couple of weeks, but if it is fun in the meantime and it is worth it to you, why not? If you buy stuff you want, and can afford, or at least you know it is a temporary fad and you can afford it, you're probably going to be fine, aren't you?

A lot of people don't want to go to the trouble of thinking about what they want, or what their buying brings them. They want an easy answer and that answer is to buy anything they fancy and assume that they want it and can afford it. When credit is easy (which it was for nearly twenty years in the UK) ignoring your motives like that seemed to work. You could always get credit, so why worry about what you want something for, or why you are buying it, the fact that you think that you want it and can have it is enough. And if you get a good feeling from finding it, buying it and/or showing it off, that's great!

But what if buying that stuff stops you buying something that you would really value?

This is where your "economise to reach your goal" comes in. If you still buy the gear that you *can* afford, but now realise that you have a better use for the money, why buy things that you don't really want?

Another spending problem comes when you try to buy yourself reassurance that you are lovable, show off your status to other people and so on, rather than think about what you really want.

So you can only cope with feeling sad (or whatever your trigger is) by feeding your habitual addiction, that is, by going shopping.

My parents didn't love me enough, My mother smothered me
I need shoes to feel secure.   I need a GPS to allow me to be free.

Talking about motives for buying particular things and having a sceptical view of credit might sound a bit old fashioned, although there is a big move now towards "thrift" and other old fashioned values.

Similarly, it seems wise after the event, since everybody now says that there was "too much" credit. But I don't think the problem is "too much" or "too easy" credit. The issue is whether what we do is sustainable. You can do what you like with money as long as you can keep it going long term.

> *We all might want more things than we can afford to buy. If we buy the bigger house, we can't also have the holiday. If we have the car, we can't also have the home entertainment system.*
>
> *We have to make choices between what we want enough to use up our*

limited resources and what we would like, but isn't worth sacrificing something else to have. With credit, we can buy a lot more than we can really afford.

But we still can't have everything!

We still have to make choices. Will we have the big house (and mortgage) and the new car (on credit) and the holiday and home entertainment system (on credit card) and realise that in addition, our children each want a pony and we would like a swimming pool and Jacuzzi?

We have to draw a line somewhere. Since that is the case, which policy makes more sense to you?

1. First, decide what you really want for yourself and your family (look at your real values from chapter 2), buy those things, then see how much is left and maybe buy some other things that you want a bit less?
2. Second, buy whatever you fancy buying because you can show it off, what a magazine says you ought to buy, what your friends have etc. irrespective of whether you want those things the most and whether, in fact you want those things at all?

Bearing in mind that you have to stop buying at some point, you probably think that the first one is sensible, but you have done (and maybe still do) the second one!

Many people also shop for, spend money on and buy not only things they haven't worked out whether they need, but to give themselves the therapy, lift from depression or whatever they get from shopping, having or showing-off itself, so the actual items they buy are completely irrelevant!

If any of this sounds like you, what do you do about it?

First of all, I'd suggest you think about what I call the Micawber rule.

"Annual income twenty pounds, annual expenditure nineteen, nineteen, six, result happiness. Annual income twenty pounds, annual expenditure twenty pounds, ought and six, result misery."

Charles Dickens, in 'David Copperfield'

That seems to me to be a good description. Mr Micawber didn't have credit cards, but was aware that, in the end, you need to have the money if you want to buy things.

If we take it as true that spending more than your income is a problem for you, what do you do?

> *Your long term solution is to think about what you really need and what buying it means that you have to give up. Then you re-organise your priorities so your life and your spending are geared to what you need, your values and happiness, not to the buttons other people have pushed for you, a desperate search for security or a delusion that somehow money is the answer so the question doesn't matter.*

However, right now, what do you do about your shopping habit? We're assuming that you buy things not only for what you are buying and whatever those symbolise for you, but also for whatever you get from shopping itself. If you can window shop, go in and try things on, have a little fantasy about it and then walk away, great. That doesn't cost you anything and hopefully you only actually buy things that you really need.

The "social event" shopper has an approach that you might use. If your idea of a good night out would cost a certain amount, you can use that as guide for what the social value of shopping is to you.

For example, I know what my idea of a good night out is and what that typically costs me. That is my overall limit for entertainment. So if

I go shopping, or I'm invited to a horse race or something where I can spend money I take my entrance money, cab costs, drink costs etc. out of my limit. What is left is my "play money". If I win something, or buy something valuable that is a bonus. If I lose it all, I've had an evening or a day's entertainment for the same price as I could have seen a show or whatever.

Incidentally, the approach of setting yourself a limit on what you will spend is an example of "mental accounting", which we'll talk about later on.

Of course, if you come into one of the other categories I mentioned earlier, it is more of a problem. When people really depend on shopping to cheer themselves up, whether it is basically about buying, having or showing off, it starts to resemble addiction. In that case it is appropriate to look at ways to change that are derived from dealing with addiction.

I'll put in a caution here. This is a book designed to allow you to "self-help". It can't be a substitute for professional assistance. If you've really got a problem with spending, you might want to consider getting professional assistance, and chapter 15 gives some guidance on where and how to look for suitable help for you.

If you are taking on your own challenges with spending too much, there are three things it is helpful to know.

1. Changing any habit or behaviour pattern tends to be difficult and there are no "magic solutions". Yes, I know you have a friend (or usually have heard of a friend of a friend of a friend) who woke up one day and gave up shopping (heroin, gambling, smoking etc.) just like that. Some of those stories are true, but
    a) they are very rare in real life as distinct from stories,
    b) you usually find that the person who gave up so quickly goes back to it just as quickly and
    c) the "overnight" cure (like overnight success) was often

contemplated for years in advance before it finally resulted in an "overnight" cure.

2. Changing any habit or behaviour is not impossible. Yes, I know you tried before and it didn't work. It is difficult, and because there are lots of people peddling "miracle cures" (like diet pills, sure fire investments, quit smoking schemes etc.) that make it sound easy, you get confused and disheartened when you haven't lost 5 stone, gained £1 million in two weeks or whatever you were promised. However, it is possible, and you can do it, but you will have to work at it.

3. People are different, and need to do different things in order to change. The same person may also need to do different things at different times in order to change. Yes, I know it would be easier if there was a magic formula to be sensible with money (or lose weight, stop smoking, banish social anxiety etc.) that everybody could use. It would also be easier if one application of one method helped you whatever sort of problem you had (buying shoes from stores, buying gadgets on the internet, buying junk generally etc.) or wherever you were with the problem (concerned about spending, contemplating the bill you can't pay, considering bankruptcy etc.). It would also be nice to end world hunger and get everybody to love one another, but that's another problem that has no simple solution, is very difficult but not impossible, and that we have to look on as a work in progress!

Think about what it is you get from shopping and what is driving your spending. Write these things down.

Then think about how much you want to change, and how much you want to stay the same. That isn't as daft as it sounds. Most people who try and fail to change haven't worked out what they get out of the behaviour they say they want to change.

Think about your "self-image". If you don't have the "relief valve" of going out and blowing more money than you actually have, what will you do when life gets a bit much? If shopping is your habitual behaviour to cure depression, what will become of you if you can't shop, will you become suicidal? If you can't show off to people all the great things you've bought, will your friends still be your friends? If your identity is tied up in possessions, if you haven't got more shoes than Imelda Marcos who will you be, will you like yourself?

That isn't because you're crazy, it's because you're human and humans are incredibly complex, unique, and, well, human! We all have an image of ourselves, and we are scared of destroying that image. If your shopping and owning patterns are part of your self-image, then changing it is hard. Remember the client I mentioned in chapter 1, whose money was "my money" and couldn't be shared with his wife even if it would save him money.

It is very easy to do with spending what many of us do with diets, stick to the new plan for a while, maybe only a few hours, maybe until it starts to work then get scared of the changes we see and feel, worry about how we'll cope under pressure and go back to our old ways because that is more familiar and seems safer.

Have a good think about what you get from spending and having "stuff", and why you want to change. I suggest to clients that they write down the situation on a piece of paper, something like this:

Changing	Staying the same
Pro	Pro
Con	Con

Incidentally, this comes from a technique called Motivational Interviewing, by Rollnick and Miller. There are a couple of books they've written that might be of interest, which are listed in the references at the end and on the website.

I ask people to consider all the things they can think of, what they get out of staying as they are in terms of their image, their concept of who they are, their health, ambitions, the outcomes they can see, costs of change, benefits of change to others, everything. Without that, you get really one-sided tables, and can try to make changes that you are not ready to make. Then it all goes wrong and you get the idea that you are really weak-willed and cannot change.

This technique is designed to get around the "weak willed" idea. We all have will power. We all have motivations. It is just that the motivation may not drive us to make the changes we say we are motivated to make. So, for example, you may say you want to be sensible with money, but actually your strongest motivation is to keep on as you are, because that is more comfortable, change is scary, etc.

So you think "I'm weak willed" but actually you're strong willed, your conscious mind is telling you to act differently, but your will (which is largely unconscious) is saying, "no way, that's far too scary, you carry on spending, you know where you are with spending. Who knows what will happen if you try to be sensible"! So your will power is actually strong, it just isn't pushing you the same way as your conscious decisions.

You need to get your motivations and your unconscious will out there in the open so you can see what is going on, and get them lined up with your conscious intentions. If you rush into it and don't think it through, you can end up with something like this:

Changing	Staying the same
Pro I'll feel more in control My family will respect me more I'll have the money to buy what I really want I'll have a better credit rating	Pro It's easier
Con It is hard to change habits	Con I'll end up in serious debt I might lose the house It will be really embarrassing

On that basis, it is really easy to decide to change. You dive right in, ban yourself from shopping, make a list of all your expenditures, cut up your credit cards and so on (all the ideas you've heard that are supposed to be magic ways to change your habits). But after the novelty wears off (usually between 24 hours and a month or so) you get some more cards, "because it is convenient". You have the odd shopping spree, "because you need some things". You buy things that aren't in your budget list, "because they are on offer". Then you have a good orgy of self-criticism about your weakness, and decide that you might as well give up.

What it needs is a bit more preparation. You probably have to spend more time to think through what you are really getting out of whatever you do now and the habits you want to change. So that table might, in reality, look more like this:

Changing	Staying the same
Pro I'll feel more in control My family will respect me more I'll have the money to buy what I really want I'll have a better credit rating	Pro It's easier I have a reputation for being generous I'm comfortable the way I am Partner/kids/friends like me as I am
Con It is hard to change habits People will think I'm stingy Friends won't want to see me Who will I actually be What if I fail	Con I'll end up in serious debt I might lose the house It will be really embarrassing

That makes it a bit trickier, doesn't it? Sorry, I said it wasn't easy! But that table is a lot more like the sort of thing that clients actually produce, usually after much prompting and heart-searching.

Write your own table, and see what you get from it.

Maybe you decide you're not ready to change your habits yet. That's fine. You know you, I don't. I can write this and it might not apply to you.

But if you think that you are not ready, work out what is going to switch the balance. Do you have to lose your job, have your house drop another 10%, get a bill you can't pay, lose sleep over how you'll pay for the holiday because you spent the holiday fund paying for rubbish you didn't really want. What is going to make you ready? Write it down.

If it happens, you've got it written down and it wasn't me that said it, it was you, and you wouldn't fib to yourself, would you?

If you decide you are going to change, we need to work on some assumptions. That is because you are unique, there isn't a solution that will fit you and everybody else as well. So you're going to have to adapt this to your own circumstances. Fortunately, there is a general approach (rather than an answer) to doing this.

An important part of this is your readiness to make a change, because the actions that are potentially useful depend very much on your readiness. That means that you need to be clear on how ready you are and only then think about what you do to change. That might sound an obvious thing to do, but failure to do it is a major reason why the "one size fits all" approach doesn't usually work, although every programme, guru or self-help book about any problem, including finance, has some success stories.

If you are ready for a particular approach, and happen to find it (you read the book, see the "Celebrity Expert", go on the programme) at the right time, then it may work. Of course, if you're not ready, it doesn't work, and you might go on reading books, going on diets or stop smoking plans or attending financial seminars until you are old and grey and never sort out the problem or have any reason for failure other than that you "lack will-power".

The stages I'm describing are contemplation, preparation, action and maintenance. The first thing to do is to work out which stage you are in. Look through the descriptions, and see what best fits your situation.

Contemplation

I'm thinking about changing my habits. I don't have to cut back a lot yet, but it is something that might come up. There might be job losses at work, or overtime bans, my own business is not as healthy as it was, but I'm OK. I do wonder whether I need to change my spending habits. I think it would be good to sort out with my partner and/or children how important the money is and how important the "quality time" is and what my "ideal life" would look like.

Planning

I'm getting a bit worried about money. Things are getting tight and it is possible I'll lose my job, or my partner will lose hers/his. I am planning to cut back. I know I need to change my spending habits. I've been looking into ways to cut back, the price-comparison websites and so on. I've done a couple of things like change energy suppliers but I'm not sure whether it is really making much difference. I know I focus too much on money, I'm a bit of a workaholic and I want a bit more balance in my life. I keep thinking about talking to my partner or somebody about money, but I'm scared to do much and am not sure how to approach it.

Action

I am taking action. I've cancelled some of the cards, cancelled the gym membership, banned myself from shopping. My or my partner's jobs are being made (or have been made) redundant. My business is going down the tubes. I really need to sort my finances out, I don't know what I owe but I'm fairly sure it is more than I've got. I have tried to discuss my finances with my partner, but it always turns into a blazing row. I keep going round in circles with the problem. I'm cutting back on overtime and starting to get a bit more balance, but I keep getting sucked back into chasing after having "stuff" instead of enjoying my life. I'm too tired to enjoy the money I've got.

Maintenance

I've taken action and it has been working. I've cut down on the money going out and found ways to get more in. I feel better about it, but sometimes still want to go out and do something mad that I can't afford. I'm starting to see how my life has improved, my relationships are better, I think less about work/money and more about what I'm really achieving, but I don't want all that effort to go to waste.

Identify which stage sounds most like you.

Incidentally, the "partner discussions" we'll look at later in more detail, but if you are contemplating your life/money balance or discussing finance with somebody at any time, you might want to look back to this section before talking about it.

*If you are **contemplating**, then there are three main categories of actions that you might use to good effect.*

The first is ***consciousness-raising***. You've already done some of that. In reading this book, you've learned some things about how people generally regard money, our motivations and defences against change, beliefs about what money is for and raised your level of awareness about what you personally get out of spending money. Some increased awareness might also be forced on you by the economic environment. It's not great if companies are collapsing and people's homes being repossessed, but it does bring it home to us all that this is not a game, it is important to have control of your money rather than have it control you.

You can look for more information, do some reading around on the books I've recommended (or any others), since knowing lots about a problem and possible solutions is very rarely a bad idea. The only caution I'd give is that you can get to what is called "chronic contemplation", where you become so fixated on learning about the problem that you either get scared to do anything at all or get into the mindset that if you can only learn "that one thing more", you could solve your issues easily. Knowledge to enable you to discuss the matter sensibly and to have some options to consider is great and gives you confidence, obsessing about trivia is almost always a waste of time.

Another thing you can do is **emotional arousal**. The stuff on TV about people made homeless by debt, or who cannot afford to buy the children anything for Christmas can make you determined to take action for yourself. A certain amount of self-disgust about not being able to pay off the credit cards is a good thing, if it fires you up so that you determine to sort yourself out. Similarly, seeing people who have realised too late that nobody on their deathbed said "I wish I'd spend more time at work", can help you get a sense of proportion. And helping other people (voluntary work, giving to charity, helping friends who have even worse problems than you) has the triple advantage of making you feel that you are doing something worthwhile, making you aware and emotional about your problems of servitude to your money and (with voluntary work) putting your own problems in a bit of perspective.

Helping others is also, as mentioned in chapter 2, a good way to gain genuine and long term happiness. But don't take it *too* far. If you end up distressed at your own failure to act, disgusted at your selfishness when others have real problems or find that the thought leaves you a weeping mess at the extent of human tragedy, you've got a bit too emotional! Getting wound up enough to be really determined that you are going to get it right, and will be a role-model for others is great; putting an emotional millstone around your neck is not going to help anyone.

The third major thing that you can do is **self re-evaluation**. This too is something you've made a start on. You've looked at why you do some things you do with money. Compare them with what you want to do. That means having an idea of the person that you want to be.

> Then have a look back at your table of pros and cons.

You have to do this for yourself. But to show how it works, we'll assume that you're like our hypothetical person filling in the table.

If you were the person you want to be, would you be bothered if "friends" only valued you because you gave them things? Would you really want friends like that, so would it bother you if you didn't see them much? If you were the person you want to be, would you assume that your partner/children/family think you are fine the way you are, or would you have the courage to check with them to see whether they worry about your spending or your inability to find any time to talk to them?

*If you are **planning**, then you are probably conscious of the problems and maybe some solutions.*

You still might want to go in for some ***emotional arousal***. That can help you with another process, ***commitment***. That is about believing that you can change and committing to it. We've already mentioned this in connection with one of the elements of setting useful goals. You might not have a problem with that. You might be wound up enough, or desperate enough to say, "I'm going to get control of my finances, whatever it takes". If you really do it, then based both on my experience and the research, you're a good part of the way there, you just need to learn skills and techniques to do it. If you aren't sure you can do it, which is what applies to most people, you have to build your confidence up so that you don't make a commitment to change with your fingers crossed behind your back! To do that some of the other techniques can help.

One of these is **environmental control**. Although it is only one of the areas you can work on, it is one of the most powerful and certainly the most commonly advised.

Chances are you haven't heard it called *environmental control*, though. What you tend to be told is "cut up your credit cards". While I would say that doing this is not always a good plan, it is a form of environmental control. What you are doing is changing the environment you operate in.

There are three main ways that you can do that. You can:

1.   change features of the environment,
2.   change the cues in the environment and
3.   give yourself different cues.

I'll provide a couple of examples of each of these, but this is where you need to use your own knowledge of yourself to adapt the ideas to your own environment and cues.

You can step away from the environment, for example, simply not going shopping. That might be useful for a while, but it is probably not practical long term. I suggest that you stay away from particularly tempting shops for a set time, and work on being able to shop without going mad on spending in a less intense situation.

For example if you have a shoe craze avoid all the shops for a while, and when you go back to "fun" shopping, make sure you avoid shoe shops. The idea is to help your self-control, and gradually increase your exposure to temptation. Don't try to do it all at once, deciding to go down Oxford Street on the first weekend and use your will power to avoid buying anything. You'll be like a child in a sweetshop, and what is the point of setting yourself up to fail? On the other hand, if you just say, "I won't go in any shop, ever", it gets like a diet. Do you know why diets fail? This is important, so let's make an issue of it:

Diets fail because they are not normal eating.

When you diet, you are, by definition "on a diet", and not eating *normally*. Eventually, the diet ends, and you go back to "*normal*" eating. But your pattern of normal eating is what got you where you were in the first place! Unless you are prepared to live on the diet forever, it won't work. The only way to do it is to change what is "*normal*" eating for you, so that you can live with an eating pattern that keeps you at the size and fitness level you are happy with and that you can continue with for life. The key is re-defining "*normal*" for you.

It is the same with money. If you say, "I won't go shopping, ever" you are basically dieting forever. Eventually, you will end up in a shop (unless you are prepared to live like a hermit). You've never learned to shop in a way that doesn't end up with spending more money than you can afford. So you have a problem.

There is another similarity between eating and shopping.

Addictions to both are alleged to be easier to deal with than addictions to drugs, alcohol, cigarettes etc. But you can stop smoking, drinking, drug taking etc. Not that it is easy, it's very hard, but you generally won't die if you stop and never do it again, so it is a simple case of do it or don't do it. It is simple, but hard.

With food and money, it is easier, but more complex. Can you just stop eating or spending any money? Maybe for a week or two, but long term? Stop eating or spending money entirely, and you'll almost certainly die. So you have to learn to do those while you live your life, and that is complex because you have to control the addiction rather than just remove it.

For the best chance of staying out of debt with shopping, by all means keep away for a while, avoid temptation, avoid the environment. Then introduce yourself to it in less risky situations, not the ones that are really tempting.

You can avoid shopping with your "shopping buddy", if the two of you normally drive one another on to spending. Be polite, explain what you are doing, but avoid them. This is where it can be hard. In the same way as the alcoholic whose social life as well as their problem, revolves around bars, your problem and a part of your social life revolves around certain types of shops and a particular social activity. You don't have to destroy your social life, but you do need to amend it, and you might feel that you are simply killing it off.

This sort of thing is an important preparation that people often fail to do. They decide that they will stop spending so much, then go shopping with "the usual suspects" and end up behaving the same way, and deciding that they can't change. If you prepare the environment (social and physical), you give yourself the best chance to help yourself change.

Going without your credit cards is a way to change cues to yourself. You *can* cut your cards up, if you find that you only spend heavily on credit cards and when you have only cash to spend, you don't spend.

However, cutting cards up always strikes me as being the same as the permanent diet. You don't train yourself to deal with credit, you just have to avoid it forever. Credit is convenient, if you can learn to use it sensibly. So I've got some other ideas for cards.

One is to put the card somewhere where it is difficult to get at. I heard of one idea, to put it in a bowl of water in the freezer, so it is encased in ice. I love the idea, but I think it might damage the card! But the idea is sound, make it difficult for yourself to go mad with the card. Do you have a friend or a parent on whom you can rely to hold the card for you? We'll come on to enlisting help later, but if you've got somebody who will give you a hard time about why you want the card, you give yourself time to calm down if you are just being self-indulgent, but still have access to the card if there is a real emergency.

Similarly, if you spend mostly at weekends, get a safety deposit box in the bank and put the card in there! You can't get at the card at weekends, when you are most likely to use it. That doesn't work particularly well if you do have an emergency at a weekend (although I'm not sure how many plumbers etc take credit cards anyway, so you'd probably need cash), but it is also little use if you spend on the internet, since once your details are on the system, you don't actually need the card and you can still run up the debts.

Have a think about how you spend, and how you can alter the cues and the environment in a way that is effective for you. My other cue related suggestion is to have a debit card linked to your bank account, rather than a credit card. They aren't so acceptable on the internet (which can be a good thing!), but you do get the convenience of not having to carry huge amounts of cash to make purchases (particularly since so many places now don't accept cheques) and you can't spend money you don't have. Again, think about what would work for you, and prepare appropriately.

Finally, you can change your own cues. Having reminders of what you're trying to do can be useful. We'll talk about what reminders you want in the next section on taking action. However, you can have in your diary, computer, phone or other organiser, reminders of what things you want to think of and do, so that you are more likely to think first and act afterwards than just go shopping because that is what you normally do without thought.

Another way to change things is to change the action you take to your own cues. If you feel depressed or bored and that automatically lights up the bit of your brain that tells you, "retail therapy is the answer, who cares about the question", then you can work out what else might help. If you still have the gym subscription, can you go and work out (if you've cancelled it, go for a run or something)? Can you tackle the project you keep putting off, phone a friend, do something other than instantly shop?

I mentioned exercise first for a reason, because it is one of the best alternatives to substitute for any bad habit. You get fitter and healthier, it takes your mind off the problem habit and has been shown to be effective in lifting mild depression (which is something a lot of people shop to lift) and, if you work out hard enough, you'll be too tired to shop until you drop, since you are already at the stage of dropping! Seriously, if you can't exercise for some reason can you take up relaxation, meditation, yoga, tai chi or something similar and use those as being a "go to" routine instead of shopping?

Yes mum, the fitness programme is going really well, I've entered us for next year's London Marathon.

*If you're at the stage of **action**, you will probably want to use some of the planning techniques.*

Environmental control is helpful as are some others, such as ***countering*** and ***helping relationships***.

Countering is around dealing with thoughts that don't help you. Part of that can be provided by things like exercise, meditation, mindfulness and other alternatives to whatever habit you are trying to break. The other major way that I'd suggest doing this is by working on your thoughts more directly. Most people have times when they think they can't do something, feel negative or anxious or in some way tell themselves to worry.

It might sounds strange that you would tell yourself to worry, but most of us have conversations with ourselves going on in our heads. Some of the time these conversations are pretty negative. So you can end up thinking things like:

- I've got to have the same things as other people.
- I've got to be able to handle my money (and do everything else) perfectly.
- It's a disaster if I make a mistake or show any weakness.
- I can't control my spending. why am I such an idiot?

Demanding perfection of yourself, expecting that the world should be the way you want and it is a calamity if it is not or feeling ashamed of being human, then repeatedly telling yourself that these things are true and unchangeable are all pretty good ways to take the joy out of life, whatever money you've got. Similarly, fantasising about how different things might be in the future, while OK sometimes, can mean that you spend your entire life looking to the future and "the day when...". Whether it is regret or expectation, past or future, it means you're not around to enjoy your life right now!

One way of getting yourself to change that pattern, by looking directly at the immediate situation, is mindfulness, which we mentioned in chapter 2.

Another way to change that pattern if you have trouble believing that you can change because of your internal conversations, is to **counter** those thoughts as they arise. This is another way to help with your own **commitment** to the changes you want to make. It isn't easy in practice, but in theory it is just taking ABC and adding D and E! These stand for:

A: Activating event, e.g. you feel depressed and want to cheer yourself up, go shopping and see something that you know you really can't afford.

B: Beliefs or thoughts, e.g. "I'm useless, I can't handle money, I ought to be able to afford it. No, I shouldn't even want it; I'm so stupid I don't even know what my problem is."

C: Consequences, emotional or behavioural, e.g. you feel depressed and stupid, are irritable with everybody, and you go back and buy it anyway, spending the next week beating yourself up for being stupid, then get depressed when the bill comes in, so you need to go shopping again, and beat yourself up and get depressed, and so on!

You train yourself to pick up those thoughts and:

D: Dispute the truth of the beliefs, e.g. "one thing I can't afford doesn't mean I can't handle money, and I'm being really responsible not putting it on credit and controlling my urge to buy, I'm doing fine".

E: Effective outlook; you generate an alternative view, e.g. you feel pleased that you are controlling your spending and also your own emotions and thoughts. You feel pretty good, so you don't need to go shopping to lift a depressive mood, and that makes you feel more in control, and so on.

The sort of disputes you produce will be things like:

- Is this thought true? What is my evidence for it?
- Does one example of something mean it is always the case?
- What other explanations are there for the situation, are they more realistic?
- If one of my friends thought like this, would I judge him/her the same way? What would I advise her/him to do or to think that I'm not telling myself?
- Does this belief, even if it is true, help me in any way to be the person I want to be?

The most difficult part of this is usually to pick up on the negative thoughts when they arise. You need to have the alarm bells ringing in your head as soon as the situation A occurs. So, for example, you've had a lousy day, you feel unloved and bored and on your way home you see something that you want. In the past, the pattern you've followed might be something like this:

"That's just what I need. I've had a lousy day, I want cheering up. I'll get it."

Then you have second thoughts that run something like:

"I'm stupid, I can't afford this. I'm hopeless with money. I really want it. Oh hell, I'll buy it, I'm never going to control my money anyway".

Then you go into the loop of self disgust, depression and more buying to lift the depression again! If you can catch the first thought, you can change your thoughts to something more like:

"That's just what I need – hang on, I don't need it, I just fancy having it because I've had a bad day. Do I really need it? No. Will I actually be better off for buying it? Maybe for a while, but then I'll feel awful. Hey, I'm getting good at this stuff. I've just saved myself £X. And I feel good, I'm controlling my thoughts and my money."

If you can make yourself conscious of your thoughts, and change them, it makes a huge difference to your mood and your money, but it isn't easy to do.

If you've got a real problem with this, and you don't believe that you can possibly do it on your own, it may be worth getting some professional help. I've made suggestions for how to look for help in chapter 15. But, if you want to tackle it yourself, two good books written for self help are: "Feeling good: the new mood therapy" by Burns and "Cognitive Behavioural Therapy for Dummies" by Willson and Branch

I mentioned **helping relationships** earlier on. In the planning stage it can be useful to enlist friends, the trustworthy ones who can help you control your credit card use, for example. Friends are also great for building **commitment** because if you tell them what you're doing, you've got that added incentive to stick with it. If you keep your attempts to change your behaviour to yourself, you can quietly go back to your old habits with nobody any the wiser. You'll remember that in terms of goals in chapter 3, where the written goals seem to help because they are a commitment that you are known to have made.

Enlisting friends can be a blessing or a curse, mind you. What you want is the friend who won't let you have the card for buying something you don't really need, who will ask you how much you really want it on a scale of one to ten, and tell you to wait until your desire is at least at a "nine" level before you have it! You want to enlist helpers who will be kind and encouraging, but firm. A story will illustrate this, it is about food, but it is the same principle.

I was coaching a woman who had constantly tried to lose weight, lost about 20 pounds each year and then later put it back on again, over the last five or six years. She was convinced she was a failure, not just because she was "so fat", but because she was "so pathetic" about regaining the weight each time.

We talked about motivation (as in the pros and cons earlier) and she decided that she was a bit scared of what she would become, what would her husband think if she lost the weight (he said he loved her now, so if she changed would he still love her)? What would her friends think ("they're all much slimmer than me") if she lost weight, would they feel she was competing with them and becoming a threat to their relationships?

She needed a supportive friend, but was having trouble sorting out who would really help and who would hinder her without meaning to. So we imagined a party, with a huge chocolate cake on the table.

The friend she needed was not the one who would say, "I'm so glad you're here. I really want a piece of that cake and I don't want to eat it on my own, you'll have a piece won't you?" She needed the one who would say, "I'm so glad you're here. You look so great and you're so strong willed. That cake is calling to me and I know you'll help me resist it".

My client knew that with the first friend, she would pretty much have to eat the cake, and that was what had always happened. She was subconsciously picking her friends to sabotage her once she started to lose some weight and get worried about the changes she was making. She could see that with the second friend she'd probably chew her arm off before eating the cake, given that build up, and she knew exactly which of her friends she needed to help her.

If you're at the maintenance stage, have a look through the previous sections for methods you can use.

You may find **environmental control** you could use, employ **countering**, enlist **helping relationships** or renew your **commitment**.

One thing that can help with commitment is rewarding yourself. Not a reward that involves spending money, at least, not the type of spending with which you have a problem!

What you are trying to do is reinforce your new behaviours. Even if it seems trivial, a mental "pat on the back", an encouraging message to yourself in your diary or planner, taking a few moments to think how well you've done today, all helps. It makes you feel more in control and builds your self-belief. It also encourages you to "keep up the good work".

You can also, with the right **helping relationships**, get some reward from friends (as with the food comment, "you look so great and you're so strong-willed" can be, "wow, you have really got things sorted, I wish I was like you with money"). In general positive reinforcement (rewards, praise etc. for getting it right) is more effective in helping people (and other animals) to learn a new behaviour than negative reinforcement (beating yourself up or being criticised when you get it wrong). That's why praising a kitten or a puppy for using a litter tray is more effective than thumping it for wetting the carpet if you want to train it. The same principle applies to toilet training infants and to adults learning to handle money!

On an ongoing basis, you will also probably want to do some ***self-evaluation***. Your current situation changes and as you move through change, your objectives (such as which shops or particular habits to avoid) may shift, your relationships with people may alter, the rewards that are appropriate may change and your goals might become different.

The idea is to shop so that you are actually buying things you want and need. It takes work, but you come out far better off financially and with a lot more respect for yourself, as well as having the things you really want and need and not a load of stuff that you never really wanted in the first place.

Notice that, again, your new control isn't from learning anything at all about finance, it's about learning more about *you*.

And now, after the chapter summary, we move on to our attitudes to money decisions and how we make them, be they good, bad or indifferent!

Summary:

- Work out what pattern of shopping you use, buy status, security or something else, have things, show them off, what is it you do?
- Decide whether you use shopping as therapy.
- Remember that you have to stop buying at some point; you can't buy everything in the world. Where do you want to stop?
- What pattern makes sense, prioritise, or just buy the first thing that comes to hand?
- Sort out your, values, goals etc. and set priorities for spending on what you need, not just stuff you fancy having, showing off etc.
- Remember, change is hard, change is possible; change requires different things, at different times, from different people.
- Look at balance, how much you want to change, how much you want to stay the same. Draw a chart of it. Include everything.
- If you are not going to change now, decide what will make you change in future and write it down.
- If you want to learn about MI, read Rollnick & Miller's books.
- Identify your stage of change. Read "Changing for Good", by Prochaska, DiClemente & Norcross for other ideas.
- Remember why diets fail, so don't put yourself on a financial "diet" that is not sustainable and well-planned.
- Money, like food, is vital – you can't go, "cold turkey" on money.
- Control your environment; don't try to do it by "will power".
- Decide what will work as control for you, in the environment, the cues that you follow, and your own cues to yourself.
- Prepare what you're doing, and pick supporting friends carefully.
- Get help if you need it.

Oops I did it again.

We all make mistakes in our decisions sometimes, particularly about money. The chapter is about why we make mistakes, what we can do about it and when there is nothing else we can do but to accept that we are human. And it shows why sometimes, logic isn't helpful, but then at other times our instincts aren't either! So we need to work out how to cope with uncertainty.

Making mistakes is human.

So is justifying them, rationalising them away, explaining to everybody why it wasn't really our mistake, but was bad luck or somebody else's fault!

Being "logical" is often said to be a way to avoid such mistakes.

It doesn't work. There are three main reasons that 100% "logic" doesn't work to eliminate mistakes.

1. There are limits to prediction, and it doesn't matter how logical you are. Some things, like weather, are unpredictable so you can't always avoid mistakes. Real life is like that. This is what chapter 7 is about.
2. The human mind simply doesn't work that way. You are not Mr Spock, a Vulcan, you are human and you can't detach your thinking from your emotions, and vice versa. That is part of what chapter 6 is about.
3. Sometimes not being totally logical (or totally emotional) can cause mistakes, but occasionally it is a positive blessing and we are better off being the way we are. The reason why we are like we are is also the subject of chapter 6.

However, the balance between "logic" and emotion – and how we can use both to make the best decisions, is the subject for this chapter.

> *Logic is an abstract concept. Abstractions can be very useful. They can also, in real life, be quite ludicrous.*
>
> *Common sense – apart from being uncommon - is severely practical. In the classroom or as part of a theory it is often untidy, ugly and without theoretical support. But in real life, it often works.*

The problem that arises for you, the person trying to Tame the Pound, is that logic looks impressive. When something is explained that is "logical" you can feel very stupid because you used a more common sense, intuitive approach. For example:

> Linda is 31years old, single, outspoken and very bright. She studied philosophy at University. As a student she was deeply concerned with issues of discrimination and social justice and participated in anti-nuclear demonstrations.
> Which of these two alternatives is more probable?
> a)   Linda is a bank cashier.
> b)   Linda is a bank cashier and an active campaigner for women's rights.

If, like most people, you think that b) is more probable, then logically, you're wrong. Imagine thousands of Linda's. All of them are bank cashiers. Many of them might also be campaigners for women's rights. But there must be some that aren't campaigners, or active, or who campaign for things other than women's rights. But all of them are bank cashiers.

So it must be more probable that Linda is a bank cashier than that she is a bank cashier *and* something else. Technically, a conjunction of events (bank cashier and...) cannot be more likely than either one of the events. Similarly, a subset (those cashiers who are also active in women's rights) cannot be bigger than the set itself (all the cashiers).

But in real life, it seems likely that Linda is an active campaigner for women's rights! Some people get quite upset about this, "I know logically it is wrong, but...". See what I mean, you feel stupid.

But look at it another way.

> Does it matter whether we are logical? What do we want to do, get the right answer in life, or provide a mathematical proof of a proposition that would get good marks in a philosophy class?

Logic says it must be more probable that she is a cashier. But what does "more probable" mean? What information do we have available? We have logic, which says ignore everything else other than, "more likely" means "a bigger proportion of every cashier in the world". But we're not going to look at every cashier in the world, all we're going to do is try to get information about Linda on which to base a decision. What we naturally do is to think, "somebody has told us some details about Linda, and they must have done that for a reason". What is Linda more likely to be?

We apply background knowledge to make sense of what information we're given. We naturally use our background knowledge to work out what is meant, despite the fact that if you take things literally (the way naive, "logic" dictates) the result is ludicrous. Some examples:

"Prostitutes appeal to Pope",

"British left waffles on Falkland Islands"

"Kids make nutritious snacks",

"British fly to discuss oil pipeline",

"Lady with little dog seeks post".

Whole books have been written on those sorts of puns; the literal and logical interpretation is so daft it's funny. If we don't have the background knowledge, the joke isn't funny. A joke about foreign politicians you don't know isn't funny to you, but it might be hysterical to a native of the country because they can use their knowledge of the context, the background, the personalities to see the contrast between logic and common sense.

What we usually think of "probable" is, "given the fact that somebody gave us the information about Linda that they did, and they must have a reason for telling us that specific information, presumably they expect us to infer what Linda sounds like based on that information". In other words, what do we think of as a typical campaigner for women's rights?

So that is what, in real life, we do.

If this were a real case, Linda is likely to be an active women's rights campaigner, if she wasn't, why were we told the information we were? Our solution isn't logical, but it makes sense in the real world.

Here's another one.

Imagine somebody is quite shy and "bookish". Are they more likely to be a librarian or a sales person?

They probably sound more like a librarian. However, logic dictates that you ask, how many librarians are there compared to how many sales people? The odds must be higher that they are a sales person because there are so many more of those. To assume the person is a librarian is to "ignore base rates", which is a logical error.

But they "sound" like a librarian. What is the stereotype we have of a sales person, and the stereotype of a librarian? Given the information, how do you categorise them?

In courses in decision making this is the point at which people start to get depressed. Not only do we do stupid things like ignoring base rates, but the choice that "feels right" is clearly wrong. And in addition, we operate on stereotypes!

OK – how else do we categorise things?

Describe a bird. It's something that flies. What, like an ostrich, a penguin or a bat? It's not simple to categorise unless you have information about every element of every item in every category.

That amount of knowledge of individuals and their detailed differences is the death of stereotypes, so ideally we'd remember all the details of every single example of every single thing. But that is impossible in the real world. So we have to categorise in some way.

However we categorise, some examples are going to be typical of a category and some will be more like fringe members. How about a tomato, is it a fruit or a vegetable? Strictly it's a fruit because it has seeds, but we use it as a vegetable. That is illogical in terms of category, but is it therefore wrong?

We might not want to categorise things by stereotypes, it has negative connotations. But stereotypes are often broadly accurate – for example, the stereotype that men tend to be bigger than women is true but doesn't exclude the fact that not *all* men are bigger than *all* women. And the alternative is either to remember every single example of every person, or to have a categorisation system that is purely logical. Which do you think is going to work best?

The thing is that in real life the logical "error" of categorising things by stereotypes and typicality works better than trying to remember every fact about every individual thing or applying logical rules to everything. For example, imagine we're talking about Lisa from the Simpsons cartoon. Is she going to be a sales person, or a librarian?

The "logic is the only way" idea requires that you ignore all the information you're given about somebody, make up totally logical categories, ignore typicality in trying to work out what something is and serve the tomatoes with the fruit course!

The way we think isn't logical – but often it works better than logic.

However, it doesn't always work better.

Let's take the same idea – " don't ignore base rates"

How likely is it the winning lottery numbers will be 1, 2, 3, 4, 5, 6?

Huge odds? Couldn't happen? Really?

Each number is as likely to come up as any other (the draw is, as far as possible, fair) and the next selection is as far as possible independent of the last (so if you have a 1 to start with, a 2 is just as likely to come next as any other number).

So the odds of getting those particular numbers are just the same as whatever numbers you pick and whatever numbers you pick, you have exactly the same odds of winning the jackpot (pretty much none!)

Obviously, somebody wins now and then and we'll talk more about understanding the odds in chapter 8, but it doesn't matter whether you pick 1-6, birthdates or the fortune tellers predictions, your odds of winning are exactly the same (practically zero!).

But we still *feel* as if 1-6 is more unlikely and as a consequence that our chances of winning by picking other numbers are, by comparison, much better than they are. Trust me, they aren't and the lottery and in fact any gambling is an area where applying logic and suppressing your instincts is going to save you a lot of money (although you can save even more by not gambling at all!)

So logic can be a real help sometimes, just don't think that because something is not logical it is automatically bad. "The logical answer is better", is usually true in the laboratory (and casino), but it may not be in real life. In life, you have to think about what you are trying to do.

Now let's think some more about fruit!

Let's say that you prefer oranges to apples. And if there is a choice between apples and pears, you'd prefer an apple. So logically, you should *always* prefer oranges to pears – because if you prefer oranges to apples, and apples to pears, then you "must" prefer oranges to pears.

So if there are apples or oranges available, you would never willingly eat a pear. By the rules of logic, that is what you *ought* to do. It's called transitivity (or transitive preference).

I've used that example because it is obviously daft.

The sort of transitivity problem that is posed in theory is something like having a choice between microwaves. Experiments have been done on this and the results are quite surprising. Preferences apparently change on the basis not of what people actually want, but on what they compare it to, and they change the points on which they compare when they get different options. That is totally illogical, probably even more so than the apples, pears and oranges example.

The conclusion often drawn is that people being illogical is surprising, and a major defect that must be eliminated.

I suggest you ask yourself:

Why does it matter whether people are logical or not in this example? Surely the key point is, are they happy with their decision, did they get the microwave they wanted at a good price?

There's actually a lot of evidence to show that people who "satisficed" (made the decision on a "that's good enough" basis, one that was, "satisfactory" rather than "best") are happier with their choice for just about any period where measurements of "satisfaction with choice" was made than those who endlessly analysed to pick, "the best".

In fact, if you let people choose then you ask half the group to explain exactly how they made those choices, the half that has to justify the decisions ends up feeling they chose badly and regret their choices and the ones who don't (who are not made to justify "logical comparison") remain happier with their choice. What do you want to be, logical or happy?

One last illustration of this point. According to logical rules, as applied in mathematics, a plus and a plus is always a plus and so is a minus and a minus, but a minus and a plus is a minus. In strictly logical terms "I ain't got none", means you have got some, because it is a double negative. In reality, it is simply an emphasis of the fact of having none (although it isn't good grammar, most people can understand what you mean).

The pompous lecturer is holding forth about logic "Two positives" he drones on, "can never be a negative". And a bored voice from the back calls out, "yeah, right"!

So don't think of logic as being holy writ. It is handy in its place, but we're not Vulcans, its place is not to dominate our entire lives. Just because somebody says — "that is illogical", even if they are right, it doesn't necessarily mean anything.

OK, so instinct isn't always wrong and logic not always right in real life, but where can lack of logic really hurt you in your finances?

One big one is with maths, such as credit card interest payments, mortgage rates etc. In fact, our ignorance of maths in many ways (but not all) is so important and ignorance is so common that there's a whole chapter on it (chapter 8). Another big one is overconfidence. This also gets a whole chapter to itself, in relation to investment, in chapter 9.

Apart from that, there are many ways to divide up the "errors". Most come from a few evolutionary adaptations that humans have that we'll talk about in chapter 6. But if we consider just those few areas and look at all the ways these can trip us up, it gets a bit hard to follow.

I've split them into twelve areas – not because of any parallel with teams or religious groups, it's just the way it came out.

The rest of this chapter is about how these twelve areas can hurt you and where you need to be aware, not simply of the "logical answer" but of your way of thinking, to be able to reduce mistakes.

Frame Dependence - *It ain't what you say, it's the way that you say it.*
Read through the first description below, imagine you're in the situation described and make a note of which option you would choose.

You're a contestant in a new game show. You've already won £1,000 and you have two options. A) You can take an additional £500 and walk away. B) You call the toss of a coin. If you call right you get an extra £1,000, if you are wrong you get nothing extra.

Make a note of which option you prefer, *before* you read the second option.

Again, you're a contestant in this new game show. You've already won £2,000 and you have two options. A) You can lose £500 and walk away. B) You call the toss of a coin. If you call right you lose nothing, if you are wrong you lose £1,000.

Make a note of what option you chose this time, *before* you read on. If you are like most people, you will have chosen option A in the first situation (you wanted the certain gain of an extra £500, giving you £1,500 in total) but in the second situation you chose option B (an even chance to lose £1,000 or to lose nothing at all, giving you either £2,000 or £1,000).

You may have noticed that in both cases, by choosing option A you end up with £1,500 and with option B you end up with either £1,000 or £2,000. So, logically, you "should" choose either A or B in both situations, depending on whether you would take a gamble or not.

This uses as an example another gamble rather than a real situation, but the general lesson is that most people make different choices depending on the way the situation is "framed", that is how the choice is expressed.

If it is framed as a possible gain, most people want security, they take the certain gain. If the situation is expressed as a possible loss, most people will take a risk to try to avoid the loss. Even if we don't know the precise odds (as we don't in real life), generally, people are "loss averse", they don't want to take a loss and would rather gamble in the hope that they won't have to.

Imagine, instead of a game show you are talking to your stockbroker, financial advisor or bank manager. You want some information about an investment.

People advising on finance are supposed to "know the customer". They should find out your goals, what your attitude to risk is and so on. We've already seen that that is tricky, *you* might not know what your real values are (as in chapter 2), let alone your goals and your plans to achieve them (chapter 3) and there is no requirement (not yet, anyway) for any advisor to understand anything we've talked about so far.

All they *have* to know about are the different products they can sell you. But they are supposed to "know" you, so they may give you an, "attitude to risk" questionnaire. That will allow them, in theory, to categorise you as a "cautious" or "adventurous" investor and various other descriptions.

Notice that this works on categories, so whether you are metaphorically a penguin, an ostrich, a falcon or a dodo, you are still a bird. Because financial advice works in the real world, abstract theories about how every person in the world would make those decisions simply don't work. Everyone (including the professionals who have to do it, not just talk about it) uses a convenient shortcut of stereotyping people and putting them into categories, just like we all do with librarians, salespeople, fruit and women's rights campaigners!

Once you're in categories of "risk profile", the theory says, the advisor can steer you towards an investment that is "appropriate" to your "risk profile".

Of course, we know that this is nonsense, because if you don't know your own goals, values, plans etc. they can't possibly find out what risks you are willing to take because you don't know yourself what winning or losing are worth to you and they have no way to help you find out (unless they've read this book too!)

The additional problem is that, even if you know what risks you are prepared to take, the way they phrase their questions (or the ones in their questionnaire) about risks will affect your answers.

So if they say – "this is 50% likely to gain you money over 3 years" – you'll have a different reaction to whether that is acceptable than if they said – "this is 50% likely to lose you money over 3 years".

Both of them are logically the same, but you'll come out as a "different" risk profile depending on how they ask the question.

There are lots of ways framing effects can confuse you – but that whole area of assessing risk is the most obvious way it can hurt your finances.

There are some other ways to work around this in chapter 14, looking at specific situations. But in general:

For you as an individual beware of thinking, "this is a risk of losing" or "this is an opportunity for gain", because both of these are two sides of the same coin. When making decisions, financial or otherwise, try to "frame" the decision for yourself as a chance of loss and separately as a chance of gain. That way, you can see if you get different answers and try to allow for your natural tendency.

By the way, if you advise others on finance, framing effects will (not might) effect the answers and therefore the categories you get, so if you want to "know the customer", you need to balance out your questions and probably need to get help to do this properly.

Unfortunately, if you don't, the authorities will eventually realise that their rules for "know the customer" were defective, will shirk the blame for not regulating properly and there will be yet another "scandal" about greedy financial salespeople conning the public!

And beware of people telling you, "just be logical", because you aren't going to be able to do that, as we'll come to in chapter 6.

Loss aversion – *This won't hurt a bit- it will hurt a lot!*
You'll sometimes hear this expressed wrongly as being that all people are "risk averse" rather than "loss averse".

Actually, some people like taking risks and will go out of their way to run them (why else would they bungee jump?), but very few people like losses.

Apart from those who chase risk, most of us will take a risk if we are faced with what we see as a loss as the only alternative.

The general consensus is that we are about twice as sensitive to the pain of loss as we are to the pleasure of gain (so a loss of £250 hurts us about as much as we are pleased by a gain of £500). That is an "average", so it is probably meaningless for you, it depends on how much money you've got, how much you stand to gain or lose, what the context is etc. But you can generally assume that you will be more upset by losing than you will be uplifted by winning a similar amount.

This causes two main problems.

The first is that, with the help of "availability", something we'll come to in a moment, when we invest we tend focus on the risks that we can see most clearly. Think about this:

You have £1,000 to invest for your old age. You hear that the stock market is likely to go up and down quite sharply over a short period (say, up to five years), but over a long term (20-40 years) it looks like it goes up fairly steadily.

On the other hand, a bank deposit account gives a steady return and shouldn't go down, but over a long term it might not even beat inflation and certainly won't give you much profit.

> Which do you go for?

If you're planning years ahead, pretty much the only way to go is to invest in the stock market (there are obviously more choices than those two alone, I've just simplified it for the sake of example).

But with our being aware of stock market crashes (and with bank deposits being "guaranteed") it looks more likely that you will lose in the stock market, we see that as "more risky" and since we are loss averse, we go for the "safe" option of the bank deposit.

Unfortunately, what appears to be safer, is actually more risky (certainly over the long term), and the apparently riskier option is probably the only one that gives a chance of safety.

There is no "risk free" option. Things are only ever more or less risky than alternatives. Everything has risks attached, even if it is supposed to be "risk free".

So one way in which "loss aversion" costs us is making us scared, so that we can't stand back and work out what the bigger risk is, it drives us towards "safe" options that are actually more dangerous.

The second way loss aversion hurts is that we develop a bit of an "ostrich" attitude to losses. We think that if we don't see it, if we don't sell something (whether it is a house, a share or anything else) at a loss we haven't made a loss. So an investment that is doing well (a share that is rising in value for example) will get sold quite early and will carry on doing well, and an investment that is doing badly (like a share that is going down steadily) will get held onto and will continue to do badly. It sounds daft, and very few people believe they do it, but there is good evidence that most of us do.

Unfortunately, people's natural tendency to be loss averse means we are all pretty good at trying to avoid loss of face as well. You can hear lots of "investment experts" rationalise their "loss aversion" mistakes if you know what to listen for.

They talk about, "taking profits. They "capitalise assets". That means they sell the winners early. They also "wait for value to re-assert itself" and look for "the bounce". This means they hang onto their losers long after they should have accepted that they were losers.

If you are trying to justify selling winners and hanging onto losers, or are so scared of investing that you run to the "safety" of the bank deposit (or other "safe" options), the chances are that you need to address your loss aversion because it is costing you money.

Availability – *Apply Occam's Razor, just don't cut yourself*

I mentioned above that we tend to misjudge risk, confusing high risk with low and vice versa. Availability is one of the reasons. It arises because we remember some things much more clearly than others, usually we remember ones that are significant for us, that are "available" when we try to think of examples.

If you are going to travel, what is the safest way, that is, which way should you travel to be least likely to die?

You can consult statistics, establish the "base rates" and so on. But that gets complicated. Figures are produced for different periods and different countries, everybody wants their own method to sound safe, etc. And then we watch QI and hear that the average person is more likely to get killed in the home than they are to be a victim of air crash!

What we usually do is think of the major losses of life involved in travel. Have a think about which means of travel is safest:

Car,

Rail

Coach

Ferry

Plane

Chances are you can think of various disasters. 9/11 or Tenerife for air, Zeebrugge for ferries, Hatfield or Potters Bar for rail, the various continental coach crashes that hit the headlines. Those are "available" to us. But there probably aren't that many road disasters involving cars that cause massive loss of life, so we don't hear about them much. They aren't "available".

If you look at the table below (from the DOT report), car travel is far more likely to result in fatality than any of the other four.

Passenger fatality rates by mode of travel: GB 2006[1,2]

	Fatality rate per 100 million		
Mode	Passenger kilometres	Passenger journeys	Passenger hours
Car	0.25	3.30	9.80
Van	0.06	1.30	2.80
Bus or coach	0.03	0.26	0.63
Rail	0.03	0.75	1.50
Water	0.02	1.10	0.61
Air	0.00	0.09	0.02

1 Rates for some modes are based on 5 or 10 year averages
2 Figures rounded to 2 significant figures (except where below 0.1)

The exact amount of, "more likely", varies depending on how you measure it, but air travel is safest, followed by water, rail and bus/coach (which are pretty similar), with cars something between 3 and 10 times more dangerous than the most dangerous other means of transport.

With money, the "available" strategy is to focus on the money and the products. That's the way all the "experts" talk about it so that's what people think of when they think of planning their finances.

Thinking what you want is more important and if you stand back from the situation and consider, it is obviously better to start with what you want before you work out how to get it.

However, starting with products, tax advantages, general purpose goals etc. is what it seems everybody does, that is the "available" option, so it is the way most people plan their finances.

Also, "be logical", despite the fact that it doesn't always help and is actually impossible, is the "available" solution to personal finance. Like a lot of "available" ideas, it isn't necessarily a good one!

Now something that is very like availability in many ways.

Recognition - *It's OK, I know this one.*
This is the foundation of advertising and marketing.

Companies spend fortunes on creating associations and brand awareness. I won't quote any, as it only encourages them, but you'll see masses of slogans, logos etc. that you know and associate with a product.

> At the supermarket – do you buy the "own brand" goods, or the ones that you've always bought? Why? Have you actually done a taste comparison, seen how white your whites come out etc.? Most people don't, they buy the things they recognise.

I had a client who didn't concern herself with quality; she just liked the labels of well-known brands, so she could show them off.

If you buy a designer label you may be confusing the value of the item with the advertising of the brand that keeps the name "recognisable". Paying for real quality is one thing, but paying for a label is another.

Paying for recognition is confusing quality you want that gives you real value with a brand label to impress your friends (that doesn't give you value but that gives a "show off potential").

Remember recognition in relation to brands when shopping and think about what it actually says about quality (often, it says little or nothing).

Because you recognise a financial product (like an ISA for example), recognise that something has "tax advantages" or recognise a company name, it doesn't mean they are appropriate for you, it doesn't even mean they are any good at all.

If you're investing, the Acme, multinational, super-duper corporation that everybody has heard of is probably more financially stable than the little corner shop. But remember, everybody recognised the name Enron, and what everybody now recognises is that it was a con.

One further illustration of recognition, I'm not famous, so to publishers, the fact that I am the only person in the world who is qualified and has practiced as both a financial advisor and a psychologist is irrelevant. This book would get more publicity and sell better if it was written by a D-list celebrity who knew nothing about finance or psychology, because more buyers (and publishers) would recognise my name!

Status quo bias – *I like what I've got, and what I've got is inertia.*

Like "more money is better", which we looked at in chapter 1, most people think more choice is better. But is it?

Imagine you go into a shop intending to buy, let's say, jam. You find they have two types of jam, an excellent, organic and expensive one, and one full of additives that is really cheap. You make your selection. A few months later, you go back to the shop to buy some more jam and they've really got interested in jam, they've got eight varieties of organic jams, several economy brands that are on sale, some "no-additives" jams from well-known companies, a few small producer, "fair trade" jams. What do you do?

In a series of experiments customers were offered either six choices of jam, or 24 choices. With less choice, (I'll make the maths easier than it's reported in the articles), out of 100 people who passed the table, 60 sampled a jam and 18 bought some. When they were given 24 choices, of 100 people passing the table, 40 sampled and only one or two bought.

These were done in real stores, in real life. The conclusions are valid, more choice isn't necessarily helpful. It makes us hesitate to make a decision, so we stick with what we've got, which may be nothing at all.

Incidentally, another result of that series of experiments was, to quote:

"participants actually reported greater subsequent satisfaction with their selections .....when their original set of options had been limited"

Iyengar and Lepper, 2000

In other words, just like I mentioned earlier that people were happier to make a "gut instinct" decision, people here were happier to make a simpler choice from less options. If you gave them lots of options then they tended to be more worried about their choice and more likely to regret it subsequently.

Making a decision that is difficult, whether it difficult because we have to focus on the reasons for our decision or because we have to choose between many options, reminds us that we made a choice. If we just pick something because we like it, or make a choice that is "obvious", it seems to relieve us of the burden of regret.

Not making a choice (even if it is obviously daft and very likely to hurt us), feels as if we haven't done anything unwise. We "feel" that a decision to do something is somehow more of a mistake than a decision to do nothing, because the decision to do nothing doesn't feel like a decision! But the opportunity cost of nothing may be higher!

This sort of "avoid regret, don't make difficult decisions" attitude obviously effects shopping and how much money we potentially waste.

It is also an issue with choices generally. "Nudge" by Thaler and Sunstein is about this. Nudge is an important book, because it is the first time most people had seen what the authors call, "decision architecture". What they mean by that is the framework in which people make real life decisions. In chapter 6, I call it "environment" (and it is "environmental control" in chapter 4) and I've seen it called decision context, but it's all basically the same thing.

It's not a new idea at all, contrary to popular opinion (the Conservative Party hired Thaler as a policy advisor on the basis that this was innovative thinking and lots of other people call it "novel" or "revolutionary"). Actually, supermarkets have used it for over forty years. The goods they want to shift are shelved at the ends of the aisles, because that is where you slow down with your trolley and tend to be more aware of what is on the shelves. And the high margin items are at normal eye level, but to see the bargains you must stoop or stretch. You're more likely to buy the high margin items than the genuine bargains. It isn't unfair, it is good business/marketing psychology!

But "Nudge", rather than using "sales and marketing psychology" to sell things is geared to social policy.

Take an example. You've probably seen calls for more organ donors, but there aren't a lot more organ donors now than there were. You can try to encourage people, but to become an organ donor, you have to think about what you believe about life-after-death, perhaps speak to loved ones about dying (never a fun conversation) then fill in a form.

It is a difficult decision, and we don't like those. We will "regret it less" if we don't decide, so we stick with the status quo, the default.

The default if you don't make the decision is that you are not an organ donor.

If we change the default to "you are an organ donor unless you opt out", then if you have religious or other convictions that mean you don't want to be an organ donor you have to take action, fill out a form etc. The result is almost certain to be a huge increase in the number of organ donors, but nobody who wants not to be one has to be.

The only difference is that it uses the inertia that we have of the "status quo" effect to get people "not to decide" to cease to be organ donors, rather than "not to decide" to become donors.

For you, the status quo makes a huge difference to your money.

If you belong to a company with a pension scheme, the "status quo" is probably that you don't join the scheme, because that gives you "more choice".

But it is a complicated choice; do you have a stakeholder pension, a personal pension, join and make AVCs etc. The result is that you probably never join.

If you consider joining, you probably have to pick a fund, perhaps one of several dozen funds. Since you don't really understand what is going on, you might decide not to join "until I've got time to figure it out", which in reality also means never joining. If you do join and pick a fund, you'll probably go for the "managed" fund which is the default. The trouble is, the managed fund is probably not the best one for you (we'll look at this in chapter 9).

Much better for pensions would be a default that suits more people, which would probably be that you're in the fund unless you opt out (rather than out unless you opt-in) and that you are in a low charge, indexed fund (which we'll talk about) rather than a managed one unless you choose otherwise.

That is just a default to help those who don't make the decisions. Ideally, of course, you should make your own decisions, which means you need to be clear on your values and goals, have a good "know the customer" profile to find out what you want from the fund, and then be able to pick a suitable fund.

The learning from all this is that when we're faced with decisions that are at all complex, that we fear we might regret or are afraid we don't really understand, we tend to go with whatever we've got. We stick with defaults, even if the default is having nothing.

Often, those defaults (like pension choices, savings plans, utility suppliers etc.) are not helping us. And one of the worse things we can do is to put off the decision because it is difficult. Chapter 14 has some ideas for getting round this issue.

Endowment effect – *Mine is bigger than yours*

We tend to be quite attached to what we've got. Remember in chapter 2 my talking about Matthiu Ricard's book, Happiness. He makes a wonderful point about this, in connection with being happy.

Imagine that you're looking in at a shop window at a beautiful work of art, a Ming vase, for example. You think, "it is really beautiful". A salesman reaches for something and knocks the vase over, breaking it into a million pieces. How do you feel? Sad, perhaps. You think, "it was such a lovely thing, now it is just so much clay dust".

Now imagine the same vase, but you have just bought it. You think, "it is beautiful and it is mine". And the salesman reaches for something and knocks the vase over, breaking it into a million pieces. How do you feel? Angry, sad, upset, furious, unbelieving, self-pitying? You think, "clumsy idiot, why does this always happen to me, it survived a thousand years, I get it, that moron breaks it, I'm going to sue, etc."

The difference is the one word, "mine". In relation to happiness, that is a vital point and worth thinking about when you look at what you really value in life.

We tend to value what we have (our "endowment") much more highly than something that we don't have.

> *If we were going to invest or buy, put new effort in a relationship, spend three years studying for a qualification we now don't really want, we wouldn't think it was worth it. We only value it so highly because it is ours already and we've invested in it and if we had to consider it anew, we wouldn't consider paying the price required!*

This might take some thinking about, after all, it is the opposite of the old sayings, "the grass is always greener on the other side of the fence" or "you don't know what you've got until it's gone".

Try looking at it this way, what sport do you like? Or if you don't like sport, what entertainment do you like, theatre, ballet, poetry reading, mud wrestling?

Imagine you've got the chance to go to the greatest event of your lifetime. It is the World cup final, and whoever you support are in it. Your favourite band of all time is doing a reunion concert. Your favourite dancer, poet or wrestler is appearing in their farewell event.

You've got a ticket for the event. A millionaire approaches you and wants to buy the ticket, what is the lowest price you would accept?

Now imagine you don't have a ticket but you find somebody willing to sell one, how much are you prepared to give them for their ticket?

People invariably want considerably more to part with something that they own, that is their "endowment", than they are prepared to pay to get exactly the same thing if they don't own it yet. The only difference is that it is "mine", or it isn't.

One impact of this effect is that it makes us hang on to stuff we ought to get rid of.

Not just money we cling to relationships, broken ornaments, old tools, all sorts of junk.

We say that "we might use them one day", or "we've invested a lot in the relationship/job/house", but what we mean is that it is "ours" and we can't bear to part with it for less than we think it is "worth".

This is the point that Matthieu Ricard was making, the thought, "ours" distorts our judgment and makes it more difficult for us to be happy and move on with our lives. We cling to the past. We're the prisoners of our own possessions and the more we have, the more imprisoned we may become. Financially that makes us vulnerable. Here's an example of why it does.

Personal finance is supposed to be going towards a more professional, fee based structure and not be about sales of products. I've still got books I bought in the early 1980's, when finance was selling, and "ability to close the sale" was vital. They have whole chapters on "closes", and one is "the puppy dog close".

If you want to sell a puppy, do you need glib sales talk, evidence of training, bloodline books and so on? No, just the puppy. You take it round, show it to the customer, let the children play with it, then you casually say, "oh, the office is closed now, I'll have to put it in the kennels over the weekend". What happens? The customer (with a horde of tearful children), insists that it is no trouble, they'll look after it and you can pick it up on Monday. On Monday, do you think they'll let you take the puppy away?

It works with any material goods, why do you think car salesmen let you have a test drive? Once you get behind the wheel and picture yourself as James Bond or Lara Croft, the car is "mine". The only question is how much I'm going to pay for it!

So beware of being hit with the "puppy dog close", and remember that once your money (or emotional energy, time or anything else) is in the pot, it isn't yours any more. We'll look at ways to avoid this in chapter 14, but don't get fooled into believing (however "logical" you think you are) that you are objective about anything you see as "mine".

Anchoring and adjustment – *Fixation, fixation, fixation*

This is another area where we can become convinced that we can't drop value, we tend to fixate on what we pay for houses, cars etc.

The problem is, the market price of something is (in most cases) the amount somebody is willing to pay for it. You might have paid £1 million for a house and feel it is worth more, but if nobody is willing to pay more than £750,000 for it, then the "value" is only £750,000.

> We "anchor" on that first figure, and once we've "put down our anchor", we find it hard to move.

As an example, Diane and I love books. We have thousands.

We had a clear out and we found about 1,500 books we weren't going to read again and didn't really need (but they were ours, so we valued them).

Have you ever tried to sell second-hand books? Even if they were all cheap paperbacks, they "should" have been worth about £5 each, so those books "should" have been worth a total of around £7,500. We must actually have paid about £10,000 for them, but we couldn't even get somebody to pay us £0.20 per book, or £300. I know about anchoring. But it is still hard to accept that the books are not worth my "anchor" figure of £7-10,000, but are actually pretty well worthless.

It doesn't seem to matter whether that initial figure is relevant or random, we still anchor on it. Now this is a problem with money for us in two ways.

1. We fixate on the price we paid, on what "our" things are worth.
2. We are influenced by the first figure we hear, whether it is relevant or not.

The first is fairly obvious, we can't sell losers, we forget our objectivity and so on.

The obvious bit of the second problem is the one that most people writing about this discuss. If somebody gives you a price for antique, a house, a car or anything else, that first figure influences you. That's why, in bargaining, it is handy to get your estimate in first, it will influence the other person.

If estate agents are shown particulars of a house, they will estimate different prices depending upon the guide price they are given. Every time this is done the agents *say* (and believe) they judge objectively and ignore the guide price. Every time, they actually anchor on the price given and use it as a guide.

> It isn't just estate agents (although, like politicians, they are prime subjects for self-delusion stories!). We all do it, anchor on what we first hear, whether we know or recognise the fact that we do or not.

Beware of this effect, you *will* be influenced, so don't try to be a Vulcan. Just recognise that it is going to happen and allow for it.

Also, think about the other aspect, which people forget. You are influenced by the first figure, even if that first figure was ages ago or in another context.

So when you buy an engagement ring, why do you think it "should" be worth two month's salary? Why do you think that everybody "should" have an "emergency fund" of three month's salary?

Those are the standard figures sales people use, they are conventions, guidelines etc. but since they are the figures people hear initially, they are the ones they anchor on.

One way round this problem is to work out what you really want and need and not take other people's estimates as a guide, because the guide will become an anchor point and you'll have trouble moving that anchor. Other ways to avoid it we'll look at in chapter 14.

You're right, metaphorically herding and being anchored are a contradiction in terms – Luigi here, he don't know from metaphorical.

Confirmation bias- *I knew it, that proves what I thought.*

This is an interesting one, and we'll look at it in more detail in later chapters (6, 7 and 9). But for now it can look similar to anchoring, because once we form an opinion of something we don't often budge from it.

This is embodied in folklore as, "you don't get a second chance at a first impression". It's a real problem if you are doing job selection interviews (something I train people to do as part of my "day job"). People like people who are "like me", that went to the same school, support the same team, have the same political views. But these factors don't have any impact on whether the person can do the job properly.

People also display what is called the "halo and horns" effect. If the first impression is favourable for whatever reason, the interviewer gives the interviewee a "halo". Everything they say or do after that is taken as evidence that they have "the right stuff". Conversely, if the initial impression is bad for any reason the interviewee gets, "horns". If that happens, anything they say or do (even if it is identical to what the person with the halo said or did) it is interpreted as a sign they are unsuitable.

That's the problem with confirmation that is actually more dangerous than anchoring. It isn't just that we fixate, it's that once we fixate we might think we're collecting information to "check" our decision, but we are looking for "proof" that we're right and ignoring anything that suggests we're wrong.

*Whether you understand or believe it, this is what you **usually** do.*

Think of the banks, pre-crash. Securitised loans from the US sub-prime market had potential to make lots of money. Therefore they were a good idea. Once they were a good idea, all the evidence was interpreted that they were a good idea and all the figures "proved" that the bankers were right, they were a wonderful investment. Banker were knighted, paid big bonuses etc.

They were wonderful until they ceased to be wonderful, when bankers suddenly became greedy, risk-taking fools. But the facts didn't change, they were always very risky as the sole investment policy. Objectively, some facts made them a good investment, some made them a bad one, but the bankers, regulators etc. only saw facts that confirmed what they started off believing.

Some people seem keen to "prove" that people *always* have a "confirmatory" bias (that is, we all look only for things that confirm, not those that disagree with our first impression). They think that it shows that people are inherently stupid and need to apply mathematical logic to all situations.

The "poster boy" application of this is something called the "Wason test", named for the psychologist who designed it.

Imagine you are given four cards, these show, respectively A, D, 3 and 4. You are told that if there is a vowel on one side there should be an even number on the other side.

Which two cards do you need to turn over to check whether the rule is obeyed?

You need to turn A and 3. If you got it right, you're among only about 25% of people.

Most people assume they need to turn 4, on the basis that if there is no vowel on the other side it proves something. But look at the question, it says that if there is a vowel on one side, there is an even number on the other. It doesn't say that if there is an even number, there has to be a vowel, the logic is one way only.

Similarly it doesn't say anything about consonants, so D isn't needed. But if you turn over 3 and the other side has a vowel, it would prove something.

It looks at first glance as if we do try to confirm our opinion, that we don't try to contradict it to check it out. But it isn't that simple!

The problem is that the reasoning involved in the problem as stated is logical, but the reasoning we use in real life isn't. The Wason test uses something similar to the Greek idea of syllogistic reasoning. The classic is:

All men are mortal
Socrates is a man
Therefore, Socrates is mortal.

The first two lines are premises, the third line is the conclusion (which is inferred from the two premises). You need to reason in a certain way to get this right. It's very elegant and can be very useful. But the (almost) equally classic version, one more commonly (mis)applied in real life is:

All tables have legs
Socrates has legs
Therefore Socrates is a table!

People aren't very good at doing it properly. If you didn't get the right answer to the vowels and numbers example, it's probably because you got the logic the wrong way round, you basically "proved" that Socrates is a table, rather than that he is mortal.

What it needs is a focus on what is asked (rather than what you infer is asked) and on trying to disprove the premise, not proving it.

All this is lovely abstract logic, and people are not very good at it.

But in real life, you don't usually have abstract problems, and the logic works both ways, not only one way round.

We make decisions almost instantly (whatever we consciously think we do) and we tend to look for information that confirms our initial decision, but we can (and sometimes do) break out of that pattern if we think of the problem in the appropriate way.

The most practical real life solution is not simply to try to use logic (which we're not good at), but to re-frame the problem, which we'll look at doing in the next few chapters.

However, once we have a solution to a problem, we tend to stick with what we know, because, having limited processing power and time, it is a lot easier to go with the idea that once seemed to work than to change to something that might not. That's another example of anchoring and the endowment effect.

> *If we find a good solution is a hammer, lots of problems suddenly resemble a nail, not a new type of problem. So we often continue to believe things that can't be true and instead of changing our beliefs, try to find the evidence to "prove" what we want to believe.*

Mental accounts *You'll have to leave a deposit.*

Read through the first description below, imagine you're in the situation described and make a note of which option you would choose.

> You buy a ticket to the Cup Final, a hit show or whatever you really want to see. At the stadium or theatre you realise you have lost the ticket that cost you £120. Do you spend another £120 to get in?

Make a note of which option you prefer, *before* you read the second option.

> It's the same situation, but you are going to buy the £120 ticket when you get there. At the stadium or theatre you realise you have dropped the £120. Fortunately, you've got enough in your wallet to buy another ticket. Do you?

Make a note of which option you prefer, *before* you read on.

Like several of the other issues we've looked at, these are logically the same, but most people don't treat them that way. Most say they wouldn't spend the money in the first case but would in the second.

The reason seems to be that we have little mental accounts in our heads.

In the first case, we have a "ticket money" account and once that money has gone, the account is empty and we don't have money to buy a new ticket.

In the second case we have money and the money can be used for lots of things. We might be sad that we've lost some, but there is nothing to stop us buying a new ticket with the money we have left.

This has several effects. One is that (in common with our symbols and taboos, from chapter 1), we are inclined to think of some money as "sacred" and some as somehow less valuable.

You get a tax refund, find some cash in the street that you can't trace to anybody particular or you win the office sweepstake. How easy is it to spend that money?

You've worked really hard for some money, you've done some overtime or a special project, had to struggle to get paid for a fraction of the value of the work you've done and then had to pay higher rate tax on the money when you finally got it. Can you splash the money on something trivial?

You've inherited money from dear old great aunt Gertie, whose favourite you always were. Can you spend that money at all?

Most people can think of "found" money in terms of "easy come, easy go", earned money we are careful about but can use in any way we consider reasonable, but our inheritance has to be saved for something worthy of great aunt Gertie's memory, like a house extension or the children's university fund.

But it is all just money! So theoretically it is all the same, but most of us don't see it that way. This can create a few problems.

First of all, look at a common idea for money, that everybody *must* have an emergency fund. For a start, the rules won't apply to a lot of people, but everybody will have "available" the idea of an emergency fund. Then, if you're thinking about your own situation, values etc. and decide it is a good idea for you, what figure will you use? Probably, you'll "anchor" on "three months salary".

What actually happens: You have a credit card and owe some money on it. You also have your emergency fund, which is "sacred", it's for emergencies so you can't spend it on something trivial like the credit card bill that was used to buy CDs and other minor purchases. So you have a small rolling balance on the credit card.

Next month there is the car tax that had to go on card because you're a bit short this month, and the regular shopping and some "sale" items that were too good to miss, but you can't pay those with your "emergency fund". Before you know it, you've had an outstanding balance running on your card for a year, and the card company are offering to increase your credit limit, give you a special card that is a different colour and makes you feel important and are offering you their first born children as hostages if you keep using the card!

In 2002 the average US household had about $3,000 on credit on which they paid about 19% and $5,000 on deposit on which they got about 5%. They were paying about $400 (plus charges) each year to have an emergency fund or the "security" of having money readily available and the "convenience" of having a credit card.

And, apart from "experts" promoting "emergency funds for all" without thinking that people are individuals, with individual needs, the problem stems from mental accounts – the belief that particular money is sacred instead of just being money.

Some money is easier to spend, like credit cards or gambling winnings. Treating cash and credit as totally different is pretty common behaviour, and mental accounting is the usual reason why; it doesn't seem like real money. We find it easier to buy things with credit than cash. The cash comes from the "hard earned money" account and is thus relatively sacred, the credit comes from the "it's sort of monopoly money or gambling winnings, it isn't really money" account and thus can be squandered.

But apart from this, we *actually spend more* on credit. I'll mention one study, because of the title, Always Leave Home Without It, a nod to the credit card advertisement that recommends the opposite!

Prelec & Simester arranged "auctions" for things like sports event tickets, and had people bid for them. Some knew they had to settle in cash and others by credit. The details are quite complex because they did variations of the auctions for different products and testing slightly different explanations, but basically, using credit people were prepared to pay between 64% and 110% more than in cash.

People would pay roughly one and three-quarters times as much if they used credit than they would in cash.

We're normally much happier if we can predict, with familiar situations (hence the "endowment effect", "recognition" and "status quo" effects). To the generations who lived through the World Wars, being in debt was a sin, it was new territory for most people and was therefore something to be avoided. But now credit is familiar, it doesn't seem strange and therefore dangerous. In fact, not being able to buy anything we want, the instant that we want it seems like the unfamiliar and dangerous thing. Now it so usual that trying to live without extensive credit (and possibly paying a lot of money for it) is seen as the "risk" and being massively in debt is the "safe" option!

Because we have mental accounts, we treat different sorts of money as being different in terms of "sacredness". We're normally loss averse, but as credit card money is not "real", it tends not to trigger our loss aversion. We misread the risks, and we use our money in potentially daft ways.

> *Fortunately, if you recognise your mental accounts, it is one of the easiest mental habits to use to your advantage.*

Bigness bias *Don't bother me with trivia, I'm looking at the big picture*

We tend to think it is much better to think big.

> *We talk about "visionary leadership" and "far-seeing" as good, while "nit-picking" and "pedantic" are negative interpretations of bothering about the details.*
>
> *On the other hand, there's the saying, "look after the pennies and the pounds look after themselves", "the devil is in the detail" and even, "many a mickle makes a muckle"!*

With your money, you may need to suppress the desire to be a visionary and look after the pennies. Think about this one:

Imagine that you go to a shop to buy a lamp, which is £100. At the shop, you find that at a branch 5 miles away it is on sale for £75.

> Do you go to the other branch to get the lower price? Note down what you'd do.

Now imagine that you go to the shop to buy a dining room set, which is £1,775. At the shop, you find that at a branch 5 miles away it is on sale for £1,750.

Do you go to the other branch this time to get the lower price?
Note down what you'd do.

Most people at least consider it in the first case, but not the
second. But there is the same £25 difference in each case, so why
the difference in choice?

The difference is that the £25 discount is quite a lot compared to
£100, but a small amount compared to £1,775. Why does that matter?

Imagine this. You're, making quite a lot of money but you're not in
the pension scheme because you don't have any money to spare since
you are paying off a big mortgage. You're also looking at buying a new
fridge freezer. You and your partner have one in mind, a big US model
that costs about £2,000, so you've spent a few weeks thinking about
exactly which one to buy, where to buy it and so on, because you may
be able to get 15% off. The discount is important, yes?

You leave home for work on Monday morning and on the way to
the station you pick up a paper and have a decent cup of coffee. Mid-
morning you send out for a cappuccino and at lunchtime (because
you're on a bit of a healthy eating programme) you get a nice organic
sandwich, a bowl of fresh fruit and an organic smoothie. During the
afternoon you get a latté and on the way home you stop for a quick
glass of wine and get an evening paper. All trivial, right?

*At a rough estimate, you've spend about £20 (in money after tax) on
coffee, papers, lunch and drinks. Do that every day and you've spent
£100 in a week. That is about £400 in a month and £4,800 in a
year.*

Rather than worry about saving £300 (15% of £2,000) on the fridge freezer you could consider making sandwiches and a thermos of coffee, get the news you're bothered about texted to your phone and drink a glass of wine at home. You'd have the money to buy a new fridge freezer at full price each year!

Or you could put the money you save into the pension scheme and, given that you'd get tax relief on that contribution and the company might match your payments, you could probably put about £20,000 a year into the pension scheme rather than say – "I don't have any money to save right now"!

We tend not to think of those small amounts, £1 or so for papers, a couple of pounds for a coffee, £3.50 for a sandwich. We look at the big picture of the £2,000 fridge freezer or the £300 discount.

But the small figures can add up to a lot more money.

This is one of the main ways to make economies when you set your goals (chapter 3) and you try to sort out spending habits (chapter 4). It also shows up how unconscious a lot of our decisions are. After all, do you think that somebody buying a paper and a coffee is deliberately deciding not to have a decent income in retirement?

Another aspect of this is the "add on" sales close. This is increasing the value of the sale with (small individually and huge collectively) added items.

So "would you like the designer trim, only £50" (this on a purchase of £1,500). You've bought that (it is important to get agreement to each item individually, because then they are treated individually). And "the special paint job, it will suit you so much better". And that is another £150. And the Y, and Z and (and this is the biggest scam going) "you'll want the extended warranty".

Individually all those things are only 5 or 10% of your purchase, so like the discount on the furniture or the coffee and papers, they seem insignificant, but you end up paying 30 or 40% more and you haven't got any discount (you anchored on their figure, not yours, didn't you!)

Remember, both the "big picture" and the "detail" can matter, don't get so lost in the woods you can't see the trees (or vice versa).

Overconfidence *Of course, I could be wrong – but I'm not.*

I said earlier that there's a whole chapter on this (chapter 9) so I'm only going to mention a couple of points.

One is that there is something you get taught in an undergraduate psychology degree called the Fundamental Attribution Error.

If we succeed, we attribute that to our intelligence, skills and all around quality.

If we fail, we attribute that to bad luck, force of circumstances or, if we are magnanimous, a momentary lapse of concentration.

If somebody else succeeds, we attribute that to luck or circumstances ("nobody could have failed, given the situation") and

If they fail we attribute that to their congenital stupidity.

Think about driving. If somebody carves you up, you know they are a homicidal maniac, question their eyesight, the legality of their driving licence and their parentage. If we carve somebody else up it is their fault, they were too slow then accelerated when we tried to pass them, the town planners are idiots as they have the road narrowing without proper signposting or, admit we momentarily took our eyes off the road but there was no reason for the other driver to honk their horn, they really are aggressive!

This is the basic state of humans. To a large extent we have to believe in ourselves, not to do so can be a sign of depression, and we'll talk about this more in chapter 6.

There are lots of ways to demonstrate this overconfidence that we have. I'll give you a trivial example.

> What is the nearest city to London?
> How sure are you that you're right?

People have been convinced that it is Paris or Amsterdam, (even Moscow!) on the belief that these are nearer than Bristol, Chichester or Ely or whatever. People have come up with all sorts of definitions of what a city is that they are convinced mean that they are right. I don't think I've ever heard anybody express themselves as less than 70% certain their answer is correct.

Actually the answer is Westminster. If you got it right, great, but the point is that everybody is pretty sure they got it, and most of them are not only wrong, but massively overconfident that they were right.

This overconfidence is a reason projects don't get done on time or to budget, we tend to be overconfident that everything is under control. It is at the root of under-insuring, since we are convinced that we are in control and "it won't happen to me, because I won't crash/let a fire start etc." We are overconfident we picked the "best" investment, etc. and if it falls, are convinced it was "bad luck".

Overconfidence is also quoted by "experts" who say you are overconfident and therefore need them to put you right.

Sadly, those who are most overconfident, make the most mistakes from overconfidence and have the greatest arrogance about their own ability are these experts themselves. They are overconfident that "other people are overconfident", but they are not!

Just to remind us all, including me, that it is easy to be overconfident.

Once scientists "knew" the earth was the centre of the universe and "It was obvious" that the body was made of "the four elements". There was "no question" that heavy materials fell faster than light ones or that Newton's equations were absolutely right and allowed prediction of the future.

Overconfidence is so common that it is useful to remember that not only you but any "expert" can be wrong, and even if everybody including all the experts agree on a point, they might still all be wrong, but be overconfident that they are right.

We'll look ways to deal with this in money later on, but for the moment, remember that Fundamental Attribution Error - you might be wrong and the other person unlucky, even if it feels like it's the other way around!

Herds – *Two (thousand) heads are better than one.*

Given that most people are overconfident most of the time, it seems strange that we might, as we apparently do, doubt our own judgment and follow everybody else like a herd of sheep, even if what they are doing is clearly inconsistent with our own reading of the situation.

In the 17th Century a phenomenon later called, "Tulip Mania" hit what is now Holland. It's generally regarded as the first "bubble". In the 1630s a single tulip bulb went from the equivalent of a few pennies to the equivalent of 10 times the yearly income of a skilled craftsman.

As with more recent property prices, internet companies etc. it "should be obvious" that although the "value of a thing is worth what people will pay for it" at some point you'll run out of people ready to pay a still higher price.

It is the same with illegal pyramid schemes, it sounds great, you get in and get paid by people who come in later, who get paid by people who come in later still and so on. But eventually everybody is in, there is nobody to pay to enter, and the scheme collapses with a few people making lots of money and most people losing a smaller (but still substantial) amount. OK, a pyramid scheme has no product, but even if you've got a product, that product isn't realistically going to go on increasing in value indefinitely.

With a bubble, as shown by the Tulips, people see "everybody" investing. Naturally, most people are sceptical, after all, we're loss averse and we wonder how the product we're buying (houses, companies, tulips or whatever) can possibly keep going up in value all of a sudden when it hasn't before.

But it seems that the prices keep rising, and we tend to compare our wealth to others (as in chapter 2), not to what we have ourselves. The "loss" we perceive is not about our own money, it is about failing to keep up. We're not in, and we aren't making profits. Everybody else (we think) is in and is making a fortune (we think). So the bigger danger of loss seems to be not getting in.

The result is people join the herd. They get a big mortgage, they buy dot com stock, they pile into the investment the "experts" tip as a winner (whether it is on the stock market, a flower or a horse race). And it goes up for a while. But perhaps some people follow their other "illogical bias" and sell the winner too soon, and the price keeps rising.

So they have to get back in again at a higher price, and curse themselves for losing their nerve and determine that this time they'll stay in. And they do. They stay in all the way to the bottom of the market after the bubble bursts!

Lots of people (particularly experts) think they can time this entry and exit. After all, it sounds really easy and we're all overconfident. They can't!

We'll look at why they can't in chapter 7, why people still think they can and what to do instead in chapter 9. And we'll have a look at why we herd at all in chapter 6.

But for now, remember the comment of your parents when, as a child, you tried to justify what you wanted to do with the "John does X and his parent's don't mind" argument.

"If John jumped off a cliff, would you do that too?"

Forget about what everybody else thinks. Work out what you want and don't worry so much about "logic" or "everybody says".

Finally, before we move on to looking at why we herd and are prone to all these other errors – don't get too upset if, despite all my reassurances, you still feel a bit stupid, illogical and predictable after reading this chapter!

Summary:

- Logic isn't always right in reality, although it is wonderful in theory.
- Common sense is very practical – it often works in real life but it is very hard to justify in theory.
- Remember Linda the bank teller, and the librarian – logic isn't always right and sometimes gives ridiculous answers.
- But also remember the base rates for the lottery – sometimes logic is spot on and our "instinct", "intuition", "gut feeling" or "common sense" is wrong.
- There isn't an easy answer – anybody who says logic is always right and intuition always wrong (or vice versa) is either an idiot or a liar.
- Look out for where logic is really useful – it might be hard to be rational, it might in some cases be impossible, but read the examples and you'll at least know when the effort is likely to pay off.
- We are conscious of the way choices are "framed" as loss or gain.
- We hate losses (including loss of "face"), but not always risks.
- Don't assume the "default", the one you recognise or the available one is best for you – know what you want.

- "Mine" is a powerful word, but doesn't mean much beyond distorting your judgment in finance, or anything else in life.
- Careful where you put your anchor, and remember it will go somewhere – you're human, you can't "float free".
- We generally look to confirm our first impressions, but it's not that simple and, as we'll discover, we will question it in some situations.
- We all have mental accounts, you can't eliminate them. But they are easy to use to help not hurt you – if you learn to understand yourself.
- You need to think about both the wood and the trees, not just one.
- You're either overconfident you are right, or you're depressed!
- Don't worry about what other people want or do, if you want a herd, create your own – the one that knows how to Tame the Pound!

A primitive man

Why we are like we are, why we do the things we do and why we make the sort of mistakes (and have the sort of successes) that we do. And how that helps us understand both how we think, and how to change.

It was hard to avoid Darwin in 2009. It was the 200th anniversary of his birth and the 150th anniversary of his theory.

I noticed that nobody ever gave the full name of the theory, and it was only ever applied to bodies (not minds) and animals (not humans). The title is more completely, "Evolution by means of Natural Selection", and it affects the human mind as well as the body.

Our money decisions are affected by those two points because:

- *Natural Selection in human evolution made us how we are.*
- *Thoughts, emotions, motivations, decision processes, personality traits were all "selected". We think like we think, act like we act and are how we are because of "Evolution by Natural Selection".*

Lots of people get confused about Natural Selection.

They look at a book like "The Selfish Gene" and think it means that people are "naturally" selfish.

Or see things about "social Darwinism" or "cultural evolution" and believe that people are "evolving" into 21st Century city dwellers.

Or hear debates about whether "genes or environment" are "more important" and get totally confused!

Actually, it's a pretty simple concept.

1. Genes are a blueprint. They set out the basics not only of hair and eye colour, eyesight, height and build, but also of the basic tendencies of personality, thinking style, emotions.
2. They might make somebody slightly smarter than others. They might give them a more selfish, or a more altruistic personality. They might make somebody very analytical and not very emotional, or the reverse. They set out general guidelines, that's why close relatives tend to look alike and behave alike, particularly identical twins who have identical genes.
3. The genes are "expressed" in us, we look, think, behave broadly in line with the "blueprint", but we develop ourselves, the blueprint doesn't dictate everything.
4. We interact with our environment and learn from those interactions (if we live long enough, and learn from experience).
5. Because we each have unique experiences and a unique environment (we are the only person who sees the world exactly the way we do) we develop unique versions of personality in the same way that even identical twins are not exactly the same, although they are very similar.
This is where "natural selection" comes in.

Imagine one of your distant ancestors millennia back in time. They had genes which gave them a certain basic physical appearance, a certain basic personality, a style of thinking and behaving. They learned from experience what worked best in their environment.

> Think about what worked for them, what would make them behave in that way again, or try something different?

Genes are passed from parents to children. You're a mix of your ancestral genes – you don't just have your mother's eyes or your father's nose, you might have Granny Brown's temper, or Auntie Doris's extraversion.

You will develop with your own experience. You can teach your children, but the only bit you truly pass on is your genes. Aspects of your personality may get passed on. The skills that you've spent thousands of hours learning for your job you can teach your children, but you can't pass skills on genetically, they've got to learn for themselves.

In human history, genes that result in the person they produce being more successful in getting food, mates and the other requirements of life (e.g. stronger bodies to hunt, personalities that attract mates, larger brains to solve problems) or producing more and better offspring (e.g. emotions that helped us find and keep a mate or protect and feed offspring so they grow up successfully) will mean that those people tend to have more offspring. Those offspring will then tend to have more children in their turn.

Remember the "selfish gene"? Imagine three people. One is very selfish, one is very altruistic and the third is in between. Now think of the fairy story, "Goldilocks"!

This person is too selfish, nobody likes them and nobody mates with them.

This person is too altruistic, everybody likes them they have lots of mates, but give away all their food to the poor, and their children die of starvation.

But this person is just right – they are pleasant and helpful enough to be well liked, but they look after themselves and their offspring.

Therefore the "just right" person has more children who survive.

> *The genes that made them like they were get passed on to lots of people in the next generation. Those children inherit a lot of the very genes that made their parent so popular and successful in reproducing. So they tend to have lots of children too.*

The less *reproductively* successful people will have less offspring who breed, so over time, the proportion of the genes that produce successful people will increase in the population, while the genes the produce less successful people decline. It's all about what behaviour is effective for reproduction.

The genes are said to be "selfish" because they don't care whether we are happy or sad, rich or poor. The genes are running a "Goldilocks" experiment on every living thing on earth.

The ones that breed most successfully pass their genes on in the greatest numbers. The result is that genes that lead us to reproduce more viable offspring will get "selected" and eventually be present in most of the population. Genes that result in us being "less fitted" to the environment and producing fewer viable offspring tend to reduce in proportion and possibly die out, although they may "pop up" again sometimes by the "random gene mixing process" (otherwise known as sexual reproduction!).

> *Note that is isn't about being "nice", "selfish", "strong", "good", "rich" or anything else, it is only about what works to drive increased numbers of offspring in the environment, that is, it is **reproductively** successful in the real world.*

It's where the expressions "selection", and "survival of the fittest" (i.e. those that fit the environment best, not necessarily those that are most physically fit) come from.

It is also where the less well known expression "selection pressure", came from. It is about the best "fit" with the environment.

Change the environment and you change the selection pressure. If a species is in an environment that gets colder or drier, if a new predator moves in that kills off some animals that are "less fit" (maybe they are slower, can't climb fast or can't outthink the predator), if somebody works out a better way to hunt a prey species and suddenly there is more competition for food, the selection pressure changes.

Of course, this takes quite a bit of time. If there is a 1% advantage in reproduction in 1% of the population and you assume 25 years for each new generation, it will take about 11,300 years for that advantage to be in the genes of 99% of the population. That's assuming that all other things, such as the selection pressure, stay the same.

If you consider human (and pre-human) history, it is something like:

Hunter-gatherers – about 1.75 million years

Agriculture – about 11,000 years

Cities – about 7,000 years

Banks – about 400 years

Modern probability theory – about 400 years

Welfare (such as the NHS) about 50 years

Now you might not agree with those exact figures, but the proportions are right – some things we assume are "normal" are less than a single lifetime old, most modern financial and "risk assessment" methods are a few hundred, city living and agriculture are several thousand and living as hunter gatherers is over a million years old.

Which environment do you think we're evolved to deal with – what sort of "environmental selection pressure" on our genetic blueprint formed the way we look, think, make decisions, register emotions?

Right, hunter-gathering.

We tend to think of hunter-gatherers as little better than beasts.

But put us down in the outback or the veldt and our lifespan is measured in hours, not years; we're just a meal on legs for some predator and we couldn't catch food if it sat on a plate and wrinkled its nose at us. Watch Ray Mears programmes if you doubt it!

Hunter-gatherers lived for hundreds of thousands of years in that environment and prospered (if they hadn't, we wouldn't be here). They were very well fitted to their environment; they had adapted successfully, over millennia, to the particular selection pressures they faced. And they are our ancestors. Do a bit of "who do you think you are?" and go back far enough, you'll find a hunter gatherer that survived environmental pressure that would kill you or me inside a day or two.

Bit short on Aga's, catch it, kill it, eat it, that's my motto.

Of course; "social Darwinism" says that we're still evolving to fit modern life. But think about how "evolution by natural selection" works.

> Does being a "successful" rich person, a banker, professional footballer etc. mean that you will have more viable offspring?
> Does being "unsuccessful", on benefits, with no home mean that you have less offspring that survive to have children of their own?

Actually, it seems that richer, more successful people have less offspring since they often defer having children until later in life, and being poor in a modern, welfare inclusive democracy doesn't mean your child mortality rate is vastly higher.

I'm not saying that is a good thing or a bad thing, it is just the way it appears from the evidence and it suggests that we aren't "evolving" into modern citizens, finance users or anything similar and even if we were, we wouldn't change much from the hunter-gatherer model for at least a few thousand years and probably several tens of thousands.

> *Our bodies, brains and emotions were "fitted", by "selection pressure" to the hunter-gatherer environment. They haven't altered much, if at all, and aren't going to alter in the immediate future. We are like we are, well adapted hunter gatherers.*

Making decisions.

The "logic is always best" school of thought says that all decisions should be logically correct. If we're going to be logical, we'd need some sort of logical process for making decisions. What about this?

We might work out a "Subjective Expected Utility" (SEU) for everything:

> *SEU*
> *Consider all the options, evaluate them in terms of their value to us and calculate a numerical value for the "utility" (value) to us of each option if it works, calculate the probability of it being successful, multiply each option's value if successful by the probability of it being successful and choose the one that looks like the best overall option.*

The SEU idea is great, and in some circumstances it produces much better results than anything else, but do you want to do it every morning to decide what to wear, think about what way to travel to work, decide what TV channel to watch?

I won't belabour the point, read "Descartes Error" by Damasio, if you want to find out what happens if people lose the ability to make instinctive decisions without going through a logical process every time.

To save you time, I'll tell you. Their life falls apart and they cease to function as human beings. If you want to know just how amazing your instinctive decisions are (again, without using SEU all the time) read "Gut Feelings" by Gigerenzer.

And if somebody tells you, "ah, but you should use it for important decisions", ask them what is more important than choosing a mate, and whether they apply SEU every time they are considering asking somebody out.

What they are really saying, and I agree, is that neither instinctive nor logical decision processes are always better, the issue is deciding when you should use each one and how much.

It isn't simply a case of "important" = "logical", life is more complex than that.

That's why logical isn't always applicable.

Here's why we can't actually do it.

Imagine you are out hunting or gathering. The grass moves and it isn't the wind. What do I want to do about it?

The main options for "what do I want to do" are:

- I want to eat it.
- I want to prevent it eating me.
- I want to mate with it.

- I want to fight with it for the right to mate with somebody else.
- I want to cooperate with it to hunt/gather/mate with/fight-off something.

That's pretty much it. Now, think about it, do you want to draw up a table and calculate probabilities of each option, based on your perception of the size of the grass movement and an estimate from that of the size of the object, and work out each option's value to you in terms of how hungry you are, whether you currently have a mate, your strength (and consequently your chances of fighting off a predator or competitor) and so on? Of course you'll still have to assign values to everything from the estimated size and consequent danger posed by different predators, your own strength relative to a range of different opponents, your charisma if it turns out to be a potential mate and so on.

So you have to guess lots of unknowns, fit them into a formula, then solve the formula (all in your head) and then go with the final probability estimate.

If you want to do all that, I'm afraid you're too late. Here's what happens:

For millions of years our ancestors made their decisions in time

If you spent longer than a fraction of a second trying to work out what might be making the long grass wave, figuring it isn't the wind, deducing that it is unlikely to be another person or a prey species that you want to eat, and concluding that it is something that you need to run away from, the time for running has passed! You are either lucky (it isn't hungry) or you're dead.

If you die, you don't pass on your genes to another generation. We're all the product of thousands of generations of people who didn't die and consequently of those who made quick decisions on very little, very ambiguous information. It was a selection pressure we adapted to, and we got extremely good at making snap decisions well.

Your brain on the plains

There are three principal parts of our brain. The oldest bit (older than people by several *billion* years) is the reptilian brain. It does things like keeping our hearts beating, speeding our hearts up when we need to run, letting us know we're hungry and getting our liver to work when our blood sugar level drops. Basically, those bits (such as the brain stem) control the basics, but don't deal with new situations, don't do much that is available to conscious thinking and don't really have any sophisticated responses.

The more sophisticated limbic system developed hundreds of millions of years ago. Another name used for that part of the brain is the "emotional brain", which suggests its main functions.

Both of these areas basically work without our being aware of them working, they normally operate pretty much entirely unconsciously.

Finally, a few million years ago the most sophisticated part of the brain, the cortex, developed and allowed our conscious minds to engage in deep and meaningful thought, acquire language, reason etc. Among those thoughts our advanced, conscious minds have is the false belief that we run the whole thing consciously, and that we make our own decisions all the time.

Actually the subconscious does the analysis, and sends us messages about what is going on (in our bodies and in the environment) and makes very strong hints (sometimes overwhelmingly so) about what we ought to do that sometimes we become aware of consciously.

For example, have you ever had the "feeling" that you were being watched?

That is your "cognitions" working sub-consciously. You've seen something in the environment. You've thought it through unconsciously, got an emotional trigger and then become aware of that "feeling" consciously.

Of course, we don't think (I use that word deliberately), it works that way. We believe that we think things through, and we then act, and then perhaps feel some emotion and our body sorts out what our heart and lungs need to do when we've decided how we will act. But we don't.

We see a situation, assess it subconsciously, get some sort of emotional and intellectual trigger and all that happens in fractions of a second.

After that, our conscious mind works on it and tries to invent a story about the situation to explain what we've done. Even if we consciously endeavour to assess a situation, our emotions, automatic responses etc. act as a "filter". We see things in a certain way. We don't see "reality", we see what our mind tells us is reality.

The parts of the brain work together. You can't separate out thinking and feeling, logic and emotion. Our "rational" cognitive thought has emotional prompts and our "feelings" have cognitions behind them. It's like a chicken, two eggs and another chicken, nobody knows which comes first.

That's why being "logical" all the time doesn't happen even if it would work; we simply can't do it.

Often we see what we expect to see, which is why visual illusions and magic tricks work. Even when we know that the "vanishing ball" or the "McGurk" effect are our brains fooling us, we still see the effect. People working with effects for 20 years still see them.

Our brains evolved to keep us safe, to predict what was going to happen so we could act in time. Visual illusions don't work the way we "know" the world works, so we don't see what is there, we see what we "know" *must* be there. What we "consciously" analyse and assess is not an objective "truth" in the world but our interpretation of it based on our evolved brains. We think we see the world "as it is", but we don't.

It's hard to convince people that this is what happens. Our conscious minds are extremely good at making up plausible explanations for things that we see, do, think, believe or feel, but those explanations don't necessarily bear any resemblance to the real reasons.

In case you think I'm wrong, and you are different, here's an excerpt from some work by Michael Gazzaniga, a psychologist who did a lot of work with "split brain" patients, who had had the two hemispheres of the brain separated (a way to control severe epilepsy)

"Each hemisphere was shown four small pictures, one of which related to a larger picture also presented to that hemisphere. The patient had to choose the most appropriate small picture. We then asked the left hemisphere - the only one that can talk - why the left hand was pointing to the object. It really did not know, because the decision to point to the card was made in the right hemisphere. Yet, quick as a flash, it made up an explanation. We dubbed this creative, narrative talent the interpreter mechanism."

Gazzaniga, 2002

So we do think like hunter gatherers and we don't think the way we think we do!

Another aspect of this shows up in "recognition", mentioned in chapter 5. Even if our subconscious makes the decision before we're consciously aware of having a decision to make, it has to work on something, it can't make decisions or give us hints in a vacuum.

People can be shown random patterns, "squiggles" that have no meaning. If they are then shown a series of these squiggles and asked to say which ones they've seen before, they don't know. The squiggles are meaningless and nobody can remember (consciously) which ones they've seen before. But when they are asked which squiggles they prefer, then despite the fact that the squiggles were meaningless and they couldn't remember which they'd seen, they "prefer" the ones they'd seen before.

Not only that, but they give all sorts of fascinating reasons as to why the squiggles they prefer are preferable. They say these were more aesthetically pleasing, more meaningful etc., but nobody says they liked the ones they had seen before, although that was the reason they preferred them. We "like" (feeling) what we've noticed (thought).

> *We make most decisions before we're even aware of having a decision to make, we don't think we do and it might (as in chapter 5) not always work very well in modern society that changes fast, but it is the way we do it.*
>
> *We make those decisions on very little information that our subconscious mind has filtered and analysed for us.*
>
> *We can't ignore that filtering and "see the world as it is", nor can we consciously pick out the details on which we base most of our decisions, we just "know" and "have a feeling" about the world.*
>
> *And we can't simply separate "feeling" from "thought" and logic, the human brain does not work that way.*

Sex (it had to come, didn't it!)
Another thing we get wrong about hunter gatherers – apart from assuming that they are stupid and that we make decisions much more "logically" than they did - is the belief they are all the same, a sort of combined "huntergatherer". They aren't, they come in two basic types.

We confuse "equal" with "identical" when we talk about men and women. Socially, it is desirable that we are equal, equal in opportunity, equal in rights, etc. and I agree with that idea. But we aren't the same.

Women bear children, which is a big investment of time and resources. For hunter-gatherers there is no baby food and no animals to milk; if the child is to grow it must be fed. A woman can't have more than one child about every two-four years, assuming she can get enough food to be able to produce milk, to look after the toddler, keep it alive and then to get pregnant again immediately. A woman can't realistically have more than, say eight children in her lifetime, given that she can first bear children at about fifteen and ceases bearing them at about forty (which is about life expectancy).

By contrast, how much investment of time has the man got? Do I hear you say, "fifteen seconds, and ten of them to get his trousers off"?! So a man can potentially have hundreds of offspring if he can persuade enough women to choose to mate with him, or is a desirable enough mate for them to choose him of their own accord.

But why does it matter whether there is "investment" in children, or if we have emotions that lead us to care for our offspring? Other animals manage without, so why should we have evolved in this way?

Humans are successful enough to be at risk of killing off most other life-forms (and ourselves) because of our intelligence. That needs a big brain, and that means a big head in proportion to the body size. That brain needs time to develop, and the size of the mother's body puts a limit on the size the infant can grow to inside her. The duration of pregnancy and the lack of opportunity for the brain to learn from experience in the womb limits the degree of maturity the brain can reach before birth.

Some animals are relatively mature at birth. For example, a

Wildebeest can stand up in a few minutes and run within half an hour of birth. All primates are relatively helpless, but a new born monkey placed on its back can probably turn over to right itself. Higher primates, such as chimpanzees will take longer, perhaps weeks, but humans take months.

Effectively, humans have to be at least three or four years old before they can survive without help because if they matured in the womb to the same physical and mental point as a Wildebeest, the mother would either explode or have to be cut open to get the baby out! Also, because they need time outside the safe environment of the womb in which the necessary learning can take place for the brain to develop fully, a lot of care is needed to help the young manage to develop well enough to have young of their own.

> *The trade off for the size and sophistication of the human brain is that it takes a long time to be able to use it well. The brain can only have so much "hard wiring", it can have "kit" to learn languages, to speak, to make quick decisions etc. but it has to experience the language being spoken, try out the muscles that control speech, learn what things to consider in making a decision, and that takes time. During that learning time the infant is relatively helpless. It will become smart enough to kill predators bigger than itself, but it has first to learn the mental and physical skills to handle the bow, spear, assault rifle or whatever weapons are in use.*

As a consequence of the different time investment needed, women evolved to be selective in choosing mates, men evolved to compete with one another to be chosen. One result is that men are generally bigger than women, because it is an advantage in male-male competition to be big, you're more likely to win and get chosen, so your "bigger bloke" gene gets passed on.

Another consequence was that a woman's goal was to receive the best viable genes for her offspring as well as secure an ongoing supply of high protein food (meat) for both herself (so she can have another baby as soon as possible) and for her offspring (so they are viable). So women had selection pressure to be good at judging people, not just the potential mates and food providers but their competition – other women.

Women competed with other women, to get a secure future for their offspring. That usually needed the support of a mate (or several) to provide good quality food for both her and her offspring. That meant inspiring loyalty so that the mate wouldn't give food to rival women in the hope that he could mate with them, ensuring that other women can't steal the protection and food the mate represented and to be able to beat the other women to the best genetic material.

Remember the symbols of money in the first chapter?

It isn't about what ought to be, or what is fair or nice or anything else, it is simply what worked for reproduction in hunter-gatherer society.

The best strategy for women was to be better at understanding people, to get the highest status, most loyal mate(s) she could and to make sure other women didn't take his (or their) attention and the food he (or even better, they), could provide. That way she could have a good number of offspring and most important, make sure they all had plenty of food and were likely to survive.

By contrast, men tended to compete with other men, looking for freedom to mate with lots of women. To get that, they need to be chosen, and what got them chosen was status and power as that demonstrated they could provide for the women's offspring.

The best strategy for a man was to have high status and to be able to provide food for several so as to be chosen by the most women (which gave freedom to father as many children as possible) and probably to be able to demonstrate that he didn't abandon the women that bore his offspring so that women would continue to accept him as a mate.

The ones who "got it right" passed on their genes to the largest numbers and those genes helped to make the offspring, like the parents, successful breeders.

Hunting and gathering

Probably since it is hard to hunt when you are six months pregnant and personally need to nurse existing babies, women tended not to go chasing off for miles after animals. They specialised in gathering.

If you want to gather ripe fruit and vegetables, it helps to have a good sense of smell. Women do have that sense, almost invariably better than men. Of course, it doesn't matter much about sense of smell if you hunt. Since the prey have a much better sense of smell anyway, the difference between success rates in hunting for men won't differ much dependent on their sense of smell.

If you are going to gather and you see a bush that you know will bear fruit later, you want to remember where it is relative to other things so you can find it again. Women's spatial sense is geared to location. Being able to go in straight lines is less use than remembering landmarks and most women are superior to most men in any tests of that "landmark" ability.

If you are hunting, you might have chased prey miles on a winding course. If you catch it, you don't want to walk all that windy way back carrying a heavy load of meat, you want to go in a straight line to save effort. Men's senses are usually geared to that ability, not to finding landmarks.

If you're hunting animals and they are trying to run away, it helps (so it is a selection pressure on your chances of producing viable offspring) for you to be good at working out instrumental problems such as, "if we chase the herd this way, we can run them towards the cliff and then they'll either fall off or we'll catch them". It isn't so critical to work out those sorts of things if you are gathering food which doesn't try to run away.

By contrast, being able to decide when somebody is lying is handy when you are trying to determine loyalty (so it is a selection pressure for you to have more viable offspring as a woman), but it isn't so critical if you are the one whose loyalty to a mate is being measured by somebody else – which is the case with men.

Obviously, it didn't hurt if you were a woman who was good at "things" or a man who was good at "people", but there wasn't much selection pressure for that, it wasn't going to make much difference to your chances of passing on the genes that made you the way you were.

Today, a woman who is an engineer or a man who is a nurse is not at a disadvantage in ability (but they might be due to social misperceptions!), but they are rarer than the other way round. But, if you were a gatherer woman who was not good at people or a hunter man who was not good at things, it makes a difference and long term your genes were likely to decline in the population as a whole.

Over hundreds of thousands of generations, that's how we developed.

Women evolved mainly around gathering food, choosing carefully for both healthy genes and particularly for loyal support in a mate and were good at empathy and people skills.

Men evolved mainly in hunting for food, competing physically to be chosen and were good at "instrumental" skills (like if-then rules).

Men generally became overtly physically competitive, aware of status and display and prepared to take risks. If they competed, risked and lived, they got status and more chance of mating. If they didn't compete they wouldn't get chosen anyway, so dying because they took risks was not, in terms of the "Goldilocks" viewpoint of genes, much worse than not competing at all.

Women usually became the driver for behaviour; controlled mate choice and had a huge investment in young. They competed with one another in much more subtle ways than men and didn't tend to such extreme behaviour, as that would compromise the safety of their children, so there was no need for extremes.

How does that effect money? Men and women, as we've seen, usually look for different things. They compete, including competition over money, in different ways, with different objectives. Men usually want to compete, even if they lose. Women usually prefer to cooperate, even when they have to share their winnings.

This doesn't mean that men or women are "better" or "worse", it was the result of selection pressure and the pressure was slightly different for the sexes. Basically, women evolved to be "better" women than men are, and men evolved to be "better" men than women are. The differences are about motivation and style, not about intelligence or mental ability.

One warning about all this. I've emphasised differences of gender in motives and behaviours to aid understanding common differences in attitudes to money, but we are all human. Much is said about human similarity to Chimpanzees since we share around 91-97% of genes (depending on whose evidence you believe), but men and women share 100% of genetic material.

Most of our behaviour patterns are similar; only a few are gendered. They persist although the environment is different today. Two million years of evolution hasn't suddenly been wiped out by a few thousand years of a social desire for equality and we still have most of the drives although the reason for them evolving (the selection pressure) has changed. And we are all human.

One thing we all evolved to do was care for our young.

There's an obvious advantage for the genes in this. If you make sacrifices for your own offspring, or other near relatives, then even if you die you will be allowing people with at least some of the same genes to survive. For example, your children will have 50% of genes they inherited from you (so in simple terms, sacrificing your life for three children means three times one half survive, so one and a half copies of your genes survive!)

Similarly, you share significant similarities in genes with your siblings, grandparents, aunts and uncles. The degree of genetic inheritance that is significant in this way (and that usually bonds family groups in hunter-gatherer society) is the same degree as in intestacy law. In other words, if somebody dies without making a will, the family who can inherit (rather than the estate going to the Crown) are the same ones that will have a marked genetic similarity. Uniquely, it is a law that follows both nature and common sense!

But of course, as humans evolved, a single family group might not be enough – so we have a tribe. What is the difference between a:

- tribal tattoo,
- religious prohibition on particular foods,
- old school tie,
- political belief,
- regional or "BBC" accent?

Not a lot.

We evolved to like people who look like us, talk like us, smell like us, eat our food and not "disgusting foreign muck" and who are "our sort of people". It is also vital that our "tribe" also think like us, like whom we like, hate what we hate, and see the world as we see it.

It is also, unfortunately, the basis of prejudice. In the Bible there is the story of the tribal war, where the defeated enemy were trying to get away and the password for the bridge across the Jordan was set by the winners as "shibboleth". The defeated tribe couldn't make the "sh" sound, they said "sibboleth". If they couldn't say the password properly they were killed. It was an easy way to tell friend from foe.

We're more sophisticated now, we don't usually kill people for having a funny accent (although we might refuse them entry to our club). We just laugh at or despise people who are different or don't speak like us.

In a more serious context we have selection interviews for jobs and find out what party they belong to, what team they support, what school they went to, what colour or gender they are and how they speak and accept or reject them on that basis. It is the root of the "like me", bias I mentioned earlier. And because we evolved to make quick decisions, the average time to make those decisions is a few seconds or less.

As humans spread out and made bigger social groups, we needed to be able to trade favours and to barter. This was before money, remember. To do this, and to be able to use specialisation (like hunting, roof fixing, etc.), we needed to develop trade mechanisms.

There seem to be four major systems that humans developed to handle trade, based on research with groups, including modern hunter-gatherers. One of these, Equality Matching, occurs where people exchange goods or favours at different times and the traded items are identical, similar or easily comparable.

Let's suppose I've hunted successfully, and I've got meat. I'll share with you if next week (when you're successful and I'm not) you share with me. It's what we intuitively understand as trade. In order for this to work, we need to remember faces and debts so we can trade favours. And we need to remember cheats so that we don't continue to trade with people who don't reciprocate.

This brings us back to the Wason test that was mentioned in the last chapter. You might remember that people were generally poor at working out which card to turn over to test something logically (it was the A, D, 3 and 4 question). Let's revisit the problem (based on what Cosmides and Tooby did).

You are given four cards that show Lemonade, Beer, 25 years old, 16 years old. On one side of the card is a drink and on the other the age of the drinker. Only those over 21 should drink alcohol. Which two cards do you need to turn over to check whether the rule is obeyed?

You need to turn over 16 years old and Beer.

Most people get this one right. The difference seems to be the "content". When it is a real situation, people can see what the issue is and use "common sense" that doesn't convert directly to "logic" with an abstract problem.

Gerd Gigerenzer and his colleague Klaus Hug, posed the problem as one of entitlement to pension. The rule was, "if an employee gets a pension, they must have worked for the firm for at least 10 years". Working on the basis of cards with something like, 9 years service, 11 years service, pension granted, no pension granted, can you work out which cards to turn over?

The interesting thing about this is that the reasoning is different depending on what the person's perspective was. Those told they were union members were better at finding entitlement without benefit, those told they were managers looked for benefit without entitlement. Each detected cheating, but from different perspectives of what was fair and what was cheating!

The logical structure is the same as in the basic task. However, people are much better at detecting cheating in a context than at using abstract logic, and they detect cheating from their own perspective. From our hunter gatherer heritage, and our need to trade/cooperate, we evolved an effective way to work out solutions to fair trade and cheating, it just doesn't work in the way abstract "logic" suggests.

People are good at "real life" problem reasoning (at least, in this context), although they are not usually good at abstract logic.

But we make decisions very fast, remember, because we had to. So for speed we avoid "second guessing" – we often look for confirmatory evidence unless we can see a good reason not to. We don't often delay to agonise over accuracy, it might kill us!

Before we leave the subject of tribes, trust, trade and cheating detection, there's another thing that is actually smart and which seems to have evolved as a way to survive, but that confuses some people and makes them assume humans are stupid and irrational about money.

Imagine you're involved in an experiment with a partner you don't know. You have £100 to split between you. You are separated and you have to make the offer of a split of that £100 without reference to your partner. If they accept the offer, you both get the amounts, but if they don't accept it, neither of you get anything. How much of the £100 would you offer them and how much would you keep for yourself?

This is called the Ultimatum Game, and there's been a huge amount of research done on it. Logically, and according to economic theory, you should offer only £1 (or perhaps only a few pence). Your partner is better off by that amount if they accept, whereas they get nothing if they refuse, so they should accept. Would you feel comfortable offering that amount?

How about if it was the other way round, if you were offered only £1 (or even £10) would you accept? If you accept you get the £1, but you know that your partner is getting £99. How about that?

What happens is that most people offer a "fair" share – even though they don't have to. So they tend to offer somewhere around £50. That causes a lot of problems for economics.

In theory (again, this is theory, that like logic has very little to do with the real world) people should "maximise", in other words they should make the most money and be totally selfish.

Of course, that is just an experiment. So think of this, why do you leave a tip in a restaurant?

The reason might be, perhaps, that it is for good service. But you don't give the tip until the end of the meal so by then there's no point giving a tip because it won't influence the service quality. Perhaps it is for future service. But are they going to recognise you, in fact, are you ever going to go there again? Despite this, most people tip even on holiday at places they've never been to before and will never go to again. In pure economic terms, that is crazy, why give away money that can't possibly give you any benefit?

As I've mentioned, our relationship to money is complicated, too complicated for theory (or economists) to be much use in the real world!

But if you remember tipping and the "offer" side of the ultimatum game are behaviours that are linked to our evolutionary past and trade, the need to detect cheats and treat honest people fairly so you can trade with them again, it makes sense.

But if you think the offer side is complex, what about the "accept" side!?

> Would you take the offer of £1?
> How about £10? Most people aren't happy to do that.
> Would you "punish" somebody who made a low offer, say £10, which means that neither of you get any money, but you "teach them a lesson". Or would you accept it, on the basis that it's £10 you didn't have before?

Theory and logic say that you "should" accept any offer. Logically, and theoretically you should also never leave tips or give a fair offer.

It seems from the cross- cultural research that every culture has a concept of "fair" offers and members of each culture are prepared to give up money to punish the selfish.

> Again, think about it. Do you want to be happy or logical?
> Could you be happy being "logical" in those circumstances?
> How well do you think society would run if everybody did that?
> And do you believe that we would have evolved like we have if there weren't advantages to being "illogical" but treating people fairly, those advantages meaning that you could have trade, trust, inter-tribal negotiation etc.?

If you think about the way we evolved, that sort of trust, inter-dependence and detection and punishment of cheats was important. If somebody cheated and got away with it, they could get food from others without paying it back.

If they always did it, the cheat would do well and everybody else would not. But if the group as a whole isolated the cheat, the cheat lost and everybody else won.

Incidentally, it is useful for humans (in terms of breeding successfully, competing with others of their gender and staying alive) to know certain things.

These include the current hierarchy of our tribe, who is "top dog", who is popular and who is not, who is mating with whom, who has the best reputation as hunter etc. Knowing allows us to avoid offending the powerful people who might cause us problems, helps us know what our status is, who is a realistic potential mate, who is available, who might have food to spare and so on.

We still like to know these things, because for millennia they were vital to survival, so our brains developed "kit" that helped us keep track.

The difference is that in modern society we imagine our tribe is bigger. We like to know what celebrities are mating with other celebrities, we are interested in reputations of footballers or clothes designers, we like to see the "rich list" or find out who is "most powerful" in the media and in business and instead of being interested in the social problems of our family and our tribe (because they had a huge impact on ourselves, our social group and those who shared our genes) we are now interested in our "extended family" that only exists in a TV soap opera!

We still make social comparisons and are vitally interested in status, power, security, reproduction etc., it is just that these have been removed from our immediate circle and extended to those people who appear in Hello magazine or on the TV.

The "kit" is there in our brains and it works, it just doesn't have the same environment to work in that it used to. We spent millennia evolving to cope with a real world, with social relationships, trust, betrayal and trade and it worked well. Only lately have we had money and dealt with abstract problems (with and without money), and been expected to react to those problems with logic, instead of something that our instincts (and large chunks of our brains) told us worked.

Now consider some of the other things required to be able to trade, particularly over long distances on a formal basis. We obviously need to communicate, and have some sense of number and proportion. I only talked a little in the last chapter about our number blindness. There's more about when it matters and what to do about it in chapter 8. But for the moment, let's look at language and numbers.

Numbers and language

Humans appear to be unique in that they can discuss the future, think (and talk) about thinking, make plans that aren't just instinctive, they can even communicate quite complex concepts to one another.

Obviously, there is selection pressure to be able to talk, to listen, to make sense of what we hear and to be able to communicate our own ideas to others.

We've evolved so that any child with normal functioning who is exposed to human communication learns how to communicate. If as a child you hear Chinese, you learn Chinese, if you hear English you learn English, if you hear Swahili and Hungarian as well, you learn all of them. You don't have to try, to concentrate, to go to school or be taught, you just learn. Admittedly, you appear to learn better if those around you simplify speech for you when you are very small and talk "parentese" with lots of repetition and gradual increase in sentence complexity as you learn. However, you'll still learn, pretty much irrespective of what they do and you'll end up fluent in whatever language is spoken around you. And if you hear and see Sign Language, you'll learn that.

How about writing, did we need that as hunter gatherers? Not really. Written language isn't much more than a few thousand years old. Compare it to spoken communication (which was subject to selection pressure) that everybody can learn, however "slow" they might be. Even if you (or your child) are a real prodigy, there is some effort involved in learning to read and write. We don't seem to have the mental "kit" for learning to read and write that enables everybody to learn spoken language pretty much effortlessly.

Now think about numbers. How much do hunter gatherers depend on numbers? What things about numbers are important enough to have been a selection pressure?

You need to have some idea of quantity – are there more of them than of us, is there enough food to go round, what is something worth in relation to something else for us to trade?

We need small numbers, and some idea of subtraction and addition. There are three lions round an antelope carcass, two go away, is it safe to approach? There are a small group of us and only one of the enemy tribe at the waterhole, but there is a small group of the other tribe just over the ridge, can we safely approach the waterhole and drive that one off?

If you read Terry Pratchett's Diskworld books (and if you don't, you should), you will know the trolls. They count like this: one, two, three, many, lots. Those numbers are pretty much all that you need.

Bears in a cave, lions round a kill, numbers up to about three are important. A single prey animal (one), a stag and doe (two), a pair and young (three), a small family group (many), a whole herd (lots), is probably all you need as long as you can make an estimate of whether there are more of 'them' than us.

There is no great need for you to be familiar with Bayes theorem, the differences between a Gaussian and a Zipf distribution or the mathematical complexities of a statistical problem with probabilities that don't sum to one.

Not that knowledge of those things will hurt you, in fact in some situations in modern life it is really helpful. However, it doesn't matter how clever you are, that stuff is not going to come as easily as learning to speak, it will take effort. For most people, in most circumstances, that effort is not worthwhile, even nowadays. It certainly wasn't needed for a million years, but being able to speak, to do simple proportions and understanding addition and subtraction with small numbers was.

There's another type of trade that human groups use, which has been labelled Market Pricing. Slightly similar to modern concepts of economics, it works on a different basis to Equality Matching.

Whereas Equality Matching is generally used *within* groups, Market Pricing is used, usually, *between* groups. So it is more explicit and formalised, there are often individuals who are designated as traders with another group.

An example is aborigine tribes. At the coast, where stingrays can be caught and the stings used as spears, but stone isn't available you'd perhaps trade three spears for one stone axe, as the axes have "rarity value". Inland, where stone is available, axes are "cheap" and stingray spears are not easily available you might give three axes to get one spear. It uses more complex concepts.

We therefore have more trouble with it!

Meanwhile, remember, we evolved to make decisions fast. To do that, we had to pick some key information from the environment. We think we look at everything and consider it, but we simply don't have time or enough short term memory (or computational power) to consider every factor in every situation.

And think about this, while you are reading these words, there will be sounds around you, objects in peripheral vision, you will have contact with a chair and some objects.

Are you aware of all of those different things all the time? How do you know which are the important ones and which you can ignore?

You use experience. For situations that are familiar, it works. Work on naturalistic decision making shows that we learn to deal very effectively with things that don't alter in form too much and on which we can get feedback. An example is fire-fighters, who become amazingly good at determining the best course of action in situations where the chemistry of fires doesn't change much. We all learn to do similar feats, like catching a ball. Try doing that by working out equations, or better, try programming a computer to do what a five year old child can do easily.

But in order to evolve to be able to do these amazing things that we can't work out how to get computers or other machines to do, our minds had to sacrifice some other things. We don't deal with big numbers easily and can't do abstract, complex, conditional probabilities, we can't think through masses of options and outcomes to pick "the best" and we don't use logic much.

We do what worked over hundreds of thousands of years, in the "Goldilocks" lottery of life. We give a lot of weight to things that were important when we were hunter gatherers, like staying alive.

So, having talked about all this, let's think about how our minds work, and how this leads to the "errors" referred to in the last chapter.

Loss aversion and frame dependence

Imagine that you're a hunter gatherer and you see a lion standing over a carcass.

Do you think you can chase it away, and get the meat for yourself and your family/tribe? How much do you want to bet? You can work out the odds of it being scared away if you want, but on what are you going to base those odds (see chapters 7 and 8) and how are you going to do those calculations?

The big question is, what is the pay-off to you? If you scare it away, you get a meal for perhaps a couple of days until the meat goes off.

That's good, your family will eat for a few days. On the other hand, if you don't scare it away and it kills you, you're dead and your family may die too. In the mathematics of the genes, that is not a good equation. And of course, you have to make that decision fast, before the lion decides not to wait for you to dither and kills you anyway!

Some people will take the risk, if they are desperate enough. But on the whole, the downside of risking and losing is huge, while the upside of risking and winning is limited. So unless you are starving and going to die if you don't take the risk, you'll generally go for the sure thing. Stay alive until tomorrow, make your mind up, run!

An aside on the "make a quick decision, be safe" policy in modern life. Think about "computer scams", the sort of thing where you're sent an e-mail that says you have won a lottery or are going to be paid money to help a refugee get money out of a country at war.

The "logic and painstakingly thinking through every problem" idea says that you have to consider this carefully.

The "intuitive, gut-feeling" school says that it sounds too good to be true, delete it.

Which person is more likely to be scammed?

Right, the big thinker. It appears that carefully considering it adds lots of false detail, you start to take it seriously and end up being suckered in. Your normal, human scepticism over trade and your intuition says it must be rubbish and keeps you safer.

Human evolution produced people who are smart, not logical but smart in the real world, and that is what mattered. Now, it is more complicated to know what will work best, but real world results are still what matter.

Most of us are the descendents of people who, in five seconds or less, reasoned, "eat for a day or two but maybe die. I don't want to die, I won't risk it". Some people were desperate and reasoned, "take a risk or die of starvation, I don't want to die, I'll risk it". The ones who risked it and died obviously didn't have offspring, but the ones who risked it and lived might have offspring that joined the rest of the population and eventually resulted in us.

That gives most of us a good head start towards reasoning, "we don't want to lose, if we are going to lose, take a risk to avoid it. Otherwise, play safe and stay alive for tomorrow".

However, sometimes taking those risks would have worked so you'd expect some relatively small proportion of people would inherit the genes for taking risk, because it paid off sometimes. So we might all be loss averse, but while most would generally be "risk averse" as well, a few wouldn't.

I wouldn't say, that explains "adrenaline junkies", but based on research into the minority who take risks for fun, it is consistent with the facts. It therefore gives a hint to why some people might do things that seem to attract the probability of financial loss (like gambling) that are needlessly risky and that contravene both "logic" (the odds never favour you, as we'll look at in chapter 7-9) and evolution (we mostly only take risks, or gamble, if there is no alternative to avoid a loss).

We react to framing of issues as loss or gain and we are loss averse (and mostly, risk averse), for perfectly sound evolutionary reasons.

The fact that generally, these days, we aren't talking about losing our lives doesn't matter to the parts of our brain that gives us the cognitive and emotional cues to make the decisions in a fraction of a second. Those parts make the decision in the way they've always done, tell us what the decision is and we then have to deal with it without much, if any, conscious input.

If the sub-conscious bits that make quick decisions waited for us to have conscious input we'd have died out ten thousand generations ago because we wouldn't have made the decision fast enough to stay alive.

Sometimes, as with the investment examples in chapter 5, we're better off standing back and thinking, but sometimes, as with the scams example in this chapter, our intuitive sense keeps us better off. It isn't a simple, "thinking hard is always better", situation.

Status quo bias, recognition, the endowment effect.
We've already seen that we are "regret averse" in the same way that we are loss averse. We've also seen that we like our own "tribe" since strangers might be dangerous and untrustworthy. Finally, we have seen that we use our experience of what is important to make decisions about what risks to take.

> What do you think is going to happen when we have to go into a strange situation, one where we have no direct experience, where there are new things or people involved and where we might suddenly find ourselves in trouble?

If we push ourselves into a new situation, discard the tools, areas or other supports with which we are familiar or get ourselves surrounded by potentially hostile strangers we might be in danger. We want to be safe. We want to have what we know, the people, the areas, the tools, the ways of thinking, the ways of seeing the world that we feel at home with.

Naturally enough, therefore, we are going to stick with what we've got, with the status quo. We're also going to want recognisable situations. Finally, we are going to stick with the tools and ideas we know, our own "endowment" and also our "tribe".

It doesn't matter whether "our" tools are really stronger than somebody else's, or "our" ideas are better. What matters is that they are "ours", they are familiar, we know them, they are useful. On the other hand, somebody else's ideas, tools, methods or whatever are not worth much, they might not work for us, we don't recognise them, they are unfamiliar and involve making a conscious decision to change that we might regret.

And that way of thinking gives us some predispositions to things. We're set up to fear the things that were dangerous in that environment. The dark, where other animals could see better than us, spiders or snakes that might be venomous and so on. We're actually genetically prepared to fear some things.

We only have to see somebody (like a parent) show fear of spiders once to acquire a fear of spiders, but they aren't actually dangerous (not in the UK at least, Australians might disagree!) But in modern society a much bigger danger is, for example, an electric toaster. We're not set up to fear those.

We're also prepared to be afraid of disasters. A reason that people have disaster information (like 9/11) "available" may be because in a small tribe a calamity like a flood or an animal stampede may kill a significant portion of the tribe and ultimately wipe it out. Regular deaths, that only kill a few at a time are less of a threat of extinction of our genes and are probably, in the reality of hunter-gather society, a normal occurrence.

So perhaps we react to disasters like plane crashes etc. with death tolls in the thousands in one incident with the same hunter-gatherer reaction of overwhelming fear; while smoking, car accidents and so on that kill millions more than plane crashes, but do it one or two at a time, don't bother us so much.

It isn't "logical", but I suspect we can understand why we might feel that way as there is a rational explanation for that "illogical" fear.

We can recognise, that "our" tools might not be better, a disaster might not be more dangerous etc. But by the time we recognise it consciously, our subconscious has already thought about it, decided not to change, told us we are afraid, will lose and done everything it can to "keep us safe". Our conscious mind has a job to do to over-rule all that.

Therefore, most of the time we don't think about it, if we do think we assume "ours" is best anyway and our conscious mind "justifies" that belief (remember the "split-brain" experiments) and it is only with a lot of hard work we manage to question that belief, accept that our decision was made by our sub-conscious, rationalised by our conscious and in fact we've been totally wrong and self-deluding. We don't like feeling like that, so mostly, we don't do it!

Availability and anchoring

Look at this list:

Table
Car
Shoe
Telephone
Candle
Dr Who
Duvet
Book
Cushion
Stool

Now look away from the list and see what you remember.

The odds are that you'll remember the first couple of items (table, car) the last couple, (cushion and stool) and the odd one out, Dr Who.

The odd one is obvious. You'll undoubtedly remember your first day at school and other exciting or unique events in your life, but you'll soon forget what you had for dinner on a particular day, it just isn't important enough or outstanding enough to remember.

Incidentally, that is why older relatives (and ourselves, as we age) can remember clearly incidents in their childhood but get hazy about last week. When we're young, there is so much new and exciting it is as if we met a Time Lord pretty well every week. When we get older we've got life sorted out, we have our habits, our routines, yesterday and today are similar and pretty much the same as last week and the week before. So why would we remember them, for they blur into one?

As hunter gatherers, we wanted to be able to predict the future to remain safe. But if we try to remember everything, we'd have too much to think about. Apart from having to store it all, we don't want to trawl through thousands of examples to find the one we need. Like the internet, there's all the information there, the difficulty is finding the right bit!

Think about all the sounds around you, the physical sensations etc. You don't want to have to store everything just in case it is useful at some point, and then not be able to find it when it is useful. What you need is to forget the normal and boring and remember the things that are likely to be helpful in predicting the future.

What do you think is most useful to make predictions?

The first time we encounter anything we expect it to be typical, that the next encounter will be like the previous one. We use the first encounter as an "anchor", it is a guide for the future until we have something more significant to go on.

Also, what happened last time, whether somebody tried to trick us, was friendly or hostile, whether something that looked dangerous wasn't, or vice versa, is important as the latest "state of play" with that object or person.

Add to those the unusual events that might be significant.

The useful stuff is the first, the latest and the odd – exactly what we do remember.

Anchoring and availability might cause us issues in modern times, in some situations. But they arise out of our "safety first" approach.

Obviously that isn't to say that in modern life, especially money, we "should" go with our instinct all the time. In the same way that "logic" is not equal to good, neither is "human nature".

Just because we evolved in a particular way doesn't mean it still works better. When people say, "natural is best" I sometimes ask them whether they eat raw meat using their hands and sitting naked on the ground and whether they like poisonous fungi, since those are "natural"!

Overconfidence

Another point about "natural", we want to believe we are good.

I mentioned the fundamental attribution error before. We mostly believe that we are a bit special, a bit better than other people. Imagine if we didn't. Imagine that we're worried about getting it wrong, about misjudging people or situations, about putting other people (and ourselves) at risk because our opinions might be wrong, our experience might not be relevant or we might not be able to perform as well as we want to. How effective would we be? How attractive a mate would we be?

That is, in very broad terms, the situation with depression, that it's all hopeless, it all goes wrong, we can't cope, we're not good enough. And the result is that we don't actually get much done.

Being overconfident is a way to cope with that. I'm not saying it's the best way. In "Learned Optimism", Martin Seligman points out that actually, those who are optimistic and more overconfident have more fun and success, but those who are pessimistic (from whom the ranks of the depressed are more likely to come) actually have a more realistic view.

> In some jobs, like being an auditor in accounting for example, it is demonstrably better to be pessimistic than optimistic, to tend towards reality and depression rather than optimism and overconfidence. How many auditors do you think there are in hunter-gatherer society?

Bigness bias

What is more important; have a meal today and perhaps die, or go hungry today, eat tomorrow and live?

> Is that a trivial question? If so, why be confused about people naturally focussing on the "big picture"?
> After all, it might be sensible to look after the pennies on the assumption that the pounds will look after themselves, but what if the pounds don't have that sense of responsibility? What if, while you're taking care of the pennies, the pounds all disappear?

Or how about if you bother about small details of hunting, of the exact nature of the tracks you are following and learn what it tells you about the age, state of health etc. of the animal you are following. That could be very useful, but it will probably be useful in a few years.

Right now, it might mean you're so bothered about the detail that you don't react fast enough to kill the animal, maybe it even kills you instead. It make sense to focus on the "big picture" a lot of the time, and on the timescale of a hunter-gather (you mainly can't afford to worry too much about next week, let alone a few year's time), "a lot of the time" is pretty well always.

By the way, this point about timescales is also an indicator of why we often find it difficult to "defer gratification", to put off good stuff for tomorrow. I'll say more about this in chapter 13, but basically we tend to want to eat the food, spend the money, open the presents, right now, this minute. We don't want to have to wait. As hunter gatherers it makes sense, we might not be alive or able to enjoy it later, so let's have it now.

It's a big reason that, as in chapter 3, we don't get excited about long term goals, find pensions boring, don't plan for next year's holiday. That wasn't a strategy that paid dividends for most of our history, at least until we developed agriculture and could start to plan food supplies.

We have trouble thinking about doing unpleasant things now (like studying, saving money, not eating sugary foods, exercising regularly) to give us benefits later (like getting promotions, having a comfortable retirement and being fit and healthy).

We much prefer to do the fun things now (like eat the sugary, fatty foods, lounge on the sofa and watch a movie rather than study) that give us "instant gratification" but that lead to problems (like obesity, boredom and lack of job prospects) in the long term.

There are ways to use bigness bias and desire for instant gratification to your advantage which we'll look at in chapter 14.

For now, remember that like the other effects, bigness bias isn't a good thing, or a bad thing, it is just a natural and human thing.

It is a departure from logic, but to me (and in terms of your personal finance) that is irrelevant. What matters is what do you want to happen? Probably, with your money, what you want or need can sometimes require a focus on the pennies, sometimes on the pounds, but all the time it is best to be aware of the way you think so that you can make the best of being human, not try the impossible task of converting yourself into Mr Spock.

Mental accounts

In keeping track of things, as we saw earlier, we categorise. It tends to be the only way we can operate. Remembering every example is too slow and uses too much memory and "mental capacity" to be practical. When we traded, having categories, for example, our tribe, others, negotiators, family members, goods to trade, food items to trade etc. was useful.

I suspect that our mental accounts come out of this. If we trade with another tribe that we don't altogether trust, we might be prepared to trade food or other goods, but not weapons we've manufactured; those weapons might get used on us! I wonder whether arms dealers and Governments who sell weapons today would be quite so keen if they thought the weapons were going to be used on the people selling, and not on some third party that the sellers don't really care about, like other nationalities (or their own soldiers!)

Therefore having a "trade goods" account, which when empty means we have nothing to trade even though we've got a surplus of perfectly good weapons makes sense.

Similarly, we might trade *within* the tribe for some items but not others and we'd probably have special rules, (like "mate's rates") for family.

In fact we might have a completely different system with family, such as "communal sharing" (which is another of the basic systems of trade identified in human society) which would mean that with some people, like kin, we wouldn't "keep count" and expect to be paid back.

If we were trading on the principle of "equality matching" we'd have to keep track of who owed whom how much, and between family, tribe, outsiders, different types of goods, favours and so on, it would get quite complex. We'd need to have a good idea of what all the respective "account balances" were and without written records, where would those balances be kept except in our heads?

Over tens of thousands of years we developed a system that allowed people to get more regular food (by trading), to protect their genetic inheritance (by having special rules for their kin) and to reduce the danger of being killed (by categorising outsiders, cheats, trustworthy people etc.) and so increased our chances of our genes surviving by making rules for interaction that depended on "accounting".

Now, obviously, the mental accounts don't always help. However, they can do, in fact they can be one of the best ways to handle your money more practically. However, in order to be able to use them effectively, you do need to understand what you are doing and why. So again, understanding your own thinking is the key to controlling your own money.

Herds

The herd instinct makes sense if you consider it in a hunter-gatherer context. Why do animals herd, or fish shoal? It makes you safer. If you are part of a group, you don't stand out and are less vulnerable.

I've had people say to me that this is ridiculous, we know we're not going to be killed by a predator or something, so herding is just another example of people not applying logic properly. Apart from the fact that our brains haven't evolved much (if at all) from the hunter-gatherer model, so current conditions are irrelevant, think of the facts instead of the theory.

Tell me if this is logical, or illogical.

Tony Dye at Philips & Drew was a fund manager who predicted in 1996 the market was overvalued. He took £7 billion out of the market and was judged by peers, the financial press, advisors and clients as mad and called, "Dr Doom". Nobody had a good word for him, no advisors supported his value based and, in hindsight, sensible move.

In 1999, with the fund 66th of 67 funds in the sector he was under increasing pressure and he left early in 2000 (some accounts say he was fired, others that he jumped before he was pushed). Before anybody changed the strategy, the stock market turned and suddenly the fund topped the performance tables over all periods up to about seven years.

> Did the advisors who recommended that clients switch to other funds lose their jobs or clients?
>
> Did the investment managers of the short-term successful, eventually disastrous funds lose theirs?
>
> Did the journalists and economists who had mocked him admit they were wrong and hail him as a genius?
>
> Did his employers kill the fatted calf, offer him his old job back at twice the salary and cut the bonuses of all the other fund managers who were in the herd and who got it wrong?

Of course not, they were all wrong, but they were in a big herd so you couldn't pick out one of them as an idiot, or fire all of them (although I would have fired them all because they *were* all idiots!).

But Tony Dye was on his own, he was a good target, so although he was dead right, he was also professionally dead, while others lived on.

Well, is it "logical" or "illogical" to stay with the herd?

Fred Goodwin (who we'll come back to in later chapters) was the "poster boy" for successful banking, European Banker of the Year, knighted for services to banking. Obviously, every banker followed his lead (some from behind, some from in front, but we think they followed him because he became the best known).

Nobody was going to stand out against successful policies and the securitised mortgage market was clearly a licence to print money. There was a bubble, but even if people could see it was a bubble, if they pulled out their own funds or their own bank, how long would they have lasted? The shareholders or the other Board members would have got rid of them. Even "Fred the Shred" himself wouldn't have lasted any longer than Tony Dye did, probably not even as long. So they all got in, and they all crashed when the bubble burst.

Even for the top people, the smartest move (throughout human history, right up to today) might be to see what others don't, but to do what others do, in other words, to join the herd even if you know it is wrong, depending on what you want.

I'm not saying that you should join herds. Just that, while it might theoretically be "illogical" to join them, in real life it makes perfect sense, so you can understand why people do it. The best strategy is to decide when it works better to make your own decisions and when to go with the herd, which is something we'll look at future chapters.

But in the meantime, remember why you make the sort of "errors" we've talked about in this chapter and the last. Quite often the "errors" can work to your advantage, but almost invariably they can only work to your advantage if you know what you want (chapter 2) and why you want it (chapter 6) and if you don't know what you want, these "errors" can really hurt you, because you won't understand what is going on in your own head.

Summary:

- We're the product of natural selection.
- From the genes point of view, breeding success is all that matters.
- The genes of the most successful breeders were passed on most, so we're all the result of genes (and hence behaviour) that produced the most offspring.
- We are, basically, adapted to hunter gathering, we haven't changed much in the last few thousand years and we're not going to change, if we do at all, for several thousand more.
- SEU is great in the right circumstances. It wastes time in the wrong ones. You have to work out what to use in the situation.
- Women and men are equal, but different.
- Women have huge investment in a child, men have little.
- Human infants need time to develop, and lots of investment.
- Women generally are good at "people", men generally are good at "things" – but it's a preference and tendency, not a law!
- Being fair, building a reputation for honesty has advantages – it might not be logically the way to maximise money, but it is the way people evolved so that is the way most of us are.
- Gossip has a function, just not the one it evolved to serve!
- All the "errors" we make are understandable and human.
- That doesn't make them right or wrong – it means you have to work out how you are thinking and feeling, so you can decide whether "logic" or "gut instinct" is going to work better, or realise when you need to blend the two.

Hurricane!

Prediction, why it is so difficult and sometimes impossible, what we can and can't predict, and why it is all so important to us. The chapter also distinguishes between "risk" and uncertainty!

Here are a couple of quotes.

"Always expect the unexpected, grasshopper".

Advice from Master Po to the young Kwai Chang Kane in the 1970's TV series, Kung Fu.

"If it is unexpected, you can't expect it, so that is nonsense!"

Typically pragmatic comment from my friend Mike.

Bearing in mind our hunter gatherer ancestors were able to predict well enough to catch prey, survive to out-compete all the other predators and expand to inhabit pretty much the whole land surface of the earth, what is the problem?

> Why should it be so difficult to predict now, when we have so much technology to use – why can't the unexpected be expected?

Prediction, where will prey move, whether the weather will be suitable tomorrow, will he or she like me, was always important. It still is, but now it is more likely to be, will the stock rise or fall, will I lose my job, can I afford to buy her or him this gift.

Here are some reasons why it causes trouble.

The value of experience.

We evolved in a world where experience was valuable. Social structures didn't change much (certainly not quickly), technology didn't move on quickly, what worked one year worked well the next.

Experience not only worked to aid predictability, it remained valid for generations. What your grandparents knew about hunting or gathering, who to trust, what foods to avoid, how to deal with drought or flood was worth knowing. Your parents could add to it, you could add to it and pass it on to your children and grandchildren and they could all use it. The accumulated knowledge stayed useful and built up over hundreds, maybe thousands of years.

What about the last few hundred years? There was the British general who, in the Crimean war, kept referring to the enemy (the Russians) as the French (the British allies) since he remembered the Napoleonic Wars against France in his own lifetime when the Russians were on his side.

Or the First World War generals who had grandfathers who had fought with the King's German Legion against the French, but were now fighting alongside the French against the Germans.

Or the Second World War where the Russians, whom the British had fought in the Crimea less than 90 years before were now on their side, while the Japanese who were on their side 25 years before in the Great War, were now against them and battleships that dominated the seas 25 years before now got sunk by carrier borne aircraft.

Who do you trust, how do you keep up with the technology?
What useful information can you get from your parents or grandparents, or pass on to your children or grandchildren about the tribes or nations on "our side", the merits and demerits of GM foods or about everyday technology like smart phones?

When we look at history, we tend to compress the timescales. This is partly because only the unusual things get remembered and we don't know of many unusual things that happened long before we were alive. We can mock Victorians for their prudishness, be appalled at their morals regarding children and women and regard them as part of a dim and distant past. That was only about 150 years ago but we regard ourselves as separate from and superior to them. How separate are we? My maternal grandfather was born in the 1880's, so my great-great grandfather on that side must have been born about 150 years ago, in the middle of Victoria's reign.

Think back further, beyond a few lifetimes. When were the Trojan wars? How near was Alexander the Great (real) to the heroes such as Achilles and Odysseus (mythical) who fought in those wars?

The Trojan wars were going on about 1,190 BC and that was 800-900 years before Alexander. If you track back from today by the amount of time between, you get somewhere around the "first English Civil War", of Steven and Maude who feature in the Cadfael novels.

But we think 150 years is a long time, because we've seen enormous change and we've got personal memoirs from relations (or at least TV) of what the Victorian era, the Blitz or the trenches of the Western Front were like. How much change do we perceive in the six times longer period between Achilles and Alexander, in terms of technology, culture etc.?

The pace of technological, cultural and other change has speeded up in the last few thousand years. As soon as people started living in cities, things changed, but compared to what we experience now, it was still very slow change. In the last few hundred years the changes have been phenomenally fast.

Now think of hunter gatherers again. How fast does their world change? If we have trouble thinking of the Trojan wars other than as a myth because they are a few thousand years ago and we confuse that with the technology, culture and events of 1,000 years or so earlier or later, how do we envisage the events of 15,000 to 25,000 years ago? What changes do we see over that period?

We had a pretty stable situation for thousands of generations. There weren't electrical gadgets, styles of music, clothing etc. dividing the generations (and even age groups). There would be different tribal conventions, but everybody in every tribe would use similar technology, have cultures based on the same things, and do the same things to survive.

Some things were difficult to predict accurately; the weather, for example. But generally, by building up knowledge of how we could hunt, gather and survive through the seasons, when gales blew, when there was drought and so on, we could pass on information to the next generation and they could assimilate useful knowledge. Even if there were sudden storms, our basic way of doing things worked and if something really unexpected did happen, well, it happened, some people died, the survivors passed on the story and moved on.

Humans developed effective ways to predict happenings, based on experience and accumulated wisdom. That's how we survived. And, by natural selection, we adapted to those happenings and came to use those new abilities automatically (like making quick decisions).

Just because those abilities don't always work well in the modern, rapidly changing world, doesn't mean we can (or should) just ignore them. Sometimes, they don't work, but sometimes they do, very well.

A wonder of our modern age is the computer. We think they are brilliant, but of course, they are actually dim. Everything has to be either yes or no (a binary system). And they can't do a lot of the things people evolved to do. For example, computers are not really very good at pattern recognition, but we people are fantastic at it.

When you see pictures of all of the dials in a modern aircraft cockpit how do you think anybody can keep track of them all?

What if something goes wrong, how would you tell?

What if it is something that wasn't anticipated, like a system being shut-off that is supposed to be impossible to shut off?

You can have a computer to warn you.

But computers can't warn you unless they are programmed in advance of what to look for. If nobody anticipates the problem the computer can't be programmed for it, so it can't recognise it. Even if there is a programme to sound an alarm to warn us that something has gone wrong, if that particular problem wasn't anticipated *or* the system is switched off, it won't work.

In most planes, the dials are set up so that when everything is going well, all the needles point the same way. If something is wrong, one needle is out of line. You wouldn't think that would make much difference.

But the human visual system, designed by evolution to detect small differences that might indicate a predator or a potential mate, picks it up automatically. We'll see that break in the pattern immediately and you can't "turn off" that system, it works all the time.

When you go into a room with patterned wallpaper, if there is a dot that is a different colour, or a section that isn't quite straight, you'll see it. It seems to jump out at you (the phenomenon is called, "cognitive pop-out" which as a label is dead accurate, if a bit uninspired). You'd probably go mad trying to programme a computer to do that, but *you* can do it with ease just by glancing at the wall for a fraction of a second.

> *You can also do it by looking at a series of dials where one has a needle at a different angle, whether you can fly a plane or not.*
>
> *You have abilities that computers can't match and many of them were designed by evolution to warn you of danger, to make predictions about the world around you.*

The downside of having an "always on" system is that we can't turn it off when we might want to. It tries to keep us safe all the time. We are constantly looking for patterns in the world, because that process will "keep us safe". Even if there is no pattern there, we'll still be subconsciously trying to find a pattern, because that's what we evolved to do.

We constantly look for patterns, and we "need" those patterns, without them, we'll be worried we've missed something.

So we have abilities we can use to make predictions, and we do have a "need" to predict. Neither of those things have changed.

What has changed is the speed of technological and cultural change. We used to have time (or at least, we had a few hundred, if not thousand years) for our systems to adapt by natural selection.

Now, the changes that once took several thousand years as hunter gatherers (so at least some of us could start to adapt by evolution) and a few hundred years in earlier centuries (so we could at least pass on a few cultural tips from grandparents and people would spend their whole lives with one set of rules) now only take a few years. We can have three or four big changes in a single lifetime and little that is learned or passed on by parents or grandparents is of remotely so much use later in life as it was at the beginning.

> *We still need to make predictions in the modern world, but we aren't naturally very good at it in this environment, as we aren't so well "fitted" to our world now – the world has changed but we haven't.*

Risk, Uncertainty and the Unknown – part 1

When we look at prediction, we are predicting a future that is unknown. It used to be "is it a predator, prey, a mate, what is it and what should I do?" Now it may be "should I take this job or when will I be financially able to retire?" But the point is we don't know for sure what is going to happen.

There's a definition of risk from insurance:

"...uncertainties where the doubt as to outcome can be measured either mathematically or statistically. More specifically it may be defined as objective doubt as to the outcome of a future event, being measured by the degree of variation in actual from expected results."

CII Tuition Service, 1976

Notice that it specifies that you have to be able to measure it mathematically or statistically.

Also, the book mentions that risk, uncertainty etc. tend to be used interchangeably and the definitions given are "frequently used" but that there is no "general agreement on terminology".

> *The problem with all this is that it leads lots of people to assume that somehow putting a probability (a defined, mathematical and statistical concept) on something that is "unknown" makes it a definable "risk".*
>
> *In other words, probability turns the unknown into something measurable and therefore predictable.*
>
> *But it doesn't!*

To simplify things, I'll define three categories of unknown events.

1. The "calculable" – which we can call risks and for which we can calculate probabilities. These are what you'll recall from chapter 5 cause some "experts" to say people are stupid because they don't stop to work out the odds, and which the insurance text book defines as being risks with which insurance is concerned.

2. The "uncertain" – which are about uncertain futures for which we can't calculate probabilities, although we might say we can, in reality we can't put mathematical or statistical processes to work.
3. The "real life unknown" – which don't get described at all because we not only can't calculate them but we don't even think about them so we don't know we even have to do calculations!

Nassim Nicholas Taleb describes the third sort as "Black Swans". His description comes from a common flaw in most people's reasoning that is a bit like the "Socrates is a table" syllogism from chapter 5. This one says:

Swans must be one colour
I've only ever seen white swans
Therefore all swans are white.

There's no basis for the "swans must be one colour" assumption, but it is the sort of assumption made all the time (such as "property prices will never fall because people need a place to live.").

The problem is that people don't notice they are making that assumption. Consequently, "because I have never seen a black swan, there *are* no black swans" and therefore all swans are white "is a fact". In fact, swans can be all sorts of colours, irrespective of what colours you may have seen.

To put it another way: "absence of evidence is not evidence of absence". The lack of evidence (no reported sighting of a black swan) is not evidence of absence (that no black swans can or do exist).

Notice it's "can or do" exist. They might not exist at the moment, but that doesn't mean they cannot exist. We might assume that there "isn't" a market bubble because we've never seen one and there isn't one at the moment; so there "cannot" be one because we aren't aware of the assumptions we have made. We'll have a look at a good example of exactly that in chapter 9.

Three other things before going on.

1. We live in a world with global interconnections. We evolved in a world where a flash flood might kill one tribe but not affect any other. Now a terrorist attack that kills (proportional to world population) an insignificant proportion of people can trigger off global events that affect nearly everybody on the planet.

2. We feel we "ought" to be able to predict accurately, because that's what we evolved doing and learned to rely on. Any counsellor, therapist or counselling psychologist will tell you that "ought" is a dangerous word in this sort of context!

3. There is some science and maths in this chapter, because those are the tools we use when we want to go beyond our intuitive abilities to try to understand and predict the world. However, don't worry about it if you regard yourself as a bit of a dunce in maths and/or physics, I'll reduce it all to common sense terms.

The Unknown and science

Now for some of the reasons why life is unpredictable: you've heard of Sir Isaac Newton. He's the "apple fell on his head and he discovered gravity" chap.

His conception of the world was way ahead of his time, but his time was ages ago. He believed that if you could measure everything accurately enough you could predict it, that the universe was a bit like a massive snooker table, and that if you could measure the position and the forces acting on each ball, you could predict where everything would end up at some future time.

Of course, he was wrong. We know now that a lot of "Newtonian physics" is wrong. But it is a pretty good approximation most of the time, it tends to go demonstrably wrong only at the very big, fast end (relativity) and the tiny, sub-atomic end (quantum mechanics).

You might also have heard of Heisenberg's Uncertainty Principle.

This shows, for example, that you can't measure and know both the position and the momentum of a sub-atomic particle.

The point is, if you were going to predict what we might call the Newtonian snooker game, and wanted to measure the positions of all the balls, you would have a problem. If we *can't* know both the position and the momentum (basically the speed, weight and direction) of even one particle, how can we measure a whole table full of balls made up of millions of particles? We might measure where they all are now, but we don't know which direction they are going in, or how fast?

This gives us another problem, we can measure their position, "now". But what is "now"? In a hundredth of a second, they will have moved, so 'now' is within a hundredth of a second. But where are they after a thousandth of a second? You end up with an infinite regression, you keep defining "now" as a smaller and smaller instant of time.

We can hope that, since this is basically quantum mechanics, which deals with very small things like sub-atomic particles, we can ignore it. After all, quantum mechanics is complex and downright weird so maybe it won't apply!

So prediction isn't possible for very small stuff by a theory that is too complex for anybody to understand fully, but maybe it works OK for bigger stuff.

There's something in physics called the "three body problem". It is about working out the orbits of three bodies under gravity. Basically, it can only be done by making assumptions that are clearly unrealistic, such as "point masses", one body having no mass and so on. You need to get infinitely accurate measurements of past positions to be able to make future predictions and, as mentioned above, you can't get infinitely accurate measurements.

So the problem doesn't just apply to sub atomic particles but "real world" items too. It is even more complicated if it is an "N body problem" where N is greater than three. Since there are millions of objects in the universe, the more complicated N body problem is more accurately a description of the real world than a simpler three body problem, which nobody can do anyway.

> *It doesn't matter what rules of the different elements of physics you use. You can't get the sort of perfect predictability that Newton hoped for when you look at any system with more than three elements or that is made up of particles (which, of course, everything in the universe is).*
>
> *And physics is fundamental, if you can't do it in physics, it would be a bit odd if you could in any other science, like economics.*

As an illustration of what goes wrong as a consequence of failure to comprehend, a leading economist was challenged on a BBC programme in September 09. He was asked about the failure of his and his colleagues' predictions about economics and the unreality of their complex equations. He ridiculed the critics, saying that people just didn't understand equations and laughingly said that people had claimed "Newton had too many equations".

But ours is a world of quantum mechanical uncertainty, not Newtonian determinism, so his equations not only don't work, they cannot possibly work. The bigger problem is, he's an influential person, Governments listen to him, he obviously suffers from the human condition of overconfidence, and he's equally obviously totally ignorant of what equations can and cannot do!

The unknown and chaos
Let's have a look at the weather, because it has a lot in common with markets, including both being "chaotic systems".

Three things they have in common: one, they operate globally;

two, people always endeavour to predict what they will do next and three, they make a pretty comprehensive hash of their predictions!

> Imagine you're trying to predict the weather, and manage to work out exactly what factors affect it. How accurate do you have to be?

Imagine you discover that you need to measure, say air pressure, to 66 decimal places. What happens if, in the 67th decimal place there is a slightly different figure? It's obviously a very small amount, so you might think it doesn't matter.

> If you put the figures into a computer, ran the programme, then did it again with the same figures but got a totally different result, would you think that you'd got it wrong, or that you'd discovered a whole new area of science?

That's what a meteorologist named Edward Lorenz thought. He put in the "parameters" (measures of particular variables) into the MIT computer in the 1960s and thought he'd got it wrong or that the computer had a bug.

But in fact it was right. The computer rounded the figures to do the calculation. Calculators and computers might display 8 places of decimals (so you see 8 figures after the decimal point) but the calculations they do are to, say, 10 places. They make the calculation on 10, then display only the first 8.

The figures Lorenz was using seemed to be identical and to an extent they were. But somewhere, in what seems an insignificant position, a digit that the computer used but didn't display was different, and it gave a significantly different end result.

That is the "butterfly effect" of chaos. It occurs because the weather, like a market, is a large, self-organising, chaotic system.

Chaos doesn't mean (in this sense) that events are random; on the contrary, they follow quite simple rules.

The problem is they are extremely sensitive to initial conditions. You can start with weather (or market) conditions that look exactly like previous conditions and measure hundreds of factors to thousands of decimal places of accuracy and they still seem identical.

But one apparently insignificant difference (a butterfly flapping its wings, for example) in an apparently insignificant factor can make a huge difference. Perhaps there is no hurricane, or Sevenoaks becomes one Oak, there is a rising market, or perhaps a crash.

Technically, weather and markets are "non-linear" systems. With linear systems the end result is more or less equal to the sum of the parts. With non-linear systems the result may be much more or much less. Sometimes small things we think don't matter can trigger huge results and at other times events that we think will drastically change things have no effect.

With the weather, actually measuring all the factors accurately is impossible, and making predictions from it is also impossible because you don't know from where you are starting and the result is so sensitive to the starting point.

And another problem, how do you know what you want to measure in the first place?

What affects the weather? Say there are 50 factors (atmospheric pressure, wind velocity, humidity, etc.). How sure are you that those 50 are the only ones that matter? Let's say you manage to make yourself believe that you've got the only 50 that have any effect. To strengthen that belief, you need to work out how accurate you are. As it said in the definition of risk, you have to work out the *"..degree of variation in actual from expected results."*

To do that, you have to analyse factors, compare them to the weather that occurred and try to work out what the features are and why you've succeeded (or failed) in previous weather predictions, so that you can confirm you've got them all. Then you can use your information as a predictor in the future.

Of course, however hard we try and however carefully we compare predictions with results, we don't always get the weather right. Even when we do get it right and we predict the hurricane, because of sensitivity to initial conditions (chaos) and the complexity and interconnectedness of the system, we predict it will stay in the Gulf of Mexico and it doesn't, it destroys New Orleans. The reality is we can't predict weather accurately more than about 24 hours ahead (even then, there's no certainty in real life as distinct from theory).

The weather hasn't changed much since we were hunter gatherers, it still does the same sort of things, even with global warming, pollution etc. We can't even get that 100% right when it is largely the same.

You can't say the same for business, and although we have more sophisticated methods to analyse than the hunter gatherers had, our world changes faster.

Uncertainty and feedback

There is a saying, "practice makes perfect", which is nonsense!

> *Practice doesn't make **perfect**, it makes **permanent**.*
>
> *If you start off really bad at something and practice enough, you'll become expert at being really bad, but you won't improve.*
>
> *To become perfect (or to improve at all), you need practice with feedback that allows you to correct what you are doing.*

Feedback is hard to come by in business. Imagine a tennis game. You serve, the ball either goes in or out, and you get feedback straight away so you can try to do better, or keep things the same if it worked

It's one reason games, with their rules, results, and boundaries are easier to learn than life. You know exactly what is possible within the rules and you get clear feedback on how you're doing.

Imagine you're a company Chief Executive. Your company grew 10% in the last year, is that good?

It depends what others did, what the market did, at what stage your business cycle was. Perhaps it was the result of luck in that foreign competition dropped off, or a tax break you got, or maybe you made a bad decisions last year but you got lucky since.

Remember the fundamental attribution error. Maybe you were skilful but perhaps you were just lucky. Maybe it was just a fluke, or something else caused the effect you saw. How will you know?

The Governors of the Bank of England weren't agreed on whether "quantitative easing" was working and they all had access to the same facts. They couldn't agree what the results they saw actually meant, or whether the results were anything much to do with the action they'd taken.

And think of the time delays with a company (or economy).

You have different policies, involving staff, sales, operations etc. that are all working on different timescales, and the effects will show up in different areas, and will emerge to affect your market results at different times.

Some of them won't have clear effects at all, for example if you hire better staff, how will that effect your results and when and how does the marketing budget actually "impact on the bottom line"?

> How do you pick out "causality"? Can you know exactly what things cause what?

And apart from the time lag between cause and effect and the complications of each single effect, in reality you have the bigger problem of untangling individual cause-effects from one another; even assuming you had some idea of what cause (or more likely, causes) had the effects at all, at any time!

We can't get the feedback to make our "practice" help produce behaviour that is anything like perfect, it just becomes permanent.

Nobody can unpick all the millions of details that make up any event in business and say for certain "this event X caused the result Y". It is just too complicated and too uncertain.

Who actually knows what makes success or failure? Maybe it was a failure to see a major shift in the market, maybe it was somebody being ill on the wrong day or maybe it was a "butterfly effect" from something that happened as a result of foreign export policy, who knows?

> If your company does well or badly (relative to the previous year) how sure are you that this was all caused by the decisions you made, what percentage is due to you, what to luck, what to the market conditions, what to changes in faraway places etc.?
>
> How sure are you about your judgment of all those factors and what they individually contributed?
>
> Remember overconfidence, the possibility that you "know" there is a city nearer to London than "Westminster" and the Fundamental Attribution Error?

And you run the company!

How clearly do you think any outside "expert" analysis is going to be over what really causes the changes in price of a share? How sure would you be that they can accurately determine exactly how the rest of the market responded (if it did anything at all), when you don't know yourself exactly what it did to your own company and you run it and are in the boardroom every day?

> So how can anybody be absolutely sure they've identified all the factors they need to take into account so that they can "practice" in a way that makes them "perfect"?

Uncertainty and hindsight

There's a saying that everybody has perfect vision in hindsight. That's also nonsense!

If it was true, we'd know, in hindsight, exactly how and why everything happened. In the Black Swan, Taleb gives an idea of this that he attributes to Aaron Brown and Paul Wilmott.

Operation 1 (the melting ice cube) Imagine an ice cube and consider how it may melt over the next two hours while you play a few rounds of poker with your friends. Try to envision the shape of the resulting puddle.

Operation 2 (where did the water come from) Consider a puddle of water on the floor. Now try to reconstruct in your mind's eye the shape of the ice cube it may once have been. Note that the puddle may not have necessarily originated from an ice cube.

> Going from ice cube to water is easy, it's a problem in thermodynamics and you can make accurate predictions and test them.

> Going the other way is also easy, you can predict any shape of ice cube and it is hard for anybody to prove you wrong, there are millions of ice cubes that could have made the pool of water.
>
> But how do you test it, how do you know which one actually did?
>
> The world, his wife and her brother can all give an explanation and say, "this is what happened and if the ice cube had been this shape it would have happened in this way" – but how do they know that's exactly why and how it happened?

When a company does well or an economy collapses you can produce millions of explanations, thousands of which *could* fit the result, the ice cube becoming that particular pool of water.

> But how do you know what combination of butterfly wings, economic policies, business decisions and so on actually leads back from the particular pool to the particular ice cube you started with?

Don't forget, from the lesson of the "split brain" patients in chapter 6, we can all justify our beliefs about the shape of the ice cube with reasons that have nothing to do with anything except our imagination.

Whatever we invent, we can carry on inventing ways for it to be right when it is questioned, and so can everybody else with their own explanation. There are millions of explanations, some are impossible but only one is the total and true story of how the pool was formed and that story could involve butterflies, heaters, hurricanes, panic in the streets and budget cuts (or all or none of them). Chaos theory says you can't predict, and you can't truly explain either.

So not only is accurately measuring all the factors in a complex system impossible and producing predictions from them impossible, but we can't even be sure we're measuring the right things in the first place or whether the things we're measuring had the effects we thought of or even had any effect at all, even afterwards!

Risk, Uncertainty and the Unknown – part 2

Risk, we said earlier, is calculable.

> *This isn't what we usually think of as risk.*
>
> *We tend to think of "risky" as being too dangerous whereas strictly, something that is "risky" is simply an event that can come out in different ways, so the outcome isn't certain (but we can measure its chance of occurring mathematically).*

Since just about anything can come out in different ways (you might die in a tea cosy related accident, your shares may go down as well as up), the whole of life is actually "risky". But if you stay in bed to "avoid" the risk, you might still be hit by space debris, choke on your water or win the pools, it is all uncertain and therefore risky!

By the way, you know what risk means in business? If the outcome is good, it was a "calculated risk". If bad it was "too risky" or "lunatic"! Nobody in history, from their personal viewpoint, has ever taken a risk that wasn't carefully calculated; only other people take stupid risks!

Most organisations that claim, "we encourage calculated risk", mean that if something pays off it will be rewarded even if it was a million to one gamble, because nobody can work out accurately what the odds were. The only way forward they can think about it is to ignore the actual degree of risk and look only at the result. That's why bankers pay themselves billions in bonus.

If there's a bad result, even if the odds were in favour beforehand, it will be "we encourage calculated risk, but this was stupid", because again, the risk is hard to assess so we just look at the result. So banks sometimes stop the bonus for a year or so because they were – "too risky"!

And if you're accused of taking unnecessary risks and you did actually calculate it carefully; the next section might help you explain what you did, just don't expect it to get you off the hook!

This indicates that regulation of finance in the UK has problems. Everybody complains that bankers took "too many risks", but certainty is impossible so they are always going to be going into uncertainty, which is only "risk" if you can calculate it mathematically. And as we'll see, you can't, so it isn't a risk anyway.

But if it was "too risky" afterwards, it must have been "too risky" before, but nobody said anything before because they judge by results, not by the risk, which they can't calculate before.

And all are herding, overconfident, subject to the Fundamental Attribution Error etc. and need to work on their blindness to the style of their own thinking, not their imperfect understanding of the nature of risk or their complete ignorance of mathematical laws!

Remember our three types of uncertainty:

- Calculable (risk) which we can calculate mathematically.
- Uncertain, which we can't, not mathematically.
- Real life unknowns, the "Black Swans" which we don't even think about.

Risk and maths.

The "risk" has two parts, which are a bit like SEU from earlier:

1, the pay-off (what the potential outcomes are) and
2, the chance of different outcomes happening.

These lead to another point:

3.   The chance of an outcome has to be expressed in some mathematical way.

To talk about anything as "risk" only in terms of the chance, without referring to the pay-off is meaningless, but that is actually what happens most of the time Another thing that happens is that people refer to the "risk" of something happening without bothering (or understanding that they need) to specify the terms in which they describe chance.

Gambling games, dice, roulette, cards etc. are used a lot to describe "risk", so let's have a look at those. I mentioned earlier that games are easier than life, because they are bounded and have rules and limits that you can rely on, which life doesn't.

Think about roulette.

> *Your pay-off if you win a bet on a single number is 35 times the bet.*
>
> *The rules mean that the ball has to land in a slot; it can't fly off into the air, change into a large gherkin or request that it not be bounced around anymore as it has a headache.*
>
> *You know there are only a certain number of things that can happen, you can work out exactly how many, what the likelihood of each is (with a fair wheel, the odds are the same for each outcome) and therefore can work out exactly what the odds of each outcome are.*
>
> *You can compare that to your "pay-off" if you win, because you know that in advance as well.*

The odds of 35 to 1 make sense, because on a standard European wheel (the US has a slightly different wheel) the numbers 1 to 36 all appear, each is equally likely, so it looks like your odds are 35 to 1. In theory, this allows you to specify both the pay-off and the chance, and it allows the chance to be expressed in a mathematically exact way.

The trouble in reality is that it only looks like your odds are 35 to 1, because the standard wheel has the number 0 as well, so there are 37 slots, the numbers 0-36 inclusive. That slot is the "house advantage". It means that you aren't going to win because your pay off is 35 to 1, but the odds of you winning are actually 36 to 1 against.

In dice, cards, anything, you get similar figures. They can be fun to work out (for geeks), but are almost totally useless in real life.

They are handy as practice and for gambling because you can work out the pay-off and the odds, and you get the odds in a very concrete, clear way. So if you can do the maths you can make quite accurate predictions.

Of course, the accurate prediction is that you will lose money by gambling, but that will happen whether you can do the maths or not!

However, lots of people talk (and write books) about the use of mathematics in gambling and suggest that because it is possible to work out the "risk" in a game of chance, the same thing applies to life.

In other words, they think people are stupid because they don't use the maths of the gambling den in their daily lives.

Maybe, from what we've said so far, you can see some flaws in this.

You can work out the odds in gambling because, if you do it right, you know what all the outcomes are.

The dice won't land on their edge, stay in the air or turn into rhubarb and you won't throw them and have them disappear with a clap of thunder leaving a smoking crater where the table was.

In gambling games you know how many outcomes there are, you know how likely they are, you know how much you win if you win.

Now think of horse racing

What are the "odds" in a horse race? That's a tricky one. What we call the odds is actually the payoff. If the horse is at 3 to 1, then if it wins you get three times the stake, plus your original stake (less tax, unless you paid it on the bet – I think – hey, let's ignore the tax!)

But what are the actual probabilities of the horse winning, what is the "uncertainty"? We don't know. We know we won't get a gazelle or camels appearing, or horses disappearing, but is each horse equally likely to win? I doubt it. So how do we work out the probabilities?

We can reason, "the going is soft, that favours horse A, but horse B won last time out and he's got the best jockey, except he's drawn on the outside and he likes to run by the rail and.....". We have a problem. We need to work out what the important factors are, and how important they are relative to one another. But for a "risk" we need some way to work this out mathematically.

Obviously, we can estimate, use experience, use our intuition and knowledge etc., but we don't *know* and we can't use maths because we don't have exact numbers to base calculations on.

If we want to work out the probabilities, we have to get some values, and those values will be subjective and based on "rules of thumb" and "gut feelings". That isn't maths, so we aren't calculating a "risk", it is an unknown that we're making guesses about.

We've also got the problem that "experts" say we must use logic and calculate carefully, but how are we going to work out what to put into our probability equation unless we use guesswork, intuition, experience etc. which are not mathematical and not logical?

This is an area where the problem I mentioned earlier exists:

> *The problem with all this is that it leads lots of people to assume that somehow putting a probability (a defined, mathematical and statistical concept) on something that is unknown makes it a definable "risk".*
>
> *In other words, probability turns the unknown into something measurable and therefore predictable.*
>
> *But it doesn't!*

Makes its presence known!

> *We're dealing with uncertainty here, which was the second of our types of unknown.*
>
> *Risk — can be expressed accurately in mathematical terms. Uncertainty can't.*
>
> *The problem is the common confusion of the two and the mindset that says gambling problems are the same as life.*
>
> *But they aren't even the same as horse racing!*

We have horses not zebras or okapi. But now we don't have the same definition of our odds. With roulette we expressed the odds as a number of outcomes that win relative to the total number of outcomes (like one way to win compared to 36 or 37 possible slots).

Now we are saying the odds are some subjective value based on the firmness of the going, whether the horse won last time out, the record of the jockey etc. We're still calling it the odds of winning, and probability theory still calls it a probability, but it isn't the same thing.

But of course real life is harder still. At least in a horse race we know what the payoff is. We might not know how likely we are to win, but we know how much we'll win if we do win.

How about in life, have you got any idea how much you'll "win"? How about in the stock market? Put in £1,000, what are your odds of winning? How much will you win if you "win"? What are your odds of losing? What will you lose if you don't win?

And that's another problem. In roulette, dice etc. (and even in horse racing to some extent) you have a complete set of events. You will win or, if you don't win, you will lose. It doesn't matter what bets you make, you will win or lose in each play and you can bank on there being no "real life unknowns" that you haven't thought about.

Those real life unknowns are, as in my quote by Mike at the beginning of the chapter, unexpected. Because they are unexpected, you cannot allow for them or predict their effects.

The horse racing equivalent might be horses becoming camels mid-race or in a game of chess the pawns declaring a republic and executing their own king. They are things that it is impossible to put into the equation because we don't even think of them!

How many factors affect your real life that you not only can't calculate accurately (they are uncertain) but are so far out of left field that you never even imagine them?

How did you meet your partner, find your job, pick a career? Are these all the result of careful consideration, or are most of them chance happenings that depend on thousands of different events; the party that you went to because your other plans for that evening fell through, the chance meeting because your train was cancelled, the conversation with the person in the check-out queue?

There are hundreds of these every day, the accident you avoid because you decide to walk another way for a change, the job opportunity you miss because the new way you drove took you into a traffic jam, the fascinating potential partner whose number you lost because you left the phone into which you'd programmed their number in your pocket when you washed those trousers!

Chance has a huge impact and apparently trivial incidents can change your whole life, and things that you expect to be life-changing actually mean nothing to you in reality. You just can't imagine what things are going to matter in the future.

Take the stock market. You think your share had a 70% chance of going up and a 30% chance of going down. What if the share doesn't move, what odds did you give that? What if the company represented by the share goes into liquidation so your share ceases to have any value, was that in your 30% loss calculation? What about if the company aims to buy another company, gives a rights issue and you end up with twice as many shares in one organisation of two linked but different trading entities that are overall worth less but have greater potential?

And that is without deliberate human intervention. Pensions were seen to be a good investment because of the tax reliefs and there was a "gentleman's agreement" that tax was not made retrospective. Then Gordon Brown became Chancellor and wasn't a gentleman, so the tax regime changed retrospectively to tax pension funds to raise money for other policies. It raised a lot of money, because nobody saw it coming. Gordon became a "real life unknown", a "Black Swan" all by himself!

Single events

Many real life events (probably most) are "single events".

This applies to any situation that is unique. In real life, chaos theory etc. dictates that the exact situation has not occurred before, so many situations are unique.

Probability (and ideas about building up experience that will be useful for prediction) works on the basis that you either know all of the possible outcomes and their probabilities or you at least have lots of events so you can get an "on average" idea and make useful mathematical calculations of "risk" .

That is the fundamental idea behind insurance, which we'll talk about in chapter 10. Without that, any "probabilities" are meaningless, at best they are a "subjective assessment of likelihood".

You might have heard of Shrödinger's cat. It is a hypothetical cat in a box. Until the box is opened, you don't know whether the cat is alive or dead. So the cat is said to be "50% alive"!

If that strikes you as daft, well done. Shrödinger was a physicist who was being ironic. He was pointing out that quantum theory, which described things in terms of probabilities such as this didn't have a sensible meaning in real life.

The cat is either alive or it is dead, it can't be 50% alive. Unfortunately, many people don't see the irony, they take it seriously (I had a fine argument in a pub after one talk I gave, when several people were trying to convince me that the cat was 50% alive)!

There isn't a body of data for single events in life with which you can use statistics the way they are supposed to be used, in the way that there are with insurance. So any estimate like, "there is X probability of..." is not a probability in the true sense, based on data or statistical calculations. It is somebody's subjective estimate of what they think is likely. They might make it sound as if it is based on solid science by calling it a "probability", but it isn't.

I mentioned that, as in insurance, you don't always have to know all the outcomes. What you can sometimes do is build up enough good data to give you a picture of what happens.

For example, every person is unique, so you can't do calculations on them like you can in gambling. To take the number of outcomes where they die because they smoke, and divide that by the total number of ways they might die on each day of the rest of their life is not only daft, it's impossible. But you can look at the data for people who smoke who are the same age, gender, general fitness level, who have a similar lifestyle etc. and work out the odds. That works well in the right situations.

The main model used for this sort of build up of data to use for probability is the "normal" distribution. That's the one that we usually see with statistics.

It's handy because lots of things are distributed like this. If you get an unrelated group of people together, measure their heights, and plot them on a graph you'll find that they will average out like this, and the more people you have, the more nearly you get the curve.

You'll get a peak at the average height, and the farther you go from that average the less people you will find at the height you are measuring. It is also symmetrical, the "taller than average" end is a mirror image of the "smaller than average end".

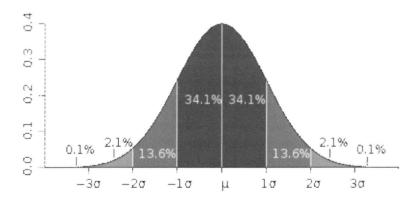

The percentages in the curve are the proportion of people (or whatever you're measuring) in that section. The symbol μ in the middle is the Greek letter mu. Mu is the mean, basically the average. The symbol θ is sigma, it stands for the standard deviation, which is a measure of variability, how much heights or totals differ from the mean.

If you know the mean and the standard deviation and see what they measure follows a normal distribution, you can tell what proportion of things fall within different parts of the curve.

It can be helpful, but we need the data and need it to stay pretty much the same. It works for gambling, but not for horse racing where the "chance" varies so much that you can't build the distribution easily.

How do we build up data on markets, the weather, life etc.? We can't even be sure what has caused a stock market crash, a hurricane, a success or failure in life.

How do we accumulate enough applicable and useful data to make our table of probabilities, our picture of the distribution etc?

Well, actually, we can't.

Another big problem is that we don't only need data (which we don't have because they are single events, we can't measure them accurately even if we could collect them and can't be sure either what figures we need to collect) we also need that data to form a "normal distribution".

The normal distribution has several assumptions that have to be met before it can validly be used; including one that the data points are independent.

There are standard measures of "risk" used in markets. They have the problem that they don't measure "risk" because markets are uncertain, not mathematically defined, and include "real life unknowns". The maths doesn't work for those. They also measure "volatility" (basically the standard deviation) as a "proxy" for risk, because we can't calculate the real risk. And apart from measuring the wrong proxy with the wrong maths in the wrong way, they are all based very firmly on a normal distribution. And the normal distribution, as above, depends on assumptions, including that of independence of observations.

Coin tosses, roulette wheels etc., are independent observations (or can be assumed to be independent). One spin of a wheel or toss of a die doesn't affect the next one. Heights are usually also independent. Measure lots of people and their heights will not be inter-dependent, there's no reason person A's height will be dependent on person B's height. But what if the people are related?

Imagine we get a big sample of people from one extended family and measure the height of all. Because the people in one family will have some shared genes and some of those genes affect height, our sample will be distorted (technically, it will be a "skewed" distribution and the data points will be "correlated").

> *The normal distribution is lovely when it is appropriate; we know lots about it and can use it really accurately. But it doesn't apply to markets.*
>
> *If it did, and markets followed a normal distribution then, as with people over nine feet tall, we'd have huge stock market swings once every 5-10,000 years. We've had seven in the last century!*

Mark Buchanan described this in an article, Power Laws & the New Science of Complexity Management. Note that he uses the other term for the normal distribution, the "bell curve", named after its shape:

"When interdependence is important, the power-law pattern frequently takes the place of the bell curve. At first glance, this may not seem very important, as the two curves do not appear to be that different. But on

closer scrutiny, there is actually an enormous difference. The "tails" of a power-law curve — the regions to either side that correspond to large fluctuations — fall off very slowly in comparison with those of the bell curve. (See Exhibit 1.) These so-called fat tails imply that large events take place far more often than one would expect on the basis of "normal" statistics. In the case of market fluctuations, for example, the bell curve predicts a one-day drop of 10 percent in the valuation of a stock just about once every 500 years. The empirical power law gives a very different and more reliable estimate: about once every five years.

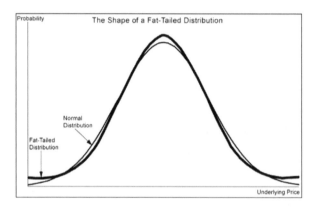

Mark Buchanan *Laws & the New Science of Complexity Management*

Power laws are a better description of markets than the normal distribution, and we'll look at them a bit more in chapter 9.

In the meantime, just to give an idea of what sort of things follow power laws, relative city populations (the biggest city, the second biggest etc. in a country), individual wealth in society, the ratios of tree trunks to main branches, branches, twigs etc and the size and frequency of volcanic eruptions show power law relationships, not "normal" ones.

> *In power law distributions, big events happen less frequently than small events,*
>
> *Single big events that happen have bigger effects than lots of small events all added together.*

Volcanoes erupt all the time, but if the super volcano under Yellowstone Park goes off, it is likely to wipe out a fair amount of life on the planet. It could go off tomorrow. Or next year, or in 10,000 years. We don't know, and we can't predict from normal statistics what the probability is because it doesn't follow those, it follows a power law. Unfortunately, simply substituting power laws for normal distributions doesn't work either, not for volcanoes or markets!

> *Like volcanic eruptions, the total movements in share prices over a year are mostly accounted for in a few days of "big events".*
>
> *That's a good reason for not trying to "time" the market, a subject we'll come back to in chapter 9.*
>
> *The problem is, the more common, small events suggest markets follow a normal distribution, so bankers etc. assume they can use ordinary statistics to predict the markets and excessively "risky" policy isn't predicted to cause a problem. Until it does!*

Just to make it even more complicated, those who want to predict the future of an economy or a market assume "diminishing returns".

It's the principle that once you've sold your product to everybody who wants it, there is nobody left to buy it. That means that, as sales grow higher, they are naturally limited and you can't get a "bubble". The trouble is, it doesn't work like that all the time in real life. Sometimes you get "positive feedback", everybody wants the product just *because* everybody else has got it. Think of particular trainers, I-phones, stock market bubbles etc.

With those, we can only "predict in arrears", so after the event everybody says it is obvious that the housing market would collapse, the Apple operating system would lose out to Windows but Apple would rise again on the I-phone or that Obama would win the US election.

Beforehand nobody knows and afterwards everybody can explain the puddle but nobody can reconstruct the ice cube.

So the maths we use for gambling, with normal distributions, simple, linear dynamics, non-chaotic systems etc. cannot work in a real, chaotic, complex, non-linear, power law distributed, non-equilibrium system like life.

Particularly when we can't measure the things we need to measure accurately enough, don't know what they are anyway and have no way of knowing which ones are important because we lack feedback.

But we have a desperate need to predict and because this is a "scientific" age, we are inclined to throw maths at problems to try to sort it out. As with the "Newtonian physics" mentioned earlier, the maths we throw is often the wrong sort of maths.

But it does give us a feeling that we are in control. And people don't like to feel they are not in control (remember, we tend to make up justifications for what we do so we can feel in control).

She wants to know our signs.

A bit more risk and maths

One mathematical technique used for analysis is regression analysis. This (and allied techniques such as SEM, Structured Equation Modelling) are really powerful techniques, when used with systems that aren't like markets, ones that are linear, have stable equilibriums etc.

What regression does is to take all of the factors (that we know about, that is) from the past and build an equation that takes into account everything that has happened (that we know about and can measure). It uses what we think has affected the outcome and all the results observed and (in theory) tells us how the factors all interact in a mathematical formula (the regression equation).

The problem is that in real life, we don't know what factors are really important or even what factors, (butterfly wings, chance meetings, etc.) have had any impact at all.

Was the fact that we raised prices vital or did it make no difference? Did the rebellion in an obscure South American country cause a plane delay that stopped somebody travelling who would have met a politician, who would not then have been the casting vote on a change of policy which changed the export tariff which......? Who knows? In terms derived from the study of acoustics, some of this is known as "noise". It is stuff that happens, but that isn't relevant to the outcome.

So we don't know which things are relevant, and which are noise and even after the event, we can assume we have understood how the ice cube melted and therefore what shape it was, but we might actually have the totally wrong shape (or indeed a spilt glass of wine or a naughty puppy that caused the puddle!).

There's a saying in marketing:

"Half every marketing budget is wasted, but we don't know which half".

The same is true of regression, the equation includes everything we can think of (while missing things that are important but that we didn't think of), so it includes lots of "noise" along with all the important factors and nobody knows which are which. They include loads of rubbish with the occasional scrap of insight but they can't tell us which is noise and which is relevant.

But the regression model "explains" the past results in terms of the data and, by comparison, makes our intuitive thoughts look very shaky in hindsight.

That is one factor that makes those who use regression (and similar techniques) on markets and other complex systems (things like the weather, real life etc.) think that they can predict. They can look back and think they can explain what happened last time.

> *But as we know, we can't be sure of any of it. The melting ice-cube, the cause/effect links, the lack of accurate feedback, all mean we don't really know what happened or why, we just think we do and have some wonderful looking equations to "prove" it!*

This causes two problems.

The first is that when we use the equations we've derived to try to project to the future, the model includes so much noise that it is pretty useless as a prediction, our simple, intuitive models usually work better! I've read whole books about how wonderful complicated calculations are for making better decisions in life, but in fact while they work very well in some situations (medical diagnosis, for example), for lots of predictions of uncertainty, they are a disaster. I'd suggest reading "Gut Feelings" by Gigerenzer if you're interested in this subject.

The second problem is that maths is so clever, and so complicated, that it convinces people it is right when it is dangerously wrong! On this point, let me ask you two questions.

Have you ever despaired when "customer services" said, "but that's what the computer says", when you queried your £14 million bill?

They think that because it has come from the computer, it must be right and the maths behind it infallible, so if it conflicts with reality, it is reality that must be wrong.

Do you think the customer services assistant is somehow a different type of human being to the people who sell the concepts and "front" the organisation (like the bank bosses, the investment "experts" and Government advisors)?

Not only is there a computer, which people think can't be wrong, but the maths involved is really complicated.

Specialists are brought in to do the maths and we'll look at that more later, with the (literal) "rocket scientists" used by market traders. But the issue is that while the people who do the actual maths and programming might understand the limitations of what they are doing, the uncertainties and assumptions, and might even be aware of the potential for "real life unknowns" outside their model because they know what formulae can and cannot do, they don't talk about it.

They are in the "back room" and the front men do the talking (mind you, when the real experts emerge, watch out; we'll talk about the Nobel Prize-winner that nearly caused the crash ten years early in chapter 9).

Even if the "front men" are told by the "back room staff" that the model is limited, they can't understand why and their human desire to be able to predict means that they neither can nor want to see anything other than the perfection of their system. When you add this to the fact that everybody else in their world is doing the same thing (herding) and the tribal instinct that says anybody saying anything different is wrong, they are going to ignore any warnings.

They carry on with securitised, sub-prime mortgages because they think the "model" says it cannot possibly result in a property crash, even when warned that this is exactly what will happen at some point.

And afterwards, the model will explain exactly why the crash happened precisely when it did and what could have been done to avert it, even though, as with the melting ice cube, the fact is that the crash could have happened at any time over about the last 20 years or we might still be waiting for it to happen. The model includes too much noise and the situation has too many real life unknowns to be sure what shape the ice cube was, given the pool of water. And even if a rocket scientist could explain it and knows that it contains uncertainty, the front man will neither understand the explanation, nor admit the possibility of error. After all, the computer said it, so it must be right!

Emergence

Humans think "top down", so we assume the patterns we see must have a designer. We are geared by evolution to seek out patterns (like "pop out" and the pattern recognition of "availability").

We call an ant egg-layer a "queen" because we think there must be a central organisation, the "queen" must organise, must be a sort of dictator. But ants don't work like that, they work bottom up. That means that things like social insect colonies (and, apparently, stock prices), produce apparently organised behaviour that is "emergent".

This property is used a lot in some places. The programmes that allow you to be sent the annoying, "if you liked that product, you'll like this" e-mails are based on emergent properties and commonalities.

They come up in less practical, but more fun areas such as the "artificial intelligence" systems that are used for the "opponents" in computer combat games

These are all principally based on the sort of "individual agent" programme that is typical of individual ants in a colony.

Of course, constructing models like this does mean we need to simplify things and use only the stuff that is obviously relevant, which is relatively easy in a game with rules, but not so easy in a simulation of the economy that is real life and doesn't have rules.

Unfortunately, despite all the knowledge that is accumulating about how bottom up processes work and how they can operate in a totally different way to produce what looks like an "organised" pattern, there are lots of people who cannot resist the tendency to view everything from the top down. So some people (often called "chartists") build very fancy (and expensive) pictures of markets that they say can predict those markets. But markets aren't "organised" in that sense, so charting prior movements in stock to predict future ones is tackling a bottom up phenomenon by top down thinking.

The specialists who are brought in to do it (needless to say, the managers who want it done can't understand the maths) are the literal "rocket scientists" I mentioned earlier. They are people with very advanced knowledge of physics and mathematics who construct models based on patterns in the data from a top down perspective. This approach is very clever, complex and based on top down thinking being applied to bottom up processes, so it is probably never going to work any better than it has up to now, which is not at all!

The issues I've outlined in this chapter make me wonder how people can say, with a straight face and without their nose growing longer like Pinocchio when he lied:

"the economy is expected to do X in the next 6 months" or "this share is Y percent likely to rise"

any more than we can say confidently, "the weather will rain at the end of next week, but by the middle of next month it is going to be fine with temperatures of Z".

And of course, the sorts of models that are used for finance require calculation of utility for any event and that has to be based on some sort of subjective evaluation.

So, as we saw in chapter 2, a general value is meaningless, the value for you is an individual one; you have to work your values out for yourself.

Maybe, one day, we'll find a system to make more accurate short term market predictions in the same way as we have fairly accurate short term weather forecasts. But they will be short term.

Even theoretically, let alone practically, getting accurate longer term predictions seems totally impossible. Having explained about "real life unknowns", I won't say it *is* impossible. The fact that nobody can imagine what it could be and although it would involve re-writing the laws of physics, it could happen. It just isn't likely!

Most of the time we don't have a clue what the odds or the pay off are and the whole thing is subject to unexpected events that, by definition, we cannot possibly anticipate.

Whatever anybody says about "probability" or "controlling market risk", they are pretending mathematical accuracy for guesswork based on inadequate data that they aren't sure are the right data, about which they've made inappropriate assumptions about proxies for "risk" that isn't a risk but an uncertainty, to which they've incorrectly applied maths that shouldn't be used on the data they've got anyway!

And after the summary, having talked about maths we can't do, we'll look at maths that we can do, how we can do it and how we might fail to do it!

Summary:

- Prediction is still important.
- Experience is of much less use than it was in predicting.
- The three types of unknown - calculable (risk), uncertain and real life, are not at all the same thing!
- Globalisation now makes the impact of the unexpected greater.
- We still want to believe we can predict, we need to do it and desperately want to, but we can't.
- Many people are so scared of the maths involved, that they won't question the bizarre assertions of those who claim, entirely falsely, they can defy the laws of science and predict accurately.
- Quantum mechanics makes accurate prediction impossible. At best it is "probabilistic", which works for quantum theory in hypothetical situations, but is dangerous if you believe it is accurate in life and markets.
- Chaos makes it impossible to predict chaotic systems accurately.
- Feedback is vital – practice doesn't make perfect without it.
- Accurate feedback doesn't happen in business or markets.
- We don't have perfect vision in hindsight, life is too complex.
- Normal distributions don't fit markets, power laws do better.
- Accurate prediction in economic markets is impossible.
- We sanctify computers and maths – we don't understand them, but if they produce an answer we think it must be right, even if it is guesswork based on inadequate data that was full of noise and was presented by a front man who can't count beyond ten without removing his shoes!
- Markets and life are not predictable, not even short term, certainly not long term.

2 4 6 8 motorway

This chapter is about the maths you need to run your personal finances. And it assumes that you don't have a maths degree or access to anything other than the calculator you have in your phone and a paper and pencil.

If you are one of the people (the majority, in my experience) who are maths phobic, don't worry about it. I know you can stay safer with your money.

I know I can help you stay safer because I'm lucky. I was good enough at maths to understand the basics (which is all you need to do everything important for personal finance) but not good enough to go beyond A-level. So I've never had the problem explaining things that some of my maths masters at school had. They found it so easy they couldn't get down to my level!

If you cast your mind back to chapters 5 and 6 you'll remember that most of us are not really good at maths beyond the simple addition and subtraction of small numbers, unless we put some effort in. Also, there are good reasons why we aren't and that not being logical doesn't always matter and nor does failure to understand more complex maths.

However, having some basic ideas is helpful, so that's what I'm going to concentrate on here.

Estimating

Having a general "feel" for what outcomes you expect with numbers, is very useful. You make an estimate of whether the answer will be hundreds, thousands, negative numbers, less than one or whatever. If it is the wrong "order of magnitude" (you get an answer of 17,000 or so when you thought you'd get an answer of under one hundred) you check your working carefully. I'll give you a real example of that later.

That sort of quick check applies to any area of maths, in the schoolroom, at work, in real life, with money, anything.

But, unless you are a certified maths genius, you must check your working every time when you deal with money, whether it is "roughly" what you expect or not.

Anything you can't work out exactly and with absolute certainty in your head in less than five seconds needs extremely careful checking, everything you can work out easily you should still check, just in case.

If you *are* a certified maths genius, then you can do what you like, but I suggest you check money very carefully at least twice because you are human and you're evidently over-confident that you are infallible!

Albert, it is a waltz – it goes 1, 2, 3, 1, 2, 3 what's the matter, can't you count?

The money illusion

This is about how we look at money and see a mathematical amount and not what that amount means.

Remember in chapter 2 we talked about your values. Those are what are really important to you; and money is not a substitute for them. Also, we're still not really used to money. We've had it long enough to get socially used to it, so we can't imagine a world without money, but we aren't "adaptively" used to it, in that we forget that its value is what it will buy rather than a fixed numerical amount.

Because of that, because we are still, basically, hunter gatherers, we don't really adapt well to inflation (what money will actually buy reducing year by year) or to compound interest (how fast amounts grow, either when you get paid interest or when you owe money).

By the way, it is called "compound" interest (as distinct from "simple" interest) because you get interest paid on the interest you've got already, it is "compounded". We'll look at this later. For the moment, here's an example of how interest works that I rather like.

You might have heard about the purchase of Manhattan (an island of New York). It is now one of the most expensive pieces of "real estate", in the world. I did some calculations, and the value of Manhattan came out to about $8 trillion at December, 2005 prices.

That is $8,000,000,000,000! That's more than some countries (it's probably more than the whole of the UK, if you take all the debts into account!)

Famously, the Dutch, "bought" the land from the Native Americans, in 1626, for the equivalent of 60 Guilders in trade goods. I did some calculations and that worked out as about $40 in 2008 money.

Now it's pretty academic, because it's probably apocryphal and anyway, the Native Americans were laughing because they didn't "own" it in that sense anyway, not having a concept of "owning" land.

But people tend either to mock the naive Native Americans who sold trillions of dollars of land for only 40 dollars or they criticise the Americans, (or the Dutch, or the British) for taking advantage of the poor, stupid savages.

> *I did some calculations about the real value of the $40.*
>
> *If you invested the money at 7% "simple" interest, you'd get $0.28 each year for nearly 400 years, so you'd have just under $1,100.*
>
> *You could perhaps buy a few meals for two at a top restaurant in Manhattan.*
>
> *If you invested the money at 7% compound each year since the Dutch paid it, you'd end up with about $7 trillion!*
>
> *So $40, by the magic of compound interest has become worth $7,000,000,000,000!*
>
> *Therefore, the paltry sum of $40 that today would barely buy you a meal at a cheap restaurant has become, over time and purely by compound interest, enough to buy not only a meal but several thousand restaurant chains (even really pretentious ones)!*

However, the Dutch/Americans still come out ahead (Manhattan is now worth 8 trillion, not 7, remember) so it was still a good bargain, although not perhaps enough for anybody to be able to laugh too much at the Native Americans.

7% is quite a high rate in some ways (certainly it is before the 20th Century) and you probably wouldn't get it in a bank deposit or something. But funnily enough, 7% is a fairly standard average growth rate for share prices in the last century or so.

> *Imagine that you had invested the $40 in shares in 1626 (OK, there wasn't a market in that sense, bear with me). And imagine that instead of getting your 7% growth annually, at the end of each year, you got the interest paid each month in dividends or something.*
>
> *You get the same rate; it just gets added more frequently, because you get 7/12 of a per cent each month instead of 7% each year.*
>
> *Do a quick estimate, what difference, if any, would that make to who got the better end of the deal?*
>
> *Well, according to my calculation, if you compound the interest each month, you end up with about $16 trillion – you could buy Manhattan twice over!*

Apart from the Native Americans laughing because they didn't "own" it anyway, what this tells us is that

a) Compound interest makes a huge difference and makes our "intuitions" and approximations about the effects look pretty silly and

b) The frequency of compounding also makes a huge difference.

Percentages

Percent (%) means, "for each hundred". It's useful because it fits our number system based around tens and hundreds.

If you've got 10%, it is "ten per hundred". If it is 8.5% it is "eight point five per hundred".

The great thing is that the numbers after the decimal point are arranged in tenths and hundredths. So 1.25 is "one, plus two tenths, plus five hundredths". Another way of saying it is "one, plus 25 hundredths". 75% is "seventy five hundredths".

This means that percentages and numbers are easy to convert.

Take 50%. It is "fifty per hundred". That means that we want fifty out of a hundred, and since we have hundredths sitting there after the decimal point we can write 50% as 0.50 because that is 50 hundredths.

Similarly, 10% is 0.10. And 5% is 0.05 (it's 5 hundredths, so you need to make sure you don't make it 50 hundredths by mistake and write 0.50).

You can convert back and forward in the same way, 3.5% is 0.035, 0.20 is 20% and so on.

Interest.

> Imagine you've got £100 that you don't need for a year
>
> You invest it and you are promised 5%. What do you end up with at the end of the year?

You have £100 and you are adding "five per hundred". So you add five pounds to you hundred and get £105 at the end of the year. It doesn't matter whether it is "simple" or "compound" interest in this case, you get the same £5.

Now imagine you are investing your £100 at 5% for two years or three. This is where simple and compound interest start to differ.

Simple interest

You get 5%, so as before, you have £105 at the end of the first year.

Then you add £5 in the second year, because the interest rate is the same and it is "five per hundred" of your £100. So at the end of the second year you have a total of £110. And the third year you have £115 and the fourth (if there was one), £120 and so on.

Compound interest

You get 5%, so as before, you have £105 at the end of the first year.

In the second year you are again going to get 5%, but because it is "compounded" you actually get "five per hundred" of your money plus the interest so far.

So you've got £105, and you add "five per hundred" of the £105.

You can do all sorts of calculations to work that out, but the easiest thing to do is to multiply the money you've got, your £105 by the rate of interest (which is 5%) plus one. As 5% is 0.05, we get 0.05 plus one, which is 1.05.

So we just multiply £105 by 1.05 and we get £110.25, and that's what you've got at the end of the second year.

If we want to know the third year figure, we multiply our money, £110.25, by our rate of interest (5%) plus one.

That is £110.25 times 1.05 which is £115.76 (plus some fractions of a penny that we'll forget about for the moment).

That's all there is to it! You can do all the calculations you need on the calculator in your phone.

Of course, if there is more compounding, for example if you want to look at ten years, or you add interest every month or every quarter, it becomes a pain. It is still dead simple, you just get a repetitive strain injury pressing the buttons!

The way you get around that is to use a mathematical trick.

A number "raised to a power", simply means the number times itself a certain number of times. It is conventionally written as a superscript, like this

Ten to the power of two is written as 10^2

So we could work out our three year compound interest at 5% per year on £100 as

100 times 1.05^3

That means 100 times 1.05 multiplied by itself three times.

Whether you do that by multiplying 1.05 together three times or use a calculator or spreadsheet that has a power function, you get the same answer, £115.76 (plus the odd fractional pennies).

> *It's worth noting that already, after only three years, compound interest has got bigger than simple interest.*
>
> *Remember simple interest in three years gave us £115 from our original £10. Compound interest gave us £115.76.*
>
> *OK, it is only 76 pence, but remember Manhattan! It adds up quickly.*

The other thing worth noting is that it is pretty easy to work these out, but it is a bit cumbersome to write it all down.

The simple way to do it is to use a formula that you can plug the numbers into, press a couple of buttons and you're away.

For that, you just have to remember another mathematical trick.

If we want to make sure we do things in the right order we put a bracket round the bit we want to do first. That's it!

The formula is:

Amount at end = amount at beginning x $(1 + Periodic\ Rate)^{number\ of\ periods}$

This says:

The amount we get at the end, which is what we want to find out, is going to be (remember to do the bit in the bracket first):

Take the interest rate each period (which was 5% with the period of a year) and add to 1.

Multiply that by itself a number of times equal to the number of periods (the number of years, which was 3)

Multiply it all by the amount at the beginning, which was our £100

And that adds up to £115.76 in our example.

The beauty of it is that you can slot anything into that formula.

E.g. 8% over 10 years on £1,000 is $1,000 \times (1 + 0.08)^{10}$ and so on.

If you want to know the interest monthly, your "periodic rate" is whatever the monthly rate is (probably the annual rate divided by 12) and the number of periods are the number of months.

All you need to do is put in the figures you have, work out one plus the periodic rate, multiply it by itself (the "power" calculation) for however many periods (months, quarters, years etc.) you want and multiply that by the money you started with.

That gives you the figure that you'll have at the end with all the compound interest added.

Maths over!

If you just couldn't bear to look – that's OK. I recommend you look over the last couple of pages a few times, because it is important. If you still can't make head nor tail of it, it might be worth getting some help because the basics are important to being safe with your money. Not understanding it at all leaves you very vulnerable to people who don't have your best interests at heart. Have a look at chapter 15 and perhaps get some help with maths.

For other important stuff, you just have to know where to look, you don't need formulae because there is a much simpler shortcut that avoids having to do any figures unless you want to.

If it was all trivial and you think I'm being condescending, sorry, but it is good to remind yourself sometimes!

As a consolation to mathematicians, I've put the a basic formula and a link to the detailed calculation below. They are handy to know if you want to check other people's figures, you don't need them, but if you find it easy you might have fun!

APR and AER

APR (Annual Premium Rate) is what you see on loan agreements and

AER (Annual Equivalent Rates) is the amount you are quoted as interest on savings accounts.

If you know about them you can get a much better idea of what loans will cost you and what income your savings will earn. That means that you can compare different offers without getting ripped off and you are a lot safer financially.

If you are confident with maths, the basic formula is:

$$APR = (1 + Periodic\ Rate)^{\ number\ of\ periods} - 1$$

If you really get keen, look at:
http://www.oft.gov.uk/shared_oft/business_leaflets/consumer_credit/oft144.pdf

If you just want to get an idea of what is going on when you look at a loan, mortgage, hire purchase agreement etc. here is what you do:

- Find the APR they are quoting. This is a standardised rate and in theory you can compare them directly.

If you can't find the APR, ask for it in writing. If they won't quote it, they tell you it is "difficult to quote", or "not needed for this type of loan", walk away! Don't discuss it, ask politely, ask to see the manager or have anything to do with them, just walk away.

- Once you've got the rate you have a percentage:

That percentage is the amount per £100 that you will pay in interest each year (your payments may or may not include paying off the actual amount you borrow, what you are being quoted is the *interest* payment).

- When you know what the APR is, think about it!

The APR is intended to allow you to compare rates. If you get a rate that sounds high, then question whether borrowing is a good idea.

The APR (which as we said, is a yearly figure) is the sum of all the monthly (or quarterly, or weekly) rates. It is a compound rate, not a simple one and not a "nominal rate" (which is basically the rate often quoted in advertisements, as a headline part of a sales pitch).

Quick sanity check:

Why bother getting APR? Surely they are all the same?

No, they can be terrifyingly different. We aren't just talking "loan sharks" we're talking about HP agreements, bank loans and all sorts of things.

Think about this one – you're offered £100 just before Christmas and you agree to pay back £125 in January, a month later. Sounds OK doesn't it?

If you're confident with maths, put the figures into the formula given for the APR. It's good practice.

If not – no problem, this is why you need to get the APR.

Plugging the figures in you end up with APR = $(1.25)^{12} - 1$

That is an APR of 1,355.19%!

That means that if you borrow that money, £100 to pay back £125 a month later, you are effectively paying back more than 1,355% interest on it in a year.

If you borrow, for example £1,000, it means you are agreeing to pay back just over £13,550 in interest each year!

But people take those loans on all the time, because they don't look at the APR. They don't look at or think about the APR because it seems complicated, they are afraid to admit they don't understand it and so on.

> *If you were frightened of maths, I hope by now you're considerably more frightened of ignoring the APR!*
>
> *Don't be scared, you don't need to do calculations, you just need to have an idea of how they work (which you now have) and an idea of how important they are and how they can help you with avoiding that aspect of the "money illusion".*

You can apply the same principles to the AER that you are quoted on investments.

The major difference is that the APR has to include all the compounding effects and also has to include charges (which you usually have to pay on loans) while AER deals only with compounding effects (because usually you don't get charged to put money into a bank or something).

Sales documents will talk about "return rates", "yields" and so on. Bear in mind that anything that you're given by a bank, advisor, investment company etc. is a sales document. It doesn't matter what it is called, if they produce it, it is a sales document. They are trying to use it to sell the product so ignore the bumph and look at the AER or APR.

The whole point of those figures is to make it relatively easy to compare different options. They are quoted on a standard basis so you can pretty much take them as read.

> *However, do remember that if you have a "fixed term" deposit or something similar and need the money early, there may be a charge for taking the money out that won't have been included in the original rate you were quoted (whether it was called an APR or an AER) because it wasn't originally anticipated that a charge would be made so it doesn't have to be put in the quote.*

This is because there has to be a bit of flexibility in the rules, to allow for differences between credit cards, loans, HP agreements etc.

Naturally, companies will use the leeway they have in the regulations to make their APR look low (they want you to believe you'll pay less than you actually will) and their AER look high (they want you to believe you'll get more than you actually do).

The easiest thing to do when looking at a loan or a deposit, is take notice of the official rates such as APR and AER, assume that they are just about accurate, but make the loan look cheaper than it really is and the interest you'll get look more attractive, and you won't go far wrong.

However, because of the leeway allowed, charges for "early redemption" can be quite misleading. So be careful with those sort of loans and try if you can to avoid anything that has any "conditional" charges (ones that depend on things like paying off early, making bigger payments early in the term etc.) because it can cost you money.

Incidentally, that is why you can often get "redemption penalties" refunded on mortgages. If, at the start of the mortgage the lender said that "returning the deeds" was a fee of £50 and you agreed to it, then you agreed to it and that is it. But since the £50 was in there already, it must have gone into the APR calculation. If they suddenly make the fee £500, they have quoted the wrong APR, so they are not acting legally and you can challenge it.

Most lenders will still try it on (they are businesses, not charities remember), and most people don't Tame their own Pound and take responsibility for their own money. However, if you point out that they have changed the rules in the middle of the game and if they don't play fair you will report them to the authorities and potentially take them to Court, they will usually back down and revert to the original agreement.

Avoid anybody who won't give you, in writing, the full and correct figures and will not allow you to take them away and think about them, show them to an advisor, accountant, counsellor etc. and come back to them with your decision at another time. And don't believe any, "one day only special offers", "you have to take the finance option now" and all that sales malarkey.

If you want whatever it is but can't afford it without their finance:

1. Go through chapter 2 and sort out what your values are and whether this fits with what you actually want in life.
2, Go through chapter 3, sort out your goals, and decide whether this really will help you with what you wish to achieve .
3, Go through chapter 4 and think about your shopping habits and whether you need to change them.

This applies to all the "0% finance" offers, "there's nothing to pay until....." etc.

Remember that you might not be paying interest but you still have to pay for the goods.

*Don't think of the interest you will **not** have to pay as a profit, think about the money you **will** have to pay at some point as a loss. You're probably loss averse, remember. Avoid losing, keep your money where it is and don't waste it.*

If after this you are *still* adamant that you must have it, and you must have it now, look again at the APR.
4. Can you really not do without it?
If after this you are *still* adamant that you must have it, and you must have it now on credit, look again at the APR.
5. Is there any way that you can get the loan at a lower APR?

There almost certainly is, so walk away and check out options!

By the way, different countries have different definitions of what an APR is! In the US, APR is more like the UK nominal rate, and what the

UK calls an APR the US describes as Annual Percentage Yield! So preferably, don't buy anything on credit abroad, if you do, make very sure exactly what you are signing up for and certainly don't sign anything without getting it checked through very thoroughly (preferably by at least two lawyers, your Embassy and a mathematician!)

> *So whether you are looking for a loan or the highest rate of return on a savings account, be absolutely sure that you understand which rates they are quoting and then compare the same rates between alternatives. In this country, the easiest way to do this is to make sure you are comparing written APR with written APR for loans, and written AER with written AER for savings. And watch out for "redemption fees" etc. that are conditional on certain things (like early repayment) and thus don't get quoted in the standard figures.*

I've focussed a lot on debt in relation to maths, money illusion, bigness bias etc.

Here's how the money illusion can effect investment

In successive years, Peter, Paul and Mary each bought a home that cost £200,000, and each ended up selling their home one year later. During Peter's year of homeownership, the country experienced a period of 25% deflation – that is, the average price of all goods and services in the UK fell by 25% - and Peter sold his house for £154,000 or 23% less than he paid. During the twelve months that Paul owned his home, the situation was reversed: the average cost of goods and services actually rose 25%, and Paul eventually sold his home for £246,000, or 23% more than he paid. As for Mary, the cost of living during her year-long stretch of owning a home stayed pretty much the same, but she ended up selling her house for £196,000, or 2% less than she paid. Soon after, the three friends met for a drink, but their bonhomie ended in anger when they couldn't agree on the answer to what seemed a simple question: Factoring in the changes in overall consumer prices, which of the three came out the best in their home sales?

Belsky and Gilovich, 1999, page 107

What do you think?

Many people assume that since Paul is the only one who actually made money (his house went up 23%) he must be the winner.

This is a bit like the distinction we made earlier between buying a house to make money, and buying one to live in. You'll remember that I pointed out that it is fine and dandy when your house gains value, but if everything else goes up as well, unless you sell up and live in a tent, you haven't gained. Anything else you buy will also be more expensive.

In this case, Paul has 23% more money, but because of inflation, the amount of money he's got is worth 25% less than it was at the start.

He's got £246,000, so he's "made" £46,000 – and that is what people fixate on, the general public, the "experts", the TV pundits on property programmes, all of the people subject to the "money illusion" (which is just about everybody).

But that money is only worth 75% of what it was (overall prices have increased by 25%).

So in terms of the money he had at the start of his year of home ownership, Paul only has 75% of £246,000, which is £184,500. So he's lost money in real terms, he's about £15,500 worse off.

Meanwhile, Peter seems to have lost most, since his house went down 23% in value, so he only got £154,000 on the sale.

But prices went down 25% remember. As prices went down 25%, Peter can buy more with less money.

In this example, his £154,000 will now buy just over £205,333 worth of goods in the values that applied when he paid £200,000 for the house, so in fact he has made just over £5,000 in real terms.

Mary is the easiest calculation, because the "nominal" (the money in pounds) is the same as the "real" (the purchasing power at different times) because there is neither inflation nor deflation, so her loss is the £4,000 quoted (£200,000 less 2%, which is £196,000).

In the modern world we are more familiar with inflation than static prices or deflation, but any of them can happen. The trouble is, although we are, sort of, used to inflation, we forget about it and think that because what we've got has gone up in nominal value it is actually worth more. In fact, like Peter, we might have made the biggest loss of all while thinking that we've made money.

Now a final example of compound interest, maths and the "money illusion". This is from Belsky and Gilovich once more (and I've adapted it slightly from the US version), because it is a nice "similar to real life" example and it doesn't have an easy answer:

Jill and John are twenty-one year old twins who had just graduated from university. Jill, immediately on entering the workforce, began contributing £50 a month to an investment fund and continued to do so for the next eight years, until she got married and found more pressing uses for money. John married immediately after graduating and soon after started to raise a family. He only began investing when he was 29. Then, he too contributed £50 a month to the same investment fund and carried on for thirty seven years until he was 65. At age 65, which of the twins had the most money, assuming they earned an average 10% compound each year?

You can try to work this out various ways, but without something like a good statistical calculator, putting it into a spreadsheet and using the appropriate functions or something similar, it is hard to estimate.

What tends to happen is that we look at Jill's eight years of contributions and (perhaps) think, "that's £50 per month for a year, which is £600, for eight years makes £4,800, that's not a lot". Meanwhile, John has put in £600 a year for 37 years, which is over £20,000, which sounds quite a lot. So it looks like a no brainer as to who ends up with more money.

But of course, Jill's £4,800 has been increasing a bit during the first eight years because interest has been added to the first year's money for 8 years, to the second for 7 years and so on. It actually adds up to just over £7,500 by the time she stops paying.

Now think about the position when the twins are 35 (after John has been paying for eight years so he will have paid in the same amount as Jill has). By this point, Jill's first eight year's contributions have accumulated to just over £16,000. So although she stopped paying eight years before, with 10% being added in interest every year, she is getting an extra £1,600 each year in interest and that is increasing at 10% each year and so on.

John, meanwhile, has made eight years contributions so his fund is just over £7,500, like Jill had. He's also now adding £50 each month and will carry on doing that for the rest of the time until they are 65.

The thing is, the interest on the accumulated amount that Jill has is £850 more than on John's fund (10 % of her fund is £1,600, 10% of his is £750 and £1,600 − £750 is £850).

*Although he is now adding £600 each year in the continuing contributions in addition to the interest on the fund, he's actually falling farther behind Jill each year. Jill finishes with £256,650 and John with £217,830, which are both much more than the money they've put in (showing the power of the compound interest) but clearly the early money Jill has put in makes a huge difference and John can never catch up without putting in a lot **more** money.*

We'll look at this again in practice in chapter 14, but for now,

- *Remember how powerful compound interest is*
- *Remember the APR and AER.*
- *Get money accumulating as early as possible.*
- *Compound interest can buy you Manhattan twice over, if you invest early enough!*

Thinking about having huge masses of money, I mentioned the odds of winning the lottery in an earlier chapter and here's a good time to look at that.

Probability, the lottery and coincidence

I mentioned that many people have trouble believing that 1-6 gives you just as good odds of winning as picking another six numbers. There are a few simple things that we need to know, before we go into why that is the case.

First, think back to what we talked about in chapter 7 with roulette; working out what all the possible outcomes are and comparing that to what outcomes "win" and seeing what happens if you run through examples.

Let's take tossing a coin. Suppose you've got a fair coin and you call heads. There are two chances (it can be heads, or tails) and one situation where you "win"; heads. So your chances of winning are ½.

Simple. Now a bit more advanced maths. You can get the chance of two events *both* happening by multiplying them together.

For example, if you toss a coin twice and call heads each time, what are your chances of winning both times?

Your chance the first time is ½, and your chance the second time is ½, if you multiply ½ by ½ you get ¼. So your chance of getting two calls right in a row is ¼.

You can extend this, if you do it a third time, you get ½, times ¼, which is 1/8 and so on.

If you think this is very basic, remember how simple it is in the next chapter, because most investment experts don't appear to have got it yet! If it is difficult to grasp, you can check it out by listing what can happen.

Imagine your three tosses of the coins. You can get

HHH

HHT

HTH

HTT

THH

THT

TTH

TTT

So there are eight possible series of three coin tosses. Only one "wins", which is HHH, the one you guessed. All the eight sequences are as likely to come up as one another since it is a fair coin. So our odds are 1/8. As I mentioned, this is quite important for money (believe it or not) so it's worth making sure you understand it.

Now let's imagine that there are two people each guessing what result you'll get from three coin tosses. One guesses, HHH, the other guesses TTT. What are the odds that one of them wins?

There are still 8 combinations of tails and heads (as we listed before). But now there are two that "win". So our odds that one of the people wins are 2/8 which is ¼. That's obviously the same as the odds of each person winning (1/8) added together (1/8 +1/8 = ¼). And in general, you can add the odds together when it is a case of "this result *or* that one", as distinct from multiplying them together when it is a case of "this result *and* that one".

However, it isn't always quite that simple!

Suppose you've got eight people guessing. If you add those eight chances of 1/8 together you get 8/8. That means the chance of a win is the same as the number of possible results, so it sounds like somebody would be certain to win.

And you'd be right if all eight people guessed a different order. If one guessed HHH, one HHT and so on all the way to TTT, whatever sequence you actually got when you tossed the coin three times, somebody would "win" by having guessed the correct sequence.

But what if two people guessed the same sequence of heads and tails? Suppose two people guessed, say HHH, and the other six people all guessed various combinations of heads and tails, but nobody guessed TTT. If HHH came up the two of them would win, if TTT came up, nobody would win and if any other sequence came up, then the one person who had guessed that particular sequence would win.

Now the important thing to note is that if there are enough people who pick different sequences (in this case we have eight) and there are only a limited number of options (in this case, again, there are eight possible sequences) it can be almost certain (or even absolutely certain) that there will be at least one winner.

If all eight guess different sequences then whichever sequence of heads and tails comes up of the eight possible ones, somebody is absolutely sure to win. On the other hand, the chance of any *particular* person winning is still only one in eight. They will win if their particular sequence comes up, but there is only one winning sequence for them and eight possible sequences. Each sequence is equally likely, so their chance of winning is 1/8 and of not winning (another sequence comes up and not theirs) is 7/8.

Now think of this in terms of the lottery. Obviously, there are lots more possible combinations, you've got 49 numbered balls and you're picking six numbers. Without going into a lot of unnecessary maths, the number of combinations is just under 14 million! But the principles are exactly the same.

> *If 14 million people play the lottery and they all pick a different six numbers, then you can be absolutely certain that, whatever numbers came up, somebody would win.*
>
> *But with any six numbers, it doesn't matter which ones, your odds of winning are still 1 in about 14 million, the same as your odds in the coin tossing were 1/8.*

And of course, in the same way as it doesn't matter whether you pick HHH, TTT, HTH or any other sequence your odds are still 1/8, it doesn't matter whether you pick 123456, 987654 or any other sequence of numbers, your odds are exactly the same, which is about 1/14,000,000.

> *It is useful to be confident about multiplying the odds, adding them etc, because once you get into bigger numbers, having to list everything in order to work out the odds takes ages! But it isn't vital, the important thing is to realise what this means in real life.*

If you've got enough people doing something, the most unlikely events are actually likely to happen. In the same way, if you do something enough times, it becomes likely even if initially it is unlikely.

As an aside, and very unfortunately for something like the lottery, to make it certain that you're going to win you'd have to buy about 14 million tickets for yourself, each with different numbers!

As an example of how the initial "unlikely" becomes an eventual "likely", take this classic maths conundrum. How many people do you need in a room for the probability of finding two people with the same birthday to be more than ½?

Most people figure, "There are 365 days in the year. So it must be about half of that. So it's about 183".

Actually, it is 23.

On the other hand the number you need in the room to have a better than ½ chance of somebody having the same birthday as *you* is 253.

I won't go into the maths (it isn't that complicated, just a bit tedious).

If somebody hasn't got the same birthday as you, or the next person, or the next, then maybe one of the next couple have the same birthday as one of the first two and so on. There are loads of chances for coincidences of birthdays and it only takes 23 people for it to be more likely to have a match *somewhere* than it is for no match at all.

However, if you look at one particular person and the chance of something unlikely happening to them specifically, it remains very unlikely. If one person doesn't have the same birthday as you, nor the next, nor the next, you just have to keep going. You need 253 people before you are more likely to find a match with your own birthday than not.

*The result is the chance of **somebody** winning the lottery is very likely, the chance of you or anybody in particular winning it is extremely unlikely.*

Take something more common than winning the lottery. Imagine you go on holiday to the Maldives, and you bump into your second cousin once removed that you only met at Cousin Sheila's wedding twenty years ago and it turns out that she's called her daughter the same name as you've called your daughter. What an amazing, unlikely coincidence, you think.

And it would be, if you were looking at the chance of meeting that particular person in that particular place and having that particular thing in common *before* you met them. But you're not looking at that. Think of all the people who used to live near you, you went to school with, worked with, that were friends of friends, distant relatives etc. There are hundreds of them. Then think of all the coincidences, you have the same birthday, you named children (or pets) the same, you have the exact same model camera, the list is endless.

Then think of all the holidays you've ever been on, the days you've gone to work, or travelled to town and met people, the people you've seen on the bus, in the library, in the hairdresser, at the big game.

It means the chance of you meeting somebody you weren't expecting to meet, at a place you weren't expecting to meet them and having in common something you weren't expecting to have in common *seems* unlikely but is actually bound to happen sometimes.

It is an example of where the driving logic of probability is really useful. People believe that this "amazing coincidence" is something rare and astonishing (and get confused about accident statistics, for example), because they confuse the prior odds (the odds before you start) of "one in a million" of a particular person being in a very specific situation on a single occasion with the odds of a "one in a million" event occurring at any time in a million examples.

It might seem an incredible coincidence, but meeting somebody at some time when you weren't expecting it is pretty well guaranteed. If you want to know the chance of meeting somebody in a particular situation with a particular common factor on a specific single occasion, and you write that down now and predict the exact situation *beforehand*, and within the time period specified it happens, that is perhaps as unlikely as winning the lottery. If you run into them and only *afterwards* think, "what are the chances", then the chances are that it is going to happen several more times to you, in the same way that the chances are good that *somebody* will win the lottery.

Informed decisions

Another mathematical issue most people have is with what is called "conditional probability". This is basically about making allowances for new information. It's a bit difficult to understand in abstract terms, so let's look at an example that comes up all the time in the media, in learned papers and in people's lives, i.e. medical diagnosis.

Imagine you've read in the newspapers about a really nasty newly discovered form of cancer. It affects only 1% of people (so only 1 person in 100 has the potential to develop this form of cancer), but without immediate treatment it is always fatal. There is a test for the precancerous cells that is 90% accurate if you've got it (so if you have the potential to get the cancer, the test will detect it early 90 times out of 100), but it sometimes gives false positives so the test will be positive 10% of the time even if you don't have the pre-cancerous cells.

You're worried, so you go to get tested and, horror, you get a positive result. What is the actual chance that you have the cells and need immediate expensive treatment?

If that is as clear as mud, don't worry. Most of the medical profession, 99.9% of journalists and (apparently) every politician and policy maker in the country (and in most of the world) will spend ten minutes or so trying to figure out the chances and end up saying, "I'd have the treatment anyway, I've probably got it but at the moment I can't quite work out the exact chance"!

But imagine that it is £20,000 or £500 a month for the rest of your life to pay for treatment. If there really is a good chance you have the cancer, that is obviously worth it, but if it is less than, say, fifty:fifty, it is worth getting tested again and checking the results. So what is the chance, and is it greater than even money that you have the cancer given a positive test?

What you can do is to apply something called Bayes' Theorum. I won't go into it in detail, it is very clever and gives accurate answers. The thing is, while it is wonderfully elegant maths and fascinating if you like that sort of thing, it's a bit impractical to use it every day, so nobody I know ever bothers! You'll see why in a minute.

Unfortunately, lots of people who don't understand it at all, use the threat of the maths as another stick to beat the poor public with and come up with nonsensical statements like, "people are bad at applying Bayesian mathematics and therefore are stupid and need us experts to tell them how to think".

Here's how Bayes Theorum would apply to that problem. The chance of actually having cancer, given that you've had a positive test is:

P (cancer) × P (pos|cancer)/(P (cancer) × P (pos|cancer)) + ((1- P (cancer)) × P (pos|no cancer))

I won't bother to explain all the terms – I assume you can see why nobody in their right mind does it that way!

The answer, if you can be bothered to do the maths is 8.33%

So although this test is 90% accurate if you have the cancer, your chance of actually having cancer, even if you have a test that is positive and says you have the cancer, is only about 8.33%

Four things:

1. It is really important for things like medical expenses, so you can really benefit from being able to work it out.
2. The result is counter intuitive, we expect the chance to be much higher because the test is quite accurate. In the real situation, if you can't work out the odds, you have a good chance of being scared to death whether you have the cancer or not!
3. The maths is very good and accurate, but it is demanding of your technical ability and understanding. Even if you are good, it takes a long time.
4. The good news is you don't need to bother, there is a really easy way to do it!

You can read Gigernzer's "Reckoning with risk", which very entertainingly goes through this whole area in a very easy to understand way. You can also read Ben Goldacre's work, such as the book (and newspaper column, blog etc.) Bad Science.

That is full of terrifying examples of the sort of distortions that come from people with vested interests (like pharmaceutical companies) trying to influence people who don't understand the maths (like everybody, but particularly politicians) to buy their products; and journalists and "bad scientists" promoting "scare stories" that present facts, but in a very confusing way. This is partly due to the journalists being ignorant of any maths and partly due to the majority involved not being concerned with the real health situation or the possibility of scaring people unnecessarily, but far more interested in selling their paper, their products or their policies!

Sorry, mini rant there but it irritates me that people who should really stay quiet until they know what they are talking about continue to go on about the complex maths they clearly don't understand, when there are simpler ways to explain things in order to help people, not panic them into wasting money and time.

You might wonder at this point what that has to do with Taming the Pound – unless you run an NHS trust, in which case, it will be obvious! But it is important for everybody for three reasons:

1. If you can understand what is going on, you can be a more intelligent consumer of news generally, which is full of "this indicates that...." statistics that are complete rubbish and incite you to waste your money.
2. Your health is probably important to your happiness and since the main application is healthy eating, exercise, cholesterol levels, medicine, surgery etc. you want to be able to make informed decisions (on which both the books I mentioned are very good).
3. Choosing what to spend your money on (do you need "exploratory surgery" or "cholesterol lowering drugs" for example), and whether you want to pay for various forms of medical fees insurance, critical illness insurance and so on, makes a big difference to the money you have available to facilitate the rest of your life interests. If you are spending £500 a month for life on something believing it is 90% certain you have a problem, and it is actually only 8.33% likely, you're not likely to be as happy as you could be!

Look at the problem again. But this time, we'll use what is called the "frequencies approach" and use pictures, both of which are more natural ways to think for humans (as distinct from mathematicians!)

Imagine there are 10,000 people. One in 100 of them has this cancer. That will mean out of all 10,000, 100 will have the cancer and the other 9,900 of them won't. Let's draw that:

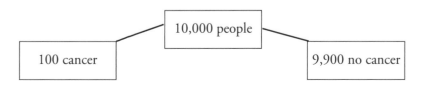

Now imagine that all these people take the test for cancer. Of the ones who have cancer, 90% will test positive. Of the ones who don't have cancer, 10% will test positive. Let's draw that in.

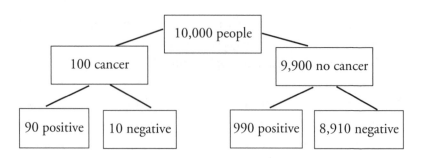

We want to know our chances of having cancer if we have a positive test result. Remember our method of working out the odds, take the number of "wins" and divide by the total number of possible results.

There is a total of 990 + 90, which equals 1,080, tests which are positive, so that is our total of possible results. And the number of people who test positive who actually have the cancer (which isn't exactly a "win" but it is the result we want to find out about) is 90. So if we take 90 and divide by 1,080 on our calculator.

We get 8.33%

So we can get exactly the same result without all the complicated maths, by drawing some pictures!

Regression to the mean
This is another thing that people get confused about with maths.

Going along with the point that pictures are easier to understand, have a look at the "normal distribution" picture from chapter 7.

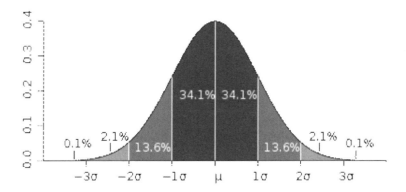

Remember, the "mean" is the μ (mu) symbol in the middle. And the height of the curve reflects the proportion of objects at that point.

Have a look at the curve. If you are out to one side, the curve is quite low, there won't be many people (or whatever you are measuring) out there.

If the curve is, say, IQ of people, somebody like Stephen Fry will be way off to the right where the curve is very low and if you measure the IQ of loads of people you won't find many others that far out. On the other hand, if you measure lots of people off the street, the chance are that about two thirds of them will be in the highest part of the curve, the two sections in the middle.

In general, you expect to find people, objects, whatever you are measuring (if they are normally distributed) grouped around the mean, not at the edges. If you get one person who is very tall, very intelligent, very anything, you'd expect that the next person will be nearer the mean than that extreme example.

So when you test Stephen Fry (who is both very tall and very clever) you would expect that the next person you measure will not be as tall or clever. They might be taller or smarter than average (or they might be a bit below average height or cleverness) but you wouldn't expect them to be even smarter and taller than Mr. Fry. That is regression to the mean. When you get an extreme result, the next result is likely to "regress" from the extreme back towards average, and the mean is the average.

You see it in parents and children, tall parents tend to have tall children, and clever parents have clever children (that's genetics for you), but usually the extremely tall or clever parents have children who are above average but not as extreme as the parents, they have "regressed to the mean". The important thing is that they tend to go towards the mean, they are less extreme, it doesn't indicate that they will fly across to the other side and "balance things up".

Look at the normal curve again. If you have two very clever parents, so they are way off to the right on the curve, you expect the children to be off to the right of centre, to be cleverer than the average person. You don't expect the child to "balance it up" by turning out to be less clever than average and being off to the left hand side of the curve.

That might seem blindingly obvious. But, if you apply this to share values and so on, people suddenly seem to be blinded by it!

Many people think that if a share has performed poorly, it is likely to bounce up again because it will "regress to the mean". The trouble with that is that if it has done extremely badly, it will probably do less badly (it will regress and not be so extreme) but "less bad" is not the same as "become good" so why should it jump across the curve to the other side? Similarly, something that has done extremely well over the year will probably regress in the next year or two, and become less extremely good, but it isn't necessarily going to do worse than average from some strange notion of "balancing things up". It will probably carry on being above average, just not as much above as it was.

This, of course, assumes that stocks follow a normal distribution, which as we've seen, they don't, but it still applies in general. Stuff that is very much bigger, faster, cleverer, better, worse or slower than average will usually become less bigger, faster, cleverer, better, worse or slower than average, but won't necessarily cross over. But people still hang on to losing stock because they think it will "bounce back" due to "regression to the mean" and "the law of averages"!

The other point about regression to the mean that I want to make is that the "mean" to which things regress is assumed in theory to be stable.

But what "mean" is it they are regressing to? Because the "true value" of a share or a stock market index or whatever is variable (is it doing well or badly, how do we know, what about chaos, what about all the traders doing daft deals etc.) nobody actually has a clue what the "mean" is. Maybe it is where it was before (the assumption that is generally made in practice and always made in theory). But maybe it has gone up or down in the meantime.

So be very wary of people quoting "regression to the mean" as an explanation for poor performance (or as a reason for investing). It might be the reason, but it is quite likely an apparent effect (it is an "emergent property" as in chapter 7) and mathematical effects like regression to the mean might not apply, particularly since the market isn't normally distributed anyway!

Quick check

Having said, "always check your working with money", here's a tip from the "order of magnitude" I mentioned at the start of the chapter. This leads into a final anecdote on why it is important, so bear with me.

If you want to get a rough idea of what something will be worth allowing for compound interest or inflation, use two figures, 7 and 10.

Adding 10% compound interest for 7 years, or 7% compound interest for 10 years, you get approximately double.

The actual figures are

10% compound for 7 years, multiply by 1.948717

7% compound for 10 years, multiply by 1.967151

Just bear in mind that it almost doubles in both cases, and think about it in terms of this story.

I was what is now termed an Independent Financial Advisor. I'd gone to a friend's office. It was an insurance company, and I got talking to two of the "broker reps", the people who called on Advisors like me to get me to use and sell their company products to my clients. They started telling me how good their rates were for a 25 year policy, how their premiums were low, the policy was great etc. I asked them how they calculated the premiums. The premiums were based on the bonuses, which is basically a form of interest, paid each year that would grow to produce a particular sum in 25 years. Once they knew the amount the client wanted in 25 years, they would work backwards to calculate the premium required each month.

They told me that they used "80% of bonus" which was what other companies used. I said, "no, others use 80% of bonus rate". They said, "that's what we said". Now can you spot the simple error there?

If you can, great. You are better at maths than those reps and in fact better than 99% of "experts" at the time (and probably 80% of "experts" now). If not, that is the problem because the vast majority of people can't see a difference. "80% of bonus" and "80% of bonus rate" sounds the same, so how can the single word "rate" make so much difference?

Here's what I said at the time. "Assume your bonus rate is 10% each year and you pay £50 per month".

At this point, I borrowed their calculator – remember, always check when you're working with money!

"If you work out what you get after 25 years," and I worked it out (using the compound interest formula at 10% over 25 years), "you end up with £66,341.67. If you take 80% of that, you've got 80% of bonus, which is £53,073.34."

"Now," I said, "look at what you get if you take 80% of bonus *rate*." And I worked that out. "Same assumptions, 10% bonus rate each year, £50 per month. Take 80% of that bonus *rate* which means 8%, and you get £47,551.32." (I got that by compounding at 8% over 25 years).

"There is a difference of about £5,500 between £53,073.34 and £47,551.32, which is about 10% of your total sum."

"That can't be right," they said.

> *But of course, it was. The difference between 80% of bonus, and 80% of bonus rate, which sound so similar, is huge.*
>
> *It is huge because the rate you compound at makes a big difference (this has big implications for all sorts of investments, where fees can cut down the compound rate substantially. We'll look at this and what you do about it in chapters 9 and 14).*

You might also think about this when people are "projecting" the value of an investment into the future, they are making assumptions about what will happen in future which nobody knows.

Assumptions have to be made, some of which will be set by the authorities and some decided by companies (like with APR).

What actually happens (as we saw in chapter 7) could be completely different from what we expect, the actual investment performance might be the same, better or worse than the projection, or bear no resemblance to it at all.

If a company is told by the authorities to use "80% of bonuses" so that the public can compare like with like, the projections don't have any relation to the reality of what will happen (they are just authority guesses about the future). And even though all projections might *look* the same they might not be.

Why not? As we said earlier, companies want to sound like they are charging a lower amount so you'll buy whatever they are selling. If you are a company and assume "80% of bonus" actually means "80% of total bonuses" you can quote a lower premium than if you assume it means "80% of bonus *rate*". People will buy more if it is cheaper, so you make it sound cheaper.

> *It doesn't matter what rate the authorities set, 10%, 3%, 50%
> whatever, you'll still get different quotes depending on what you assume
> "80%" means, and whatever you use, it may bear no resemblance to
> what actually happens anyway.*
>
> *Naturally enough, lots of companies used the most favourable
> interpretation to sell more business. They still do, as with APR.*
>
> *After all it is within the legal "margin for error" and is perfectly true.
> And the authorities don't usually notice the difference between "bonus"
> and "bonus rate" anyway!*

Now just in case you think I'm being clever after the event, or that I'm a total geek and studied all the policies in detail when I should have been out drinking, I'll tell you what made me question it at the time.

Remember the 7 and 10 point I made. I did a very rough "order of magnitude" check (one thing for school, it made me do stuff automatically!). I can't honestly remember exactly, but I must have reasoned roughly like this:

"At 10% it will double every 7 years. So in 25 years it will double three times, which takes 21 years, and it will have another four years, which is about half of another 7. So if we have, say, £100, that will double three times, this is 200, 400, 800 and another half, which makes about 1,200. If we have 80% of that, it will be 8 × 12, which is 96, so we'll have about 960.

At 8% it is a bit more than 7%, so it will double a bit quicker than every 10 years. So it will double twice which takes 20 years, plus another half for the other 5 years, plus a bit. So it will double something between 2 ½ and 3 times. So if we start with 100 it will be 200, 400, and between 600 and 800.

Therefore, if we use 80% of total bonus, we get about £960, but if we use 80% of bonus rate, we get somewhere between £600 and £800. Based on £100 to start, that sounds like quite a big difference, better check it." So I did.

I didn't know for sure whether it would work out very differently, and I certainly wouldn't have put any money on how much any difference would be. However, it looked to me from a very approximate "order of magnitude" check that there was going to be a difference that needed to be checked.

I swear this is absolutely true. I didn't prepare for it, I just used some simple maths, then checked with a calculator as I've suggested that you do. Fair enough, I was taught (and forced to practice) mental arithmetic, but even if you can't do it as fast as me, there's no reason you can't make an estimate and then check with a calculator.

Also, the reps (who were supposed to be experts) *really* had no idea that there was a difference. But don't be too hard on them, I don't suppose *any* of the reps I met knew either. I just happened to raise the issue with those two.

The bigger problem, of course, was that the investment performance didn't match up even to the projections that the "experts" at the official regulators said were reasonable, which is why there was the "endowment scandal" that happened, which we'll talk about later.

I think this illustrates:

a) chapter 7 on unpredictability should be compulsory reading for everybody involved in finance, especially regulators,
b) sensible maths, as in this chapter, should be taught in schools and
c) ignorance of unpredictability *or* maths should be an instantly dismissible offence in every Financial Advisor, Bank, Government Department or Financial Regulator (this would produce huge public sector cost savings since about 99% of staff would have to go)!

Unfortunately, being cynical, I know that the authorities will say that the loopholes I've described are now closed, ignoring the fact that other ones are out there. The trouble is they are "Black Swans", the regulators won't see them because they don't recognise that they need to look for them and wouldn't recognise them if they did. Anyway, they are too busy trying to make impressive sounding guesses about what happened last time and lock the doors of all the empty stables!

On that note, well done! You survived the maths lesson and if you do those simple things, that only require a bit of practice and a simple calculator (if you can use one with power functions or can set up a spreadsheet or something, even better) you can keep your finances safer, understand much better than most professionals what is going on and check out the "deals" you're offered.

Summary:

- The maths you need for personal finance is pretty simple.
- Make estimates, it helps avoid errors, but check your estimates.
- We don't deal very well with inflation or compound interest, you need to think about what is going on and check your figures.
- Compound interest is amazingly powerful!
- APR and AER shouldn't be ignored.
- The "money illusion" gets all of us.
- Make sure you understand the basics, they really are useful.
- Probabilities are worth knowing about.
- The odds of predicting a particular unlikely event happening to a particular person at a particular time are very low; the odds of looking back and finding an extremely unlikely event happening to somebody at some time are so high it is almost a certainty.
- Drawing pictures can save you a lot of worry and money – and save you having to use Bayes' Theorum!
- Regression to the mean is an effect that is much misunderstood.
- Learn to estimate and check things – just because it is officially approved doesn't mean much, regulators aren't very well informed about maths and know nothing at all about how their own minds or anybody else's actually work.

So now, let's have a look at some of the "deals" and how the (misplaced) confidence that lots of people around markets have can lose you enough money to make the lottery look like a good deal!

Into the woods

This chapter is about venturing into the world of investment and the overconfidence, self justification and self delusion that everybody (expert or not) has about their abilities. It lists some mistakes we make, and suggests a general approach to investing more intelligently.

Have you ever watched a sports event and discussed an incident in the game with a friend afterwards?

Did you notice that you can watch the same thing and reach completely different conclusions? For example, watch a replay (with the aid of "Hawkeye") and you know that the English player was in and the Australian out, while your Aussie "friend" was equally convinced, but had each player's status wrong?

The world of finance might be a closed book to you and you'd prefer to talk about sport. If you are a devout reader of financial journals, a professional money manager etc. you might be happy with finance. But the delusions, self justifications and overconfidence apply equally to them both.

On sports; as I write we're only part of the way through 2010, but my favourite quote is made. Frank Lampard had a "goal" disallowed, the ball crossed the line, it was a mistake by the assistant referee, England went out of the World Cup four goals to one. And in an interview, Frank said, "nobody can tell me that we lost that game 4-1".

Frank, have a look at the scoreboard! It might not have been fair, or right, or just, it might have put a dent in our feeling of superiority over the Germans, it might mean that new goal-line technology is introduced, it might be seen in Germany as God's vengeance for the Russian linesman in 1966 not disallowing Geoff Hurst's goal, but England *did* lose the game 4-1. Whether you like it or not, that is reality.

> *The question is, what are you going to do about reality, not can you ignore it, explain it away, blame somebody else or deny it?*

So we'll look at people's perceptions and their conviction that reality is less important than what they wanted to happen or think should have happened which are, frankly (pun intended), delusional!

The world stage

I'll start with a comment on the economic crash.

Alan Greenspan was head of the US Federal Reserve (like the Bank of England, but bigger, much bigger).

We talked about the difficulty of prediction in chapter 7 and the ability of people to justify their own prejudices, blindness, reliance on prior experience that may not be valid etc. in chapters 5 and 6.

When Mr. Greenspan was being asked about the chance of a crash, his own powers of prediction were being questioned or the validity of his own (very extensive) prior experience was being doubted, you might think that he would at least have considered the possibility that he could be wrong about the future. Given that he was regarded (and still is by many) as a financial genius and had spent about 40 years in finance at a high level, you might think he might have worked out some of the points I've made in the book so far. See what you think his grasp of the facts actually was, as reported in the New York Times.

'But there was something else going on: a general belief that bubbles just don't happen. What's striking, when you reread Greenspan's assurances, is that they weren't based on evidence — they were based on the a priori assertion that there simply can't be a bubble in housing. And the finance theorists were even

more adamant on this point. In a 2007 interview, Eugene Fama, the father of the efficient-market hypothesis, declared that 'the word 'bubble' drives me nuts,' and went on to explain why we can trust the housing market:'

Krugman, 2009

Fama is another economist of the same "school" mentioned earlier that think their equations are too complicated for ordinary people. Evidently, since there *was* a bubble in housing, either the equations themselves are wrong or they are too complicated for Mr Fama and his school as well (probably both)!

Clearly, both Messrs Fama and Greenspan are making assumptions of the "all swans are white" variety, and choose to deny it.

Enter the media

When the BBC ran a series of programmes about the crash, they gave lots of airtime to these people (and to Gordon Brown) and seemed terribly impressed with their explanations of how it wasn't their fault, it was bad luck and not bad predictions or faulty theories and believed what the two (or three) said about what would happen next.

I think that is a bit disappointing for us, the public. There *was* a bubble, Fama, the expert was wrong, Greenspan, the man who praised bankers and relaxed regulation in US financial markets was wrong. Gordon Brown, who made Fred Goodwin (who we mentioned earlier) a role-model (he was Knighted and made "European Banker of the Year") and allowed further relaxation of UK regulation was wrong.

> But the media were desperate to find out what these people said had happened and thought would happen next. Why?

Neither the "experts" nor the politicians predicted the biggest crash in living memory, they were in denial over its happening, and had set up the conditions for it to multiply its effect (by relaxing regulations) and clearly had absolutely no idea of the existing magnitude of disaster, let alone what was coming next. And they didn't know why it had happened.

> They are just people, they don't have a crystal ball any more than you do. Why do the media worship them and ask their advice?

Of course, both the US and UK Governments subsequently condemned "greedy bankers" (like Fred Goodwin) and said regulations had to be tightened.

> But if they think regulation would have been effective, why did they remove or relax it in the first place, and if they removed it because it wasn't needed or effective, why do they think it will be needed or effective in future?

These people got it wrong, can't predict (chapter 7), can't explain (the melting ice cube) and are therefore totally blind about the future just like us ordinary mortals. They know more than most of us about economics, like footballers can kick a ball better, but they can't tell the future or explain the past any better and refuse to accept that fact (just like the rest of us).

They believe their own publicity. When reality conflicts with their belief in their own divinity, they say, "nobody can tell me we lost 4-1":

> *Everyone, whether sports fan, "expert", media, or whoever, whenever reality conflicts with what we want to believe, we reject reality and go with belief.*
>
> *The "experts" also believe their own hype,*
>
> *The media desperately want somebody, anybody, to predict the future.*
>
> *We are all afraid of the fact, but we can't predict the future.*

Of course, pundits and politicians are easy targets. They have to say something and since, as I've hopefully demonstrated, it isn't humanly possible to predict the future and be right all the time, they are inevitably going to get it wrong and frequently look rather stupid.

> But when experts, politicians and media still cling to the bizarre belief that somebody can do the impossible and predict and control the future, where does it leave us and our money, whom do we trust?

We may be disillusioned with the theorists and politicians, but surely there is another kind of expert who is more realistic and humble; the "working man" (or woman) who is a professional investor.

After all, the fund managers, dealers, wealth managers, stockbrokers etc. have to make their living. They aren't up for re-election and they aren't separated from the consequences of their mistakes by lives in academia. If they get it wrong their clients lose money and they will go out of business (unless they hide in the herd, as in chapter 6).

Actually, they don't come out that well either and I'm going to try to explain why by means of the three Rs

The three Rs (Required return, Risk and Reading)
What **return** do you **require** from your money?

> What would you rather have?
>
> 2% p/a guaranteed by a central bank?
>
> 5% p/a "safely"?
>
> 8% p/a with "some risk"?
>
> 12% p/a with "extreme risk"?

If you've read the book so far, you have some thoughts about what you want to achieve. You'll know what you value and what your goals are and therefore have an idea of what, financially, you need to get there.

Forget about the "risk" factor. Forget the uncertainties. What return do you want? Do you want to choose now, or would your choice depend on what you need?

> Would you take extra risk to get 10% p/a when all you need to be happy is 5% p/a? You'd add to your risk for no value? Really?
>
> Would you still try for "the best return" and take extra risk if you don't know what return you actually need? Why would you do that?

Which is what most people do, chase the "best" return, without bothering to work out what they want or need. As we'll discuss in a moment, that leads to them taking bigger and bigger risks that they can't control or predict (or even calculate).

> *The professional fund manager is in a different position. She, or he, doesn't have a value that requires a particular return. He/she has to be in the crowd so as not to be cast out if he/she is right and the rest wrong (like Tony Dye), but preferably a bit better than the crowd so she/he stands out as a bit better so he/she is better rewarded.*

That doesn't mean that professional fund management is dishonest, far from it. They have to work to high standards, know their job etc. But their goal as a fund manager is nothing like your goal as a private investor.

> *The private investor has a value that dictates a goal, which requires a particular investment performance irrespective of anything else.*
>
> *The fund manager has a goal to beat the other fund managers, but not to get too far out of step that they become isolated and vulnerable.*

People, individuals or fund managers, forget what their requirement is. They chase ever better returns and take ever bigger risks.

There is some justification for fund managers doing that, to an extent they have to in order to achieve their goal

*But ignoring the **Required return** and forgetting that the requirement is different for individual and fund manager, is a cause of problems for you – the investor.*

Risk

I'll call it risk because that's the convention, although we can't express it mathematically so it is uncertainty, not risk. Remember chapters 7 and 8, and information about the normal distribution, the mean and so on.

If, instead of heights, IQs etc., you collect together the performance data for lots of shares in companies, you can set up an "index". Examples are things like the "all share" or the "Footsie" (Financial Times Stock Exchange 100), both of which are indexes.

"Beating the index" is a good thing to do. It is a bit like, but not the same as, being at the "Stephen Fry" end of the normal IQ curve!

You can also get "funds" which are groups of shares in different companies all in one package. They sometimes get called "collective investment schemes", because they are, well, schemes where a range of investments are collected together!

With funds, instead of buying 100 shares of company X, 100 of company Y and so on, you buy an amount of the fund (usually called "units" of a fund), and that holds some shares of X, Y, Z and various others. This "spreads the risk" and avoids you having, in common parlance, "all your eggs in one basket".

There are also data on funds, so you can see who is doing well and who is doing badly. For example if an index for a market has gone up 5% and the particular fund you're in which invests in that market has gone up 7%, your fund has "beaten the index".

> *You can also track the funds and form a distribution curve of them, find a mean (or average) etc. If some funds (or fund managers) beat the average some other funds must have done worse, because the curve is pretty much symmetrical. So if there are 20 funds available, you're going to have about 10 ahead of the average and 10 falling behind.*

You might remember from chapter 7, the more "samples" you take, the more your data tend to fit the theoretical curve. So if you've got 1,000 "samples", or examples of a fund performance, you'll get a more reliable measure of the data than if you only have 100. Generally, relying on a year or two's data is not going to tell you much, it is better to go for at least five years and preferably a lot more.

Think about the maths. Some funds will beat the average and some will trail it. Imagine that you picked one at random.

It is like a coin toss, you have a fund, and it will beat the average or trail it (so there are two events possible) and you want to know your chance of beating it (which is one chance). Your odds are therefore approximately ½. But that is only one year. That doesn't mean a lot, so what happens if you do a second year?

Remember you can multiply the odds. So for two years the odds of you beating the average both years are about ¼, for three years running are 1/8 and so on. The odds of beating the average every year for ten years in a row are approximately 1 in 1,024. That is pretty unlikely isn't it?

Therefore a fund manager who beats the average fund performance for ten years in a row must be very good, because the chance of them doing that by luck are only one in more than a thousand, right?

> *The general opinion is that above average performance for even six or seven years in a row is a sign of a good fund manager.*

There are over 6,000 funds in the UK alone. I don't think any of them regularly beat the average every year for ten years, they might do seven or eight out of ten. But let's assume they do it for ten years running.

Remember the lottery, or the birthdays from chapter 8. It is unlikely that *you in particular* will meet somebody who has the same birthday as you in a small crowd, that *you in particular* will win the lottery or that a *particular* fund manager will beat the average ten years in a row. But it is extremely likely that *somebody* will win the lottery, two of the people in a group will have the same birthday or *some* fund manager will beat the average every year for ten years in a row.

> *By luck and blind chance several fund managers ought to beat the average every year for ten years. But none do.*

The problem is that, like picking the lottery winning numbers, you have to pick the fund manager beforehand. The odds of you picking the right one (even if there was a "right one", which there isn't) who could reliably be better than average ten years in a row in the next ten years are apparently more than 1,000 to one against, even if you have as a guide that some of them are lucky enough to have beaten it for the last ten years (which they haven't done anyway).

I'll explain why fund managers, some of whom ought by luck to beat the average regularly don't do it, in a moment. Part of it is to do with the fact that the goals of the fund manager and the investor are different.

> *But for now, the argument I've just made is about risk, it is a calculation of probability (so it is strictly risk) and is about beating the average of other fund managers.*

> That is a theoretical point. What is the practical experience of fund performance compared to actual markets?

First, there are funds available that are called "index tracker" funds. They are very simple in principle, they just buy shares to mimic the relevant index. So if you buy into the fund, you'll effectively have a portion of all the shares that make up the index. Therefore, your investment will perform like the index.

Most funds are "actively managed". The managers buy and sell the shares to include in the fund, using their expertise, judgment, experience, research etc. to "time the market" and buy low and sell high, thus making more money.

Now to real performance.

In one study, the average "managed" fund underperformed the relevant index in seven of nine categories, and one of the remaining two essentially tied the index.

An expert analysis of lots of studies indicates that index funds outperform 75% of actively managed funds over virtually any time period. And half of the remaining 25% of managed funds only outperformed their relevant index by chance.

And that doesn't include the thousands of failed funds that are folded or merged. That is relevant because companies often fold up unsuccessful funds, or merge one fund into another. That way, they can wipe out their really obvious mistakes and pretend that they are doing better than they are.

However, it isn't just about fund performance. There are also charges and transaction costs.

> *Because the "managed funds" are "actively managed" they do a lot more research, trading and boasting about how good they are.*
>
> *You'd think that would mean better performance, but they don't beat the index, they trail it.*
>
> *On the other hand, it does mean they have greater admin costs, more trading costs, more research costs, more bonuses, more adverts.*
>
> *The fact is that the charges on an actively managed fund tend to be about 2% or more higher than an index tracker fund.*
>
> *The performance is usually worse, it certainly isn't consistently better and if any fund is better, it would have to be consistently at least 2% better to justify the extra costs.*

That 2% difference doesn't sound a lot, although you might think that it is a bit much to pay anything extra when the performance is probably worse anyway. But of course, as we saw in the maths chapter, 2% makes quite a difference. Think of the 80% of bonus, and 80% of bonus rate issue.

I did some quick calculations on a £10,000 investment and worked out what the extra 2% did to the final fund (assuming the performance was the same). What do you think it did to the fund over 5, 10 and 15 years?

After 5 years, the difference is £1,411.82. After ten years the difference is £4,348.17 and is up to more than £15,000 after 15 years.

The extra 2% charge for "active management" that doesn't often produce better results before you take off the charges anyway, costs you more money than the total amount you started with over 15 years!

The experts can't actually beat an index most of the time, so they can't and don't often justify their fees.

They know more about it than the public, so is it realistic to think that you can do better on your own?

*We know **somebody** is going to look like an investment genius by pure fluke in the same way as some people will win the lottery.*

But you have to pick the manager beforehand. You don't know which one is going to be lucky, picking the lucky one seems more likely than picking one who is so skilful that they can outperform the index by more than 2% when nobody is that skilful, so the odds are thousands to one against you "beating the index".

As we said, the fund manager has an objective, to beat the index. If they gamble to do it and lose, they are no worse off, if they get lucky and win, they are hailed as a genius. If they just track the index, the question becomes, "what are they paid for" and they probably lose their job. So where is the incentive for them to give up the hunt for the crystal ball and just track the index?

The investors goal isn't (or shouldn't be) to beat the index, it is to get the return they need. The investor is sucked into a gamble on which manager is going to be lucky over the next ten years or whatever period.

Don't gamble on picking the one manager lucky enough to take increasing risks and win – you're more likely to win the lottery!

*Another aspect of **risk** is the "Chinese whispers" effect of the separation of the front men from the "rocket scientists" that I mentioned in an earlier chapter. And it involves the scandal that I also mentioned earlier, that is interesting, but a bit sad.*

The idea that comes from the rocket scientist may be perfectly sound. So it gets used. And the "front men" use it a bit more. Then they add a bit of something else and they give it some spin. And they market it heavily.

Now all the while the rocket scientists know that their basic ideas are sound. What they don't know is that several of their ideas which make some fundamental incompatible assumptions, are all getting put together. Here's an example. As it is sad, I'll tell it like a fairy story so it doesn't seem as awful.

Are you sitting comfortably? Then I'll begin.

Once upon a time, in fairyland, you got tax relief on the interest you paid on a mortgage but not on paying back the capital amount you borrowed. It made sense to leave the interest outstanding, to maximise tax relief (yes, that is tax cart before the reason for investing horse, but as it is a fairy story, suspend disbelief for a bit can't you?).

You also got tax relief on the premiums you paid for certain types of life assurance policy. Some of these policies gave you a tax free sum if you died, and also gave you tax free sum at the end of the policy, say, after 25 years. What's more, you could get ones that paid you the sum at the end plus "bonuses", which was like interest being paid on top of what you were guaranteed.

> *What a great deal; you got tax relief on the payments, tax relief on the interest, then after 25 years the policy pays you a tax free lump sum that pays off the mortgage in one go and gives you some money to spend how you want.*
>
> *And the peasants of fairyland all thought they would live happily ever after in their nice houses.*

These life assurance policies were wonderful. But some people were very sad, because they couldn't afford them, having to pay to get all the bonuses and so on. So the handsome prince (who was, coincidentally, a rocket scientist) realised that if you made the life assurance large enough to pay off the mortgage if you died, but made the investment for a smaller amount, the bonuses would pay the loan off at the end but the policy would be cheaper.

So, say you had a £50,000 mortgage, you could have life assurance of £50,000 in case you died but have a policy that would guarantee £35,000 that, with bonuses, would give you more than £50,000 to pay off the mortgage after 25 years. So the new policies were truly magical. And even more people were going to live happily ever after.

Then the wicked Baron decided to limit the tax relief on mortgage interest, first to only £30,000, then to only basic rate. That meant that the interest cost more so the people couldn't afford so much.

Still the peasants wanted their big houses, so the clever and handsome prince worked out that you could make the assurance policy even cheaper if you calculated the rates differently.

But the wicked Baron first limited, then removed the tax relief on the life assurance policies. This meant that the amount the peasants could pay for the assurance policies would only be enough to pay off the loan if they were very, very lucky and the bonuses were absolutely huge and kept getting bigger.

By this time, of course, the assurance companies had got used to selling the policies, and the peasants had got used to buying them – the status quo effect.

And although the clever, handsome prince knew that the assumptions made for the bonuses were now unbelievably high, the people selling the policies to the peasants in fairyland were so far away from the prince's castle that they hadn't actually realised the ludicrous assumptions. Nor had they connected this with the fact that people might as well pay the mortgage off a bit at a time anyway since there was no advantage now in leaving the capital outstanding and only paying interest.

But the peasants never found out. And then the ogre came and threw them out of their houses because they couldn't pay off their mortgages.

> *If you substitute actuary for prince, chancellor for baron, with profits endowment assurance for the policy with full bonus, low cost endowment for the "magic" policy, the "80% of bonus" issue from chapter 8 for "calculate the rates differently" and people for peasants, you get the basic story of the "endowment sales scandal". Oh, and you substitute, "reality intruding on the theory that things will go on as they are forever and that denying reality means it doesn't happen", for the ogre.*

It doesn't take much for something that is a good idea at one point to get distorted into a really stupid idea; just a few changes in the environment, a few more "tweaks" by the sales people, a few "improvements" by the back room experts. By gradual stages, all of which seem perfectly sensible at the time, the good idea becomes a stupid idea.

You can apply a similar process to that of the endowment scandal to most disasters. Like the credit crisis.

> *People say, in hindsight, "oh stupid bankers, they took too many risks". But there's nothing intrinsically wrong with the idea of a securitised market (parcelling up things, a bit like a unit trust or other collective investment scheme).*
>
> *Similarly, charging higher rates for mortgages for people who are more likely to default is basic banking practice. It was a standing joke 40 years ago that a banker was a person who would lend you exactly as much as you could prove you didn't need.*

Each step, each idea, each twist makes sense on its own. The problem is that by the time banks, investment companies, actuaries, accountants, financiers, venture capitalists, Governments, civil servants, bank employees, sales people, estate agents and Uncle Tom Cobbleigh and all have got involved, all putting their own spin and layer of complexity on it, and each trying to maximise their cut, the cake has not only to be huge (which it was) but growing all the time.

We saw earlier on that Fama, Greenspan and the rest all thought the cake would grow indefinitely and could never shrink. That was their "all swans are white" assumption and it was extremely stupid.

But everybody had their own white swan assumption, lots of people believed Fama, Greenspan etc. that property could never go down. It is the cult of the expert, they are idiotic experts, but what does that make everybody who believed they could do the impossible and predict the future accurately and that reality can be ignored? Like the media, most still believe it. Do you?

Reading

Part of the risk inherent in "managing funds" (whether it is DIY or via a professional manager) is trying to "read" what the market will do.

Investment in markets is theoretically easy. You just buy at the bottom, and sell at the top.

If it is so easy, why can't the professional fund managers with all their computers and rocket scientists etc. do it reliably?

If market prices were often irrational and if market returns were as predictable as some critics have claimed, then professionally managed investment funds should easily be able to outdistance a passive index fund.

Malkiel 2005

The problem is that you have to time the investments just right, which seems to be simple in theory and pretty much impossible in practice. If you time it right, if you predict the future movements, you make money. If you get it wrong, you might win some, you might lose some. If you get it very wrong, there is a black swan, or you are unlucky, etc. you might lose a great deal.

It sounds as if it ought to be possible. That with enough research, intelligence and experience, you could predict what was going to happen and time things right. Nobody can do it in reality, and in chapter 7 we saw that it seems to be impossible in theory as well, but is reality as powerful as the desire to predict the future? What do you think?

I said in a previous chapter that I'd talk about the time the "predict and maximise profits" approach went wrong and nearly caused the crash early. This is a good time for it.

In markets you get "derivatives". They are "derived" from actual shares. They include ways to trade so that you get a guaranteed buying or selling price at some point in the future, "put" and "call" options etc.

You'll remember that we used to do this by barter, but modern markets are a lot more sophisticated. If you're trying to buy enough wheat to feed a city for a week and the seed for the wheat hasn't been sown yet, how do you work out how much it is worth? So pricing becomes really important.

The purpose of doing the price calculations went through three stages.

Originally they were for things like feeding cities.

Then a way to reduce risk. You can "hedge your bets" for example, having an option to buy or sell something at a particular price in the future and balance this against the assets you actually own.

Finally they were a speculation, effectively, gambling on your guesses about the future, as in the common idea of a "hedge fund".

When you "hedge your bets" you are making sure that whatever happens (which you can't predict) you have something left. It is a "lose on the roundabouts, gain on the swings" principle.

That seems sensible to me, as nobody knows what is going to happen.

But another view is that it is wasteful, if you predict accurately, you can gain on the roundabouts *and* on the swings.

Lots of people now use this idea and think the losing side can be eliminated. They try to work it so that they don't have any money invested in the losing part of the equation, it is all a winner. If the market goes the way they expect, they make more than they would have made if they hedged. They get lucky and win. So they do it again, and again they are lucky. It worked for about 20 years to 2008.

They assume they are geniuses, and think they can control and predict the way the market will go. They bet on it rising, it rises. They bet on it falling, it falls. They make lots of money. They reason that they can get out when they want to (just like gambling addicts) and keep doing it. Then they get it badly wrong. They haven't balanced their bets, they have no "hedge" because they saw that as being a "loss" instead of a precaution. They lose on both sides, have no investment rising, they are bankrupt! Think it can't happen to experts?

It is really helpful to be able to price derivatives accurately, but it is extremely difficult. Then two really smart guys, Fischer Black and Myron Scholes, worked out a theory of how to do it. This was developed further into the Black Scholes options pricing model and in 1997 Robert Merton won the Nobel Prize for economics together with Scholes, (Black, sadly having died before the prize was awarded and Nobel Prizes not being given posthumously).

This was really clever. Richard Thaler (whom we met as the author of "Nudge") and Werner De Bondt (who was the analyst of the "75% of funds trail the index and of the ones that don't half keep up only by luck") said, in 1995:

"The Black Sholes formula serves admirably well both as a characterisation of option prices in a rational world and as a description of real prices"

Of course, since it was so good, people had to use it, and in 1994 Scholes set up a company with a former trader, John Merriweather, called Long Term Capital Markets (LTCM). An experienced trader plus a genius and Nobel Lauriate, with a sure fire system, it couldn't fail.

They made immense profits. Everybody was impressed and "sophisticated investors", including many large investment banks, flocked in putting up $1.3 billion.

And then it started to unravel. There are various excellent explanations of why, although everybody gives a slightly different reason for what went wrong; the ice cube melted, everybody is sure they know what shape it was etc. But anyway, the wheels came off and in 1998 LTCM was on the edge of defaulting on its obligations. Alan Greenspan and the US Federal Reserve stepped in to stave off what is described as a "systemic crisis in the world financial system".

Notice the similarity to the events of 2008? The Federal Reserve put together a package of about $3.5 billion (getting on for three times what LTCM has been worth) and basically bailed it out to stop the whole system failing ten years earlier than it actually did.

It may not be true, and I can't prove it, but I wouldn't be at all surprised if, in 2008, Mr Greenspan and others thought ,"Oh no, not again, I'm not going to bail them out this time, they've got to learn to be a bit more responsible" and delayed that little bit longer before stepping in to try to stop the crash.

Some say if they had stepped in earlier it would have stopped, others that it would have made no difference. I don't think it matters. If it wasn't 1998 and wasn't 2008 it was going to happen sometime, because people can't resist thinking they can predict the future and that they can "read" the market in their crystal ball! And since they are "experts", people (particularly media people) believe them.

Ignore him your majesty, he's mad, our scientists have proved the world is flat!

BRIDaL

This is way to think about investment that fits in with what we know about human thinking and decision making, including overconfidence and our other habits and abilities.

It is not a "get rich quick scheme" or a guaranteed way to make money in the markets – and it doesn't tell you what to invest in.

It's a way to approach financial decisions that make sense in reality.

Balance

Required return

Indexing

Diversification and

Leave it alone!

Balance

First, rid yourself of any notion that there are "safe" investments and "risky" investments, they are all risky.

The future is uncertain, so the "Risk" is in the balance, not in the investment itself.

Many people look at the guaranteed return on gilts, "guaranteed bonds", National Savings products, bank deposits etc. and think: "ah, that's safe". People also have "available" the stock market crashes, the bubbles etc. and they think "the stock market is risky".

Remember that we don't like having to choose between many, complex options and we decide quickly. So we simplify. We say "this option is risky, this one is safe". The conclusion is, "I want safety, so I need X which is safe and not Y which is 'risky'". No, *it is all risky*. It is all uncertain.

The risk of a "safe investment", for example, cash in the bank up to the guarantee limit, is usually that with inflation you will lose money.

The risk is actually, expressed as a probability, a certainty. You *will* lose money (remember the money illusion, we don't deal with inflation very well). By the time the bank has loaned the money out, paid its administration expenses and taken its profits, the amount it can pay you cannot possibly give you a long term profit in real terms.

Does that mean that money shouldn't go into "safe" investments?

> *No, it means you have to think about:*
> *What return you want*
> *What your overall risk is to achieve the return you want.*

If you chase the "best" return, you are trying to make it all a winner. If you do that, you have to predict what will happen, and unbalance your investments to take advantage of your guesses being right. If it turns out you have guessed wrongly, you lose on both sides, not win on both.

That is your risk. You have turned it into a gamble. Even if you pick all "safe" investments, you are piling up risk on one side.

You actually need to diversify, which we'll come to later.

The aim is to make profits *all* the time, not to prove you can guess right *most* of the time.

A big problem is that people still insist they can **Read** the market.

I have great admiration for people who follow what is the one method of investing (other than actually using decent psychology!) that comes close to working, value investing. That is geared to finding the true "value" of shares, rather than following fashion, "hot tips" etc. It means you don't have to "time" the market, you work out the value and let the market eventually "correct" to your true valuation, at which point you make money.

As I mentioned earlier, it is hard to find the true value, even the people who run the company don't really know that, so how can an outsider? But in theory, the value is calculable.

> *The big problem is that in fact it isn't calculable and anyway, stock markets are not about the real "value" of a company.*

Imagine a celebrity talent show where you get a prize for voting for the eventual winner. The eventual winner will be the one who gets the most votes. You happen to like contestant A. You know that your friends prefer contestants B or C. Will you vote for A, knowing that they probably won't win and you won't win the prize? Vote for B or C, knowing that they are more popular and therefore more likely to win? Or vote for, say F, because you've read that they make huge charity donations and you think that most people will like them and vote for them?

> *Whatever you do, notice that you don't care about who is the "best" any more, you are thinking about "who do other people think is the best", or more accurately "who are they going to vote for"? The real "value" is irrelevant, you're trying to read the mind of everybody else, work out who will win and vote accordingly.*

To buy low and sell high while avoiding having to "time" the market precisely you have to work out the "true value". That is hard enough anyway (probably impossible to do accurately). But you aren't even doing that, you are trying evaluate the reaction of some people to what they think other people think about the market and your view of whether those people think the market thinks the same as you think. I think!

Pound cost averaging – for balance.

This is a method to avoid having to "time" investments. It is handy if you have some idea of the "true value" of the investment because it makes the system work even better. However, it isn't essential.

I'm not going to give complicated technical explanations, if you don't know how to do it, get a good advisor, but I'll give an example of how I used it with a client in a moment.

First, imagine you are buying into a fund. Remember, it could be a tracker fund, one of shares, property, gilts, and all sorts of things or it could be an actively managed fund; it could even be direct shares.

Let's say that the fund has a price per unit of £10. If you invest £1,000 you buy 100 units. If the fund goes up steadily for five years, to £20 unit price, you'd have £2,000. That is the "gamble, time the market" way.

The risk is that if the fund value goes down during the five years, you are operating at a loss. You've paid out at a price of £10, and until prices go back up above £10, you're losing (and you have to pay the fund costs as well!)

Now imagine that instead of putting all £1,000 into the fund at the start, you spread it out so you put in £200 at the start and £200 each year following. If values just go steadily up, you are buying at an increasing price each year, so you won't buy so many units, so you won't make so much profit. That is, effectively, your "hedge", if you gamble and win, you win more, if you hedge and win, you don't make so much.

However, you will still have made a profit. If you "hedge" your bets with pound cost averaging you don't do as well if you guess right. But if you guess wrong, and fund values fall, you can still end up with a profit on your hedging, but the gamble that goes wrong loses you money. Look at the table below.

	Pound cost average		Purchase at start	
Year	Price	Units bought	Price	Units bought
Start	10	20	10	100
Start year 2	15	13.33		
Start year 3	12	16.67		
Start year 4	5	40		
Start year 5	8	25		
End year 5 total	10	115	10	100
Total value	1,150		1,000	

In this (imaginary but typical) example, you make £150 over five years, even though the price started at £10, went up a bit, down a bit and finished at 10. You've made a 15% profit.

If you want to chase the "best return", you can gamble on the prices going up steadily by putting in all the money at the start. If you guess right you make more money, but if you guess wrong (as above) you either lose or don't make as much.

Pound cost averaging doesn't guarantee you a profit, nothing does, remember it is all risky.

But it gives more balance, it helps to stop you getting into a gamble on predicting what the market will do and without an operative crystal ball that is usually a good thing.

You get the same effects if you don't have a big lump sum to invest at the start, you just put in regular amounts anyway. Remember the example of John and Jill in chapter 8. Putting away regular small amounts early on, with the magic of compound interest, means you can end up with a lot of money. So even if you can't put away masses, it is still worth using regular contributions and "drip feeding" the money for longer term investment into markets. It gives you the potential for building up money without the same gamble of putting in one big amount (that you may not have anyway).

I said I'd give an example of a real client.

When I was an IFA I had a client who was recently divorced. She needed an income, she was trying to get a job but hadn't worked for several years (she'd been a full time mother), still had the children to look after and wasn't going to be sure of getting longer term financial support from her ex-husband.

This was a time of high inflation. If we put her money into "safe" investments, she would have been using up the capital to live on (the interest wouldn't be enough) and she would have been going backwards with inflation reducing her money further.

If we put the money into the stock market, that would be great if it went up, but if it fell when she needed the money, she'd be wiped out, and what was she going to live on in the meantime?

I tried to look at the balance of the investments (without thinking of it in those terms at that time). I also looked at what she actually wanted, and needed (as in chapters 2 and 3). I reasoned that as inflation was high and interest rates were high, then probably annuity rates would be high. We'll talk a bit more about annuities in chapter 10, but basically this type meant that for a lump sum she got a monthly income paid out for five years, and because the rates were good, the client could pay a lump sum of money, get an adequate income to live on and some extra money to invest each year.

I could then put the extra money for investment into something called a PEP (which was a bit like an ISA, a way to hold shares free of tax). The client could have enough to live on, net of tax, could try to find work, get a part time job, build up her hours as the children became less dependent and after 5 years it was likely that the money we invested would leave her with a similar amount of capital (in real terms allowing for inflation) as she'd started with.

If she built up her job income she wouldn't need so much of the income from the annuity, could invest more of it and that would boost the amount she got back at the end.

> *Think of that as part of the "adaptability" in the CHEAP SMART PLAN mnemonic for goals in chapter 3.*

By way of comparison, the rate that the "bonds" some colleagues had tried to sell would have needed to grow at about 12% each year to give the client her money back (and wouldn't have given her enough income anyway) while the PEP needed to grow at only about 8% because of the preferential tax, lower charges etc. I was lucky with the result, it worked out even better than I thought it could because the funds kept going up and she had the income for five years and got more back in real terms than she'd started with as well.

The point is that I could have been unlucky and had a lot of things go wrong (inflation going up or down, stock markets rising or falling, interest rates rising or falling) and she would still have had the income and only a big market fall just at the five year point would have been a real problem. Even then, she might have been able to live on her earnings until the PEP value recovered, and that really bad luck in the market was going to be a problem irrespective of what we'd done.

My point isn't to show how great I am, it's to demonstrate that, something that isn't necessarily seen as "safe" (a stock market investment) used intelligently can provide as safe an investment to meet the actual need as it was possible to do. I didn't have to time the market or predict it, and I didn't need to be lucky, I just did things sensibly.

The post-script is that I was criticised by my employers for not making enough commission! Then I was told that somebody from head office wanted to talk to me about "risky and non conventional" investments, because I hadn't sold a pre-packaged product. I duly met the "compliance officer" from head office and had a bit of a job to explain how it worked. When he finally understood it (because I showed him from his own figures that it worked better than any alternative) he looked a bit thoughtful and told me I didn't have anything to worry about.

A week or two later I got a call asking me if I thought we could "productise" the annuity and PEP combination! Of course, it was too late, there was a particular set of circumstances of interest rates, inflation etc. that made it work for that particular client and her requirements and the "time window" had passed. There was a specific reason why doing things in a particular way made what might otherwise be seen as risky, the safest option. But I'm not sure to this day that head office really understood what happened or why "their idea" of a new *product* wouldn't work!

Required rate of Return

I've already hammered home the point that if you don't know what you want, it is impossible to get it.

Sort out your values, read the archer analogy, work out what will make you happy. Then sort out your financial goals. At that point, you have an idea what you want your money to do for you, you know how you want to use it. So you can determine what return you require.

If you start with "maximise the return", your money is using you, you get drawn into bigger and bigger gambles and eventually you lose. And you never even knew what you were after.

I'll mention here that if you are assessing advisors, avoid any who will tell you without your asking, "what is a good investment", because that is a meaningless question. It depends on what you want to get from it and when and how much you have as spare funds to achieve it. If you have the idea, or are given the advice, not to "take too many risks" or "don't play too safe", remember that the risk is not determined by the investment, but by the balance. The usual measure of "risk" (actually a "proxy" or substitute for risk) is volatility, the proportional amount the share goes up or down. This is measured as a standard deviation, which isn't appropriate to something like a stock market that isn't normally distributed. Volatility of a share isn't the same as its "risk" anyway.

Your risk is determined by what you want (your target) and what you have to do to achieve it your required rate, not by the investment (the bow) that you might use. And your investments are "risky" in terms of balance, not volatility.

In order to control the risk, to get the balance that suits you, you have to know what you can invest and what you want and when. After that you can work out the appropriate balance because you can work out what return you need to go from where you are to where you want to be.

Indexing

I said in the earlier part of the chapter that index tracker funds seem to outperform, and are certainly cheaper than, the alternatives. If you bear in mind that you don't have to time the market and you can use pound cost averaging, they are, quite honestly, the best option for most people

It is human nature to think that you are, like Jose Mourinho, "the special one", that you can time the market, predict the future, beat the experts, outperform the index etc. But the evidence is that you can't.

If you really think you can, fine. Have a go, and keep really good records. In fact, it is fun (and instructive) to work with a friend, record all your dealing costs, transactions etc. and see how well you do over five to ten years. It is more fun with two and you tend to keep one another honest about your losses! Most of the professionals can't beat the index reliably but I genuinely hope you do.

But do remember the lottery, somebody will win, but the laws of maths say it is several thousand (or million) to one against it being you.

As Scotty said in Star Trek:
"You canna change the laws of physics."
And you canna change the laws of maths either!

As a final comment on this point, if you want a master investor as a role model, you need look no further than one of the richest men in the world, Warren Buffet.

"Most investors, both institutional and individual, will find that the best way to own common stocks [shares] is through an index fund that charges minimal fees. Those following this path are sure to beat the net results (after fees and expenses) of the great majority of investment professionals."

Warren Buffett—Berkshire Hathaway Annual Report, 1996.

Diversification

There's a lot of misunderstanding of this, people tend to think it just means having a lot of different funds, or having not just shares but a variety of things like works of art, gold, property, race-horses and so on. They also misunderstand why it is usually a bad idea not to diversify.

You remember from chapter 7 that members of one family have heights that are correlated; if one person is tall, the others will probably be tall. Two people from different families will have heights that are not correlated, one being tall won't affect whether the other one is tall. I can't see how heights would be negatively correlated (it would mean that if one person is tall, it would suggest that another person will probably be short) so let's look at some investments as examples.

Diversification isn't just, "have lots of different stuff". It is about investments that are not correlated or even better, are negatively correlated.

Take shares in two oil companies. They are probably correlated. If one goes up or down, the other is more likely to go up or down as well because the things that push one company's price up or down will tend to push the other company's price in the same direction. That's like heights within the family.

Cash deposits (money in the bank) and shares are usually held to be pretty well uncorrelated, although if interest rates go down (meaning that you get less interest on your cash in the bank) then borrowing is cheaper so it might help companies borrow to expand, so shares might go up a bit. That's a bit like heights within people who are unrelated (but might be distant cousins or something!)

I won't give a technical explanation (talk to a financial advisor or read one of the books recommended) but gilts and cash are pretty well negatively correlated. If interest rates go up, you get more interest paid from your bank money. But at the same time your gilts probably go down in value. If interest rates go down, you get less interest from the bank, but your gilts probably increase in value. So as one goes up, the other goes down.

The "unbalanced" solution is that if you guess that interest rates will go up, you put all your money in cash and are right, you'll do well because your money will earn more. If you are wrong and interest rates go down, you will lose out because you'll get a worse rate of interest than you thought. You get the reverse effect if you go into gilts, you guess rates will go down, they do, your gilts rise in price; but if you get it wrong and rates rise, the gilts look less attractive and fall in price.

This is, in simple terms, what is traditionally thought of as "diversification", having a good spread of shares and a balance of shares, gilts and cash. The shares are, largely, uncorrelated with the gilts and cash, and the cash is negatively correlated with the gilts. Of course, the shares will all tend to correlate in some situations. A major market crash will pull all the shares down and a "bull market" will push them up, but news about new taxes on retail that will affect, say, shares in a supermarket, will not have the same effect as on shares in a shipping company, and news of change in oil supply will have different effects on an oil company and a consumer of oil such as an energy producing company.

Whether interest rates go up or down, whether there is good news of oil prices, retail stores, foreign mining or whatever, there is a reasonable prospect that something you've invested in will go well and balance up the things that don't go so well. It is the more practical end of the general principal of balancing your investments.

> *A big misconception about "diversity" is that a "volatile" share is "risky" in that it will go up or down sharply depending on the news.*
>
> *Technically, the "volatility" (worked out using the wrong maths, on the wrong data, etc.) stands as proxy for "risk", but it isn't even close.*
>
> *It isn't risky if the same news that will cause it to drop like a stone will cause something else you own to rise like a rocket.*
>
> *That is the point of diversity. You want your investments to react differently to the same events, to be negatively correlated.*

I'm not going to give a technical explanation of how to do it, that isn't what this book is about and there are several books that explain it really well. The one I'd recommend you read if you want to understand what diversity is (or you want to ask intelligent questions of anybody you hire) is "The long and the short of it" by John Kay.

He shows what diversity really is and how it works throughout the book, but particularly in chapter 7. There he shows how a share that unthinking "experts" would class as "risky" because it was volatile, Mr. Kay could invest in totally safely because he diversified properly.

By diversifying properly he could obtain balance so that, whatever happened in the market, he would make a profit. It might not be quite as great a profit as if he gambled and got it right, but he was smart enough to avoid having to gamble and risk getting it wrong!

I've tended to talk about funds, particularly index tracking funds, because for the vast majority of people they are much better. You've got some immediate diversification because you've got a fund that invests in a whole range of companies and if it is an index tracker it is potentially going to invest across a lot of different industries. You can also get that diversification in funds that invest in foreign markets (an example are some Exchange Traded Funds, ETFs) which give you more spread rather than being entirely in the UK, for example.

But get advice, learn what you're doing and look for real diversity, not just buying "lots of funds" because that is just like buying "lots of different stuff", it isn't really diversification. Similarly think about "geographical diversification". Again, you will probably be better off with a diversity of areas and not counting on "it is obvious that X area will grow", and trying to "read" markets.

Apart from funds you can do it through shares themselves. There are some good books on that, notably John Kay's and Peter Lynch's. But in general, I'd suggest that you really shouldn't go for direct share investment as part of a properly diversified portfolio unless you have most things covered already and you are either

a) putting the icing on the cake to get some diversification you can't get from tracker funds or

b) using money you've set aside to play with because you can afford to lose it and you will get some fun out of having a go (in which case it is the activity that is the goal and any profit is secondary).

> *There is an old joke about share investment, "how do you make a small fortune in the markets?"*
>
> *The answer, "start with a large fortune". So do your preparation.*

Understand, this isn't a way to become an overnight millionaire, it is a way to get a similar results to a tracker (and better than a managed fund), but possibly slightly better than a tracker because you potentially save on dealing costs by doing it yourself, and can get more "real" diversification. If you are interested or you get a real sense of satisfaction out of it, then done sensibly (that is, trying to get a reasonable return whatever happens, not to "break the bank" if you guess the future right), it can be both profitable and fun.

Do remember, if you are going to invest in shares, you still need diversification. You will also, almost certainly, need to work out the "value" of shares, which as we've seen is very hard to do in practice.

It also means that you have to have the courage to wait for the "value to assert itself". That might take five years, or ten or twenty. Some of Lynch's shares, for example, went up phenomenally, but not for years after he bought them. They languished, bobbing up and down for eight or ten years before taking off. And sometimes, they never did take off (some "fell off" instead).

> *Again, it isn't a recipe for overnight success; it is a long term investment philosophy. I'd only suggest you use it if you have enough spare money to be able to wait for the market to realise that you were right about the share's true value and for your prediction to come true. That could take years, and in the end the market might decide you were wrong, and your money disappears.*

The point in both cases, and with any funds you look at, including trackers, is that you are investing for the long term. You are trying to make a reasonable profit on the back of shares rising over the long term. You aren't trying to make a quick buck by diving in and out of the market. "Day trading", swapping in and out in a day so the deals are in one accounting period, looks like a way to make a fast million. It is, for the very rare individual who stays lucky long enough.

For most people, it is a way to lose a fast million they don't have. Remember how you can make a small fortune!

and Leave it alone

That leads to another piece of advice, don't look at your holdings too often, certainly not daily or weekly. Who cares what the shares (or funds) you are going to hold for five years are doing day to day?

I'll quote Warren Buffet again,

"W*e don't need a daily quote on our 100% position in See's or HH Brown [companies of which Buffet's Berkshire Hathaway Group own 100%] why, then, should we need a quote on our 7% interest in Coke?*"

Buffet 1993.

Since Warren Buffet isn't bothered, (he's actually said that once he's bought, he wouldn't care if the market closed for a couple of years) do you really think that you are a better investor and can out think him?

As a final note, you'll probably ignore everything I've said and chase "the best return", believe in "risky" and "safe" investments, ignore your real values and goals, gamble on your predictions, try to "beat the index" and check your investments daily (and trade lots in order to "buy low and sell high").

The fact is you lose by doing it, that is reality.

But people will still try, that is human nature.

I'd just suggest that you remember that for every gambler in games of chance who wins, millions lose.

The market (futures, options, property, bullion, stock whatever) is basically a gamble in a game of chance. You might think you can predict it and have a perfect system, but so does everybody who goes to Vegas and every racetrack tipster who tries to handicap the ponies!

And after the summary, let's have a look at another way to "hedge our bets" – insurance.

Summary:

- Don't ignore reality, what you want or expect or would have liked to have happened doesn't matter – only what does happen.
- Nobody can predict accurately – the media might desperately want to have a fortune teller, but they don't exist.
- Remember the three Rs.
- Look at the return you require and remember that an investor and an investment fund manager have different objectives.
- People misunderstand risk – risk is mathematical, the market isn't, it is uncertain and that is not calculable. The only risk you can calculate is the strong chance that you won't beat the index.
- Reading the market is impossible, Nobel Prize winners can't do it, professional traders can't do it. Trying to get all wins and no losses isn't clever investing, it is brainless gambling.
- At least think about BRIDaL as an idea.
- Risk is not in "risky" or "safe" investments, it is in balance. Chasing all "upside" is not a balanced approach.
- Market values are not about real value, they are a talent contest.
- Use pound cost averaging if you can.
- Look at your required return, it tells you what risks you need to take.
- Use indexation, if you don't understand index tracker funds, get good, professional advice on them.

- Diversification isn't about "lots of stuff" it is about non-correlated, or even better, negatively correlated investments. Read "The long and the short of it".
- Don't keep peeking at investments and don't fiddle with them once bought!
- I don't want to be rude, but you are not "the special one" and it is millions to one against you gambling and winning!

High risk insurance

Insurance, when it is worth it, when it isn't and how it works. The chapter starts with the basic principles, and then explains how you can decide whether a policy is worthwhile for you.

Insurance is, in essence, simple.

It's a way to exchange a known cost (the premium you pay) for a potentially calamitous loss (the sum assured that the insurer pays you if the event you've insured against happens). When I did my first exams (back in the late 70's), this was the classic example:

In a country village there are ten farmers who each have a pig. They live well because a piglet only costs £1, but by the time they've fattened it up for market the pig is worth £9.

The trouble is, if the pig dies it obviously won't grow and they probably can't sell the meat because it may be diseased. For years, most of the farmers make a good living, but sometimes one or two are unlucky, their pig dies and they see their children go hungry.

One year somebody new comes to the village. She works out that on average, one farmer has a pig die each year (it might be one, it might be two, some years it is none, but on average it is one a year).

She offers the farmers a deal. If they each pay her £1 every year, she will guarantee that she'll buy them a fattened pig if their pig dies during the year. It makes sense, they are guaranteed to get £9 whether their pig dies or not and at a cost of only £1.

They know that they will get £7 profit whatever happens (£9 for the sale of the fattened pig, less £1 to buy the piglet at the start and £1 for the insurance), so their children will definitely not go hungry

They all agree. At the start of the year they each pay £1 to this lady, and sure enough during the year, one farmer has a pig die. The lady buys him a new pig for £9 and gives it to him. The lady gets £10 in premiums (£1 from each of the ten farmers), pays out £9 for the pig, and she makes £1 profit for arranging the whole thing.

That's it. I said it was simple and I could leave it right there.

However, you'll have noticed that it assumes quite a lot. It ignores fluctuations in pig price, inflation, unexpected problems or advances (such as cures for pig diseases or outbreaks of swine flu), the lady having enough cash to buy four or five pigs in one year if lots die – all sorts of things.

However, there are a few basics to note:

It is worth it for the farmers if the loss of a pig is a potential calamity and the premium is relatively small.

It is worth it for the insurer if there are adequate data to be confident what the risk is (remember in chapter 7, you need to have good enough data to work out probabilities).

Therefore, the premium has to be small enough to be worthwhile as a regular expense for the farmer, but big enough to cover the risk to the insurer and give them a profit margin.

If the premium is too much it isn't worth the farmers' money and they shouldn't take part.

If it is too low the insurer doesn't have the cash flow to deal with bad years and still make a profit, so they shouldn't offer the insurance.

As an aid to working out whether insurance is worth it, think about it from the insurer's point of view. There's a chance of the event happening (the house burning down, the pig dying) etc. Nobody knows exactly what that is (remember chapter 7) but it is possible to make a fair estimate because good data are available about most events to be insured (like pig death, fires, people of different ages dying etc.).

If they estimate that the chance of loss is, say, 1 in 1,000 and multiply that by what they'd pay (sum assured) if there is a loss, they get what's called the "pure premium". But they have to cover not just the claims, but admin costs, their profit, plus a margin in case they get it slightly wrong. They have to charge more than the minimum to cover the risk of the loss they are insuring.

So, for you, it is about calamity; losing your house, your life etc. (life is a bit odd, because obviously you're not around to deal with the calamity, so we'll look at that in a minute), and we've got a bit of a hunter gatherer situation in that it is wise to be "loss averse".

> *According to economic theory, insurance shouldn't exist, because it can never be a good deal. The premium you have to pay must be more than the chance of you needing to claim times the amount you'd get back if you did claim.*

Houses, cars, life, whatever else you may wish to insure, all work on the basis that if an insurer offers a policy, they have got to be making enough to ensure it is not worthwhile for you unless it allows you to deal with a calamity you couldn't cope with otherwise or get some other benefit than money.

> *A real disaster is worth paying the inevitable "over the odds" premium for.*
>
> *If it isn't going to cause a disaster, then paying the premium cannot be financially worthwhile and insuring against something that is only an inconvenience not a calamity only makes sense if it brings you peace of mind or something else that isn't directly equivalent to money, but is more valuable to you.*
>
> *That's really all you need to know, in theory, about insurance!*

I mentioned having good data. If you have data that form a regular pattern, that doesn't change too much (unlike markets) you can build up a good "table of expectations" or a distribution curve even if it isn't strictly a "normal" distribution.

Take life assurance as an example. If you have lots of data for how many people die, at what ages, what gender, by what cause etc. you can work out what proportion of people are likely to die each year. And people don't change that much, what killed us a thousand years ago (like plague) might not kill us now, but we'll still die of something (perhaps heart disease, which killed people thousands of years ago too, only not as much because we didn't have a lousy diet then!) and we can reliably work out how many people are likely to die in a given period, and make good predictions based on their age, gender etc.

*This doesn't tell you **who** will die. Like the lottery, some people will win, in life some will die, you can work out odds and roughly **how many** people will win, die or whatever. But you don't know **which people are which**. It just gives you a pretty reliable estimate of how many people in a particular category will die in a given period.*

If you smoke, for example, the figures will show that for people of your age, sex and so on (so all other things that we can think of apart from smoking are the same), more people who smoke die than people who don't smoke. Say that means that 5 people per thousand die who smoke, and only 3 per thousand die who don't. It doesn't mean that a specific smoker will die young, we've all met the chap who has smoked 40 capstan full strength from the age of 12 and is still healthy at 90. It means that, other things being equal, more people who smoke are likely to die over a given period than people who don't.

This is all the insurers need. They work out what the chance of dying is (5 in 1,000, 3 in 1,000 or whatever), and that figure is based on the evidence of hundreds of thousands of deaths. That chance is multiplied by the amount they have to pay out, their expenses, margin and profit are added and there is the premium.

In fact, from the insurer's point of view, it works out slightly better than this because the information on deaths they work on is obviously in the past. If, as tends to happen, medical science finds better ways to treat illnesses, not so many people actually die in the future as you would expect from the data of the past. There is an extra bit of profit, they don't have to pay out as often as they expected when they set the premium.

Of course, if things go the other way, it causes a problem. When AIDS hit the insurance market a couple of decades ago, there was near panic. For years the life insurance companies had worked on the assumption that life expectancy will rise over the years. So they always had that extra profit from less people dying in future than would be expected from the data of the past. Suddenly, it looked as if many *more* people would die, they would probably be younger, and the insurers could expect huge numbers of death claims from groups where past data suggested that they would have very few claims.

Any change in medical technology, epidemics such as swine flu that would kill off pigs in our initial example, cultural trends towards or away from things like smoking etc. that affects the incidence of claims will have an impact on premiums.

This description is obviously very much simplified. The people who work these sort of things out for insurance companies are actuaries. They have to take into account inflation, all the odds of various different things happening, the claims experience, the likely future and so on. They are basically solving very complex equations with dozens of unknowns. Each of the unknowns depends on several assumptions. As we saw in chapter 7, that introduces some problems in theory and, as we saw in chapter 8 (in the anecdote about the endowment policies), these sort of predictions cause problems in practice.

By the way, I mentioned an annuity in the last chapter. That was a temporary annuity (because it is "temporary", only paid for a limited period). The more common ones in connection with retirement incomes are usually called simply "annuities", but technically, they are life annuities. They are a life assurance in reverse. You are paying money to get a guaranteed income in case you live so long that your savings run out while you are still alive. It's insurance against outliving your capital.

Because women tend to live longer than men, the life assurance rates for women tend to be lower (the women are less likely to die, so the assurance company have to pay out less frequently). However, an annuity for a woman is probably going to have to last longer, which means the assurance company have to have more money to be sure of keeping up the payments for longer, so annuity rates for women give a lower income for an amount of purchase price than they do for men.

Whether you are talking about life assurance or annuities, there are lots of assumptions that have to be made. And you don't have good data for them because they are unpredictable. When you've made the assumptions and taken into account dozens of different variables you have to do incredibly complex calculations. So the actuaries need to be amazingly good at working out different possibilities and keeping the insurer safe. That led to a saying:

"*ask most people what do two and two equal, they will say 'four'. Ask a mathematician, they will say 'plus or minus four'. Ask an actuary, they will say 'what do you want it to equal'*"!

So don't try to do the maths for yourself. Just remember that the insurance company have the data and they will set a premium that allows them to make a profit, so you cannot "win" any more than you can in a casino. All you are trying to do is to use the insurance to protect yourself from calamity.

After I wrote this the European Court of Justice (ECJ) decided that men and women were identical, presumably because they've never learned to read, or look at the pictures in a biology textbook.

So from December 2012 women pay more for life insurance than they should, men get less annuity than they should and women pay more for car insurance (which we'll come to in a moment) than they should. In theory, some rates will come down to compensate, but as the insurers are unsure what it will all mean and have to play safe, need to reprint the literature, spend a lot of expensive time and money recalculating, masses of money will be lost and you will pay for it. Don't complain to me, complain to the ECJ. The "identity" element they've proved is that, male or female, the ECJ members are identically stupid and have identical lack of contact with the world outside their tiny, demented minds.

It's similar for other insurances. If there are enough data on fires, car thefts etc. you can construct the same sort of tables or distribution curves and perform the same sort of calculations and work out what premium to charge.

For example, if you're a teenage boy wanting car insurance, as I once was, you will pay a huge premium because teenage boys tend to have a lot of accidents (the "claims experience" is bad and the insurers know the chances of having to pay claims is high). The insurers don't know *which* particular teenage boys will have accidents, they just know that a high proportion will, so although *you* know you won't have an accident (you're human, therefore convinced you're better than average, etc.) you will be tarred with the same brush as other boys and pay a high premium to insure your car! As you will, from December 2012, if you're a girl!

As you get older, the tables suggest that you become safer and your premium falls. It doesn't mean every older driver is safer than every younger one, if it did Top Gear wouldn't be worth watching! It just means that, on average, older drivers have fewer accidents than younger ones and the insurer is only worried about the amount they have to pay. As are the ECJ, who are apparently fine with discrimination on grounds of age.

> *It's the same with "no-claims bonus", fitting smoke alarms, better locks on the doors etc. If something makes the chances of a claim lower, the insurers tend to encourage it with lower premiums as it reduces their chances of having to pay out.*
>
> *Do remember, however, that the insurer will still build in their profit margin etc. so it is never going to be worth insuring (in financial terms) unless it prevents a calamity, or unless it gives you something other than money such as peace of mind.*

The alternative to insuring is to "self insure". What it means is that instead of paying money to the insurance company so they will pay you if you have a loss, you save the money yourself and build up a fund to pay for any losses. I'll give you a couple of examples to show how this might work.

I've already said that Diane and I like books. We've got huge numbers of them. If our house was burgled, I can't see somebody stealing the books. They might take the TV, computer etc. easy stuff to carry and fairly valuable individually, but they aren't going to try to remove several hundredweight of books that aren't individually worth much. So if theft was the only consideration, we wouldn't bother with contents insurance.

If we would have to pay £250 or so each year for contents insurance and put that money into a high interest account instead of paying a premium, we'd have over £2,500 in 10 years, more than enough to replace all the electrical goods that might be stolen. If that is the premium the insurance company charge, the odds must be pretty good that we won't get burgled more than once in 10 years. So we're better off not having contents insurance. If we were burgled this year, true, we might lose say, £1,500 but that is an inconvenience, not a calamity. Over the next ten or fifteen years we'd save the premiums we would have paid, and in the end we'll have more money than we would if we paid for insurance.

But that isn't the whole story. It might be very unlikely the house will catch fire and even if it does it probably won't destroy everything in the house. The premium doesn't seem to allow much for that, so obviously the insurance company (with all their good data that I don't have) thinks it is unlikely. But if it did burn down and all the books were destroyed by fire or smoke damage, that would be a calamity. We'd want to replace them and that would cost a huge amount of money, more than we'd save and more than we'd be able to find at short notice. So we insure.

Apart from the books, we've also got cats. They are very important to us so we make sure they are healthy. That means vets bills. We could insure them. But most of the regular check-ups, vaccinations and so on are not covered by insurance. And with multiple cats our premiums would be, say, £100 per month. Sometimes one of the cats is ill and needs special care. We once had a bill for about £850 that we could have got back from the insurers if we insured. But those bills don't come along all the time.

We might go for three years, during which we would have paid about £3,500 in premiums for insurance, then we get bills of perhaps £1,200. That £1,200 hurts, but it isn't a calamity. In the long run, we actually save money. We save because a big bill in those terms isn't a calamity that we can't deal with and we're effectively keeping the money we would pay to the insurers for their expenses and profit. So we "self insure" for the cats.

Remember, the point is to cover calamity, such as the death of the farmer's pig that would mean the children go hungry. If you insure everything just because you can, or people sell it to you, it is probably going to cost you money. So work out what the position is for you. And remember, if you are "self insuring" you want to do something sensible with the money you're not paying in premiums. That's where the "mental accounts" come in. Sort out what you are going to do with the money instead (see chapter 14).

If you are going to insure something, the big factor in what you are going to pay, apart from the number of claims is the size of the claims. Remember, the insurer cannot afford to offer you a premium that is equal to the amount they expect to pay times the chance of paying (the pure premium), they have to charge more to cover expenses and profit. So if you decide you need the insurance, you might want to reduce the size of the potential claim so that it just covers a calamity. This should reduce the premium. The best way to do this is usually to set the "excess" as high as you can.

> The "excess" is the bit that you pay out of a claim. The name comes from the fact that it is the amount "in excess of" this that the insurer pays out. There's usually a compulsory excess (so you have to pay the first £50 or something) but you can usually increase this in the form of a "voluntary excess".
>
> What that means is the insurers eliminate some small claims; it saves them administration costs and means they don't have to pay out so often or so much.
>
> Generally, you'll get a lower premium in exchange for a higher excess (if not, change insurers!).

Let's take a simple, hypothetical example.

Imagine you are insuring your car. To replace it would cost, say, £15,000. If it is written off by an uninsured driver, or if it is your fault (obviously, it won't be!) you won't get it replaced if you only have third party cover. Say the third party premium is £150 and the comprehensive premium (so you can claim even if it is your fault, the other driver isn't insured etc.) is £400. By law, you have to have third party cover. Whether it is worth insuring comprehensive depends on you. If the £15,000 for a new car is a calamity, then maybe you need comprehensive cover. You'll pay an extra £250 p/a for it (£400 less the £150 you'd have to pay anyway). So it would take about 50 or 60 years to make a saving as big as the cost of the car if you invested the money.

Perhaps, as things stand, your policy has a £100 excess. Suppose you increase that to £300. Maybe that reduces your premium from £400 to £350. So do the maths again. Not insuring at all still puts you at risk of losing £15,000, so that is too big a loss to handle and you will have trouble trying to get that money back just in savings. But you save £50 each year (£400 less £350) by increasing the excess. If you have a claim, you pay £300 towards it rather than £100. But you can cope with an extra £200, as it is less than a year's premium. And in four years you'll have saved over £200 (four years of a saving of £50, plus interest on your savings) so you're better off unless you get claims more frequently than that.

If you are going to insure, look at ways you can reduce the number of claims (better locks, burglar alarms, smoke detectors, healthy lifestyle etc.) depending upon what you're insuring. And look for ways to reduce the claim, particularly making the excess bigger. These will reduce the premiums without turning a loss into a calamity.

A few other words about insurance.

It was livestock cover I wanted. Then we thought about loss of profits in case it died.
But then they saw Babe, so I suppose we need pet insurance

Markets are unpredictable. Anything that is unpredictable is dangerous for insurers, they can't use existing data to work out the premiums accurately. For example, when AIDS became a factor, it messed up the tables. Insurers aren't charities, they are businesses, so if they aren't sure of their figures, they'll put in a big safety margin in case they are wrong.

It used to be that Lloyd's of London (the insurer has an apostrophe, the bank, which is a totally different organisation, doesn't) would insure just about anything. There were policies on Betty Grable's legs, violinists' hands, there was even a policy written for a stern parent against the danger of his daughter losing her virginity before marriage! To an extent anybody can use accident data (or data on sexual activity) to work out a theoretical premium for this sort of risk, but it is a bit of a stretch from "sound underwriting practice".

When you get to situations where there aren't adequate data, insurers either avoid the situation or play it safe. Therefore "odd" risks will either not be possible to insure at all or you will pay a very high premium, because the insurers who take it on are going to make sure that if unreliable data mean they have to pay out more than they thought, they will have collected enough money to do it. They will build in a big safety margin for themselves, and they'll collect it from you.

They will also avoid anything where the only people who will want to insure are the ones who are almost certain to claim. That's the reason you can't get unemployment cover.

There used to be (in the 1980's) a few companies that in return for a monthly premium would provide a monthly payment if your job was made redundant and you had to claim unemployment benefits. It was a fairly stupid idea, based on the mistaken assumption that as things seemed to be going well with employment at that point, there consequently wouldn't be many claims. Of course, most people didn't buy a policy because they felt their job was secure. The ones who did buy a policy were those whose jobs were at risk. So the claims experience was much worse than the general unemployment figures suggested. The insurers thought they'd get, say, 10% claims based on existing figures and they actually got perhaps 60% because nearly all the policies were sold to people who thought they would shortly be out of work.

That's the same type of explanation for why most life assurance needs medical declarations (not necessarily a medical examination, but a confirmation that you don't already know you are terminally ill). The insurers don't want to write policies only for people who know perfectly well they are going to claim, for it means all the data on which they base the premiums are useless.

The other aspect of this is the "good faith" point. You will have information the insurer doesn't know. You'll know the motor claim that you sorted out in cash to avoid telling your insurer, the suspicious lump you've found that prompted you to go and get life cover before you went to the doctor etc. The proposal forms will always have a declaration that you have disclosed all "material facts" and a material fact is one that would affect the judgment of a prudent underwriter. So if you know you are terminally ill, will lose your job, are medically unfit to drive or whatever, you either have to declare it or tell lies on the form. Lying almost invariably invalidates the policy.

It might sound harsh, but the insurers are protecting themselves against being cheated, against people changing the odds and they are naturally sensitive about it. So do make sure that if you are insuring, you declare any relevant information; if the premium goes up too high as a result, you can always self-insure, but if you don't mention a material fact, have to make a claim and the insurer refuses the claim on the basis of a false declaration, you get the worst of both worlds, you've lost the premium and suffered the calamity, as well as broken the law.

> *When you're buying insurance, make sure it is you buying it, not somebody selling it.*

There used to be a saying "life assurance is never bought, always sold". That saying gave rise to another one "life has no endurance, like the guy who sells insurance"!

I mentioned in chapter 5 about the four times salary life cover that has become standard. That is a sales convention. In the same way that you can be made to feel a cheapskate if you don't spend two month's salary on an engagement ring, you can be made to feel stingy if you don't have at least four times salary life cover, "for the wife and children". Ignore that, work out whether you need life cover in the same way as you do anything else, and work out how much you need if you decide you do need it.

Another anecdote. When I worked for Lloyds (the bank, not the insurance organisation) I was part of the independent financial side. One of my jobs was to give technical support to the bank staff. I was talking to staff at a branch and was asked "how do you sell life assurance to a 25 year old, single person, living on their own". Here's how the conversation went, the points are still valid.

Me: "Do you want the official answer, or the real life one?"

Staff member, after a bit of thought: "Both"

Me: "The official answer is that you 'create the need', you emphasise how important life cover is, talk about how upset their parents would be and so on. You can try that if you want."

Staff member: "Does it work?"

Me: "Of course not, even if you can bring yourself to do it, it makes you feel like a second hand car salesman, it isn't very good customer service, and most people are not daft enough to fall for it."

Staff member: "So how do you sell it in real life?"

Me: "You don't. Think about it. They are single, no dependents, they don't live at home. If they die, their friends and family will be sad. No amount of money is going to compensate their parents for the loss of their child, you're not supposed to outlive your children, the parents will be distraught. Unless they have some dependents, like their parents are in a care home, they have a child of their own, a partner who depends on their income, then their death will be sad, but nobody is worse off. So since they are dead, who is going to benefit from life assurance? On the other hand, having no dependents means they probably don't depend on anybody else. They are not living at home with mum and dad so they have some freedom. If they were seriously ill, had a car accident or something, what would happen? Since they've become independent, would they want to lose that independence and move back in with mum and dad, give up their own place, be a child again?"

Staff member: "No"

Me: "Why not forget about life assurance and look at income protection? That way if they are injured, which they are more likely to be than killed, they can still maintain their independence."

I'll talk about income protection shortly, but there are a few useful things from that dialogue.

1. Just like everything else to do with money, simply accepting what people tell you that you "ought" to do with money without considering what you actually need or want, is a bad move.
2. If you don't make your own decisions you will be "sold" life assurance (or whatever people want to sell you) rather than you deciding what you need.
3. What they will sell you has nothing to do with what you want to buy, but what they happen to have to sell to you. That applies not only to insurance, but phones, internet services and other rubbish you neither need nor want.
4. It also applies to ideas; "what most people do", "expert opinion", "the wise thing to do is.." and all those other barking mad opinions

that you can be *sold* but that if you think for yourself and make your own decisions, you wouldn't *buy* into in a million years!

On life assurance itself, if you have a partner with whom you have a mortgage, you have children or other dependent relatives etc. or anybody who would lose out financially if you died then you probably need life assurance. If that is the case, work out what would be needed. I'm not going to dictate how you do this. Check out chapter 15 for how to get help working it out. But basically you want to replace the money you were bringing in or enough income to cover all the debts, probably whichever number is higher. Don't fixate on four times salary, or anything else.

It is usually best to take out what is called "term" assurance unless there's a good reason for doing something else (for example, for inheritance tax planning you might use a "whole life" policy). Term assurance just means you pay a premium each month or year for a given term (10 years, 25 years, whatever) and a particular amount (the sum assured) is paid to your dependents (tax free), if you die during that term, but you don't get anything back if the term ends and you're still alive. You aren't investing in the policy, it is purely to protect your dependents if there is the calamity of you dying.

You can buy life assurance that is paid out as an income (it used to be called family income benefit), so instead of having a single sum of, say, £200,000 if you die within, say 25 years (perhaps until the children have left university and are earning), you get a policy that pays £25,000 each year for the rest of the 25 years. The advantages of this are that it is easier to work out what you need, you simply replace the income rather than having to work out how much you could earn by investing a lump sum, and if you die early on there is income available for longer (while it is still needed) than if you died towards the end of the term when the dependents don't need the full amount.

I don't want to get into all the different forms of life assurance. If you want to find out more, have a look at chapter 15 and find yourself the right advisor, make sure they are independent and are properly qualified, and pay them to give you a course in the basics such as the policies mentioned above, convertible term assurance, reducing term, whole life and so on. It will only take about an hour or so and you'll learn all you need to make your own decisions. You can always ask them to help you, but it is handy to know the basics before you get somebody to get quotes for you, so that you know what questions to ask.

I mentioned income protection assurance above. This also gets called IPP (Income Protection Policy), PHI (Permanent Health Insurance) or PSI (Permanent Sickness Insurance). It's a type of insurance that covers income if you can't work due to illness or injury. In my view it is massively under-used, probably because it is:

a. more expensive,
b. more complicated so the public don't understand it, and
c. for the previous reasons harder to sell so sales people don't try to understand or sell it.

The point is, you are far more likely to be injured than you are to be killed. Think of the figures reported on accidents, it is always "two died and twenty-seven were injured". The figures I used to carry around with me showed that in a working lifetime you were about six times more likely to be ill or injured badly enough to be unable to work for more than a year than you were to die.

But people still don't buy it, or rather, are still not sold it.

It is expensive by comparison with life assurance for two main reasons.

1. They pay out for the rest of your working life (usually to age 60 or 65) so the insurer could be looking at having to pay out £25,000 or something every year for 30 or 40 years (about a million pounds in total).
2. Something like a "bad back" or other injury that is in no way life

threatening could stop you working for an extended period so there are a lot more potential claims. This also means that the medical underwriting (the amount of information needed on forms, the likelihood of needing a medical or a doctor's report etc.) is much higher on an income protection than a life assurance policy.

Another thing that affects how much you pay for income protection (and life cover, come to that) is your job. Jobs that make injury more likely tend to make it more expensive and jobs where a small injury will stop you working (like injuring your finger if you are a surgeon) make it more expensive.

Another consideration is the "deferred period", which is the time you have to be unable to work before the policy starts paying. This is a bit like the excess on car insurance. If you are only paid by the policy after, say, six months off work (if you're employed, your contract might give you some sort of pay in the event of illness) the premium will be cheaper than if you are paid after one month, because there will be a lot more claims to pay out after a month, so the insurers have to pay out less the longer the deferred period.

The word "permanent" in the title "permanent health" means that the policy is not cancellable by the insurer if there is bad claims experience. Income protection sometimes gets mixed up (by the "professionals", as well as the public) with a personal accident (PA) policy. PA is, usually, an annual policy, like car insurance. If you claim on it and cost the insurer money, they can refuse to renew it. With income protection, as long as you've told the truth on the forms, have declared any existing problems and any material facts and you pay the premiums, they can't cancel the policy.

As I mentioned, I think this type of insurance is massively underused. It can come in useful (although it can be hard to find) for somebody who is what the Americans call a domestic engineer. You get various calculations for what a house based partner is worth, in terms of what you'd have to pay for a child minder, cleaner, cook, driver, personal shopper, budget planner, waiter-in for the gas man, etc. Typically, it is a rare couple who even has life cover for the partner at home, "they don't earn any money"! Try getting all that labour for free if they died and see how far you get! Same thing applies to them being ill, you only need a bad fall or a whiplash injury and they aren't going to be doing any heavy lifting, like groceries, children or vacuum cleaners for a few months. Work out what that costs.

> *Again, don't simply accept what I say any more than you would any other "expert" – don't dash out and buy income protection, family income benefit etc. because I think they are often a good idea.*

Work out whether you, your partner or anybody else on whom you depend or who depends on you being ill or dead is a calamity or an inconvenience.

Probably, death or long term disability will be a calamity for somebody, because the income they bring in or the work they do will cease, although if you both work and have no dependents, death is sad but may not matter much financially. On the other hand, shorter term disability is probably only an inconvenience unless even a short term interruption (if you are launching a business together perhaps) would be a disaster. Work out the situation for your family, dependents and those you depend on, and insure, or self insure, accordingly. And if you need help to work it out, get the help. If a calamity happens while you're dithering, you'll only have yourself to blame.

With other forms of insurance, again, work out what you need for yourself, but bear in mind the issues raised in chapter 5. Things like special travel insurance (the sort where you get extra life cover on plane trips), insurance against Ebola, SARS etc. are almost always daft and are sold on the basis of "availability" and people's natural fear of disaster. I don't know if it happened, but I would guess that somebody who issued a "cover for being attacked by a shark" in the year after Jaws came out would have got millions in premiums, and probably wouldn't pay out more than one claim every ten years or so.

I wouldn't rule them out, but think very carefully about "critical illness" cover, medical fees cover (like BUPA), and things like pet insurance and drains/central heating/boiler cover. The chances are high that you'll actually be better off self-insuring so unless there is the potential for calamity, you are paying a high price for the peace of mind they bring. Also bear in mind the calculations in chapter 8 about medical conditions if you are being scared into paying money.

> *The forms of insurance that are almost certainly a waste of money are the "extended warranties" on electrical goods, white goods etc. The chances of the loss of your phone or washing machine being a calamity are pretty well zero, so you'd normally be better off "self-insuring".*

A lot of the time you can claim things like this on your household insurance anyway (if you've got it, that's why you need to work out the whole package to suit yourself). The main thing is that the chances of something going wrong in the first year or so (during the normal guarantee period) are very small, otherwise the manufacturers or retailers wouldn't offer the guarantee, it would cost them too much if loads of stuff went wrong that they had to fix for free.

If it hasn't gone wrong in the first year or so, the chances are slim that it is suddenly going to go wrong until it gets a bit worn, say in five to ten years. The insurers know that, they know that the number of claims will be very small. They also know that compared to £200 for a phone or £600 for a washing machine, an extra £17 p/a for an extended warranty will play to your "bigness bias", you won't see it. But if the chance of a claim is 1 in 1,000 per annum (it's probably less) even a £5 premium for all three years is huge.

Multiply the chance of loss by the amount of the claim, the chance of loss each year is 1 in 1,000 and the claim will be, let's say, £600 to buy you a new washing machine. So the "pure premium" is about £0.60 p/a. All the rest of the £17 p/a premium is profit and expenses for the insurer. These sort of insurances are almost always a waste of your money, but don't take my word for it, do the maths yourself.

One thing you can do with this sort of situation is ask the sales people what percentage of goods they are selling goes wrong. They probably won't know, but will almost certainly tell you that they only sell reliable stuff. That means that the extended warranty isn't needed, because it won't go wrong anyway. They'll try (if they've got good sales training and bad morals) to focus you on the amount you'll lose if it does go wrong working on your loss aversion and on the "cheapness" of the warranty, working on your bigness bias, but stick to your guns and ask them for the claims figures and then do the maths.

It's a fact of life that if you say to a business, "if you do X, you will make lots more money", they will probably do X. If X happens to be "sell some warranties or policies" using people's susceptibility to bigness bias and loss aversion, then that's what they'll do.

Another point about being sold anything, including insurance, always check what the sales people make from the sale.

They will give incentives to the staff to sell policies, tell them that it is genuinely a good idea for people to take out extended warranties etc. You saw that in chapter 8 with the broker reps. They were honest enough people, they just weren't that bright and genuinely believed that their company offered a good deal because that was what their company training had told them. They were quite upset when I told them the truth. Probably the people who trained them didn't know the truth either. Obviously, somebody in the company knew that what they were doing was misleading, but

a) they might have pointed out the problems but because they were in the back room (chapter 9) nobody listened or

b) they knew that it would go through managers, trainers, reps, brokers etc. so they figured by the time the public were conned it wasn't their problem!

There's regular press comment about commission hungry sales people who miss-sell pensions, endowments etc. and undoubtedly some is due to individuals who want the money, know what they are selling is no good and sell it anyway. But in my experience most people really don't know what they are doing and that is also true of most shop assistants. They are just doing what they are told, most of them believe it is a good idea (maybe they even buy warranties themselves) and they would be horrified if they did the maths and realised that the customer is paying money for nothing of value. But most people don't do the maths, they can't, can't be bothered or whatever, but they don't make their own decisions. Most people don't "Tame the Pound".

If you're buying insurance that *you* choose to buy, shop around. If you are getting independent advice, shop around for the advice to measure whether it going to be helpful. After you've chosen an advisor, you are paying them to do the shopping around for you and to help you to make better decisions.

If you are doing it for yourself, look at the price, but don't forget the claims handling. If you've ever been burgled, had a car stolen or anything like that, you'll know it is pretty traumatic. You want to have people who advise you and get you the money and help you need quickly and without fuss. The last thing you want is some petty officious idiot who can't speak in clear English and won't listen to you.

The situation is even worse with death or disability. If you are laid up in hospital wondering whether you'll ever walk again, or contemplating life without somebody you loved, having an obstructive and ill-mannered insurance rep, broker or whatever to deal with is not going to help.

So beware of the apparently cheap policy. There used to be some syndicates at Lloyd's the insurers who specialised in motor insurance for teenage boys. They were very cheap, the apparent reason being they never paid any claims, they always found a way to avoid it!

That's another important reason for being honest and declaring any material facts as it is the only chance you have of getting any dodgy company to pay out. As you're now in a position to avoid the dodgy ones and pick the good ones, if you're playing fair with them then if calamity happens you're likely to get things sorted out much quicker and more easily.

If you're looking things up on comparison websites, good luck! I've got a post graduate diploma in computing and I can never get any sense out of most of them. There was a Which? report (June 2010) that said much the same.

The problem is that most of them have some sponsored links, so you have the commission element coming in and the rankings aren't necessarily correct. They will also miss out companies that won't pay them to be included. Some companies even make a point of saying that they don't appear on comparison sites so you need to find out which they are and try them.

And you can't get specific details into most of the sites unless they fit their generalised lists. For example, we've got some wine that we include in the house contents in case we have a fire or something. Most comparison sites simply don't have a space to record it, I end up calling it a "work of art" or something if I bother to use the site.

The basic problem is that comparison sites are set up to deal with standardised policies for large numbers, they don't really deal with individual needs very well. If you can get what you really need at a good price, great. But don't accept what they want to sell, if they don't allow for the larger excess you want, if they can't cover what you want to cover or won't let you split things up the way you want, then usually you're better off shopping around or, if you really can't be bothered, getting a broker to do it for you (see chapter 15)

> *What you need to do is work out what you really want, what matters to you, what is a calamity and what is an inconvenience and do some very simple maths. If you do that, and if necessary get the right advice, you'll save yourself a lot of money to spend on things you actually want, but you'll have the cover there to ensure that if a disaster happens, you've at least got some money to try to cope with the consequences.*

So insurance is basically fairly simple. It might require some complex maths to work out the premium, but you don't have to do that.

But of course, that is just a part of your whole plan for Taming the Pound. So after the summary we'll look at how to deal with it going wrong, in a situation of redundancy or debt.

Summary:

- Insurance is to cover calamity, not inconvenience.
- The insurer will charge the "pure premium" plus admin costs and profit, so you can't "win" on insurance.
- Do the maths. See if you should "self insure". Insure stuff that would be a calamity, not (usually) an inconvenience.
- Do things to reduce premiums, fit locks, smoke detectors, etc. and look at the excess on the policy.
- Work out what you want and need and buy that; don't buy what they want to sell.
- Protection, like life assurance and PHI should at least be considered if you have dependents or anybody who will suffer financially (or if you'd have big problems paying your bills if you were ill or injured).
- Extended warranties are usually a waste of money.
- But as with everything else, do the maths (or hire somebody independent to do it for you).

Buddy can you spare a dime

This chapter starts on redundancy, the way we see it, how we can react positively to it and what we can do about it. It then moves on to debt (which is sometimes a result of the loss of income from redundancy) and what can be done about it.

Redundancy: general points.

Some people say that "I've been made redundant" or, "lots of people are being made redundant", you hear it on the news all the time.

But people do not become redundant, only jobs do, the word redundant means not required. Your job may be redundant, you cannot be.

To many people, that sounds like bad "pop psychology". Their reaction is, *"it doesn't matter what you call it, I've lost my job and no fancy wording is going to get it back"*

I can understand that, I've had my job made redundant between four and six times (it depends on whether you include the ones where we agreed I'd leave, or only the ones where the employer made the decision without my input!) It hurts. But what it hurts is your pride, not you.

We said earlier that people define themselves by their job. If you take the job away, you take away part of them.

We think a job isn't just a way to earn money; it is a symbol of what we are worth. If you have no job, are you now worthless?

So although it sounds like a semantic quibble, there is a big emotional difference between "my job is redundant", and the incorrect, "I am redundant". And that difference effects what we look for.

I mentioned earlier that we often see what we look for. Visual illusions depend on it, we decide about people in a few seconds and give them "halo" or "horns", we simplify situations to make them easier for us to deal with. If what we are looking for is a problem, what we'll tend to see is a problem. If what we are looking for is an opportunity, what we'll tend to see is an opportunity. Remember the two clients from chapter 3.

This becomes a bit intellectual if you focus on all the research evidence that it is true, or sounds like mindless Disney, "Pollyanna" thinking if you just try to "think of the positives".

So here's a joke that, hopefully, makes the serious point, without getting too stodgy. I heard it told by Dave Allen, whom you might remember told wonderful "shaggy dog" stories sitting on a stool, sipping a drink.

A man is out driving one night, there is a terrible storm blowing. Suddenly, his car blows a tyre, he skids to a halt, luckily not crashing and he gets out into the driving rain and howling wind, and is promptly up to his ankles in mud.

He struggles to the boot of the car, gets out the spare and the car jack, and tries to change the wheel. The jack won't work. He can't get a signal on his phone, he is soaked, muddy, oily, cold and fed up and it looks like he is stuck for the night. Then he sees a light in the distance. It looks like a house.

He thinks, "the home owner might have a jack, I'll walk over there and get help". He climbs over the fence into a field, cutting his hand and ripping his trousers on the wire. As he walks along, he thinks, "he'll probably be annoyed at being woken at this time of night. Or there will be nobody in".

He walks on through the field, getting muddier and colder. He thinks "what if he has got a jack but doesn't want to lend it to me? He's way out in the middle of nowhere, he probably likes solitude and doesn't welcome visitors."

He trudges on, gets a foot stuck in the mud and loses his shoe which he can't find in the dark. He thinks, "he's probably a total recluse, hates people, maybe he's mad." He drags himself on, trips in the mud and ends up sprawling in a puddle. He heaves himself up, muddy, wet, cold, bleeding and thoroughly fed up.

"He's probably got a fortress there, mantraps, alarms all sorts of stuff to keep people at a distance. He'll probably look out of an upstairs window, laugh and tell me to **** off".

The motorist trudges on, getting nearer so that he can see the outline of the house more clearly. "He's sitting in there, nice and warm and dry, probably enjoying a drink, while I'm out here soaked, muddy and cold, his stupid fence has cut me, his stupid field has taken my shoe, rotten little ***".

He gets nearer and thinks, "I bet he'll tell me to go to hell and threaten to call the police. There's no way he's going to offer to help me, look at the state of me and it's all his fault". He gets a bit nearer and thinks "what's the point, he's not going to help me, he doesn't care about my tyre or my jack not working, he's a selfish pig that's what he is. Even if he opens the door and has a jack, he won't lend it to me, what a *******".

He gets to the door and wonders whether it is even worth knocking, he thinks "he's sitting in there, warm, dry, got a wonderful jack, he could help me but will he, will he Hell, he's a rotten *******.

But he rings the bell anyway and a very pleasant man comes to the door and asks what the visitor wants. And the motorist says, "you can keep your jack, you selfish ****" and storms off!

You had to hear Dave Allan tell it for the real comedy, but hopefully you recognise the reaction!

We build up problems in our minds, rehearse things going wrong, ruminate on how it is awful, nobody will help us, life is dreadful. And when we actually get to a situation where we can get help, we're so taken up with our own private fantasy of how awful it all is, we don't ask for help or even look for friends, we see problems and enemies and "get our retaliation in first"!

The general human response to any threat is fight or flight. If you are supposed to have "outplacement counselling", "get out and network", "chat to the people who matter" etc. you might find yourself trying to "fly". You might avoid them, feel you're not ready, you don't want to, there is plenty of time and so on. That is your flight response.

You want to run and hide, and maybe the threat (like the predator that might have killed our ancestors) will move off and we can come out of hiding and things will be like they were before. Unfortunately, in modern life, the monster won't go away, and things won't go back to where they were. Things might actually be better in the long run, but the clock definitely won't turn back, however fast you run away and hide.

Or, as above, we might get ready to fight, push people away when they are trying to help us (sometimes not by direct aggression, but with "you don't really want to help me, you're just feeling guilty" etc. kind, which is a more indirect form of being aggressive).

If you've ever lost a loved one, or tried to comfort somebody who has, you might have seen this sort of pattern before. Denial, anger, bargaining, depression and acceptance can be applied to redundancy just as much as death. If you face redundancy you might not go through all or any of the stages, the edges might overlap, or you might skip some stages, then go back to them. But it's quite likely that you will experience at least some of them. Be prepared for your mood to swing a lot. You might get (apparently) irrationally angry or tearful, or all sorts of things might happen. It is grief, it is a normal process and it will pass.

Redundancy: planning a response

I've adapted the basic plan of this from a friend of mine, an occupational psychologist named Dai Williams who has done a lot of work around "career transitions", particularly redundancy. He's got a lot of other good stuff on his website (www.eoslifework.co.uk).

1. What is the problem - concern or crisis?

People talk a lot about stress, but there aren't very clear definitions of stress in most places. The way I describe it is based on what the Health and Safety Executive (HSE) do.

Strain or pressure are neutral, they are the demands of a situation. That can be like the "flow" situation we talked about in chapter 2. You can have just the right amount of pressure so you are excited by it, you get a sense of achievement, you are in "flow" and you love it. That is great.

If there are too many demands (you are rushed), demands you can't meet (no time, not the right skills), things are out of your control (you are told what to do and have no say in it, your job is being axed and there is nothing you can do) or you simply don't know how to cope, then the demands are too high and you feel out of control.

On the other hand if there isn't enough challenge you can end up under insufficient pressure to achieve much, you feel pointless, the demands are too low and you get bored.

> Stress is the bad stuff; it is the boredom or the "out of control" feeling where the pressure is too much or too little for you.

In the same way that people don't actually die from AIDS, but from some other disease that they can't fight off because of the virus, people don't actually die or get ill from stress itself. What happens is, for example, that because of the stress they experience they stay continually in the "fight or flight" mode and their body (which isn't designed to live like that for more than a few hours at a time) gets tired. The chemicals in the body get out of balance and their system gets weakened.

This can lead to disturbed sleep, becoming susceptible to loads of minor illnesses, skin problems etc. and can also push people to rely on coping strategies that are not helpful, like drinking heavily or drug use.

It isn't "stress" as such that hurts them; it is the body's response (and their actions) in response to a strain or pressure that they experience as stress that do the damage.

If we have an obvious problem we become concerned. That is a strain or pressure.

What we do with such a concern, with the fear, the uncertainty, the anxiety is to try to clear the uncertainty. We try to give ourselves a future that we can predict and remove the fear and tension.

That can motivate us to find answers. Having a concern can be the good side of redundancy, it can make you think about what you really want, what you value, what options you have for the future. Using the concern as a springboard to action usually helps.

We can also try to clear the uncertainty by interpreting redundancy as meaning we're worthless, and imagining we'll never work again, everybody will laugh at or ignore us (or possibly worse, pity us), etc. We can say we never liked the job anyway, they were stupid, we were only doing it until something better came along and so on.

Denial, despair or anger usually leave the issues unresolved and the uncertainty can produce stress symptoms. Unresolved issues lead to more problems, which can lead to more stress and become a vicious circle where the problems build up faster than you can solve them.

Sooner or later there is a crisis, and at that point you are too stressed to deal effectively with anything.

Whether you are simply concerned or already in a crisis, the first task is to stabilize the situation, with help or advice from others if needed. Chapter 15 has some pointers for good sources of help or advice.

2. Stabilise the situation - take care of yourself and manage stress

The first priority is to manage the symptoms of stress to get back in control and think clearly. Three key tasks are:

fitness,
training for stressful situations and
relaxation (stress dumping).

Regular, quality exercise (walking, cycling, swimming etc.) half an hour each day can make a big difference, especially if your sleep is affected. This can save you an hour a day with clearer thinking and fewer mistakes. It is also a good way to relax.

Practice relaxing and breathing easily several times a day and before stressful tasks e.g. meetings or interviews. Get coached or take relaxation or meditation classes if necessary. Take regular breaks and find "still moments" in your day. Take care when driving and working, there is a greater risk of errors or accidents when you are stressed.

Both exercise as a "go to" routine, as in chapter 4, and mindfulness as a way to focus and balance your mind (as in chapter 2) can be helpful.

3. Support your friends

Harassment and scapegoating are common in stressed organisations. Confront anybody doing this firmly and stand by your friends. Remember, you may be next!

This also keeps up the relationships that are so important both for networking to find opportunities, and for your own happiness (remember in chapter 2 how vital friends, family and relationships are).

So it is important not to cut yourself off. Anybody bereaved (by death, loss of a job, relationship breakdown), needs human contact. You might not feel like seeing people, but if you lock yourself away and ruminate on your own failings, the stupidity of former employers, the unfairness of life and so on it is easy to make a job loss, that might turn into a great opportunity for you, into an absolute disaster.

Helping and supporting others not only gives both of you that contact, but it also helps to make you feel better (because you're helping others) and it helps you keep things in proportion (both of which we mentioned in chapter 4 about changing behaviours).

After all, at the end of the day, it is only a job. Maybe it symbolises to you how successful you were, but that is just a symbol. Like Gerald the company Director (from the Full Monty, in chapter 1) you can get involved in the symbol of a lifestyle, or you can live your life; it is difficult to do both at the same time.

4. *Seek help and information for immediate problems*
   Check your facts and seek help.

   Some situations need prompt action or referral for the right kind of expert advice e.g. legal or financial advice, medical advice for illness or severe distress, counselling for relationships and advice from someone you trust and respect in difficult work situations.

> *Early action may prevent a problem from getting worse. You don't have to cope on your own, there are no prizes for being John Wayne and "doing what a man (or woman) has gotta do". This is not a film, it is your life. In real life the best results usually come from getting help when needed.*

If you really feel bad about asking for help (even if you have professional help available), here's a point that my dad made to me when I was about ten. I'd managed to get lost and was scared to ask anybody for directions because I didn't want to bother them or look stupid. When I finally got found again, dad asked me some questions that I suggest you ask yourself.

How do you feel if you can help somebody?

Say somebody asks for directions because they are lost, or asks your advice because they know you are knowledgeable about something they don't know about. Do you feel bad, or do you feel flattered that they asked you?

If you can't help them, do you resent them asking you, or do you feel a bit guilty and wish you could help?

And if you can help them, does it make you feel good, or do you hate them for taking up your valuable time?

Most people are much like you. Most of them will be pleased to help if you ask them, it isn't costing them more than a small amount of time and they get to feel good and kind and clever and get lots of gratitude. Why not help them feel that way and ask them for help if you need it, and whether they can help or not, thank them for trying?

5   *Buy time for major decisions*

As mentioned above, stress can affect our judgement and our ability to think ahead and to think clearly.

Buy yourself time when you can, take a break, re-schedule tasks. If possible put off major decisions for a few weeks until you can think clearly again. This applies to stressed groups and families as well as individuals.

Your "flight" response may kick in but try to control it and give yourself time, don't quit jobs or relationships, at least until you have checked all your options and preferably until after you've taken a break from the pressure to see if things still look the same.

If you have to make a major decision under stress check your options with someone you trust. You're trying to "respond not react", giving yourself the time and the emotional distance to make the best decision.

6   *Check your options*

By checking options, even hypothetical ones, we can make better quality decisions and feel more in control.

Remember the "O" of the GROW idea of chapter 3, it is part of your goal setting to generate options. Most problems have more than one solution. For example you have the option to struggle on at work or take a day off, to act now or later, to have a main plan and a fallback position.

When we are under stress it is even more important to check options to reduce the chance of making mistakes. Checking several options and discussing them with others helps to sharpen your ideas about what really matters to you.

You might want to go over the things you really value (chapter 2) to remind yourself of what you want and to help yourself generate options looking forward, rather than regrets looking back.

7 Don't give up - your future starts today

Hard times show us life from a new perspective. It is a chance to rediscover what we really value, and who our real friends are.

Remember the first client from chapter 3 who told me that this was the best thing that had ever happened. That is a true story, and what I told you is exactly what he said. But if you'd asked him the week before the redundancies were announced to leave his job and take the risk of setting up on his own, he would certainly have given you a fairly robust (if not downright rude) answer!

Remember how you survived past changes or disappointments, and taking courage from that, you can deal with it. Sometimes we just need a crisis to let go of old ways and come to terms with a new realities.

> Actually, and this will be no compensation at all if you're in that situation (not yet anyway) it is a good opportunity to stand back and think about what you really want. What does the job give you, what do you want from life (your values, as in chapter 2).

That's why I said at the start of the chapter that redundancy can be a good thing. But while it is a good opportunity to re-evaluate our lives and it is very helpful to stand back and consider, knowing that to think dispassionately about it all will help doesn't make it any easier actually to do!

8   *"Eat your elephant a spoonful at a time"*
Sometimes a major problem seems to be blocking us completely. Find the smallest, easiest thing that you can do successfully and try it.

Small victories give us confidence to move forward again. Recall the point in chapter three that good goals need to have little steps and be actions, not wishes (the LA of PLAN in the mnemonic).

The little actions get you moving, you can tick off accomplishments, feel good about yourself and move on. And you know that you are doing something, you are not a helpless victim, taking little actions gives you back some control.

9.   *Have something you can look forward to*
Plan things you enjoy, time for yourself and to be with people you like every week, starting today!

The relationships are a way to be happy as in chapter 2, planning time for yourself is rewarding yourself as in chapter 4, planning it for every week is part of goal setting to motivate you as in chapter 3 and getting started today is living in the moment, as in mindfulness in chapter 2. So by doing that one thing, you can put a lot of your "Taming the Pound" skills into action and have some fun while doing it!

Talking of putting skills into action, there are some particular points regarding money (that we've already mentioned) that become even more important when redundancy looms.

Heading for debt
You know perfectly well that £1 is £1 from chapter 1, but you also know that you probably treat it differently depending on whether you

earn it, win it, find it, inherit it or get it as a tax rebate. That isn't logical (chapter 5) but often it is harmless (chapter 6).

If you might be facing redundancy or serious debt it isn't harmless.

If you have emergency funds, or Auntie Gertie's inheritance etc. earning 2% and any debts at a higher rate, even possibly a mortgage, you almost certainly need to kill the debts

You might not want to part with the money; it represents your security, dad's favourite sister or something; but £1 is just £1 and 2% is less than 5% let alone 23% or something.

So look at your borrowing and the rates of interest, do the maths (chapter 8) and sort out what is best. If the roof blows off the house, you can stick it onto a bank loan or a credit card if you have to, but at least you only pay interest on the money after you borrow it. If you don't get rid of loans immediately you are paying a lot more to borrow than you can possibly get in return for your savings.

Generally, it will be a good idea to use any cash you have to reduce or eliminate any debts. Check it out and do the maths, though. Don't assume that it is best because I (or anybody else) says it is so in general. You're an individual, your situation may not be like the "general" one.

Also, remember that on the way up we change our comparators fast. The pay rise of £5,000 seemed great, but within a month or two we got used to it and measured our success against wealthier standards.

On the way down, we cling to what we had. Particularly with a cash pay-out on redundancy, it is easy for you to try to maintain a show. Most people (as the current figures show) couldn't afford their lifestyle anyway without huge credit. Most of us already need to stop worrying what car our brother in law drives, what the bloke at the golf club thinks or whether our parents or siblings will respect us if we don't have lavish holidays. We need to work out what we really want for ourselves. In redundancy situations, we definitely need to work out what is important to us and our family, not what the Jones's think.

Budgets and personality.

One of the common pieces of advice given about budgeting is to "write down everything you spend for two months" to get a picture of what you spend. That's not bad advice, but it does ignore what people are really like, their complexities and differences.

People, as I've said several times, are really complex. Psychology is the scientific study of human behaviour and it encounters the problems arising from that complexity. To paraphrase Abe Lincoln:

"you may explain some of the people all of the time, you can even explain all of the people some of the time, but you cannot explain all of the people all of the time."

With real people, no theory works for everybody, in every context, every time. It doesn't matter how clever the theory is, how much research has gone into the way of measuring aspects of personality or even whether those dimensions and the descriptions they give of people reflect anything real at all, nothing works all the time.

So when I say, "making a list of everything you spend for two months ignores what people are really like", you have to understand I don't even know what I'm really like all of the time, let alone you or "people" in general!

However, most people have some pretty abiding personality characteristics. In one well accepted model, one of those is called conscientiousness. It is basically about how much somebody *tends* to complete tasks, follow through, keep to commitments etc. The scale is regarded as a continuum, you might be very high or very low on conscientiousness. It isn't a case of "this is the way you are and you cannot change", these are tendencies rather than fixed behaviours.

One end of the scale (being very conscientious or not conscientious at all) is not better than the other, they are simply different ways to operate. People aren't likely to change dramatically from one extreme to the other, but most people aren't at the extremes anyway, they vary a bit all the time and everybody acts differently in different situations.

Because what works best depends on the context, getting all the details right to dot the I's and cross the T's, following through until the job is fully complete and so on might be very useful in some contexts. In other situations it might be obsessive and time-wasting.

So if you are trying to budget to find out where you stand, because you might be losing income or because you are in serious debt, you might find it really easy to write down all your costs or it might be nearly impossible, but you still need to do it.

You probably have a good idea of how easy you'll find it, but you don't know until you try, so try!

If you find it easy, good for you.

If it is hard work for you, that means you need to adopt different tactics, not that you should give up.

Tactics for budget making.

If you can, go through all your bank statements, credit card slips etc. and set up a list of everything you spent in the last year. Keep a diary or notebook with you, and record every single penny you pay out for a couple of months (or at least a couple of "typical" weeks), the newspaper purchases, the pack of sweets, the donation for "The Big Issue", everything.

Make a note of all the bills you have to pay monthly, quarterly and annually, utilities, Council Tax, insurances, subscriptions etc. Make sure you've allowed for all of them.

It's easy to forget things, so there are a couple of handy tools that you can use. One is connected to Credit Action and the Consumer Credit Counselling Service, sister charities that are brilliant and that I'll say more about later. The free site they've set up is MoneyBasics and it has lots of good advice, downloads and helpful contact numbers:

http://www.moneybasics.co.uk/en/

Within that site is a budget calculator.

Another useful one (also free) is run by Martin Lewis, under the name Money Saving Expert. This budget tool is at:

http://www.moneysavingexpert.com/banking/Budget-planning

Both planners are good because they recognise that a "month" of spending is not a lot of help, you need to include all the little daily cash purchases, the annual bills, the sudden costs that have come up etc.

One thing though. I think what Mr. Lewis does is great; I even talk in seminars and in training financial advisors about "Martin Lewis skills", meaning the ability to keep an eye on the bargains, economise, avoid wasting money and so on. These are things that aren't part of the standard financial advisor training (any more than psychology is) and are not something that I'd claim to be expert on either.

What I'd be careful of is that it can lead you into starting with the budget, making economies before you have worked out what you want from your life.

> So please, don't get sucked into thinking a budget is where you start. The place to start is with working out what you really want.
>
> Then do the budget, work out where you are, are you within the "Micawber rules". Where is the money coming from (accumulating) and where is it going?
>
> Then you can make economies, change priorities etc.

If you find you are spending £500 more than you are getting in income, particularly now your overtime has stopped and you are concerned for your job, you might look at changing your energy supplier or something. That means that you find a saving of £750 say, and you are again within your budget. But you still could be buying loads of things you don't need, and you are still probably ignoring what you really want from your life.

If the mere idea of doing a budget, digging through bank statements, credit card statements, bills etc. is scary, you've got a choice.

1. You can "feel the fear, and do it anyway", or
2. You can pay somebody else to do it.

If you're a couple, one of you might sort it out this once and be responsible for it (then you both need to know about how it works, as we'll look at in chapter 12). But you really have to have an idea of what is going on (after you've worked out what you really want from life, naturally).

If you don't have the slips, statements etc. (you've burned them, lost them, the dog has eaten them etc.) then get in touch with the banks and credit card companies and get duplicate statements for the past year. That will cost you money. In future, don't lose them!

> Even if you don't want to look at them regularly, put them in a particular drawer, shoe box, something to keep them together so you can dig them out when you need them. It is a lot easier to keep them together and keep the statements filed (I use a ring binder) in date order and tick off the cheque stubs and credit slips as you go along.
>
> Each time you get a bill, check things off, query anything that doesn't seem right (you don't have a slip for a credit card debit that is on the account, for example).

If you're low on conscientiousness, this might be hard for you. I'm sorry, but that's life! As I said, personality is adaptable and nobody knows exactly how things work for different people in different contexts, but it is generally true that some people have more trouble with following through on this routine than others. You are one of the ones who finds it harder. If you want to control your money, you have to learn how to cope.

Trust me, I don't find it easy myself, I get bored with doing all the details. Years of training mean I know *what* I need to do, I just don't, in terms of my personality, *want* to do it. However, it shows that training and effort can make a difference to what we do. After all, there's nothing special about me and if I can alter my personal style in a particular context for good enough reasons, so can you.

If you want to pay somebody to do it, and can afford it, fine. If you can't afford it, then you have to do it yourself, and as a first economy drive, it's probably better to do it yourself since you will understand it better if you do.

Get that "past year" budget sorted out! If necessary, promise yourself a treat when you've finished, get the papers together, spread them out on the dining room table, (or the floor, or whatever) and get on with it.

Incidentally, if you think that, as you are losing your job, doing this doesn't matter, I'm afraid it is even more vital. This is your chance. You are going to be taking up exciting new challenges, to achieve your real values, things that will make you happy.

If you don't know how you dealt with what you were earning and spending, how are you going to know what you can do in future? If you don't know how you lived on your old salary, and don't even know whether you were going backwards or forwards, how can you work out whether you can take the new job (or start the new business) that gives excitement and prospects but less money initially? If you don't have any idea how you spent the money in the past, how can you work out what you can economise on to give you the funds to achieve your dreams? If you have no idea where the money went, how can you work out whether you can use the redundancy money to fund the course of study for your dream job? So get on and do it!

As far as recording everything is concerned, that is trickier. Some people can carry a notebook with them, always have a pen or pencil and remember to write everything down. Diane is like that, she can maintain a food diary and record every single thing she eats or drinks. I find it incredibly difficult. I'll have a notebook, but it's in a jacket and the weather was warm so I didn't wear it. I had a pen, but I lent it to somebody and don't have it with me. Or I remember in the evening that I forgot to note down things during the day.

So basic personality comes into it more. Checking credit card statements isn't something that comes naturally, but I can do it, particularly since I get a reminder each month when bills arrive. Recording things daily takes a lot more organisation, it requires having something to note things down on as well as remembering to do it every time. So I have to change my behaviour in more contexts, with less cues and it is therefore harder.

> *If you struggle with recording spending, maybe try these ideas.*

- Take only a known amount of cash with you. If you've got odd change, put it in a charity box or a savings tin at home or something. Have a set amount and make a note of how much it is. For all the small things, drinks, papers or magazines, snacks etc. everything small that you might normally pay with cash or stick on a card "because it is easier" and then lose the card slip, pay with cash.

  In the evening, when you take things out of your pockets or your bag, or whatever, check how much you've got and record it. The difference is the money you spent that day.

If somebody gives you cash for something, put it straight in the bank, give it to your partner or a trusted friend or something, don't get the cash mixed up. When you need more cash, take an amount out of the bank, from you savings tin or wherever, but make sure you know how much you've added.

After a week or two, you might be vague over what you've spent it all on, you might not be entirely clear on which days you spent how much (although you'll have more idea than you normally do), but you will be able to say something like, "I had £50 on Monday, on Friday I got another £100 to see me through the weekend. Tuesday night I checked and I've got £65.37. So I started with a total of £150 and now I've got £65.37, so I spent £84.63 between Monday morning and the following Tuesday evening." It's not exact, it's not foolproof, but it works, and if you keep at it you can start to get a realistic idea of just how much money drifts away from you that you didn't normally notice.

• You can do the opposite, use a debit card only.

Note that this is not "use a credit card". That is a debt set up and (from chapter 3) you know how easily that can spiral out of control.

Get (if you haven't got one) a debit card that debits amounts directly to your bank account. Most of them won't work if you don't have funds to cover it, so it is a bit like writing cheques with a very strict bank manager who won't let you go into overdraft.

This is quite a good substitute (temporary or permanent) for credit cards if you really have trouble with spending. However, *checking your small spending by that means is can be a problem* because people like the newspaper seller won't take cards.

Therefore, either you can't buy stuff (which is usually no bad thing) or you end up having to carry cash as well. As soon as you have two different things to check, it becomes harder to keep track. You have spent an unknown amount of cash, have a debit card and cheque stubs and maybe some credit card receipts, the task of untangling it all is so horrific that you give up before you start. So either carry cash, or decide that if they won't take your debit card, you won't buy it.

- If you have joined the modern world you don't need paper and pencil. You can make notes (possibly verbal memos) on your phone, Blackberry, virtual computer or whatever. Technology being what it is, you can probably put them straight into a spreadsheet to give you a running balance of what you've spent.

  This is probably the easiest way to do it, but you still have to remember to do it!

  I just use my phone as a phone so I don't know, but I imagine you can get whatever device you use that is capable of storing the information about what you've spent also to remind you to record it and to tell you to make sure you've downloaded all the information at the end of the day.

  If you are somebody who says, "I'd be lost without my phone", then this works since you'll always have it with you and you depend on it anyway. Just make sure (as in chapter 10) you've got the vital devices insured and all the data backed up!

There might be other things you can do to get a clear idea of where the money goes. The website (www.tamingthepound.com) is there and if you've got strategies that have helped you, please share them with others through the site, or let me know and I'll put the ideas out there to help others.

All of this, you might have noticed, ties in very much to the R of our GROW mnemonic; it is about reality, where you are, what situation you are in.

Notice the first part is G, where do you want to get to. Bear in mind your values, what you want from your life, what your goals might be etc. This is where partner, friends, family might be of help. What are those dreams you have always talked about, what do you really, really want?

When you've got that idea, and have a clear idea of your "reality", you can start working out options. Professional advice might help there. But the options depend on what the reality is. And maybe the reality is debt.

Debt

People get into debt for all sorts of reasons, sometimes including having lost their job.

Some quick 'Don'ts' first.

- Don't get advice on debt from anybody who is getting paid to advise only on debt.
- Don't bother with the "IVA"s, "easy bankruptcy", or "we'll do the negotiations with creditors" people that advertise on TV.
- Don't even consider bankruptcy, signing any agreements etc. until you've talked to somebody from one of the organisations I'll mention.
- Don't go for a "consolidation loan" or extend the term of a loan until you've talked to somebody from one of the organisations I'll mention. These are connected.

Businesses are there to make money. If somebody is going to do legal or accountancy work for you (setting up some agreement, drafting bankruptcy proceedings) or is going to act as your agent (negotiating with people on your behalf) they have got to get paid for it. If you aren't paying them, the other side is. That means they are acting as the other side's agent, not yours. What is probably going to happen is that you are going to pay for it one way or another, and you are going to pay far more than whatever they do can possibly be worth (particularly bearing in mind that mostly, what they do is worse than useless).

TV advertising is expensive. Even in the daytime when there is nothing on worth watching, it is expensive. If you deal with the people hawking their services to those in financial trouble, who do you think is paying for the advertising? Right, the people in financial trouble. Life is hard, and the Bible was right,

"To him that hath shall be given. Him that hath not, even that which he hath shall be taken away."

If you're one of the "hath not's" don't give all your money to the advertisers who "hath"!

And ignore people who try to scare you by quoting statistics on how overstretched the legitimate services are. They will quote accurate figures and suggest that they come from legitimate sources, like Credit Action, which may well be true. What they want you to assume is that they are connected to one of the honest, charitable institutions. They're not, and if the Government actually protected its citizens, they would go to gaol for peddling scare stories.

I know the adverts and scare stories make you think you've got to get their help, but you don't, there are better places to go for help that will cost you a lot less money. Also, while consolidating all your little difficult-to-pay loans into one, big, impossible-to-pay loan sounds great, don't do it until you've worked out what you want and where you are financially (as in the earlier part of this chapter) and if you're in debt, checked it out with the organisations that will help you, not charge you.

Loans

If you are going to take out a loan, ignore the "payday loans" and all those high interest, short term things (remember the maths chapter and all the stuff on APR). They often won't quote you an APR for a start, so you should walk away. If they do it will be hundreds of per cent, and it is financial suicide to take those loans on.

If you need short term finance, go to a bank or better still a Credit

Union, which I'll describe in a moment. If they won't lend to you because you have such a poor credit rating, why do you think that is? It's because you can't pay the loan back, so you are a bad risk.

> If you are such a bad risk, is it likely you can pay back this "short term" loan from a payday loan company at a far higher rate of interest than the bank would charge?

Of course not. What you will do is get a "small, short-term" loan that will gradually become a permanent rolling loan that will get bigger and bigger until it destroys your finances and eventually you.

If you think you've got debt problems now, wait until you have had a "short term" loan for a year and are facing the 1,000 per cent plus interest rate. You'll regard your current situation as being wealth!

Far and away the best sources of small loans (and encouragement to savings) are Credit Unions. Hardly anybody in the UK has heard of them, but they are great. Basically, they are financial co-operatives owned and controlled by their members. They offer savings schemes and reasonably priced loans organised on a non-profit, local basis. You can find out more about them via the Association of British Credit Unions (ABCUL) at Holyoake House, Hanover Street, Manchester, M60 OAS Tel: 0161 832 3694, E Mail: info@abul.org Website: www.abcul.coop

Of course, there is a problem, namely that despite allegedly supporting them (while ignoring loan sharks, "payday loan" companies and other parasites), successive UK Governments have managed to keep them a secret, which is why very few have heard of them.

Then, in July 2010 it the Credit Union Legislative Reform Order was delayed until 2011. Because Britain has such an archaic and restrictive bureaucracy, UK membership lags behind membership in just about every other civilized country anyway. So rather than being able to expand to serve a wider area, most Credit Unions are restricted to a single borough, locality, employer or association and it will stay like that for at least another year. I sometimes despair of the UK Government!

ABCUL have a search facility for Credit Unions by area at: http://www.abcul.org/page/members.cfm, hopefully, whether you need a loan now or not, there is one that you can join and it is very well worth finding out about them.

> *Similar to payday loans, it might sound great to reduce payments by extending the term of the loan. Don't. Again, at least not until you've worked out what you want and where you are, have checked out other options like Credit Unions and have got advice from an ethical organisation if you are seriously in debt.*

I talked earlier about the reason for this last point, the effects of compound interest and so on. But I've got another true story for you that is an even better word of warning about extending loan repayment periods, and as a bonus it gives an example of why you are unwise to go to "commercial" loan or debt advisors.

You remember my friend Mike, whose pragmatic quote started chapter 7? You might also remember in chapter 9 I talked about the strange, fairy land where endowment mortgages were used. I'd taken out a couple of low cost endowments for myself, when they still got the tax relief, mortgage interest was tax free etc. so they were a good idea. I'd also suggested them for various friends and family including Mike.

It came out in conversation that he was thinking of cashing his in, which was very rarely a good idea. It turned out that somebody had told him about an "even better" deal. This had lower premiums each month, and sounded too good to be true, so being a pragmatic and clever chap, he figured it probably was, became suspicious, asked me about it.

This was a type of policy where the premiums went up each year for the first five years of a 25 year policy. I knew about those and thought they were daft. They were supposedly designed for the first time buyer, to make the purchase even cheaper in the early years and were called, "low start, low cost endowment assurances". Instead of paying, say, £50 each month, you'd pay only £40 each month the first year, £45 each month the second, and so on, and end up at £60 per month after the fifth year. This was to "help" the borrower!

Hopefully by this stage of the book, if you wouldn't have before, you can work out that this is a bad deal. You are paying a bit less for two years, but after the third year and for the next 22 years you pay more. You end up paying a lot more (I'll leave you to work out how much, it's good practice!).

I never used them, on the basis that they were such a bad deal and if, as they were intended, they allowed people to buy a house too big for them that they could only afford today by taking a lousy deal for tomorrow and ever after, they were accidents waiting to happen.

That isn't because I predicted a crash, disaster in housing or anything. Put simply, for a deal like that to be worthwhile we would have to have high inflation and huge house price rises every year for 25 years. Those were the conditions we had at the time, and there seemed no reason why they wouldn't go on, but I could see that if things changed at some point, particularly in the first few years, the person lost a job, had their income reduced or any sort of other problem, then they would lose the house.

Therefore, *knowing even then* that life was unpredictable and things rarely stay the same for decades on end, these policies were not a good idea.

So I asked Mike why he would even consider doing it. Apart from anything else he had started the policy a year or so before so it only had 24 years to run and he could cope with the premium. Why would he need a lower premium and why would he throw away what he'd paid already and start to pay for another 25 years? What he said made my blood run cold. He was told he could run the new policy for two years, then cancel it and start a new one. That way, he'd always have lower premiums!

I hope you can see at least one of the problems there.

1. You probably got this one since I've dropped some fairly big hints. If you keep cancelling the policies, you never get them to run to the end to get the bonuses, so you never actually pay off the mortgage.

   You pay and pay and pay on the interest, so whatever you might have saved in premiums, you pay far more in interest. That is what happens when you extend the term, you pay less each month, but you continue to pay for years longer, so you end up paying out thousands of pounds more.

   It's quite easy to double or triple the amount you pay on a loan by extending the term. Again, do the maths as it is good practice, but have some smelling salts or a good strong drink ready because you are likely to need something when you find out just how much you were going to lose!

2. If you're way smarter than most people you'll have worked out that as you get older, the premium goes up (because you're more likely to die, see chapter 10) so although it is cheaper than the equivalent premium you'd pay at your age now, it is still more than you'd have to pay for the policy when you were younger.

   For example, say you're 20 at the beginning and the premiums are the same as our example above, £50 normal and £40 low start. By the time you're 30 your normal premium that was £50 when you were 20 is now £70 per month. So the low start premium at that point will be about £55 per month rising to £85. But if you'd kept your first policy going, you'd have still been paying £50 each month, and the policy would have been running for 10 years, with only 15 to go. The "cheaper" option actually becomes more expensive, and you have nothing to show for paying more money!

3. (And if you got this, you are either a good IFA or should apply to be appointed as Stephen Fry's stand in) the "initial commission paying" period was two years.

   That meant that the guy trying to sell it was looking to pick up about 70% (maybe more) of the first years premium (so perhaps £420 at a time when the average monthly salary was about £600), paid over two years, as his commission for the sale. After two years, the "renewal" commission would only be about 2%, so his solution was to sell lots of policies that lasted two years! He wasn't in the business of letting them buy what they needed, he was in the business of selling what he had to sell, because what he had to sell was what made him lots of money.

Help and advice on debt

Specific advice is always useful if you are a victim of this sort of thing and in terms of your rights, whether relating to finance, your house, or anything else there is a legal advice service, Community Legal Advice. It is a free, confidential service paid for by legal aid so there are conditions applied to who qualifies, but it may be worth contacting them to check. Their phone number is: 0845 345 4 345 and website: www.communitylegaladvice.org.uk

There are many sources of advice about debt, rights and general matters, and before we get to the debt ones I'd recommend, here are two that are commonly encountered that might also be useful.

Local advice centres. These can be good if they are free, are run as a charity etc. Usually they can't give you advice on the positives such as helping you to firm up your life values but can be great if you are having problems and the aim is simply to get out of financial trouble. They may also be very good on Options in terms of ways to economise and also Reality in terms of what bills to deal with. They differ a lot in terms of the quality of the advisors; the staff are almost always very considerate and want to help, but don't always have much technical knowledge about finance.

Government advice is usually in the form of websites or official bodies. It can be good, but limited. There is a huge amount of red-tape involved and the mills grind exceedingly slowly, but don't always grind very small. Often you can't find somebody who will give you specific help, it tends to be generic and everybody is too scared to step out of line and give you a definite answer in case they are held responsible. So it is usually more productive to use the resources to find general information and then research it yourself. The resources can usually be found via Directgov "the website of the UK government for its citizens, providing information and online services for the public all in one place" at: www.direct.gov.uk

If you are in debt contact one of the four organisations below as a first step.

I've already mentioned, **Credit Action**. They are the national money education charity promoting better thinking about money. I'll admit some bias because I've worked with them on some of my research and they are great. They specialise in education, so they don't give direct advice, they do things like training organisations (public and private), schools, prison staff etc. in how to deal with debt and credit and how to help staff and others with it.

Their website is www.creditaction.org.uk, through which, or via www.moneybasics.co.uk or phone 0207 380 3390, you can get various guides to help you sort out your own finances. Their good, popular self-help aid is their 'Dealing with Debt' guide which includes a 7-step process for you to work through:

The steps in that process are:

Step 1 Contact all creditors

Step 2 Decide priorities

Step 3 Prepare financial statement

Step 4 Maximise income

Step 5 Review expenditure

Step 6 Negotiate with priority creditors
Step 7 Negotiate with secondary creditors

If you want to know what, Priority Creditors are, there's a useful mnemonic to guide you (and lots of other good advice) in the book, The Money Secret, by Rob Parsons. Essentially, the priorities are ones that might jeopardise your home, fuel supplies or your liberty if they are not paid.

Some principle ones are represented by THEM FIRST, standing for:

Tax
Hire Purchase
Electricity/Gas
Maintenance or child support
Fines
Income tax
Rent/Mortgage
Second mortgage
TV licence

A second organisation, which is great if you want to talk through your situation in person with an expert who is not trying to sell to you, is **Citizens Advice** (www.citizensadvice.org.uk). They operate locally (but are a nationally organised charity), so you can go and see somebody if that suits you better than "do it yourself" or telephone help. They deal with lots of other things than debt, such as legal problems, so you might find you have to wait a while. This is often the case, many good organisations are charities where people are expert volunteers and there is, sadly, a lot of demand for their help. But you will get help, and it will be help that is free, unbiased and given in your best interests, not to make somebody else money at your expense.

If you are happy to deal with somebody by telephone, you can contact **National Debt Line** (0808 808 4000, website www.nationaldebtline.co.uk). They offer free debt counselling over the phone; also via their website you can contact them by e-mail.

Finally, there is the sister organisation to Credit action, the **Consumer Credit Counselling Service** (CCCS). This is the leading debt-counselling charity and provides free and confidential advice on debt issues by phone (0800 138 1111). They also have a website (www.cccs.co.uk) and, which is great, a web based service which allows you to work through the debt counselling process in your own time, anonymously.

If you can't face somebody in person or on the phone, you want to handle it yourself etc. there is a "work through" guide that was developed over three years, works really effectively and is proving very popular. The guide is at https://debtremedy.cccs.co.uk/.

So if you do have debt issues, get on those websites, they have some great resources, guides, budget planners, contact numbers, sources of specific advice for particular problems etc.

As final points on debt, copied straight from the Credit Action guide are some do's and don'ts that I heartily endorse for anybody looking at debts or a "Micawber crisis":

DO be realistic, face up to your true situation and resolve to deal with it using the help available to you.

DO get in touch with your creditors immediately to explain your difficulties.

DO give priority to those debts which may result in you losing your home, fuel supplies or your liberty.

DO remember that your creditors prefer small payments regularly rather than larger, irregular payments that you cannot sustain.

DO reply to creditors' letters and court documents within the time period specified and let them have all the facts.

DO keep copies of all correspondence, financial statements, debt schedules etc.

DO attend and/or be represented at court hearings and take all relevant correspondence with you, including your current financial statement.

DON'T ignore the problem – it won't go away.

DON'T give up trying to reach agreement with your creditors even if they are difficult and refuse your initial offers.

DON'T be threatened or bullied into making promises which you cannot fulfil.

DON'T borrow more money to pay off your debts, especially by taking on more credit or store cards.

DON'T be afraid to ask for specialist advice – it's FREE

And a final word from me. You *can* control what goes on with your finances.

The money isn't a scary monster, it is a trainable resource and when it is trained, it is a means for you to lead the life you want. But you have to train it, so if you need help to do that, get the help, there are no prizes for battling on alone, but there are lots of prizes for Taming your Pound, notably the life you actually want.

Summary:

- People don't become redundant, only jobs do.
- A job is just a job – it is not your value and it does not define you as a human being.
- Be aware of "fight or flight".
- We see what we expect to see – look for problems you'll see problems, look for opportunities you'll see opportunities.
- Is this a concern or a crisis?
- Stabilise the situation - take care of yourself and manage stress.
- Support your friends.
- Seek help and information for immediate problems.
- Buy time for major decisions.
- Check your options.
- Don't give up - your future starts today.

- "Eat your elephant a spoonful at a time".
- Have something you can look forward to.
- Make a budget – after you've sorted out what you are budgeting for.
- You might find it hard, but you need to do it, so whether you must knuckle down and do it, find it easy, or pay somebody to do it, you need to sort out a budget to know where you are.
- Get help if you need it.
- Don't get debt advice from commercial companies; their interests are not the same as yours.
- Go to one of the organisations I've mentioned (or another charity) to get debt advice. Or use their websites.

And now, we'll look at discussing these things (including debt) with your partner!

Love and marriage

This chapter is about discussing and arranging finance with your partner. It can be hard discussing money with anybody, since it is often taboo or sacred or the source of fear. It can be harder still talking about it with the person that you love most, when all the other triumphs and disasters of the relationship can creep in at the edges of the money.

Let me start by telling you the story of the one time in my life when I intentionally sold something.

I was taught to sell. I was never very good at it, which is why more than half of my 4-6 jobs that ended in redundancy worked out that way, I couldn't earn enough commission to keep employers happy! I always wanted to be an "expert", somebody you asked for advice, not somebody who sold things, even things that people wanted to buy. I never felt comfortable selling. I always gave people advice and waited for them to buy products or more of my advice.

I was due to see a couple about their finances. They were coming in to my office, but we had a big open plan "aeroplane hanger" with paper everywhere. I was wondering about taking them to the nearest coffee bar and saying that the office was being repainted or something. Then the couple turned up with their three children in tow, saying "sorry, is that OK, my sister was supposed to have the children, but something came up". Fortunately my boss was out, so I grabbed his office. I sat at the desk with the couple, while the three children slowly but efficiently wrecked everything in the office under two feet high.

It wasn't actually a requirement then (it definitely is now) but I always liked to get a full picture of what was going on. Even if somebody "just wanted a mortgage" I'd find out what else was going on for them, partly because there were often things that they didn't realise they could use, partly because it is the professional thing to do but mainly because I'm incurably nosy.

So we went through various questions about their finances, what they planned etc. And after about half an hour, several apologies from mother, three admonitions, "George, don't do that, the man will take it away from you if you do that" and so on, we got to life cover. Father was obviously a bit uneasy.

You'll remember from earlier that I believe you need to work out what income you need to provide if you're ill or dead, and death is a problem when you have dependents or you have commitments like a house with an outstanding mortgage. The wife didn't go out to work (three children under five strikes me as being more work and longer hours than a junior doctor anyway) so the sole breadwinner was the husband. They'd got a mortgage. They'd got three dependent children. So I figured they should have life and health insurance on both of the adults, because if something happened to either of them, the survivor was going to be in a lot of trouble.

I asked about life cover on the wife. She looked at the husband; "No, well, she doesn't work." I wasn't a psychologist then, but even I could see the warning lights flashing in her eyes. But he was oblivious.

"Have you got any income protection insurance on either of you?" I asked. There was a bit of confusion, so I explained that this wasn't medical fees cover, but so they had an income if one of them was ill or in an accident. He said he'd be paid by work if he was ill. I asked, "For how long?" she was obviously very interested in the answer and this time, he realised that she was interested. "For a long time, they'll look after me, it's OK." I asked, all innocence, whether they would pay him until the children were old enough to leave home if he was in a car accident, say, and unable to work.

There was more hesitation. He mumbled the usual lines about being a careful driver, he wouldn't be injured, "never had a day sick in my life, ha, ha!" Her interest deepened, so much so that as one of the brood tried to chew his way through the bookcase, her attention was entirely on her spouse.

"All right," I said, "I think it would be a good idea to check on the period for which you'd get paid, and perhaps arrange something for when your pay would stop." He agreed, very quickly. He obviously wanted to get out of there, even though his wife's expression suggested that leaving would be very much out of the frying pan into the fire.

"The other thing," I said, "is life cover on you. Do you know how much cover you have through work?" Panic flared up in his eyes. "It's OK," he said, very slowly, "I've taken care of it."

Often, in the past, I'd left things there. But with three children I really thought I'd got to get something sorted out for them. It wasn't about me being scared of selling, it was about being professional. If he wasn't going to deal with his own responsibilities over money voluntarily, maybe I'd have to prompt him to do it. "You've taken care of it?" I echoed. He nodded. "Fine," I said, poising my pen over my notepad, "how much is it you've arranged?"

There was a pause. She shifted in her seat, looking from my face to his and back again. He looked down. "I've got it in hand, you don't need to worry about it," then he shouted at the only child who wasn't currently trying to destroy something and said they'd better be going.

It was decision time. I'd been taught to sell. I knew what I needed to do. I just had to have the courage to do it. I made my decision.

"That's fine. But could you do me a small favour?" Yes, he said, grateful that I'd let him off the hook. "Just so that I understand things, I'd like to do a little bit of acting. What I'd like, Mr Client, is for you to be me. And Mrs Client, I'd like you to be your husband, just for a moment, and if it is OK, I'll be you. Now, I'm afraid, Mrs Client, that you don't have much to do, because you – that is, Mr Client – have just died. So I'm Mrs Client, and I've come to you, Mr Client, as my financial advisor, to find out what to do. I've got no income, I have three children under five and my husband has just died," and I indicated Mrs Client, who by this time was a rather more menacing corpse than "The Mummy". "Now," I said, looking at Mr Client, "as my advisor, what do you suggest I do about feeding and housing the children?"

And, for once in my life, I stopped talking.

This was straight out of the textbook. The secret was, let them speak. Whoever speaks first has lost. I had never seen it as a game of win or lose, but this time, I did. The books said you might have to wait five seconds, it might be as much as a minute. But even if it was an hour, don't say anything. Don't say, "well", clear your throat or anything, just let the silence work on them.

After what was probably five seconds (it seemed like a minute or two) he cleared his throat, started to speak but tailed off.

I waited.

After another ten seconds or so (this pause seemed like at least twenty minutes) his nerve started to crack and he began to say something. At that point, the "corpse" returned from the dead.

"Shut up," she said to him, forcefully enough to stop the children momentarily, even the one attempting to dismember her handbag. "You told me you'd sorted this out." On the receiving end he tried to dig his way backwards through his chair, "well..." he said.

"I trusted you to sort it out,' she went on, 'you said you had. How would we be if you had died. What would have happened to me, to your children?"

I wondered about intervening. It seemed possible that she would a) kill him before any policy could go into force and b) use her handbag as the handiest blunt instrument with which to do the deed, which would involve projecting the child clinging to it either into its father's head or the wall behind him.

But he tried to save the day; "I'm sorry, can we ....." he started.

"Shut up", she said. Turning to me, she asked "Mr Stephenson, what should we do?"

We got some details sorted out, I made a couple of phone calls, we arranged a medical, I got the details of his company's HR department so I could check what cover he'd already got and gave them some literature on "housewife" health insurance policies. Any time it looked like he was going to protest, she gave him a "if you think you're in trouble now, just you wait until we're out of earshot of third parties and children and you'll understand what trouble is," look and he subsided.

I don't honestly know whether they ever needed to use the insurance we arranged that day at any time before the children grew up. I hope not, because I hold the family in great affection as the only people with whom I ever used a sales technique. I'd be sad to think that one of them died or was injured before their time. But of course, if they were, the survivor and the children would be upset, but at least they wouldn't be in financial trouble as well.

There are several useful lessons for couples in that story – and by the way it is true. OK, maybe the children weren't quite that cutesy, and the dialogue isn't word for word (I didn't tape it) but the basic situation, events and outcome are all completely true.

The four big lessons I'd pick out of it make a nice structure for the rest of the chapter. These are:

1. *Honest Communication,*

2. *Agreeing plans*

3. *Taking responsibility jointly for what happens*

4. *Both knowing what is going on.*

Honest Communication.

This is probably the most important. And it is tricky! We're not just talking about the accidental lack of communication, but deliberate deceit. In 2009 there were two surveys that indicated that 19% of Britons kept secret debts hidden from partners, 10% lied about the number of credit cards they had and 15% said they kept their partner in the dark about how much they earned.

At the same time, people apparently wanted to know what was going on, since 27% had read their partner's bank statements or pay slips without them knowing.

Oh, and 89% thought financial honesty was important in a relationship!

By April, 2010, research indicated that one in three people hid financial problems from the family.

So it appears to be getting worse, if it went from around a fifth (19%) to a third of people (33%) less than a year later.

> *There seem to be three major reasons why couple's don't communicate honestly (or are tempted not to) and they all come from being reluctant to trust the other person. Those three are:*
>
> - *It might put you in their power if they know so much about you, they might not feel you are "pulling your weight" (or that you feel they don't pull theirs!)*
>
> - *It might mean admitting to something you're ashamed of, like big debts or a secret passion for shoes or gadgets.*
>
> - *You want an "exit door", a means to get away if things go wrong.*

I'm not going to moralise about it. But I do think it is a shame when couples don't trust one another. After all, if you get married you make vows about that sort of thing and if you have children you'd probably like to set them an example you want them to follow; and suspecting the one person you're closest to will betray you is probably not the example of relating to others that you want to set them.

Still, that is imagining an ideal world, and the world is the way it is, the point is how do you deal with it?

One thing about "being in somebody's power" and power relationships themselves are "gender roles". As I mentioned in chapter 6, equality is a fine concept, but it is an abstract concept.

What does it mean?

We can all say, "equal work for equal pay" and mean it, but what is equal work? Since the man cannot bear children, does that mean that he's actually doing less work? Since maternity leave means the woman is not available in the work place all the time, does that mean that her work is not "equal"?

I'm not saying either is right, just that different people can have set ideas about what is right. That's just one, pretty simple, point of "equality".

If you are a couple and your fundamental beliefs (formed by your genes, your family, your history and experience, your political and religious beliefs etc.) are different, then you could view what the other one regards as "equal" as being grossly "unequal".

I got asked by a journalist once whether I thought the increasing earning power of women affected how couples deal with money issues? I said it did, and made it a lot more complicated.

Not that it necessarily made it more unfair, just more complex. I certainly wouldn't want to go backwards. Personally, I don't think we're anywhere near "equal" in terms of "pay for work" between the sexes yet, but it is much "better" now than years ago.

The problem is that gender roles are far more loosely defined than they were, so it is harder to work out what to do to be "fair". When my parents married in the 1950's my mother earned more, but once a 'married' woman she was automatically no longer considered suitable as an employee (even that far from the immediate post war era there was still concern about women "taking" men's jobs); it was still seen as a man's duty to be the main breadwinner and the woman's to keep the home. Therefore, my mother had to budget the household on my father's income and there was nothing to argue about.

It might not be fair in the abstract and it might horrify you as it does me by its Palaeolithic stereotyping, but that was the way it was. My parents could just get on with it, with nobody telling them that whatever they did was wrong. We've moved on from there (I think) to a more equitable society. That is great, but the only thing that is truly equal is that whatever we do, both women and men seem to feel equally guilty that we should have done something else!

> Now there is greater variability, so what is the role of either partner (and how does that affect same sex couples?) and what "should" their roles be?
>
> It isn't just about who earns more and whether the pay scales are fair, but who makes the money decisions, whose job is "less important" so they have time for taking pets to the vet or to oversee the builders, as well as who should ask for a raise and who pays whom how much for study time or for giving up work for childcare?

So it is far more complicated, not just because of greater pay equality but because of changing gender roles, changing social norms and the reality of people. For example, most women are more likely to take time off to look after children, even if their job is "more important" or higher paid, because of our evolutionary past. It isn't "logical" in a modern society but it persists because it is the way that evolution and selection pressure shaped us. That is the reality (read Susan Pinker's "Sexual Paradox" for dozens of examples and studies demonstrating it) and we have to work round it because the irrationality, unfairness and feelings of guilt all round aren't going to go away.

> *So, in keeping with the importance of values, work out what the two of you really want, not what society, your friends, your parents or anybody else says you "ought" to want.*

If what the pair of you are happier doing, like the man being the principle breadwinner and the woman being the housekeeper, bringer up of children etc. is conventional then that is nobody else's business and just because it is what your grandparents did doesn't make it immoral or mean you are "letting down your sisters" or being a Neanderthal or something. By the same token, if the woman has a well paid, high pressure job that she loves and the man would like to stay at home and be the housekeeper, bring up the children (now we have baby milk, breast pumps etc. it isn't essential that the woman does huge amounts beyond actually carrying the baby for nine months) why not?

> *If other people tease the man, or say the woman is "unnatural" or something, then that is their problem. Personally I think any critic should probably have a good look at their own situation and how they have been weak enough to feel threatened by anybody who breaks the convention of either doing what your parents did or deliberately not doing what they did. Who cares what they did or what other people think, do what you both want to do.*

But in order to do that, you have to be honest about what *you* want to do. If you really hate your conventional role, or really want it, or whatever, you need to share that honestly with your partner. If you suffer in silence, you're very likely to have a problem with it at some point.

It tells me what society thinks.

That's what they say.

It's even trickier if you're ashamed of what you do with money. If you have been deceiving your partner for years, it is hard to "come clean". I think it is better in the long run, but then I would, wouldn't I, because I don't have to do the confessing!

If you can make it a mutual confession, and start off with a clean slate, deal with the problems and both go forward with more honesty and a better picture of what is really going on, that is great. You may find that the relationship is even better. I contributed to an article in the Guardian by Kate Hilpern in 2008 which reported on the number of couples splitting up over money problems. I pointed out then that good relationships can often get stronger under pressure; you fight together, look after one another and come out the other side with an even better relationship. However the same pressure that can weld you together can also split you apart along any fault lines that exist if the relationship is shaky to start with.

There aren't, as with most of these things, "one size fits all" answers. If you have a basically strong relationship, then on balance you are probably better off trying to get more honest rather than less. If the relationship is less trusting, for example if you are thinking about your "exit door", then maybe being totally honest in one go, while desirable in theory might be too much for the relationship in practice. I'd suggest in that case that maybe you get some professional counselling (see chapter 15).

> *If you want "exit money" etc. fine. That's what you want. It isn't the same as having separate accounts (which we'll come to in a minute). This is more about keeping a degree of independence. Just because you're a couple, doesn't mean you're joined at the hip, you are still individuals.*

If things are at the point where you are scared to admit what you've done (or do) with money, are ashamed of yourself (or angry with your partner) and don't really see how you are going to get to a point where honesty is an option, then perhaps the relationship generally needs to be thought about. Financial worries are the number one reason for families to seek help from Relate (http://www.relate.org.uk/home/index.html), a charity that provides relationship help. But is the money the real issue, or is the relationship the issue and the money guilt, shame, anger etc. just an obvious and easy way to focus all your doubts?

The difference I'd see between having honest, agreed "independence money in case it all goes wrong" and having the same fund that you squirrel away secretly is what it means to you. If what it means is, "I'm realistic, I know people can change as they grow, couples can grow apart, whatever their intentions." then maybe that is sensible. Perhaps you've had a partner who ran up debts and lumbered you with them, maybe you saw your parents or other relatives have problems and don't want to be trapped. There might be many good reasons why it makes sense to you. But can you tell your partner, and explain why it is important to you?

On the other hand, if the "independence fund" means that you can't trust your partner and predict that the relationship is going to end in the foreseeable future, what then? This may be something you don't want to share with them, since basically you don't trust them enough to dare tell them that you don't trust them!

Again, there isn't a simple answer. But generally, if you can tell your partner why you want to have "escape money" or whatever, if the relationship is reasonably good and they actually care about you and want you to be happy, maybe they are going to understand that and perhaps even want the same thing themselves but were scared to say so because it sounded as if they didn't trust you.

If you feel you have to keep money a secret, ask yourself why. If you think the relationship is so dodgy that implying you don't trust them will finish it, what is going to happen if you don't trust them, have secret funds and they then find out? Obviously, it has to be your decision, you are the one who knows you and your partner (I don't know either of you), but in general, honest communication is likely to be better, and if honest communication about money is not an option, think about why not and whether you need to do some work on the relationship, like seeing a counsellor or something.

Honesty in communications also applies to your values generally. If you aren't sure yet where the relationship is going, whether you want to get married, have children etc. there is no problem deferring big decisions and just enjoying the time together.

But if you're taking on commitments such as mortgages, children, moving to a different area because of one partner's job offer etc. you probably need either to sort out where you are going or decide when you will sit down and discuss it. After all, you can't plan your finances if neither of you know what you yourself are trying to achieve, and if you haven't even shared the vague dreams you have of taking a year off and travelling, having 17 children or buying the Taj Mahal, when are you going to break it to them!

I'm not talking just about practical things like wills when you have children, buy a house or get married. I mean your ideas and values. What do you both want from life, what would make you happy?

Are jobs of vital importance to both, one or neither of you?

Do either or both of you dream of doing something different, maybe travelling or conversely being centres of the local community?

What is going to make you happy, and what is going to make your partner happy – do you know and do you ever talk about it?

Also, as we saw in chapters 1 and 2, men and women often have different symbols for money that frequently get confused with real values. If he wants the big house because it says "status" and she wants it because it says "security" (or vice versa), that might be OK, but it might be that you both think your aim of the big house is the same and unless you talk through what you both really value and want, you might not be as "like minded" as you think.

For example, what is more important, the swimming pool and gym complex, the walled vegetable garden or the child friendly surface and surround to the trampoline and "kiddie gym"? If you've only got the money for one at a time, which one gets priority?

And, as we saw in chapter 1, money is a taboo, probably bigger than sex nowadays. Since sex is less taboo, and more fun, let's think about sex!

If you feel unattractive, or undesired what does that do to your preparedness to be open and honest about your (or your partner's) good and bad points and what you would like to happen in bed (or elsewhere come to that)? It's not as if money is realistically as big a threat to feelings of masculinity or femininity or to your personal identity as, for example, mastectomy or impotence. But with so much weight placed on money by society (again, like sex, are you getting enough, are your habits normal, do you get as many kicks out of it as others), there's a lot of anxiety.

And many people get the idea that just as you "ought" to have wild sex every night, you "ought" to be in control of your money; so the perception is that if you don't or can't you're defective. It's emotive, you're worried about whether you're getting enough and it is tied up with your self-perception and sense of worth. Lots of us are in denial, "Money worries, what money worries, not me!" We're scared to be open and honest, even (especially) with our partner.

If you are going to have discussions about values, being honest etc. then read through chapter 2 again and maybe do some of the exercises together, it sometimes works out to be a good bonding experience.

If it is hard to have that conversation and you tend to get into arguments whenever you discuss it, don't despair! I've been told by people who deal with couples (like specialist couples counsellors) that many people worry about their clashes with their partner over money, afraid that it's a signal of impending doom and that it means they have no future together.

Most couples argue about money to some extent, but don't tell their friends about it. It would be even more embarrassing than admitting sexual dysfunction, so you don't hear about their problems!

People may have arguments because they haven't talked about what money means, what it symbolises for them, what they really value. They are trying to sort out who pays for what and how the finances are arranged before they work out what they want the finances to do. Therefore, some couples row because they are talking about the "best" way to do it, and neither has asked, "what are we trying to do"?

> *Do remember, if you have a row about it, at least you are talking!*
>
> *The conversation may involve airborne crockery, but it is still a conversation. Suffering in silence and never finding out what is going on with one another is only "absence of evidence of rows", it isn't "evidence of absence of rows"!*

A few practical points of advice for having serious conversations about money. Things that often work well are:

- Giving ideas as possibilities and asking what your partner thinks about that idea. It gives them time to think rather than putting them on the spot for an immediate answer, and it means they don't have to disagree. You aren't proposing it as your plan, you are offering it as an option you wondered about and wanted to know their opinion, you're showing them respect.

- Take responsibility and accept that you, personally, need help. You need to be prepared to admit that you'd like some help and maybe some professional advice might be good, for example, "I'm concerned about this, because of X, and I'm not sure what to do. I wondered about getting some information about it from Y, what do you think?" It gives them the chance to be seen to help you, but at the same time admit they don't feel in control either and also want help, without having the feeling that they are weak.

- Keep it in proportion. Money is a means to an end, not an end in itself. At the end of the day, if you're both happy and healthy does it matter if you're living in a tent, who said you have to be rich? If you are miserable and think that "if only" you had more money or more control over money life would be perfect, you maybe want to get together and have a look at your priorities before you worry over much about the money. If either of you is taking it so seriously that failure to agree on everything or have it all pinned down immediately seems like the end of the world and/or the relationship, lighten up, you're talking without flying crockery, it's a start!

On the other hand, some things that tend not to work so well are:

- Hitting your partner with a request for a serious talk about money when they've just had a row with the boss, have lost their major client, a patient has just died, etc. If they (or you) are already stressed, anxious, upset or generally on edge, the chances are that neither of you will think clearly and one or both of you will say something you regret later. As in chapter 11, give yourself a bit of time to think about these things. If you are under stress over money and are anxious all the time, then start off by both acknowledging the fact. Reassure one another that it's human to be anxious, that nobody makes their best decisions when they are upset and that you can put some ideas out there and then maybe both sleep on them. You don't have to dive in and do everything the instant you think of it.

- It's not usually a good idea to involve other people such as well meaning friends who are "sorted financially" at this stage. However much they try to help, they are almost certainly going to imply (or you will infer) that the only way to organise your finances is their way. That is a pretty good way to mess up your own finances even more, you turn a potentially first class financial agreement between yourself and your partner into an, at best, second rate copy of somebody else's agreement. You are unique, so is your partner, together you are – well, you can't be "very unique", it's either unique or not, but if you could do it, the pair of you would be even more unique than you are individually! You need your own system that works for you as a couple and it doesn't matter what anybody else does.

- For the same sorts of reasons, comparing your partner or yourself to other people is often a way to turn a discussion into a row. For example; saying, "you're just like X, head in the sand," or "Y and Z have got it sussed, why can't we be like that," is probably not going to help because it immediately tends to put your partner on the defensive.

Agreeing plans

This happens after you sort out your individual and joint values and communicate them. As with personal values, budgeting etc. lots of people try to do this first, often because "experts" lay down the law and say "you should do X with your money".

Just like whether you have "escape money", who is the main breadwinner, or who takes time off for things, the way you handle the practicalities are up to you. Just because somebody you admire has separate accounts, a joint account for expenses with separate accounts for private money, one central account or whatever, doesn't mean you should or that if you do it will work for you. Your parents were right, just because Jon or Jean was allowed £25 a week pocket money doesn't mean you should have it too! You and your partner are unique (or "very unique" if you insist) and you need your own agreement.

We all fear that other people are better sorted, because we only see our own problems and the chaos in our own heads, not the equal or greater problems and chaos elsewhere. We all think that everybody else is better paid, has their finances sorted, credit cards paid off, holidays booked and paid for 18 months in advance. It's a fallacy. Lots of people are living a lie, they can't afford their lifestyle and live in dread of stuff being re-possessed and that their image of being wealthy, carefree, in control of their money is going to fall apart.

It is also a reason to have that debate on how you handle money as a private discussion. Just as you don't care how other people do it, they don't need to know how you do. Airing your private financial details to other people is usually not a good move. Don't worry about what other people do, you don't actually know if their finances are in any better state than yours and if they are, copying their style isn't going to help. Sort out your own style, discuss it honestly and openly with the only people concerned, you and your partner.

> *One reason you need to sort out your values, discuss them honestly and determine how much trust you have first is that, often I hear, "my partner probably would/wouldn't....", followed by some breach of trust, fib, etc. 'Probably' is probably not enough, you probably need to find out what they really think rather than assume.*

Once you are in the position of having *talked* about what you both want, not merely assume that you know, you can get on to the practicalities of money. Some things you can do are:

Have totally separate finances. That is great if you want to be independent. You can work out a rent for one of you to pay the other if you live together while the other pays the mortgage and maintenance, for example. Or you can split all the costs down the middle. Small technical point with that, you can also have a tenancy in the house called, Tenants-in-common, which basically means you own your own shares independent of one another and your share forms part of your estate if you die rather than going to the survivor as with the more usual Joint tenants. One aspect of this is that it can make it easier to work out who gets the profit if the house goes up in value and you split up and want to sell (or who takes the loss if it goes down), another reason you need proper legal advice over property!

Other advantages of separate finances are that you can each pay your own way so you're not spending one another's money, presents are genuine presents from your own money, etc. It starts to get a bit more elaborate with joint expenses, but you can, for example, furnish the room and split all the costs down the middle.

This starts to get more complicated if you have children.

What does the person who gives up more time do if they don't have paid work because of children?

Do they get to feel like a freeloader because they are not paying their share anymore, does the one who is earning more pay them for their time, and if so, how much?

What about if you earn different amounts to start with; do you allocate the value of the house in proportion to the amount you put in (so if one pays 2/3 of the mortgage and the bills, do they get 2/3) and what happens if the relative incomes change, one of you loses your job etc.?

Also, what about cars, do you have a better car because you have more money, so your partner isn't allowed to drive your car?

What about if one of you wants to study for advanced qualifications or to get another job, and has to take a cut in salary to do it; do they give up their share while they are not earning, do they get paid a proportion that they pay back, how does it work?

I'm not saying it is a bad idea, it is just that with the apparent simplicity of having separate finances come complications when you have liabilities, responsibilities or assets that are not separate but joint.

If you and your partner looked at that and thought, "that's daft, we'd agree it as we went along, we know what we both value and what we don't", fine.

That's one reason why, when people say to me that "if we get married I'd insist on a pre-nuptial agreement" I tend to ask how many hundred pages they think it will need to cover everything. Not that pre-nuptial agreements are a bad idea inherently, it is just that if you haven't sorted out the values in the relationship (do you want children, what are your values that you want your money to help you achieve, how important to happiness are your jobs, etc.) you will have a hard time setting everything out.

You can't rely on "we have shared values about .....," you can't use a shared common sense approach; you have to nail it all down in writing.

That doesn't tend to engender trust, so if you *start* to write it all down, you have to write it *all* down. That doesn't just take the romance out of it, you end up with something the length of war and peace to argue about on cold winter nights!

On the other hand you can make the assumption that your partner sees it all the same way that you do without even talking about it, and if you find you don't share the values, either the sketchy pre-nuptial agreement isn't going to give you the answer or you have to decide to rewrite it every few months.

> *So I'd suggest talking about your values in depth, then if you want to put it in writing afterwards, fine.*
>
> *Go into legal deals first off and you'll probably never get as far as values, you'll be too busy drawing up battle lines. The only people who make money from disputes are lawyers, not the two of you.*

You can go to the other extreme, *share everything, have one account.* That works for some couples. It makes things simple, you don't have "mine and yours", you have "ours".

It does get tricky buying presents. Do you give up birthdays and Christmas because most or all of the money is provided by your partner and anyway, both of you know whatever comes out so there are no surprises? You need a lot of trust to do that. If you've got anything to buy without making an issue of it, you can't really do that without having some secret money you don't tell your partner about. Good for you both if you are that honest and trusting, but it might be a bit too much of a good thing for many people.

It may also, for those who have had bad experiences in the past, be too scary. There is too much risk of the partner taking more than their share, absconding with the common money, running up debts etc.

There's also the issue with spending (particularly on children). If one of you persistently uses the common funds to pay for things the other one doesn't want or think are worthwhile (the monthly professional carpet cleaning because you're obsessional/careful about cleanliness, the treats for the children because you are a good/overindulgent parent, the money for clothes or hobbies because you are well-dressed/keen/poor with money) then you might trigger rows about what and how much "ought" to be spent.

You can also go for a *mix of accounts*. Again, it isn't perfect but it does give you more flexibility. You might have a joint account that is for the major bills into which you both pay most of your money, and have individual accounts that get your individual "pocket money". You have to adjust that if one earns more than the other, one gives up or reduces time on work for any reason etc. so you still need to have worked out what you're trying to do first. You might have a housekeeping account that the "sole breadwinner" pays into (and that is topped up with any benefits etc.), then two separate individual accounts also paid from the breadwinners salary.

On course, you need to work out what is a joint expense and what isn't, are toys for the baby, dry cleaning bills, gadgets for the car, basic clothing etc. joint expenses or individual ones?

Are all clothes individual expenses, or only really impractical ones?

You can buy presents for one another out of "your own" money, but what about treats for both of you?

Is a luxury evening out a treat from one of you to the other or a joint expense, and if it is a joint expense who is responsible for making up the shortfall if you can't pay the mortgage or the joint credit card for essential shopping this month?

Taking responsibility jointly for what happens

Basically, whatever system you use, you need to know how you will handle small indulgences and how small is "small". You'll probably also need a limit on personal spending, over which you discuss it. That means a limit for "impulse buying". And it has to be a limit for impulsive spending, not just impulsive timing. If you've agreed that you'll spend money on something at some point, and the point happens to be tomorrow, fine. If you've agreed that you'll spend £500 and you spend £5,000 that is probably not so fine!

OK, the coat (three piece suite, whatever) is a bargain, but it is £500 and you don't have that much.

Fine, it was for "us" not "you", I accept it was a bargain, I know that you can stick it on a credit card and pay it off next month. But the fact remains that the money isn't available and if you're going to do it this time, what happens when you see the Versace bag that is a snip at only £3,000 or the Aston Martin Volante, an absolute steal at only £25,000?

Whose money is it anyway?

So know what you are trying to achieve (your joint values), discuss your joint goals and then arrange your finances with flexibility and guidelines (or absolute rules, whatever you need) to suit yourselves.

There are a few things you almost certainly both need to do, as I mentioned earlier, when you get a mortgage, a partner or children.

One is to get wills made. It isn't fun to think about, but death is going to happen. We hope it doesn't happen soon, but it is going to. So discuss what you want, particularly if you aren't actually married, since the intestacy laws are downright weird regarding non-married couples!

And don't think just about the money, but also who is going to look after the children (are you going to care for them full time, and work full time, all on your own), who do you want as guardians for them if neither of you are around, who is going to help out your parents when they are getting on in years if you aren't around to do it and what should happen to your property. Not fun, but important to think about.

Also, insurance becomes more important when you have a mortgage, children or a partner. So have a look at chapter 10, discuss it, and if necessary get some professional help.

Some "experts" (and a lot of people who confuse convention with motivation and/or good sense) assume that all couples "should" make all the financial decisions jointly. Ignore them. If you want to do that, great, do it, but do it because it suits you, not because it indicates that you are a "new age" couple or some daft abstract theory that says true equality can only come from being identical. We're not identical, we're unique (and that applies to same sex couples just as much as different sex ones).

Various people (idiots) think that somehow men are "naturally better" at finances than women. That is just downright wrong, as we saw in chapter 6, any sex differences are about interests and motivation not ability and you'll note in chapter 8 there was no reference to gender in terms of maths. I know of absolutely no evidence which says there is any systematic ability difference between the genders that can't be explained by different treatment. Any average differences in mathematical ability between the sexes are swamped by the differences within. In other words two men, or two women, are likely to differ in ability as much or more than one man and one woman.

What might differ will be interest, and since finance wasn't relevant to hunter gatherers (they didn't have money), it will be an interest that somebody has acquired in their own lifetime because they thought they ought to know about it, not because it gave them an advantage in breeding that got passed on. It's social, not genetic. Actually, in my experience more women than men are interested in understanding finances, but that is coincidence and possibly because I'm a man so women can admit interest and ignorance to me without feeling weak, while men can't, because I'm male and potential competition.

Anyway, since there isn't any particular ability difference, I'd suggest that if one of you is interested and the other not, you let the one who is interested lead, since they will have the motivation to do a good job and not cut corners.

Even more often than one being interested (usually, neither partner I see really wants to bother, they both just want to spend it!), one will have more need for control. It isn't necessarily linked to spending, you can be obsessional about keeping receipts, ticking off cheque stubs etc. and still spend like a drunken sailor on shore leave and you can be totally haphazard with paperwork and be tighter than a very tight thing.

One partner will often be more organised, have the spreadsheets, the knowledge of where papers are, file everything away neatly etc.

If you take that away from them, they will probably worry endlessly. If you hand it to the partner who doesn't like doing it, they won't do it "properly", the one who is organised will get upset and start, "I'm not criticizing, but...." and, as they say, "confusion ensues" as well as resentment and potential financial meltdown.

So as with the organisation of roles and bank accounts, the way you organise the paperwork and keep track of debts etc. is entirely up to the pair of you. It is nobody else's business and whether you want to make all decisions jointly, leave it to one of you, take it in turns, all of the above or none, it doesn't matter, as long as it gets done.

But it does have to get done!

Both knowing what is going on.

Whether you do everything together or one takes the lead, let's assume you've sorted out your values, know what makes each other happy, have set your goals, made your plans and your wills, and insurance etc. are arranged to protect what you've got in case of disaster. You've also got your accounts arranged to suit yourselves, know what you can spend impulsively, what comes out of the joint account, what is your own expense etc.

Great. Only one more thing. What happens if one of you dies suddenly? Horrible thing to think about, but it is important. Apart from the grief, the awful hole in your life, the possibility of having to explain to the in-laws (or worse, the children) what has happened, you need to sort out the legal issues, the property and the money, all at a time when you probably want to sit and cry or get blind drunk.

> What happens if the one who did all the finances, who knew where the deeds to the house, the wills, the children's savings accounts, the life assurance policies, the account details for the bank, the reference numbers for the ISAs etc. is the one who died?

> It's OK being bored by finance. It's OK not really having a clue. It's OK (in many ways it is quite heart-warming) that you can totally trust your partner (now your late partner) to do "all that stuff". But what are you going to do now?

Apart from all the new pressures, your grief and all the aftermath of a death, you'd have to learn all about all the money. When you are explaining to the lender how you're going to pay off the remainder of the mortgage, who is explaining it to you? When you're telling the children about how it is going to be fun to have a nanny, it will be like Mary Poppins and they'll get to stay with Auntie Polly sometimes, won't that be nice, who will be telling you how you'll afford the nanny and how you'll get the children over to Auntie Polly's in the car you can't drive because it's manual and you can only drive an automatic?

> *Sorry, but you both have to know what is going on. If one of you has and likes control, they can write out detailed instructions as to where everything is, what is needed, how things will work. The control freak part of you will probably like that. Even if you are the one who loathes thinking about money, you can certainly learn where one bit of paper is kept.*

But mainly, you need to discuss the possibilities. Neither of you need to have every detail committed to memory, but one or both of you needs the full picture in outline and the detail on paper, and the other one needs at least enough knowledge to know how to cope if something awful happens.

Probably, however, nothing awful will happen – but if you're prepared, you've blunted the worst effects of it and that is well worth doing. What you'll also have done, by preparing, by sorting out your values, communicating them honestly, agreeing your plans, jointly taking responsibility and knowing what is going on, is to have moved a long way towards achieving your values and getting the things in life that will really make both of you happy. And you'll probably have a lot stronger, more enjoyable relationship so you'll start off the rest of your life happier as well.

And then, after the summary, we move on to those little bundles of joy – children, and what you say to them about the money.

Summary:

- Communicate honestly
- One size doesn't fit all couples, do what suits you.
- Ignore "ought's" what others do etc. you are the important ones.
- Work out your values together, not just financially but in life.

- If you plan changes, children, new jobs, studying etc. work out together how the relationship needs to change.
- Agree plans.
- Sort out how you hold money, separate, joint, a mixture. Do you have "exit money"? What is a joint expense and what is a personal indulgence? Set out rules, guidelines or holy writ (whatever suits you) that you both know and can work with.
- Take responsibility jointly for what happens.
- If one partner is interested, let them take the lead, it doesn't matter what sex they are, equality applies with handling money.
- Organise your finances how you want, but it has to be done!
- Both should know what is going on.
- In case, Heaven forefend, one of you dies, know where the key details are.

Teach the children

What do you tell children about money, and how do you do it? This chapter looks at the way children develop attitudes to money, what resources you have to help them and practical ideas of helping your children to Tame their own Pound.

There are many sayings about children and their parents. For example "chip off the old block" and "the apple doesn't fall far from the tree". If they are true, are you happy about that? Do you think it would be a good thing if your children grew up to be like you are when handling money?

What do you figure the problem is dad, my genes or my home environment?

Genetics and environment
Like most things about people, the way children are influenced is complicated.

Maybe Philip Larkin was right, and whatever you mean to do, you – to put it politely – mix your children up!

> *However, I wouldn't forget that they are not just "your children" they are small individual people and they make their own choices, you don't run their whole lives for them. Even a small child reacts to you in their own way. If you have more than one child you will know that they will respond differently to the "same" treatment.*

Our personalities are influenced by genetics. Very emotionally stable people tend to have emotionally stable children, very extravert people tend to have extravert children. However, bear in mind that:

1. There is a random genetic mix, so each person is unique and we're all a mix of our two parent's gene structures.
2. The personalities may well "regress to the mean".
3. The way that each child develops will affect the way their personality comes out.

In this respect, point 3 is important. The "is genetics or environment more important" argument is pointless, they interact.

The genes set some limits. We all come with "kit" that enables us to learn whatever language is spoken around us, move our limbs and coordinate with vision to catch a ball, and we have built in facilities to detect edges and patterns, judge distances etc. (which is why we can see visual illusions and see "depth" in a flat TV screen etc.). If the kit isn't there or is defective we can't do some things. You can't train somebody who is blind to see, any more than you can grow taller or change your eye colour by training.

But even with the "kit" built in we have to learn how to use it to do those things. Some things, like some elements of our personality, seem to be "hard wired", but most of it is learned by experience. We have to learn the language, learn to focus our eyes, learn to catch the ball, learn how to deal with people. We can only learn the things we have the opportunities for. If you never hear a language it is hard to learn it, if you are kept in a dark room you may never learn to use your eyes and if you don't get the chance to play with a ball you may have trouble learning to catch.

For some of these things (language is a good example) there seem to be critical ages after which it becomes tougher. If you've ever tried to learn a language as an adult, I bet you found it a lot harder than you did to learn when you were aged less than ten. Also, we tend to get better at things we like doing or are interested in, for the simple reason that we do them more, get more experience and more practice, this in turn makes it easier, we get greater mastery, which makes it more fun, which means we practice more, and so on.

Think about how experience develops, and what our motives are.

What do parents actually "want" in terms of their motivation to invest time and effort in their children? They want each of the children to survive and thrive (that way they pass more of their genes on). So they probably "want" to invest equal time and effort in each child.

Note that this isn't a piece of theoretical "we love each of our children equally" twee nonsense. It is the "best" option from a genetic point of view as hunter gatherers. If you rely on only one child and that one dies or for some reason is not successful in reproducing, your genes reduce in future generations. If you help several children, so all breed in their turn, you end up with more of your genes in future generations, so your attitudes are carried on along with everything else.

By contrast, what does each child want? Obviously, it is in the interests of each child to get maximum support, the investment of time and energy for themselves. You might love your siblings, but they are rivals for your parents' attention. You want your parents to invest 100% in you, but your siblings all want 100% for themselves. There is only 100% in total to go round.

Each child wants as much as they can get and parents want to distribute investment of time and energy equally. You have a conflict between what each child wants to have and what the parent wants to give.

One way to get more attention, to outcompete siblings is to be unique in some way. Older siblings are bigger, have more experience, have already claimed the territory. There isn't much point trying to compete on their strong areas, you'll lose. For that reason, children in one family tend to be different and get into different roles.

If you are the youngest of four children, and the roles of "good student", "black sheep", "not academic but very practical" are already filled, what are you going to do, become the joker? So Larkin might be right, but it doesn't only matter what your parents do, it also matters what your siblings do.

Then, when you go to school, you'll have a different group to compete with. If there is already a strong, powerful leader in a group a child joining that group either has to be even stronger and more powerful or adopt another role. The role they have in the family might not work at school, or they might be members of different groups in the locality (which might include one or more siblings) and at school (which might also include siblings). Most children are involved in various groups with their siblings and peers, trying to forge an identity, compete successfully and get the maximum support they can from parents or other authority figures.

Everybody starts with a set of genes that set basic parameters like size, build, basic personality. But they develop and forge an identity in an environment including not only parents but siblings, peers, society and the physical environment (e.g. growing up in city and country is different).

It's not that parents are not important, they obviously are, particularly for young children; since parents and family are the only "social group" they have. But as they get older, children have others to deal with. As hunter gatherers we'd have been dealing with our peer group, learning skills to compete in life (outside a "school"), competing with our own sex, trying to attract the opposite sex, seeking status, security or whatever. So we become increasingly influenced by our peers, it is them we compete with, not our parents.

Most people naturally try to "fit in" with their peer group.

For example, think what accent children acquire, do they copy their parents or their peer group at school?

Similarly, why do children want particular things; because their parents have them or because their peer group do?

If we wanted to "be like" our parents we'd spend time paying bills, moaning about the Government and doing routine boring stuff, we wouldn't bother about great bands our parents have never heard of, buy clothes they think are horrible or like activities they don't understand!

You have parents but whatever they do it is *your* life. If your parents got it wrong you just have to deal with it! Similarly, your children are individuals, not clones of you, they will become their own people. All you can do is try to help them be themselves, you can't mould them in any way that you want.

So beyond the facts that:

- if you are careless with money it doesn't mean your children necessarily will be,

- or that they will be careful,

- or that all your children will react identically to the "same" parental treatment,

- or that you can "make them" do something or be something,

what can you do to "help them"?

The key seems to be experience with feedback. That's the way we all learn. If a tactic works for us or we see it work for others, we remember it and tend to try it out. So if screaming and crying get us what we want (parental attention, food, whatever) then maybe we figure screaming and crying are a good way to handle problems. If they work at school as well, great. But screaming and crying is unlikely to work as "grown ups".

We need something else, but maybe we don't know anything else, we've never been exposed to alternative tactics or had a need to try them out. If being irresponsible, materialistic or overcautious with money seems to work for our parents, or we don't see any other way to handle money, maybe we do it.

But it is about experience, not just words. What children can easily learn about, and perhaps copy is what you or other people do that they see, not just what you say.

And they need feedback, to learn that actions have consequences.

In the show, Into the Woods, The Witch (who points out at one stage, "I'm not good, I'm not bad, I'm just right"!) is explaining the relationship of children to parents. Her message is:

Careful the things you say, children will listen.
Careful the things you do, children will see.
And learn.
Sondheim, 1987

Your children are going to learn something, whatever you do. Therefore, ideally, you want to set your children a good example, and whether you do or don't, you also want to give them experience of observing and experiencing different ways to handle money, and the consequences. That way, they can build up a repertoire of behavioural experiences that will, hopefully, allow them to adapt to situations in the future and always handle their money effectively.

If you show that you regularly discuss family finances, and you have honest communications, there is no shame or anger about money (or lack of it), and this means that (as the children find out and you point out the links to them to help them make connections) this allows some nice holidays, attention from mum and dad etc. then that is behaviour which works.

So maybe being honest about money, thinking responsibly about it and its uses is useful behaviour for them to try out.

If you bury your concerns because of debt worries, and only discuss money in the form of a shouting match, or you whinge constantly about not having sufficient money to buy the children things (but buy them anyway to stop them whinging then whinge yourself about "spoiling" them) then they in turn learn to whinge in order to get what they want. They learn that whinging is a tactic that works and also that money is something that causes distress, anger, whinging, and maybe it's not a good thing to think about other than to whinge to get more. When they become adults, what ways of thinking about and handling money have they learned?

If the whinging doesn't work for the child, they need something else to try. If you don't show them an example that seems to work, maybe they try the opposite (if there is one). You're careless, so they become a total miser – but what options are you giving them to find and try out behaviour that works?

It doesn't all have to come from you. Whether they are influenced by parents, family or peer group, school or media they are going to learn something from what they see. They might not use it at the time, but they'll potentially remember it. If your example isn't that good, can you give them the opportunity to observe and/or try out behaviour that might be more effective?

Gender differences
As we've said, physical differences might be obvious but mental ones are

very small and are about motivation not ability. Therefore,

- There is next to no difference as infants except possibly very slight ones in interests.
- There are no significant differences in ability – except where we tend to get better with practice (if we get useful feedback), and tend to practice what we are interested in.
- People are individuals, so females can have typically "male" interests and vice versa.
- People are individuals, so they will try to express themselves, whether they are "typical" in their interests or "atypical", but,
- People can only develop the use of their "kit" if they have opportunities.

So don't assume, for example, that boys can or ought to, handle money and girls can't or shouldn't! That is nonsense.

Similarly, don't try to force a child to fit your conception of what they should do, and don't shut either sex off from learning about things, whether they are regarded as typically "female" or "male" subjects. If you try to mould children to your conception of what they "ought" to be (whether it is that the boys (or girls) should be "tough and not cry" or that girls (or boys) should not play with dolls even if they really want to) you're probably going to be disappointed.

You can shut them off from experiences and probably make them unhappy, but you aren't going to make them into something they are not. So if you give your daughter an Action Man and your son some dolls, don't be surprised if she has tea parties with the soldiers and he sets Charlie's Angels up to fight Lara Croft because they are just doing what they are interested in. Alternatively, they might play the way you want, but that isn't because you "moulded" them, it is because that is what they are interested in doing.

They are going to express their interests if they can, so just give them the chance to discover what they are interested in naturally, and try to expose each child to using and understanding money because that is important in modern society.

Deferring gratification

Any child is likely to have problems "deferring gratification". I mentioned earlier that we all tend to have difficulty with this, but it was first demonstrated in children.

There is a classic experiment where children were offered a sweet and told that they could eat it now, but if they waited to eat the sweet they would get a second sweet (or a bag of sweets, or a better sweet, depending on the particular experiment) in ten minutes or so when the experimenter came back. In theory, around a particular age children learn to "defer gratification", to take less reward (or none) now, in order to have a bigger reward later. In theory!

Now *you* try doing it with shoes, gadgets or whatever your favourite "impulse buy" is! Not easy to do, is it, even though you are no longer a child?

It's one reason why adults don't save for pensions, we still like the sweet now instead of the bag of sweets in 10 minutes, we just buy a car instead of a single sweet now and have an income of £25,000 a year less pension instead of a bag of sweets in 30 years.

The scary bit about this solid result of research is that children who could best defer gratification when young were more successful later in life, they got higher school grades, better incomes etc.

It doesn't mean one causes the other, there could be other factors involved and it is always dangerous to assume that because two things are correlated (in this case, childhood ability to defer gratification and adult success) that one causes the other.

> *However, it does suggest that being exposed to situations where deferment of gratification is useful and can be practiced is helpful. And seeing, practicing and learning strategies for doing it effectively are particularly handy things for children (and adults) to do.*

The common factor in the analysis of children who did manage it is that they "covered up" the sweet and got involved in doing something else. Those two tactics helped the children to avoid thinking about how nice the sweet would be, how much they wanted it, how hungry they were. By contrast, the children who couldn't do it kept looking at the sweet, thought about eating it and tried simply to resist by "will power".

You might recall this pattern from chapter 4. People on diets, with shopping addictions etc. try to resist by willpower alone and fail, and decide that they are "weak".

> *It isn't weakness; it is just an ineffective tactic.*
>
> *You may remember, I suggested not exposing yourself to particular shops for which you have a weakness, which is the equivalent of "covering" the sweet.*
>
> *Getting busy, doing other things, giving yourself other rewards (as in the CBT ideas) or controlling the environment to give yourself different cues are all ways to keep your thinking away from the immediate joy of eating the sweet now.*

That's also why I said you have to think of things for yourself. What will distract a child and allow them to ignore the sweet for ten minutes depends on the individual child. The general tactic is the same but the details are individual. In the same way, you can develop your own methods for yourself (if you don't do it, who will?) and you can help your child to work out how they can develop their own methods. A general "this is what you must do" will not work for the majority of people, whatever age they are.

> *Some of this "future orientation" is part of our genetic make-up. As I mentioned in chapter 12, if you are not naturally organised and conscientious about records, it is harder to deal with record keeping.*
>
> *By the same token it is harder for a child to defer gratification if they inherit genes that make them naturally less oriented to the future (because you're like that and your children inherit your genes).*
>
> *But the key word is "harder", it's not impossible or pre-ordained, it just requires more effort for some than others. It's worth doing, and if you have trouble with it yourself, all the more reason that you should help your children to cope better than you do.*

Some ideas for giving children experiences and tactics to use are coming up, but in case you think the whole point about planning for the future seems to contradict the points in chapter 2 about "mindfulness" and being "in the moment", here's how I'd suggest thinking about it.

Future planning is important. Even our hunter gatherer ancestors had to do some planning; how do you think you would successfully hunt anything or find plant food if you didn't organise yourself? Our timescales are longer in modern life, we are often thinking years ahead (with qualifications, savings, housing etc.) rather than what area to hunt in tomorrow as we would have done forty thousand years ago. But we still have a need to organise in advance, think what we need, plan our steps to get there (as in chapter 3).

At the same time, planning is not day dreaming or vague wishing. If you are planning, then plan. If you are enjoying a sunset, enjoy it. Be where you are, and do what you are doing. If what you are doing is to "be" rather than to "do" (a big feature of being mindful is not worrying about what you "ought" to *do*, but focussing on *being*) then simply be.

If you are planning, then be conscious of planning, focus on what you are doing. Be present in your planning. That way, what you are doing at any moment is appropriate to that moment. If you are planning what you are going to do next year, and determining how you will afford it, how you will work towards the goal, you are "covering the sweet" and engaging yourself in activity, you are not thinking about how nice the sweet will be. That way, you plan and defer gratification.

And you can demonstrate, discuss and give opportunities to your children to learn the same thing. That way, you all get more fun out of what you are doing now, have better plans for the future and you also have children who can focus and better defer gratification.

Parenting styles

There are a lot of books, TV programmes etc. about styles of parenting, whether you should be strict or laissez-faire, punish or reward and all that. There's a study from the US that indicates that, over there at least, there are really only two major types of parenting.

In one style (generally associated with the better off), parents are involved in their child's activities, helping to structure their experiences, getting them more involved in pastimes that engage them in critical thinking and experiencing interactions with others. There are also, (often because these parents have more money and more education themselves), more opportunities for children to learn, such as visits to museums or books available around the house that enable these children to develop skills they may need later.

The other style, (whether it is due to having less time or money or some other reason), is to leave children more to their own devices. That can encourage self reliance, but it can also mean the children may not develop so much useful experience for life in the future.

This is bolstered by another set of studies that looked at performance in schools. A lot of children from poorer backgrounds fell behind those from wealthier backgrounds. This isn't a new finding, but typically it is said either to be because of inherited differences in intelligence (that don't exist) or because the schools in poorer areas are short of resources (which sounds more plausible).

However, it is pretty clear that it wasn't due to lack of teachers, books or other resources and it wasn't about intelligence.

The children from some families fell behind during holidays, they didn't have the structure, the activities to stretch them, the books to read, the adult help to try out strategies that would work in the world. While these children were often amusing themselves during holidays, the children from wealthier backgrounds were involved in clubs, societies, family visits, they had access to books and sources of information.

The "deprived" children kept pace with the "wealthier" ones during the school year (and this applies even in really poor areas, where there most certainly *is* a lack of resources). It was a "level playing field" when all the children were having lessons.

When the children were at home in the holidays and the differences were in access to experiences and in the attitude of the parents, differences between the "have's and the have not's" increased. In fact, while the wealthier children moved on a bit during the holidays, some of the poorer children actually went backwards, they "unlearned" things that would subsequently be useful.

Now you can argue that it is a political issue, it shows how unfair the system is and that "something should be done". And I wouldn't disagree with you.

But until the world becomes a better and fairer place, what do you want to do about it?

This and other good evidence indicates that helping children to structure experience, involving them in decision making, critical thinking, analysing problems etc. helps them develop skills that are useful in life. So that is exactly the sort of thing that I'd suggest you do with your children, to allow them to experiment with and develop useful skills for handling money, because handling money is a useful skill for later in life.

Resources

Of course, this suggests that it would be useful if schools taught "experiential" lessons in relation to money. That means the teachers have to understand it first! The "financial capacity" idea that I mentioned in chapter 3 will help a bit. But the education will be about national economics, not personal finance, which are not at all the same thing. And it will be about practical, "how to", not "why would you", once the teachers learn it.

I think it less important that teachers and pupils know about the mechanics of finance (how to buy the best phone contract, how to get a credit card etc.) than, why you might not want one, whether it is actually useful (as in our archer analogy in chapter 3) and if it is something that will make them happy.

If children know why they want something, can plan and organise themselves to pursue a goal and have a range of ways to think about how to achieve that goal, then they can work out or find out "how" to do what they need, or "what" to do to achieve it. Like using a mobile phone or Facebook.

If all they know is "what" to do for a particular situation, they have to learn hundreds of "how to" skills for thousands of circumstances, most of which are entirely irrelevant to them as they don't have any motivation for those particular goals and are not in those situations.

So how interested will they be to learn all those irrelevant skills?

It's unfortunate, because this means that even when financial education is increased, the major teaching about finance most children get from school will be about "the economy" not their own finance and about "what" and "how" not "why". So most children will still learn their real lessons about finance by competing with their peers to have the coolest smart phone, the latest fashions, etc. They'll learn to keep up with the Jones's on material things, which will tend to make most of them unhappy and the influence will come from peers and the media who don't care about them, not from their parents, who do.

If you want to help your children, help them structure experience and find peer groups and roles in those groups. This will help them learn productive values, behaviours etc. likely to be useful for them. So what do you do?

There aren't any really informative UK books on children and finance. There are several US based ones (Furnham, 2008, mentions at least a dozen). The problem being, they are now well out of date (written in the 1990's, so assume that the stock market will rise forever, individual shares are great etc.) and are entirely geared to the US tax system, refer to US benefits, schooling etc. and tend to think that "more money is automatically better".

One quite good one is by Bodnar which has a self assessment quiz to assess "money smarts". It correlates quite well with the "helping attitude" I've talked about above. Higher scorers, the "money smart" parents, tended to approve more of being involved in socialising their children about money.

Such parents also tended to be less liberal but felt it was their responsibility to model sensible behaviour, discuss money with children and were not against "pay for work" to teach children about how money works in reality.

This doesn't demonstrate conclusively that being involved in this way with children will definitely, 100%, make your children better handlers of money in later life, but it looks like it helps.

It seems that taking your responsibilities seriously, trying to set a good example and at least being involved and helping children understand what is going on (maybe even learning together if you're really lost with money yourself) is going to stand them in much better stead than just letting them get on with it and hoping they'll learn some useful and practical ways to handle money from school, their peers, the media and unstructured experience.

Practical moves

First of all, if you are a couple bringing up children, sort out what you are doing yourselves, which means getting wills sorted out, having sufficient life cover, health insurance (income protection) etc. Make sure that, if both of you were to die, you've got something sorted out for the children, not just money but also somebody who will look after them and bring them up taking into account what you wanted. Try to get your own finances sorted out so that you can discuss money without rowing and hence set a good example.

If you are separated, the same things apply, only more so. Sort out what happens if one of you dies etc. because it is hard enough for a child having parents separate, without then having one die and perhaps being raised by the other parent's new partner who doesn't particularly want or like them. If you are separated but on reasonably good terms, it becomes even more important than if you are together to agree on what is going on with the children.

Children are small individuals; if they can play one parent off against the other to get what they want, they will. "But mum said I could", works if the parents don't actually discuss it, and it works even better if the parents don't live together or even speak to one another except to argue. And if you have a custody battle or are otherwise competing, the child is in a good position to use guilt, rivalry, one-upmanship etc. to get what they want and play the "poor me" card to pressurise one of the parents into giving them whatever they want.

It's not that children are bad, they will just try, like everybody, to get what they want. If you show them that the way to get what they want is to play you off against your former partner, to say "she/he said I could have it", or get you to buy them things and "show up" the former partner, then naturally what they learn is that the way to handle money is to use emotional blackmail.

Is that what you want them to learn?

If you discuss it and demonstrate that "no" from one partner means "no" from the other, that discussions about money are held like adults, that "emotional blackmail" gets treated by both parents with "I thought better of you than that, we've discussed it and we agreed X, you can't get round it by trying to make me feel guilty", children learn that money is something that you discuss sensibly and agree on, then you stick to the agreements you've made.

If you want to get help with your family relationships, counselling might help, (see chapter 15 for sources) or you can get some resources from relate, http://www.relateforparents.org.uk/, which is good on families, not just couples.

Sort out what you are going to do about pocket money, involvement in making financial decisions, the amount of discretion children have with spending (whether they keep all of their earnings or pocket money or have to pay into a "family kitty", save some of it etc.), what you want them to value (do they have to have the latest gadgets, trainers etc., where do you and they draw the line etc.) and both stick to it.

If you are forming a "new family unit", possibly with children from previous relationships and perhaps children you've had together, again, you have to sort out what the children are expected to do and are not permitted to do. The situation with ex-partners has to be taken into account, but you need to discuss what you are doing and saying to the children, and then treat the children as equally as possible. If one child gets to go on the school trip, or is funded for special lessons then the others should have the opportunity too. If one gets rewarded for passing exams, so should the others. Inequality between "your" children and the ones you've "inherited" is a pretty good way to distort a child's beliefs about life, the value of people as people and what is reasonable and effective behaviour in relation to money.

If you are on your own raising children, you've at least got the simpler situation of not having to agree things with another person, but you've got all the responsibility. So you particularly need to have insurance, a will, guardians sorted out etc.

And whatever situation you've got, it's a good idea to speak to relatives (particularly doting grandparents) about how you want to handle finances. If you say to a child they have to save up for something expensive, then Auntie Ethel buys it for them, or you've said that they need to show they are responsible enough to look after a pet and Grandma buys them one, what lesson do you think the children learn about responsibility, caring for things, the value of life (whether it is human or animal) and so on?

There's a whole book to be written about all this, but it would be a UK version of Bodnar, merely giving practical examples of what other people have done. Because you and your family are unique you need a personal solution for you, so my aim is to get you to think about the issues.

If you want to see what other people do in the UK in terms of pocket money etc. you can look up http://www.statistics.gov.uk/glance/uk-snapshots.asp which is a website of statistics about the country. It gives masses of tables about different things including pocket money, which is at http://www.statistics.gov.uk/cci/nugget.asp?id=2198

If you want some ideas now, here are some indications. Bear in mind that children are individuals. I haven't given specific "ages" because that immediately worries people that their child is "slow" or "precocious" or whatever and gets them to compare their own children with one another.

Each person is unique. Because one child was reading the FT and planning hostile takeovers of multi-nationals at the age of six doesn't mean your other children should as well. However, if you have trouble with these things yourself, do bear in mind they are handy things to know about so you might want to learn them with the children (or try to stay a page ahead, if you must!)

Young:

- Play with money. Small children "think" in quantity, five pennies is five, one pound is one, so clearly the pennies are worth more. Make it fun, but as soon as possible teach them the values of coins in terms of what things will buy. My cousin demonstrated this when, as a child and given a half-crown (12.5 pence) by Grandma he pointed out that he preferred paper money!

- Take them shopping, get them to pick up the things you want. It is harder now because prices are not marked on packets so reliably, but mum used to do this with me. I'd be sent to get a packet of flour or whatever and I'd come back to her and tell her the price, she'd tell me what we'd spent so far and I'd tell her what that meant the total was with the flour added. Remember, that was in pounds, shillings and pence so it was a bit harder than with decimal coinage! If they are expected to do it, children can learn phenomenally fast, and it stops them running round like lunatics and wrecking the shop!

- As they get more sophisticated, get them to select the best options under a certain price, make specifications to have the minimum salt or sugar content or something. It gets them to get used to comparison shopping, reading labels, doing a budget.

- Get them involved in planning shopping, perhaps they run a little brand test, is the supermarket own brand distinguishable from the one we usually buy? Can they interview their parents and siblings to see if the fabric conditioner is better worse or the same as the one we usually buy? Can we economise on things without sacrificing quality? It gets them used to comparing what you pay for brand labels with what is actually worth having.

- Discuss what they want, and what they really need. They will have values of their own, but children's memories tend to be fairly short-term for this sort of thing, what is desirable this week has been forgotten the next. So write them down and discuss with them how that works. Dad used to talk with me about saving up for big things that I really wanted. If he was convinced (I thought) that I really wanted it, he would agree to put in half the money if I saved half. I think that before he died he'd only ever had to match my savings for two things in thirteen years, as I got bored with waiting and decided I didn't really want the other things!

- This also works with savings, when children have the idea of how money saved can grow, offer to match their savings. They can get more money in the long run by saving some of their pocket money, because you add to it. This gives them experience of deferring gratification and gets them into the habit of saving.

- Get them to understand chores around the house. Start with simple things like putting their dirty clothes in the appropriate place. Gradually increase their responsibility, children often get bored with really simple things. If it is a mark of being grown up to be on the "setting the table" rota, to take their turn at washing up, to be responsible for cleaning, it becomes a matter of honour to do the job properly. If you have more than one child you can end up with it resembling being allowed a later bedtime; at a certain age each child gets to check through the cupboard to determine what shopping is needed and is relied on to get it right. This isn't directly connected to money, but Diane tells the story of having her own first home and realising that the "toilet paper fairy" didn't exist. Being able to plan and execute shopping, cleaning, laundry etc. are important life skills!

- If the children are doing chores, you can use a variety of systems of pocket money, you can separate payment entirely, you can pay them for any "extra" work they do above the standard things that are expected, you can give them payments for satisfactorily done chores (but not ones that are half done, neglected or inadequate) whatever suits your family. The point is to be consistent and that requires discussions and the setting of family standards that everybody (including you) has to stick to.

- Similarly, discuss things like holidays, budgets etc. (seriously, if you explain this stuff to children they will take an interest and potentially offer alternatives that you haven't thought of), but you need to have involved them in simpler things and make them feel that they understand the money and the whole issue of needs, wants and being "happy" or it will all be a bit too much in one go.

- Involve them in changes, querying options, setting budgets for school trips etc. and again let them handle increasing responsibility. If they get things wrong (they spend money on sweets that should have bought lunch) they will learn that they get the consequences (like being hungry most of the day) and you know that they learn from something that is less serious and not going to produce a huge problem (like blowing their whole university allowance and student loan in the first two weeks because they've never learned to handle a budget).

- Talk about charity and giving to others. Children can (like adults) be selfish about their toys but they can also be amazingly generous in giving things away if they realise that other people need them more.

- Keep to the limits you've discussed. 'No more' means no more, one item that they want the most means one, not two. Remember what example you are giving them about financial decisions.

- Watch the media together, discuss the hype in TV and magazine advertising. Get them to work out whether the stuff that is advertised really is as good as the advertisements claim. It can be a nice project for them to test out wonderful food advertised and see if anybody in the family actually likes it! Or look at the toys that are advertised and see if the fantastic toys shown on TV are actually like the product that sits in the shops. And get them to do the sums, add the cost of the batteries, any accessories, the refills, electricity etc. and how that compares to their pocket money. It's all good practice at learning the difference between price and value.

As the children get older increase the level of responsibility they have. My dad's mother had a long spell in hospital when my dad and aunt were young, and nobody knew what to do. Nanna made sure they all learned! So dad taught me. It turned out useful because mum died when I was nine and dad when I was 13, by which time my elder sister and I could run a household. I even made it a feature of being "grown up" in talking to girls when I was 14 or so. None of my friends could even boil an egg, while I could not only boil and roast but make pastry, clean, plan a shopping trip, do the laundry, iron, and comparison shop as well as pin up hems, change tyres and do a manicure! Since most of my girlfriends at the time couldn't do a tenth of that, although I'm not exactly Brad Pitt or George Clooney, I was at least worth talking to!

Make those skills part of children's experience, a mark of growing ability and maturity. If they can organise and carry out chores, handle budgets and work within them, then they can effectively defer gratification, plan and execute a project and work out what are needs and what are wants. These are skills that most people have to learn in their twenties in their first home or at university, if they ever learn them at all.

Older (but still pre-teen):

- Set them up with a bank account for savings.

- Consider savings into shares (it's not going to do any harm to have some Disney shares or something similar if it gets them to understand the basic concepts of the stock market through something that they are interested in). Or put some money into a tracker fund because then they probably get more reliable growth (but it might not be as much fun or as interesting, and the point is to excite their interest so they will be motivated to learn about it, not to make a fortune).

- Being young the children have time for the market to bounce around and they still come out ahead, and as a place to put regular portions of pocket money and the occasional boost of birthday or Christmas money they get the benefits of pound cost averaging as well. It's not likely to pay their way through university or something, but it might be a deposit on a house or car and, most important, teaches them how these things work. If they see how it grows (hopefully) and get interested they will be motivated to learn and, being more "plastic" and less set in their ways than adults, will probably know more about it than you in six months if they find it interesting!

- Explain banking and interest, and things like personal identification, NI numbers, NHS registration etc. the things you need to function in society. You can make games out of it, set it as an age related thing for each child so it becomes a badge of maturity or get them to do it as a project they get rewarded for, but make sure they understand these things.

- Involve them in details around the household budget like phone, heating, light etc. so they have an interest in saving power and know how much chatting to their friends costs! It increases their understanding of money in general, living expenses in particular, and familiarises them with the idea of economy and cutting waste to have more for things that are important.

- Model values like charity giving and voluntary work. If you do football coaching, guides or whatever, involve your children, explain and discuss what you get from it in a personal sense. It gives them values around "bigger purpose" and "helping others" that are important to happiness and gets them thinking about the relationships between money, values and happiness in life.

- Look at what their conception of being "happy" is. One of my friends (an occupational psychologist) told me a story of one of her children. At about age 11 he felt that his parents were not really giving him all the things they could, as one of his friends had lots of good "stuff" that he wanted, and "mum and dad won't let me have it". He even made a list of all the things he thought he ought to have. She discussed it with him and said that she and his dad loved him and would buy him all the things on the list. But she wanted to know one thing, if they got him all of the things, right now, was that going to make him happy all the way until he was 18 and went off to university? He thought seriously about it, and decided it wouldn't. And he thought that maybe he didn't really want all those things.

- Then she asked him if he wanted to change places with his friend, even for a day. That meant everything was changed, he would have all the stuff he wanted, but he'd also have the friend's parents who seemed to give their son money and toys rather than their time and affection. Again, her son thought about this, and decided that he wouldn't want to swap, not even for 24 hours. Obviously, it doesn't mean that they will never again have any problems about him wanting material goods, money, what is permitted and what isn't and so on. But it does show that understanding and discussing money, material goods, happiness and what those things mean helps you both to understand your children and to get them to think about what is really important in life.

- Mind you, it does need you to have listened to your children before and to know how mature they are and whether they will give serious thought to something. This depends on being involved with your children and helping to give them structured experiences and aiding them to understand what those experiences can teach them.

- You can extend the model of chores, responsibility, pay etc. to a full "citizen of the household" concept. You make the children an increasing part of the household economy, discuss how household finances work, plan holidays as a "board" etc. You can leave that as a general household management tool (which teaches the children as well as making sure jobs get done and the household runs effectively) but you can make it into a more extensive way of dealing with money. You can set out rules for advances, loans etc. so children can borrow against their future pocket money, chore money etc. but they pay interest on it on agreed terms and pay back at set times (and you do the same, if you borrow, you pay interest to the household as well).

- Less extensive than that is the idea of loans or "top ups" that are agreed. Dad would potentially give me half, but I could never assume that he would, I'd have to agree it with him beforehand.

- You can also introduce the idea (if you have household account, or "bank" that has rates of interest) of borrowing from yourself. If a child has a concept of borrowing from a bank and paying interest, or from mum and dad, and paying the household interest, it makes it very appealing to have your own savings from which you can borrow and pay yourself interest! This encourages savings, because in order to be able to pay yourself interest and build up your money, you need to have put some money away first, so it also means having to learn ways to defer gratification.

- Discuss with children the morals of money (as in chapter 1) what you do about things like tipping, stealing by finding, giving to charity etc.

- Explain tax, you don't need to go into great detail (you probably don't know it anyway unless you are an accountant or a financial advisor and the rules change with monotonous regularity) but the basics. So why we have taxes (and if you don't know, find out!), what the major taxes are (income, VAT, capital gains tax, inheritance tax, corporation tax are the main ones that will affect you) and roughly how they work (income tax is progressive, there are differences between direct tax like that on incomes that are charged directly to the individual and indirect taxes like VAT that only apply indirectly if you buy something that carries VAT and so on).

- If this stuff is a closed book to you, then get some lessons and invite your children to sit in and understand what goes on. A good accountant or IFA could teach you (and the children) the basics.

- Remember the Sondheim admonition – "careful the things you say, children will listen". I've read lots about how much we rely on "Voices from the Past", we pass on sayings that our parents or others said. I've mentioned the problems with some of these (practice doesn't make perfect, time is not money) and there are plenty more. For example "A penny saved is a penny earned", but it isn't, because a penny earned is taxable, a penny saved is net, so a penny saved is worth considerably more than a penny earned.

If you don't understand tax it is easy to forget that (another reason to understand what is going on in general terms), but the main point is that before you trot out phrases to the children that you learned or rely on, think about them and see if they are actually true.

Adolescent

You get a lot more demands for "peer group" material. Younger children might desperately want the Wii and the trainers and so on to keep up with their friends, but teenagers *have* to have the leather coat or whatever, even if it means they have no money for other clothes and would rather go to school naked but for their new coat than be seen in old and boring clothes.

In adolescence the primitive, hunter-gatherer stuff really cuts in. We all desperately want to appeal to the opposite sex (or our own, the same desire to be desired applies) and to compete with our peers for attention. Having status, looking good, being the centre of attention (or having a good friend or group of friends who really like us) and so on are vital.

We also get into the whole issue of raging hormones, which is often a bit like bi-polar disorder, one minute we feel great and confident and desirable, next minute we're on the point of suicide and it doesn't take a lot to shift. If you are lucky enough to have children who remain fairly stable all the way through, great, but if your children are unpredictable, unreliable, and basically downright weird, welcome to the experience of the majority!

As with most things involving people, there are no simple universal answers (or if there are, I have no idea what they are and have never met anybody who knows any of them). But keeping on with mature discussions, modelling sensible behaviour, building their responsibility and being consistent are likely to be useful.

- As children get more mature, they understand responsibility better (even if sometimes they don't seem to) and learn to handle money, so make sure they are responsible for their own expenses.
- If they have a phone, for example, they are responsible for the debts on it. Teach them there is no fairy that will bail them out – well,

maybe once, but after that tell them they have to be mature enough to handle their own responsibilities. If they regress to being as mature as an eight year old and expecting you to pick up the mess for them, then make sure they know they'll be treated like an eight year old.

- Little lesson on responsibility. At about 16 or 17 my sister didn't like having to tell dad where she was going, who she was going with, how she was getting home, what time she was getting home. Fairly standard teenage behaviour. After a few rows about being treated like a child, dad explained that he wasn't treating her like a child, it was up to her, but he would be the one who was dragged out of bed at two in the morning to identify the corpse pulled out of the river, so until she was 18 he needed to know what was going on. After that, she could do what she liked because the law said she was not his responsibility any more.

  After her 18th, the first time she went out, she waited for the string of questions. It didn't come. He just hoped she'd have a good time and kissed her goodnight. This went on for a couple of weeks. Then she got into the habit of telling dad where she was going, who with, how she was getting home, what time she was getting home, allegedly to "stop him worrying". She was smart enough to know that he'd manipulated her, smart enough to know that he was probably worried sick but would never show or admit it and also smart enough to make sure dad knew where she was in case anything went wrong. Children will listen, children will see, and children will learn.

- In the same way, you don't have to treat adolescents like children, you can give them adult privileges and let them take the adult responsibilities (clothes, phones, chores, financial contributions to the household etc.). If they have no credit on their phone, or can't pay the bill, then they can't use the phone. If they want to be treated like an adult, they have to accept the responsibilities of an adult. Their "job" is to do well at school. If they can't do that because they are too tired from partying or part-time working that they use to buy clothes etc, then they're going to get "fired" and not get free board and lodgings.

As they get older they will start to understand that rent and household expenses eat up a lot of money and if they don't want to live by the rules you've negotiated they can try to work out how they afford all the non-essentials they want as well as all the household expenses they have to meet as an adult.

Help them do it, work with them on a budget that allows them their own space. They'll work out that they are much better off negotiating with you and making a smaller contribution to the family economy than is needed for themselves alone, keeping to their agreements about savings etc. and still having a reasonable amount free to spend on clothes, phone etc. but controlling their spending. The alternative is that all their money goes on their own apartment, bills, etc. and they don't have any money at all for a car, a phone, clothes or going out. If you've shared the household budgets and expenses with them as they've grown up, they know you're not being mean, this is just the way it is and if they want the perks of being an adult, they have to accept the problems too.

- They've got to understand priorities, you do them no favours by giving them everything. Even if you can afford to give them a place of their own at 16 then I'd suggest that you find out what they really value and what they really want, then negotiate around it. If you and they want them to be a "rich kid" with no idea of the value of life, money or anything else – OK, it's their life, but I'm not sure it is a terribly good idea.

- Keep working on things like planning their wardrobe, give them a budget and discuss the items they've got to have, like school clothes and things they'd like to have like fashion items. You can sort out different ways to arrange it, you settle the whole budget and get all the things together, or you buy the essentials and they get a smaller amount for non-essentials to buy themselves. But either way, start off by working with them on how to budget, prioritise and shop sensibly. As they get older they might resent the help, but if they learn how to handle money sensibly themselves, you can explain that you won't need to help them, they can do it all for themselves. But they first need to prove that they won't blow the whole budget on something ludicrous and leave you with the choice of keeping them off school, sending them in with no decent clothes, forking out for an entire wardrobe or marching them back to the shop to get their money back.

- If they are interested in the stock market, perhaps you can match the money they save, help them, read up on things and compare notes and you can both learn together how to research companies, pick stocks, deal at low costs etc. (I'd recommend that you both read chapter 9 and the books I've mentioned there as part of the programme). It's a great interest to encourage, as is the idea of starting business. Lots of successful entrepreneurs started young. Also, as we've said before, children learn fast and they learn what they are interested in, so even if the world of business and finance leaves you cold, encourage the children to understand what is going on if they want to.

- As they get older involve them in the financial decisions, insurance, wills etc. It sounds like taking childhood away but early mid teens is a good time to make sure they know this stuff, it makes going away to university and having a first home of your own a lot easier. And if calamity does strike I can tell you from personal experience that it is hard enough to cope emotionally with the death of your parents way before you are ready for it. You don't want your children to face the problems of having no idea how to handle money, manage a household or look after themselves if you're not there, in addition to trying to deal with their grief.

- Model credit card use! It's up to you, you know your children and I don't, but I'd be very careful about letting children loose with a credit or a debit card – they are hard enough to control for a lot of adults. But if you show them how they can be used sensibly, you keep the credit slips, tick them off, pay off the bill in full each month etc. they then see that as an effective way to use a card and that is the only model they have. It doesn't mean that, as soon as they get a card they won't run up £20,000 in debt, but it makes it a lot less likely and if you've given them experience of budgeting and thinking sensibly about money all their lives they are obviously a lot more likely to use the convenience, the free interest period and other advantages of a card and not to fall into daft habits.

As a final point, the same thing applies to children as to partners. Children may have different priorities and interests to adults, but they are each unique just like adults and they are basically only smaller, more mentally flexible and less experienced adults. Honest communication and treating them as each being a unique and valuable individual person is usually as good a policy with your child as it is with your partner.

So after the chapter summary, having looked at how important values are, at goals, at our obsessions with shopping, our strange symbolic beliefs and departures from logic, the unpredictability of life and markets, the human desire for prediction and fear of maths and ways to "hedge our bets" with insurance; at debt and redundancy and the relationships of money to the whole family – let's look at how it might all fit together!

Summary:

- Genes set outlines, but each person is a unique mix.
- The outline gets developed by experience, the roles you take, your peers, parents etc. influence you and that interacts with your basic personality.
- You can't "mould" your children; you can only help them to develop.
- There are no gender differences in the ability to handle money.
- Some people find it hard to defer gratification, plan, do details etc. If you are like that, work on it! Not just for you but for your children, help them be better at it than you are.
- Structuring experience, being involved, helping children to learn the lessons from their experience helps them.
- Children learn very fast, they can usually cope with more information and variety than adults can, and they learn a lot more, and quicker, than adults give them credit for.
- Children learn from everything, what they see done, what they hear. You can try "do what I say, not what I do", but they are going to learn both anyway!
- One of the best gifts you can give is consistency, it enables children to learn where boundaries are so they can make decisions and experiment with different ways to behave and get consistent feedback on how things work.
- Be honest – being honest and treating each child as a unique, valuable individual (and treating your partner and others in the same way) are probably the most important things you can possibly teach by example.

Putting it together

This chapter is different to the others in the book. Elsewhere I've looked at broad, general approaches– what is known in military circles as strategy. Here, I'm looking at specific things that you can do, usually called tactics.

I've made it things you *could* do, not ones you *ought* to or *should* do. You still have to make the choices about what you want to do with your life, then decide how you are going to achieve them. But when you come to the detail of planning, you might want to consider this chapter.

All the ideas rely on what people are actually like, not what they might be like if the world were different, so they take account of the "errors" we looked at in chapter 5 and the other habits we often have.

When you are at the W stage of GROW, pick out the methods that will work for you (bearing in mind both the way you tend to think and behave and what you are trying to do) and that will work in the situation that you're in.

I've broken the advice into the broad areas of accumulating and reducing money that I mentioned earlier.

Finally, I've given some approaches to making good decisions and choices, both financial and general – but first, a story with a moral.

I had a client who was really organised with money. She had spreadsheets for everything, ticked bills off the moment they came in, had standing orders to pay bills, was a model of "conventional" good handling of money. She also had a very well paid job in finance and owned a rented property to provide extra income and as a capital asset.

And she worried constantly about money, lost sleep over the rental property, worried about what would happen if the income went down or she lost her job (she had a big mortgage) and felt like an idiot because she "ought to be happy".

What do you think? Was she an idiot?

I think she did all the conventional things right and did them very well. She just didn't know how to work out what she wanted, so she did what she thought she ought to do, and followed her training in finance and conventional advice so that all the processes and practical elements were done perfectly.

It would be very hard for her to "stop worrying", for that was the way she was and all the technically correct finance advice in the world wasn't going to make her happy or stop her worrying. Maybe she could learn to be less anxious with a good counsellor, or I could help her do some relaxation exercises, mindfulness, visualisation etc. but that was going to take time and I'm not sure it would have been all that effective anyway.

So I suggested that she have an emergency fund. That contradicts my previous advice since she would earn less on the emergency money than she paid on the mortgage. But the difference wasn't great, and the idea was to give her peace of mind, it was for happiness, not money. When she lay awake at night worrying about sudden emergencies, she'd know she had money to cover them.

The biggest financial change I suggested was that she consider getting rid of the investment property and put the money into another type of investment. She had spreadsheets of costs and income that worked out her tax liability, her profitability, the whole thing. All the TV "property experts" said property was great. And it kept her awake nights.

Maybe she wouldn't make as much money in another investment (although tracker funds and feeding the money in gradually would probably be better anyway) but what mattered was whether she was happy. The property might generate money, but also generated anxiety for her.

She had enough money to do what she wanted, so why maximise the distress to maximise money she didn't need? To me, that doesn't make sense. It didn't make a lot of sense to her either when we discussed it.

In a way I gave her "permission" to do that, to break with her training and focus on herself instead of the money. The result was that she started to sleep nights and enjoy her life.

> What is it that you want? It is about *you* as an individual remember, not about what is generally best in financial terms.

Therefore, don't worry what "experts", including me, say. Look at the reasoning, if an idea makes sense for you, maybe try it.

Paying off credit cards with "emergency funds" is nearly always a good idea financially and so is paying off loans, but as above, it might not be in your particular case. If it makes you really uncomfortable, consider the financial situation and see if you can work out how to live with what is financially sensible. If it just isn't going to work for you, ignore it.

The idea isn't to be a financial show-off, or to be unconventional or a "smart investor" or anything like that, the idea is to be happy!

Accumulating: save to build up funds,
Make savings "sacred".

We all have different symbols for money. And we all treat money as different if we earn it, win it, find it, inherit it etc. So use that. If you need to save for something (you've worked out your values, set your goals and are working out GROW and your financial plans) you might find it tricky to put enough away. Or you might find you save it, but then dip into savings at the slightest excuse.

Make that saving sacred. Whether you have to class it as Auntie Gertie's money, as the children's college fund, as your "escape money", as the seed corn for your new business, whatever it is that is needed, make that fund something that you will not touch. Make it so you'd rather sell a kidney than touch that money.

This is one reason why pension schemes can be handy. The main differences between a pension fund and other forms of savings are:

a) the tax relief and

b) the accessibility of the money.

The common idea is that tax relief is good but not being able to get at the money is bad. But if you need to save and not use that money, not being able to get at it under any circumstances until a certain time is a real benefit.

So check out whether you can use either a plan that makes the money legally unavailable, or that you can make yourself regard as unavailable. That way, you keep the savings by using your "failing" of having different symbols for different types of money and holding mental accounts.

Pay yourself first

If you need to save, what is going to work better, putting the amount aside first and spend what is left, or spend money first and save whatever is left?

Human nature (particularly reluctance to defer gratification) dictates that we'll save more if we save first and spend later, because if we spend first and save what is left we won't have anything left. If you say, "I'll start that savings plan/pension/fund for my holiday etc. at the end of the month if I've got £50", how often do you think you'll do it?

If you pay yourself first, you decide "the first £50 goes into the savings plan. I'm sure I can spend whatever I've got left". You might finish the month on three days of beans on toast because you're out of money, but you will have put the savings away.

Use your bank account

If you are trying to save; set up a direct debit or standing order into the savings account (or wherever you are saving, savings do not have to be bank accounts and for longer term, they probably shouldn't be). It gives you a virtuous habit of saving without having to do any work on changing your behaviour. You make a virtue out of your defaults, your "status quo" becomes, "I am a saver", not "I would be a saver if...." (which means you're not).

You just have to make sure that when the money comes out it goes somewhere where you aren't promptly going to grab it back!

Decide what is sacred – treat the rest as earned money

If you start off by isolating the money you cannot spend, your "sacred" money, you are in control.

The problem which still exists is our human capacity to treat some money (credit cards, tax rebates, "found money" etc) as being much easier to spend than money we earn.

So treat everything that isn't sacred as "earned money". Try sticking a "post-it" note to your credit card to tell you to think "would you buy it, and how much would you pay, if you had to pay cash?"

Try waiting a week to see if you really want something, and in the meantime put the money into a special purpose account (as below). The idea is to make you treat all your money that isn't sacred as being something that must be spent carefully, so none of it is just frittered away.

Try thinking of money as usable or as "special purpose"

Most money will be usable. That means you can use it to pay day-to-day expenses etc. You'll have your "sacred" money for your long term goals.

You might also want a "special purpose" fund. That money is set aside for the big things, reducing the debts or covering the credit card (!), paying for the holidays etc. that are important, but not enough that the "sacred" money goes into them and/or to cover utilities. You put into it enough money to cover those amounts (so you need to read chapter 12 and sort out what you pay out each month for the car, the mortgage, to reduce debts etc.). Then the big bills and regular expenses, the holiday fund etc. are taken care of. It can be tricky to stick to, but if you set up your sacred and special purpose funds and think of them as being important, it might surprise you how reluctant you are to dip into them for trivial things, so you tend to accumulate money a lot faster.

Also, if you insist that the special fund is only used to pay bills that it is designated to cover, you will not tend to spend money when you get a good month without bills (when the Council Tax isn't levied in some months, for example) and then be drastically short when you get a bigger heating bill than usual a couple of months later. The money will accumulate in the special fund and the usable money will be all you spend. And then it becomes a habit, it is your "status quo" and it will become hard to change it and waste your money.

If you want to spend money, think about what you want to spend it on.

Is it a long term goal (so it might be out of the "sacred" money)?

Is it covered by what you put into the special fund?

If not, whether it is for an emergency, it is something you fancy having, or whatever, it ought to come from your usable money.

If you can't afford the thing you fancy from the usable money, then you can't afford it. If you don't contribute to the special fund to cover your holiday, then the holiday has to come out of your usable money or you can't afford it. If the fund won't cover your credit card, you can't use the card.

Set up a "tithe" to yourself of any windfall

This can be tithing in the traditional sense (paying a sum, usually a tenth, of your money to a charity, typically the church). It is a good way to increase happiness and sense of worth.

But why not "tithe" to yourself? Rather than get a tax rebate, bonus, gift, overtime payment or whatever and have it burn a hole in your pocket, put a tenth or whatever fraction, maybe all of it (but see the idea about treating yourself, later on), into your savings plan or account or into your "sacred" or "special purpose" account. Again, if it becomes "the way I do things" then your natural inertia kicks in and it becomes automatic.

Make your default position that you save something every month

We stick with defaults, even if the default is having nothing. If you think, "I'll have to sort out a savings plan" your default is not having one. If you save, think of money in terms of sacred, special funds and usable, have standing orders and tithe your windfall cash, your default is to have a savings plan right now. It may not be the best, but it is a lot better than nothing.

Pre-designate pay-rises to savings

This has been used in the US, prompted by Richard Thaler and mentioned prominently in "Nudge" under the title SMT, standing for Save More Tomorrow. It is used in the US, because it works.

If you are going to get a pay-rise, get a regular bonus etc. pre-commit to having a portion of that money (or all of it) put into savings. The usual way to do this is at work where the money is put into the pension scheme directly. It uses the endowment effect (the money is never "mine" to spend, so it doesn't trigger the distortions that owning something produces), it plays into bigness bias (it is a small amount compared to your full salary) and it makes the default that you save some money.

It works, and really isn't that difficult to set up. There are other great advantages of it in use with pensions.

First, quite often your company will add extra money up to a certain point, so that if you put in money, they will match it up to 5%, for example. In that case, if you put in only 2% of salary, they match it and your total contribution is 4%, but if you put in 5% they match that so you get a total of 10%.

It's like adding to children's savings in chapter 13. When you remember that pension contributions usually get you marginal rate tax relief (basically, relief at your highest rate) you can end up with lots of money becoming savings for you at a minimum loss to what you would have in your pocket otherwise.

Second, it makes you join the pension scheme. As in chapter 5, most people put off the decision and end up starting too late. If you are going to increase (or start) contributions, you have to fill in forms, decide on funds etc. It might be hard to make yourself do it, but it is almost certainly a good move.

Start as early as possible

Compound interest (like the Jill and John example from chapter 8) means that a small amount of money early beats a huge amount put in late. If you want to accumulate money, even if you can only put away £10 a month or something, do it. Do it now!

If you know it is a good idea, do it now, today.

It might not be the very best thing, but it will be better than doing nothing. Remember, when we have lots of choices we tend not to decide. The failure to decide and to do nothing is the real risk, because the opportunity cost is that you will leave it too late.

So use the other ideas, pay yourself first, tithe to yourself to add to it, set up standing orders etc. but start as early as possible.

If you borrow, borrow from yourself

If you've set up some funds, you can have the fun of paying interest to yourself instead of to the bank. And you get to keep all the profits. It's a great way to set up children to learn to save as well (see chapter 13). But you do have to have some money saved to start with!

Remember pound cost averaging for the longer term

Whether you are reducing the risk of a lump sum by "drip feeding" a large amount of money into investments over a long term, or you only have small amounts to put away, long term investment benefits from regular payments. You're then in a position that if prices go down, you buy more, so you potentially gain more as long as you can leave the money in the market. It counteracts the tendency to misinterpret "risk".

Remember the 3 Rs

If you don't know what **return** *you require, you are in trouble. There's a concept in investment called, "Risk/Reward Ratio". Basically, no risk means no reward, lots of risk means exactly what it sounds like.*

It isn't really risk, because it is uncertainty and not mathematically calculable but the principle is true. You just keep stepping up the odds and the pay-off until you lose a bet that you can't cover.

If there is a mathematical **risk** *to be calculated, it is that nobody beats the index as often as they mathematically should. The odds are against you and the more you gamble in the market, the worse the odds become.*

Nobody can **read** *the market; nobody can predict the future accurately. Anybody who says they can is either insane or a liar.*

Use BRIDaL as a guide (but not as Holy Writ!)
Balance

You can't get only the upside unless you can accurately predict the future and you can't do that. Accept that some investments will lose ground or stay static while other things go up and you can create a balance that can protect you (but not totally, it's all risky, remember) against the unexpected.

Work out your values and get your Required Return.

Work out what you want to accumulate money to achieve. If you can do it with no risk at all, why take a risk? Aim for what you want and try to generate a return that allows you to get it as safely as possible, don't try to gamble to get more money just to have more, it isn't a good way to be happy (or make money long term).

Use index tracking

All the research, all the experts (like Malkiel, Buffet etc.) says it is better. The only people who disagree are those with a vested interest in having you place funds with somebody else. What advice do you want to take, neutral expert advice, or biased sales pitches?

Set up a properly diversified portfolio.

Look into getting a portfolio set up that isn't correlated, get the right help to do it, or find out how to do it for yourself if you need to. Do your homework on the best rates if you are going into cash (that's where the Martin Lewis skills and some of the IFA's access to rates information may be helpful) and remember that if something sounds too good to be true it probably is.

Once a market portfolio is set up, leave it alone!

The big challenge most people have is doing all the work to get it right. Do the work, then leave the portfolio for at least six months or so.

All you need to do is rebalance it every so often, and perhaps get advice for that if you need to.

You're more likely to make a loss through overtrading, trying to follow hot tips, reacting to news, than you are to letting the fundamental balance work for you. Everybody wants control, but you get your control from your initial setting up of something that works whatever happens.

Don't waste money on hot tips, avoid the herd

If a tip on a stock or whatever has value, it will still have value tomorrow, so there is no desperate panic to get in. If you will "miss the boat" waiting a week to check it out then it is a short term boom and you're taking a hell of a chance in investing in it.

That's the way pyramid schemes and bubbles work, people are so scared they'll miss out that they pile in and push the price up artificially.

Avoid the herd. You want to start early, but not before you know how long the race is going to be or what the starting gun sounds like!

If you have cash and short term investment, keep an eye on them

If you want the money within a year (or maybe two or three years) then keep an eye on rates. Pay somebody to do it for you if you really can't be bothered, but banks etc. rely on you being lazy and leaving money in accounts that don't give you a good return.

There's no point in carefully picking a good return, then finding out in three years time that you did really badly and haven't got the money you need, when if you'd just had a look every quarter you could have been sure of reaching your goal.

Once you're in a market – don't look at it every day.

Whilst trying to lose weight it is a mistake to weigh yourself every day, as it tends to be depressing and doesn't help you. If you look at the stock prices daily, you'll panic or get over excited or scared and undo all your good work. Warren Buffet isn't bothered, why should you be?

If you need to change things – change them

When you do a review, you may find that you need to get rid of something. You may need to balance the portfolio again, but you may have decided to buy a "tip" that hasn't worked out. If you need to sell a loser, you'll probably be reluctant to do it, you'll sell the winners and keep the losers. If it is to balance the portfolio and that is the only reason, fine. If you are reluctant to sell a loser because it triggers loss aversion, regret etc. look at it this way. If you sell it, you've got a loss to set against your Capital Gains Tax bill. Isn't that great, you've made a killing against HMRC! Get rid of what you need to get rid of.

Accumulating: protect what you've got

Have a reward account.

Particularly if you are trying to train yourself to act differently, tithe from your income or any windfalls into a special account for treats.

Don't go mad with it, but if you want to buy something special, use that as a short term goal, put away a bit of money each month and treat yourself. It teaches you to defer gratification (you can get a great sense of accomplishment from saving up for something and feeling the virtuous glow of having done it) and it means you protect your important savings rather than stick things on credit then have to deal with the problems that causes. And it gives you a reward, so it reinforces your good behaviour (remember how to train puppies)!

Check on what would happen if you died or were ill

Have you got wills, life assurance, health insurance? It's a frightening thought, so we don't *want* to, but *need* to think about it. If somebody is going to be in trouble if you are not there, remember the start of chapter 13, then sort it out. You don't always need to spend a huge amount, but you do need to think about what is going to happen if you are unlucky. And keep things up to date by reviewing them when anything changes (births, moves, marriage etc.)

Protect your assets

Remember from chapter 10 that you can insure or self insure. If you are self insuring, boost your "special purpose" funds by what you would have spent. You know the washing machine will conk out one day. If the warranty premium would be £60 a year, put that into your special purpose fund or other savings so that you've got the money there for when it does.

Accumulating: generate more

Brainstorm your options

Generating money usually requires creativity. Are there things you can sell that you don't need? Car boot sales and E-bay were set up for that. Have you got a hobby or interest that could produce earnings; website designing, cake making, gardening; these are things that can produce income from activities that you'd do for free in your spare time anyway. There are books on options for home businesses and other extra sources of income, so try the local library. The key is doing what is going to suit you. You need to generate the ideas because you are the one who knows you best.

Reducing money

I've set out ideas under general areas of spending, so spending money on non-essentials and using it to live are mixed together. Most people mix them together anyway so it makes sense. But first of all you need to distinguish between them.

> *Make sure you know what money you need to live, which purchases are about your real values, and which you just fancy having.*
>
> *If you don't know that, go back over chapters 2-4 until you are clear!*

Buying

Start by working out what you really want and need

Don't take other people's estimates as a guide or that will be your anchor. You are going to anchor anyway, so make sure it is your own anchor, not somebody else's.

Don't buy stuff just because it is cheap. If you don't want a mobile phone, don't have one, if you can get two for the price of one, only buy them if you'll use two. Similarly, if you can get broadband that you don't want and TV stations that you don't use, for only £5 per month more than you pay now, why waste £5? There's no point in spending money you could use to buy things you do want to get a bargain on things that you don't!

Do research, check what it is reasonable to pay for what you want.

Then you can negotiate from that figure, not the one the salesperson sets. It is a way to use anchoring to your advantage.

Check up what the sales people make from the sale.

If you're buying double glazing, insurance, domestic appliances, whatever, find out what sort of margin they make.

It's not uncommon (particularly around home improvements) that if you say you can't afford something, you will be offered a discount. For example double glazing firms almost invariably put in an initial quote, then offer a 40% discount. That makes the new price sound a real bargain (they are using anchoring) when in fact the new price is still a lot higher than the real value.

If you stick with them and the standard company discount is 40%, then the sales person also has a big stake in the sale and you can probably get another reduction (it will just cut the sales commission and their company's profit margin) and it is in their interests to close the sale even at a lower margin.

Use one company to tell you about another.

Ask who their competition is. They will promptly tell you what is wrong with the other companies. Then ask the other companies who their competition is. They will tell you what is wrong with the first company. That way you find out what the strengths and weaknesses are.

Nobody is best at everything, if there were perfect products there would only be one product on the market and no sales people!

The job of sales people is to make you believe that the product is perfect for you when in fact there are hundreds of products that are all pretty much the same, none are perfect but most are OK. What you want to know is the best combination for you in particular, and you only know that if you know what is important to you and can find out the flaws and strong points of each.

They want you to believe that the flaws are things that don't matter to you and it has all the strengths you need. So work out what you need first, then get the story from the competition who will be only too keen to tell you what is wrong with the opposition products.

Get technical people to tell you what to look for

If you are buying technical equipment like computers or want work done that you don't understand, like car repairs, house repairs or improvements etc. it is hard to know what questions to ask.

Get a couple of quotes and ask one person to critique what the other has said. For example, if one is telling you that "X is going to burn out and needs replacing" ask the other one what they think. Then go back to the first one and say that another "expert" told you that "X wasn't going to burn out" so that was a waste of money, but that you needed Y done because it would save wear on Z. It takes patience, but by going round to more than one expert you get a clearer idea of the technical points that matter.

Similarly, with buying new equipment, if one person tells you that you need X amount of computing power to do what you want, ask the others how much you need. You can then make a more reasonable estimate, allowing for "room for growth" and not end up paying for something that you are not going to use.

Be aware of sales psychology and "design architecture"

The model here are supermarkets. There are examples in Tim Harford's, The Undercover Economist, including the whole of the second chapter!

The common element to sales, whether it is supermarkets, estate agents, car sales people or whatever, is that they use psychology very well. This is the principle of "Nudge". However, unlike "Nudge" that outlines theory that Governments would apply if they actually worked or cared, it is a business policy that successful businesses follow as a matter of course.

In a supermarket, children's items will be on lower shelves so they can grab them, "women's stuff" on shelves that are usually a few inches lower than "men's stuff" (because their heights are, on average different) and so on. Therefore, as mentioned in chapter 5, the ones with the high margin are the first ones you see, those with the lower margin are harder to find, harder to reach, aren't necessarily labelled clearly etc. so unless you are conscious of it they make a higher profit margin on each item and you pay more than you need.

Similarly, the fresh fruit is at the front, it welcomes you, makes you feel healthy and virtuous. Milk and bread, that you nip in to get every day or so, are right at the back, so you'll see as many products as possible that you might buy and end up spending more.

Look at purchases as if they are all separate.

You know about bigness bias. When you are buying anything, think about the "add-ons" as a new item. So think of the "cheap" extended warranty as a separate insurance. What would it cost to put it on your household cover, or to self insure? The sun roof in the car is an extra £1,500 on your new £20,000 car, would you pay that to put a sun roof into your existing car?

Don't let people use your tendency to focus on the "big picture" and think of the pounds, blind you to where the pennies are going.

Economising

Distinguish between cost and value to you

An idea from Martin Lewis, trade down on goods. If you always buy named brands, try the standard ones. If you buy the standard ones, try the economy. It is a good project to give to children to teach them about how to compare (see chapter 13). But you can do it for yourself: can you actually taste the difference between one brand and another; are your whites whiter, does the branded clothing look or fit better?

Go for value

If the family don't like the cheap stuff, or find food is stiff with sugar and artificial preservatives, don't buy it because it is cheap. Saving money to get bad nutrition or clothes that fall apart is not saving, it is wasting.

Don't pay for the label alone. Save your money to pay for the things where you can appreciate the quality that costs a bit more. If you shop with a consciousness that you and your family are individuals, you can go for what suits you individually, not what suits the mob or what you've done in the past.

If you've got to keep up appearances, make economy fashionable

Can't afford a foreign holiday, you're being "green" and having a working holiday clearing canals, it's environmentally friendly and keeps you healthy. Can't afford new clothes, buying from charity shops is chic and you are concerned about sweatshop labour.

Personally, I'd be honest about it, who cares what anybody else thinks. However, if it really bothers you then economise, make the economies into a virtue for their own sake (not out of necessity) and use some of the money you save for a good counsellor to help you sort out what is really important in life!

Learn to cook!

The number of people who buy expensive, nutritionally awful, "ready meals" is terrifying. Most people say they buy them because they think it saves time, but often it is because they can't cook from scratch. Money is spent on things they could do for themselves, and produces meals stuffed with salt and sugar which then contribute to poor health.

It might take longer (although there are plenty of meals that can be cooked in less time than it takes to remove the packaging and bung something in a microwave) but it doesn't take that much longer and you know what you are eating is healthier. And the most relevant point here, it saves cartloads of money over the year. Remember how all the small amounts of money add up.

Go for power saving

Turn off the lights when you leave the room, boil only the water you need, turn down the thermostat a degree or two, insulate the house. There's loads of guidance on this stuff – use it!

Use the past to budget.

We often think in emotional terms, "I always spend too much on X" rather than practical terms like, "can I use my usual spending as a budgeting tool?"

Look at last time's bills to know what you really spent, work out what a realistic budget is, allocate it appropriately, and stick to it.

Budget special occasions

If birthdays and Christmas become a status event not a celebration, we can end up buying ever more expensive items to compete with friends and family.

Set spending limits on presents for everybody's use, "it's £X for friends' children, £Y for nieces and nephews, £Z for adults" or whatever.

Ensure everybody is clear on who is being bought for, it is embarrassing to have your children bought gifts when you have nothing for the giver or their children.

Make a "wish list" and get others to do so too. If you must get people surprises, keep these to close family members or people that you know (and who know you) really well. That way people get what they really value, costs don't escalate and you can work out what it all will cost in advance.

Give the (cheap) gift of happiness!

Try to give (and appreciate) experiences rather than "things". Material things don't make people happy, materialistic attitudes are linked to unhappiness.

We don't tell stories about or remember the expensive gifts, we remember the experiences of sharing and companionship. Those are what make us happy (remember chapter 2). Give experiences and real thought, not pre-packaged, expensive gifts that show you substitute money for love.

Making gifts shows real care and consideration, and is cheaper, so if you are talented in that way (artistically, can produce video on the computer etc.) you can give a precious gift at a fraction of the cost.

Think cash, use a debit card

We spend more on credit cards. Work out how to use your credit cards (if you have them) in a way that uses their advantages without having you waste money. Or use a debit card linked to your bank account or cash.

Work out a budget and check the small spending

Read chapter 11 and make sure you know what you are actually spending. Look at how much just drifts away from you (chapter 11). When you recover, work out how you're going to control that spending (chapter 4)!

Remember the Martin Lewis skills

Once you have separated the real needs from the "like to have's" and know what your values are, you know what you actually need to spend. Things like energy suppliers, car servicing, mortgage deals etc. are needed, but there is huge variation in price. So check out what is going to be best for you.

However, do remember to work out what you need first, or you'll end up with a cheap mobile you don't want, a dozen free channels you don't watch and boxes of cheap cigarettes you don't smoke!

Pay debts early

Compound interest applies to paying off debts as well as savings. For example, by paying £10 per month more than the "minimum" on a credit card balance of £3,300 at 18%, you pay off the debt in four years instead of nineteen and save nearly £2,800.

Getting rid of debts as early as possible (but watching for and calculating early redemption penalties) is usually a good move.

General financial decisions

You want to ignore the crowd, do what you really need and take responsibility for what you do. Those skills of independent thinking and responsibility are exactly the ones that you want to teach children (chapter 13). But how do you pick out the best choices?

A method to use (but not the absolute answer) is to try to balance out your emotions, reasoning and intuitive senses: We all get enthusiastic or depressed, feel we're right or we're stupid, that everybody is right or they are all idiots. We see things in absolutes, but it's seldom that simple.

So here are some things you can do in making decisions about money. Pick the ones that work for you, you don't have to do them all.

- Work out whether recognition, availability, overconfidence etc. are traps you fall into in when making your decision.

- For example, it is easy to think that if you research and do your homework, you will know all you need. But even when you are quite expert on the subject you are still likely to fixate on the wrong stuff. Then you get overconfident that you are right while ignoring all the contradictory evidence.

- Look at conflicting ideas. Actively seek out those who have opposite opinion, a good source often being rival salespeople.

- Try to keep the people you use as advisors independent. If you ask a group, they will come to a consensus and merge to give you a "what everybody knows" view. If you ask them separately, and if you pick your people right, you'll get some mainstream views, some really wild and wacky ones and some well to either side of the mainstream. So you get a wide range of options and that makes it easier to see the Black Swans coming. Read Surowiecki's "*The wisdom of crowds*" to get the full picture.

- Check on others' reasoning. Ask them not just what they'd do but what they'd look at, how they would weigh up the options, the pros and cons. What do they think are the key things to consider and why? It gives you different ways to think and makes you notice different features of the environment.

- Watch out for the possibility of "Black Swans" or real life unknowns, whichever analogy you prefer. What does "everybody says" prove?

- Don't assume the past is necessarily a good guide to the future even if everybody thinks it is. Look for the assumptions they are all making, the "white swan assumptions" that will prove Socrates is a table.

- Allow for unpredictability. If you are investing, look at the upside and the downside, and reduce them by ¼ to 1/2. So if you *think* you'll make £10,000 over three years, and the risk is that you'll lose at most £2,000 if it goes wrong, see if it is still a good idea if you might make between £5,000 and £7,500 and you might lose £3,000. That's more likely to be a true estimate (but is still a guess, remember!).

- The longer the term, the more uncertainty so make the ranges broader the farther ahead you are looking.

- Avoid making the decision during periods of anxiety or enthusiasm, you'll either panic or get overconfident. Remember framing effects like "this is a risk of losing" or "this is an opportunity for gain" that are two sides of the same coin. Generate different perspectives, perhaps by:

  * De-personalising. Imagine you're a consultant- what advice would you give somebody else if it was their money, "if I was telling somebody else about it, what would I say?"

  * Imagining different situations. If you are buying, think of what you'd sell for and vice versa (remember the endowment effect). Also, if you already owned it, would that effect your decision to buy, if you are going to hold it, would you buy it at the same price?

  * Think about it from the opposite emotional point of view. If you are thinking of gains (greed) then think about loss (fear) and vice versa.

  * Imagining "if I look back on it from a year ahead, what will I most like/dislike about it".

* Re-framing things like selling losers, buying and holding an investment and similar decisions, think what you'd have to lose or gain to change your opinion.

- Apply common sense. People go for risks when it seems riskier not to be "in", but that is how bubbles start. Check out different scenarios with different people and check whether things are as guaranteed as they seem. Remember tulip mania, the dot com bubble and the property crash; a few people might have seen that these were daft, but the herd carried on anyway.

- Be sceptical – if it sounds too good, it usually is.

- Remember, everybody is biased (like the TV series "House" mantra, "everybody lies"!) If you fixate on one expert or school of thought you will probably find they lead you astray because nobody can foretell the future and nobody is right all the time.

- If you end up with the decision that what the herd is doing seems sensible, then fine. The herd is not always wrong. But it makes sense to check before you sign up!

One final point on decision making. If you really don't know what you *want* to do, you might be in the "Zone of indifference" as Paul Klein calls it.

There are situations where you've thought about it, you have choices and you really don't know which one you are leaning towards. What I've suggested to clients in that situation is, literally, to toss a coin or throw a die. You don't have to go with what it suggests, but if you are genuinely not bothered, then why not (you might get less regret with less analysis).

What usually happens is people find they are hoping the coin comes up with a particular decision made, or the die lands on a specific number. It doesn't make the decision, but it tells you something you didn't know before about yourself, about what you wanted to have happen.

And that is useful information when you are trying to make a decision.

Summary:

- Work out what you want to do in principle, the strategy, then work out your tactics.
- Remember the broad things (the 3 Rs, BRIDaL) and pick the tactical elements that you can do most readily.
- Involve the family in comparison shopping, testing out different brands, economising.
- When you're making decisions, remember the principles. You are biased, you are not logical, you can't evaluate everything perfectly. But nor are you necessarily wrong because, after analysis, you don't agree with the majority. Get different views, imagine yourself in different situations and see where the flaws in the reasoning appear.

Hopefully it is clear that you really *are* the most important part of handling money, with the money trailing home a very poor second.

But there are times when "what and how" to handle money are important, and there are times when you can't, or don't want to, learn those things. There might also be times when you really don't feel able to think straight or able even to toss a coin to decide what to do. So where do you go for help?

Help!

Help is there if you want it. This chapter suggests where to look for help, what qualifications are relevant in advisors, where to check that they are genuine and what to do if it seems they aren't.

There are several areas where you might want help:

- Defining your values, goals, the symbols you use for money etc. around the areas from chapters 1-4 and their application, chapter 14.

- Problems you have around your personal style, any compulsions you have over spending and your particular habits of thought, the areas of chapters 4-8 and 14.

- Issues of overconfidence, belief in accurate prediction and generally "reading" the market in chapters 7 and 9.

- The financial detail throughout the book, for example in determining the reality of plans in chapter 3, redundancy in chapter 11 and the actual investment figures in chapter 9, but also in insurance in chapter 10, financial training in chapters 12 and 13 and in practical application from chapter 14.

- Problems over stress related to debt or redundancy worries, as in chapter 11.

- Advice on careers, making the best of your abilities, seeking out new directions, either as a result of your evaluation of your values and goals in chapters 2 or 3, or that are forced on you by redundancy, in chapter 11.

- Negotiation with your partner, establishing a system of finances that will work for you, chapter 12.
- To educate your children in the reality of finance, chapter 13

There is nobody in the world who is really expert on all of those. I'm probably the best qualified overall, and I would still want to call in other help to advise people on some of those areas, particularly the financial detail.

> *Again, this emphasises the importance of finding out about yourself, there is no "one stop shop" to go to, you need to know what help you want and need before you can get it.*

Those eight areas break down into five basic needs you might have.

a) Coaching about your personal style, to help you with goals, interacting with others etc.
b) Careers advice, looking for your options for new jobs or opportunities.
c) Help with stress, or serious behavioural change that is needed whether it is about your money behaviour or in dealing with other people.
d) Financial advice, possibly including elements of:
e) Debt (other resources for which we covered in chapter 11).

If you don't know whether to spend time or money on advice, ask yourself.

How much money would you want to forego a day of your holiday (and how much would you pay to buy another day)?

If the free time is really valuable, maybe you want to pay somebody to do things for you.

If you want the money, then maybe you want to put in more time yourself, study, work on it, and save your money.

If you decide on help, what you want from professionals in any or all of the five areas is that the person has:

Technical knowledge. I'd say you want at least a degree level, preferably masters or doctoral level. You wouldn't go to a Doctor who was not qualified or employ a solicitor who didn't have a law degree, so why have other professional help at a lower level?

Supervised, assessed experience. Architects, Engineers and Doctors (and Psychologists), as part of their qualifications have to have practical experience, recorded by log book or observation and independently assessed. It isn't enough to know the theory, you have also to prove you can apply it in practice.

Contextual knowledge. You might be very "good with people" but if you don't really know how people operate in that context, how will you help them? For example, a coach might have great skills in finding out what people's values are, helping them set goals etc. but if they know nothing about motivation about finance, the way that people think about money, the symbols they use etc. how useful will they be?

Ethical standards and code of conduct Unless the advisor has a code of ethics to follow, and somebody to make sure they do it right, you can't be sure of the quality of advice, or their motives..

Relating to these, three things about professional help that I want to outline.

1. Protection of title
2. Regulation of standards
3. Method of payment

1, Medical Doctor is a protected title, it is an offence to represent yourself as a Doctor if you are not one. But you can call yourself an accountant with no qualifications, as in turf accountants! You can't call yourself a Chartered Accountant or a Certified Accountant, as those are protected titles.

For the protected ones, you have to have qualifications, agree to abide by the codes of ethics, have appropriate insurances etc. It doesn't mean that the person is necessarily going to be honest or ethical, but it does mean they must be of a particular technical level and they can be prevented from practicing if they aren't licensed.

If they don't have the registration etc. it is an offence just to claim the title, irrespective of whether they are (or think they are) "good enough".

2. Regulation can be complex but basically it is about what you can reasonably expect from an advisor and who you complain to if they don't live up to what it says on the tin.

Regulated businesses should have levels of technical competence, usually assessed by exams that mean the person advising you is at least technically competent.

Of course, being technically competent doesn't mean that the person is honest or genuinely motivated to help you. Regulatory organisations also have codes of conduct and ethics with which their members must comply, but that doesn't mean much if there are no consequences to breaking the code. If there isn't a universally accepted central authority to complain to or if the code is voluntary, there isn't in reality any protection.

3. Commercial companies (or professional advice businesses) are intended to be profit-making ventures. Most advisors want and expect to be paid. One old adage that is very true is that "there is no such thing as a free lunch". It might not seem that you are the one who is paying, but *somebody* is paying for the lunch.

Charities may use volunteers who give their time free, but some costs have to be met (office space, copying, phones etc.) and those have to come from somewhere, such as donations.

If it is a commercial organisation then somebody is definitely paying for all of it and nobody is giving their time free. So no commercial organisation is giving "free" advice, it is all *always* paid for by somebody.

Now let's look at sources of advice, bearing those things in mind.

Coaching

There is no universal regulation or protection of title for coaches. Being a Coach, Accredited Coach, Psychological Coach, Member of X Coaching Institute, Graduate of Y Coaching University etc. means nothing. Anybody can be a coach, or claim to be "trained" or "qualified" with no training whatsoever.

Apart from meaning there is no minimum technical standard, this also means that there are no legal or ethical standards, nobody that you can complain to and no legal sanctions if they do it wrongly.

Technically, you still want somebody who has at least a Masters degree. Coaching is not simple, despite lots of cheap courses that train you to be a "life coach".

I'd avoid people who advertise only one specific technique (e.g. NLP or hypnosis) for coaching. Let me add that lots of these techniques (including NLP and hypnotherapy) can be very helpful for some things and as part of a coaching repertoire there is nothing wrong with them. But they are usually too limited to be useful to you on their own. My concern is that people often advertise "qualified master X" because they don't know anything else, they haven't got the depth of knowledge or training to know any alternatives. If all they have is a hammer, any person starts to look like a nail, even if you are actually a left hand thread bolt! They are usually below degree level anyway.

One way to ensure technical quality, ethics etc. is to go to a psychologist who coaches. The trouble with that is "psychologist" is not a protected title either!

There are nine meaningful titles for psychologists. These are

Chartered Psychologist,

Registered Psychologist,

Occupational Psychologist,

Clinical Psychologist,

Counselling Psychologist,

Educational Psychologist,

Forensic Psychologist,

Health Psychologist,

Sport and Exercise Psychologist.

Anybody can call themselves anything else, Psychologist, Qualified Psychologist, Coaching psychologist, or Financial psychologist. Those four are meaningless, they indicate nothing about qualifications, training, ethics or anything else and are not recognised by the British Psychological Society (BPS) or anybody else.

The protected titles (the nine I've listed above) mean somebody has got a doctoral level qualification (they have spent at least 6 years training including time applying skills under supervision), they've got to abide by the code of ethics and be insured, you can complain about them and they can lose their right to practice if they get it wrong and they are obliged not to take on work for which they are not qualified, so they have to have contextual knowledge (they can't give "careers advice" if they aren't competent, for example).

You can find BPS Chartered psychologists in your area via:

http://www.bps.org.uk/e-services/find-a-psychologist/directory.cfm

If you look under the "personal" section, it gives those who offer life/personal coaching, but the list is very limited.

You can check with the regulator, the Health Professions Council (HPC) to see whether somebody is subject to disqualification if they get things wrong at:

http://hpc-portal.co.uk/online-register//

Choose "Practitioner Psychologist" on the drop down menu under "step1: Select a profession" and put in the name. It tells you whether the person is currently registered with the HPC (who take any disciplinary action against psychologists who are registered). If somebody isn't on that register and they mess you about, you have no more protection than you do with a "coach", it doesn't matter what they claim.

Not that psychologists are the only good ones, there are many good coaches. The problem is that there are also many poor ones and until a proper register, protection of title etc. is established, it is hard to know what you've got unless you have a huge amount of specialist knowledge.

I am setting up a list on the website (tamingthepound.com). I'd rather have an official list that is policed by an independent authority such as the, BPS or HPC. If I do it, it is my opinion and I'm not qualified to judge everybody in the country. But it is a start, and hopefully it will prompt the powers that be to take regulation and policing of standards seriously, since they should protect the public from the incompetent and the dishonest.

Coaching is almost always fee based. Get a fee estimate before you start and an idea of the number of sessions needed. Some people will happily keep you as a client forever, since you are an income stream. A good coach is trying to make themselves redundant from the start, they want to make sure you don't need them by helping you develop the skills that you need.

By the same token, they will, and should, want to be paid. If somebody offers to give you "free" coaching, be very careful. There is no such thing as a "free lunch" remember.

Careers advice

If you're being offered career guidance as part of a redundancy package, take it. You can always ignore it, but it might be really helpful or at least give you some new ideas.

As with coaches, careers advisors, career coaches, career counsellors or whatever are not regulated. There are some very good ones around but some absolutely appalling ones as well.

In this instance the BPS list doesn't help at all, since there is no category for career advisors. I have asked several times for one to be set up but it hasn't happened yet.

I'd still suggest looking at a Chartered, Registered Psychologist (you can check up with the HPC site whether they are registered). You probably want an Occupational or Educational Psychologist, but the main consideration is that they do specialise in career advice, life transitions (such as redundancy etc.)

There is an Institute of Career Guidance. Their registered members are at NVQ 3 or 4 or above (about A-level, towards first year degree level). I don't think that is enough, so I'd go for Registered Psychologist who specialises, and ideally is a member of the ICG as well. There is a search facility for Institute members at: http://www.icg-uk.org/find_a_careers_adviser.html

In careers advice, you are not looking for somebody who deals with the trauma of redundancy, that's a different issue. You're looking for somebody who can help you determine what you would really enjoy doing, work with you on how you decide what to do, how to get into your chosen type of job etc. which could be in the case of redundancy but it might be because in looking at your values you decided to change.

Careers advice (or other coaching, to some extent) might include using psychometric instruments to look at your personal style, work preferences etc. Alternatively, it might be more of a life story based method or a combination of the two. All can be effective, but you want somebody that you feel confident about, and comfortable with and who is using tools because they suit you and your situation, not because it is the only thing they know or are qualified to use or who doesn't use them because they don't know how!

If somebody is talking about using a test or questionnaire to help you, you can find whether it has been registered with the BPS and can get reviews of instruments, although usually you have to pay for the reviews. The value of this is that some psychometric tests are terrific and some are about as accurate as a newspaper horoscope. The register and reviews are at: http://www.psychtesting.org.uk/test-registration and test-reviews/test-reviews-and-test-registration_home.cfm

That's another reason I'd try to find somebody who is actually a Psychologist (a real one, not somebody who claims to be one). They have to follow the code of ethics, have your interests at heart and if they let you down, you've got somebody to complain to about their conduct. An unqualified career coach might be very good, but if they aren't, for example if they use a really bad psychometric, you can't do anything about it, they've got your money and they can just carry on doing whatever they do, since nobody can stop them.

Again, I'm setting up a list of career coaches that are Registered and Chartered Psychologists and who specialise in career advice on tamingthepound.com. Once again, I'd rather some official body did it, so hopefully this is just an interim measure.

If you're looking at particular jobs or courses (before or after you've had some guidance), not all the advisors around are going to have massive databases of what is available. That isn't a problem, you can find the information, in fact it is often better (and I often set it as "homework") for people to look things up themselves. This lets you find out whether you are really interested when you have to do a bit of work to dig out key facts about job availability in your location or the cost and duration of part time courses.

But don't expect that, just because you've got some advice, the advisor is going to tell you what you will enjoy and be good at, find you the relevant job, help you fill in the application, give you a letter of introduction, and generally nursemaid you. I or anybody else can only help you so far, the drive has got to come from you.

Stress or major behavioural change

This moves into the area of counselling.

Some coaches can help with this, for example, the ideas in chapter 4 about behaviour change and motivational interviewing, CBT, mindfulness etc. are things I use in coaching. There is a blurring of the lines between coaching and counselling.

However, I am an Occupational Psychologist and I know what I'm competent to do and what I'm not. Some coaches (usually the ones who haven't actually got much formal training and assessment) think they can deal with clinical depression, trauma, a whole raft of issues. They can't, and they are dangerous.

I'm comfortable advising somebody who is a bit worried, has the odd fit of the blues, is generally coping but wants to be "better than average". If somebody is really at their wits' end, is depressed most of the time and is getting into self-destructive behaviour (drinking, drug taking, etc) then even as a psychologist I would refer them to a counsellor who has the full skill set to deal with those sort of issues.

Unfortunately, there is no regulation of counselling either! Anybody can say they are a counsellor, therapist, healer or whatever, it means nothing.

Fortunately, there are two recognised professional organisations that provide you with security.

One organisation is the BPS Counselling and Clinical Psychologists. They are essentially like me with a different specialisation, they deal with counselling and mental health issues (and some also coach, as I said the lines are blurred). They've got doctoral level qualifications, are required to have insurance, abide by a code of ethics, do continuous professional development and they also have to have ongoing supervision.

The other body is the British Association of Counselling and Psychotherapy (BACP). Some qualified psychologist may be members of this as well, the requirements aren't as high as for psychology, but they are still a very good standard both technically and practically.

You can check a Clinical or Counselling Psychologist on the BPS and HPC websites given earlier.

The equivalent site for BACP counsellors is:

http://wam.bacp.co.uk/wam/SeekTherapist.exe?NEWSEARCH

They may be able to help with the coaching issues, such as values, motivation etc. Where they can be uniquely useful is in dealing with anxieties, distress, grief and other problems you have with "getting your head right".

> *There's no shame in talking to a counsellor, it is the quickest and cheapest way to get back to feeling OK again and when you are able to think straight you can deal with the situation and move forward.*
>
> *If you struggle on without help you make it more difficult for yourself to tackle problems as they come up and you end up taking far more time getting back to being able to enjoy life again.*

It can be complicated because you get "debt counsellors" who are people who advise on finance, and "counsellors" who help with the stress that you show because of the debt! Don't confuse the two.

For the practical side of debt, use the advice lines, self help, debt charities etc from chapter 11. But sort out your thinking and feeling (the psychological bit) before (or at least while) you tackle the money, because if you can't think straight, you might dig yourself in deeper.

Another thing you might want a counsellor for is relating to partners or children (chapters 12 and 13). A counsellor is unlikely to be able to help you with the technical details of money itself. But one who specialises in couples or families may be very helpful in dealing with honest communication between couples, how to deal with children where the relationship is a problem or in similar situations. You need to check whether the counsellor deals with couples, families etc., people are complicated and nobody is an expert on everything.

Financial advice

For specialist financial information (such as insurance, diversifying investment portfolios or making the most use of tax allowances in your financial planning) you want a Financial Advisor.

The good news is that they are regulated (usually by the Financial Services Authority (FSA)), and specifically those giving advice on investments, savings, pensions life insurance and mortgages have to be registered. There is a minimum technical standard, they have to comply with accounting controls and there are codes of ethics and conduct. You can check this via their website **www.FSA.gov.uk**

Unfortunately, they don't (yet) have to know either the psychological aspects in this book or what I've called the "Martin Lewis" skills of saving money. This means there are no exams on any of these elements and problems arise such as the "attitude to risk" questionnaires I mentioned earlier being inconsistent and nobody having any motive to do anything about it.

Attitudes are beginning to change a bit and, once again, I'll be setting up a list of advisors on the Taming the Pound website who have done some training.

It won't be an official list, (unless I can persuade the FSA to take it more seriously) but at least it will give you a steer towards a financial advisor who not only knows the money, but can also help you work out your values and goals, knows about the ways that people commonly think about money and can help you turn these to your advantage, instead of your habits hurting you.

On the technical side, the current requirement is only something like an A-level. I don't think that is enough. From 2012, advisors will have to have a qualification that is about first year degree level, which is a bit better. However, to put it in perspective, I got that qualification in 1993!

If you are paying for advice, you want a good advisor. That includes technical qualifications at the same level (Masters) as other advisors. The qualifications are mostly monitored by the Personal Finance Society (PFS) which has a website: http://www.thepfs.org/pfs.aspx. The PFS in turn is part of the Chartered Insurance Institute (CII). There is a search facility for advisors via www.findanadviser.org.

What you are ideally looking for is Chartered Financial Planner. That is assessed at Masters level. There are various titles around that level such as Associate or Fellow of the Personal Finance Society (APFS and FPFS). Check on the PFS website to see what those mean.

To make things a bit more complicated there is an international organisation (principally US, but it does operate in other countries) called the Institute of Financial Planning (IFP). They have a qualification called Certified Financial Planner which seems to be at a similar level to the Chartered Financial Planner, although it doesn't seem to be assessed by examination. You can find out about that on their website http://www.financialplanning.org.uk/consumers/

There are three main types of adviser available:

- Tied - can only recommend the products of one company. They must "select and recommend products that are most appropriate" for you from that range. .
- Multi-Tied - can only advise on products from the range offered by a few organisations to which they are "tied" and must "select and recommend those that are most appropriate" from that ranges. .
- Independent Financial Adviser (IFA) - can advise you on products from the entire market.

Note, it is all dominated by products, not outcomes, values, interpersonal or budgeting skills or technical knowledge of what approach might be good. It is all about what product to flog to you!

Personally, I wouldn't bother with an advisor who is not independent; I can't see any advantage in it for you.

The point does get made that a limited range means they know it better, but if you pick an advisor who is well qualified, they should know the whole market and the full range of products from all suppliers.

There remains the question of payment.

Traditionally, you would pay by commission. You can also pay a percentage of money invested (like 1% of funds etc.). I'd usually suggest that you forget about both of those options. The amount you pay is usually greater than the value of the work required. In fact, in the case of a percentage charge on funds invested, you are probably paying a huge amount more than the work required.

Think of the charges for "actively managed" funds against those for "index tracking". If you've got, say, £500,000, you're paying £5,000 a year (at 1%) for somebody to give you some statements and potentially "manage" you out of some performance. If you pay £150 an hour, that is about a full weeks work – it might be worth it, but then it might not. You need to do the maths.

For those reasons, among others, you'll generally get better advice if you pay a fee, either based on an hourly rate or a fixed fee quoted on a project basis.

You usually have the option of paying the agreed fee for the work carried out and potentially have the commission that would be paid offset against the fees to reduce or cover the fee quoted.

Check that out, because the offset might apparently save you money, but if it comes out of the money that would be invested, it might be better to pay the fee and have the commission re-invested on your behalf – it depends on the situation.

The only exception on commission is possibly with life cover such as term assurance, where the amount of work involved in sorting out all the details is actually quite high in proportion to the premium, so the fee might be more than you'll pay in a year or two for the assurance itself.

It is difficult, but in that case it is probably worth offsetting the commission against the fee as you are unlikely to get a "net" rate anyway, so the fact that the advisor gets the commission doesn't alter the premium you pay.

So if you are going to get a financial advisor:

1. Get an IFA.
2. Ideally one who is a Chartered or Certified Financial Planner.
3. Preferably one who has training in the material in this book.
4. Sort out a fee and ask them when it would be fair for them and advantageous for you to look at offsetting commissions
5. Know what you are trying to do, your values, goals etc. so you can give them a really detailed idea of what you want.
6. Get them to give you lessons in maths (if you need them) understanding how markets work (if you are interested), tax (if it is relevant), work with them on diversification (see chapter 9) and make sure you know what things you are going to research and do and what you are paying them to do.

Summary:

- For values, goals etc. or for careers advice. get a coach, preferably a psychologist who has one of the nine titles and who specialises and has qualifications in the area (such as career guidance or coaching).
- If you are using anybody else, make sure they have at least a Master's level qualification that includes experience and the

application of theory to real people, and who has been independently assessed. Check what they claim as qualification, professional membership etc. are true. Ensure they have indemnity insurance, a code of ethics and are regulated so they can be kicked out if they do things wrongly.

- If you're looking for a financial advisor, see if they know any of the content in this book, check them out with the PFS and make sure they are independent and preferably a chartered or certified financial planner.

- Look on the tamingthepound.com site to see if there is a list of those who have the appropriate credentials.

- Check that any counsellor you want to see in relation to stress etc. is either a counselling or clinical psychologist, or is BACP registered.

- Speak to the advisor and see if you get on with them. You are going to have to trust them with private information about yourself and if the "chemistry" is wrong, you won't be able to do that. No good advisor, coach, counsellor etc. will mind – professionals appreciate that the relationship is really important and if you don't feel right it isn't a reflection on them, it is a matter of people and their relationships being very complex.

- Don't part with money until you know what sort of fees you're paying, for how long and exactly what for.

- And don't confirm appointments until you've had time to check out any claims they make.

Exit line

I hope you enjoyed the book.

But most of all, I hope that you do something with the ideas, because that's the only way it will be really useful to you.

If you want to check anything that wasn't in the book, have a look at the website: www.tamingthepound.com, and feel free to get in touch.

I hope that you now *know* that *you* are bigger and more important than money, and that you are well on your way from

This   to this

Best of luck!

References

Adams, D (1979) *The hitch-hikers guide to the galaxy*, Heinemann.

Akerlof, G.A & Shiller, R.J. (2009) *Animal Spirits*, Princeton

Alexander G. (2006) *Behavioural Coaching- the GROW model*, In Passmore, J (ed) (2006) *Excellence in coaching*. London: Kogan Page;

Allen, W (1978) *Without Feathers*, Sphere books.

Allan W & Hample, S (1979) *Inside Woody Allen*, Hodder & Stoughton

Allan W (1991) *Getting even*, Random House

Ambady, N & Rosenthal, R (1992) *Thin slices of expressive behaviour as predictors of interpersonal consequences: A meta-analysis*. Psychological Bulletin, Vol 111(2), 256-274.

Arkes, H.R and Hammond, K.R Eds (1986), *Judgment and Decision making*, New York, Cambridge University Press

Bajekal, M (2005) *Healthy life expectancy by area deprivation: Magnitude and trends in England, 1994-9*, Health Statistics Quarterly, 25, 18-27

Bamford, M (2006) *The Money Tree*, Prentice Hall.

Barber, B.M & Odean, T; (2001) *Boys Will be Boys: Gender, Overconfidence, and Common Stock Investment*; Quarterly J of Economics, February, Vol. 116, No. 1, Pages 261-292.

Barber, B.M & Odean, T; (2000) *Trading Is Hazardous to Your Wealth: The Common Stock Investment Performance of Individual Investors;* The Journal of Finance, Vol. 55, No. 2 (Apr., 2000), pp. 773-806

Barber, B.M & Odean, T; (1999) *The Courage of Misguided Convictions,* Financial Analysts Journal, November/December 1999, Vol. 55, No. 6 pp. 41-55

Barkow, J.H (1992) *Beneath New Culture is Old Psychology: Gossip and Social Stratification*, in Barkow, J.H, Cosmides, L and Tooby, J, Eds; (1992) *The Adapted Mind*, Oxford University Press.

REFERENCES

Barkow, J.H, Cosmides, L and Tooby, J, Eds; (1992) *The Adapted Mind*, Oxford University Press.

Baron-Cohen, S, (2003) *The Essential Difference*, Penguin.

Beinhocker, E; (2007) *The Origin of Wealth: Evolution, Complexity, and the Radical Remaking of Economics;* Random House Business Books.

Belsky, G & Gilovich, T; (1999) *Why smart people make big money mistakes and how to correct them;* Simon and Schuster.

Bolles, R (1997) *What Colour is Your Parachute?: A Practical Manual for Job-Hunters and Career Changers,* Ten Speed Press

Brennan, T. J. and Lo, A.W., *The Origin of Behaviour* http://papers.ssrn.com/sol3/papers.cfm?abstract_id=1506264

Bernstein, P.L, (1996) *Against the Gods: The remarkable story of risk*, Wiley.

Brickman, P., Coates, D & Janoff-Bulman, R (1978), *Lottery winners and accident victims: Is happiness relative?* Journal of Personality and Social Psychology. Vol 36(8), 917-927.

Brown, K.W., Kasser, T, Ryan, R.M, Linley, P.A & Orzech, K; (2009) *When what one has is enough: Mindfulness, financial desire discrepancy, and subjective well-being;* Journal of Research in Personality; Volume 43, Issue 5, Pages 727-736

Buettner, D (2009) *The Blue Zones: Lessons for Living Longer from the People Who've Lived the Longest,* National Geographic Society; Reprint edition

Burns, D.D; (1980/99) *Feeling good: the new mood therapy;* Avon.

Buchanan, Mark, (2002) *Nexus: Small Worlds and the Groundbreaking New Science of Networks* W.W. Norton & Company.

Buchanan, Mark *Power Laws & the New Science of Complexity Management* at http://www.optimalenterprise.com/docs/Power%20Laws%20-%20Complexity%20Mgmt%20sb34_04107.pdf

Buchanan, M (2002) *The Physics of the Trading Floor*, Nature, Volume 415, January 3,

Calderwood, R; Klein, G.A & Crandall, B.W. (1988) *Time pressure, skill and move quality in chess*; American Journal of Psychology 101, 481-493.

Carver, C.S & Baird E (1998) *The American Dream Revisited: Is It What You Want or Why You Want It That Matters?*, Psychological Science, Volume 9 Issue 4, Pages 289- 292

Cavalli-Sforza L.L, Menozzi, P and Piazza, A; (1994) *The history and geography of human genes,* Princeton University Press.

Chalmers, A.F; (1982) *What is this thing called science: Second Edition*; Open University.

CII Tuition Service (1976) *Elements of Insurance*, CII Tuition Service, London.

Claxton, G (1998) *Hare Brain, Tortoise Mind: Why Intelligence Increases When You Think Less*, Fourth Estate.

Cosmides, L & Tooby, J; (1992) *Cognitive Adaptations for Social Exchange*; In Barkow, J.H, Cosmides, L and Tooby, J, editors; (1992) *The Adapted Mind*, Oxford University Press.

Credit Action debt statistics (2007), (http://www.creditaction.org.uk/debt-statistics.html) accessed 21/1/08

Csikszentmihalhyi, M (2002) *Flow*, Rider

Csikszentmihalhyi, M (1997) *Finding Flow – the psychology of engagement with everyday life*, Basic books.

Darling A, (2007) reported on BBC Radio 4's Today, see for example http://news.bbc.co.uk/1/hi/uk_politics/7078487.stm http://www.publications.parliament.uk/pa/cm200809/cmhansrd/cm 090119/debtext/90119-0006.htm

Davidson, R.J., Kabat-Zinn, Schumacher, J, Rosenkranz,M, Muller, D, Santorelli, S.F, Urbanowski, F, Harrington, A, Bonus, K & Sheridan, J.F (2003) *Alterations in Brain and Immune Function Produced by Mindfulness Meditation*, Psychosomatic medicine, 65, 564-70,

Davis, G.F., Yoo, M. & Baker, W.E., (2003) *The Small World of the Corporate Elite*, Strategic Organization, Vol. 1, No. 3, 301-326.

REFERENCES

D'Adamo, P.J. (1998) *Eat right for your type*, Century.

Dawe, R.M; (1979) *The Robust Beauty of Improper Linear Models in Decision Making;* American Psychologist; Vol. 34, No. 7, 571-582.

Dawkins, R; (1976/89) *The Selfish Gene,* New edition, Oxford University Press.

Dawkins, R (1988) *The Blind Watchmaker*, Penguin.

Damasio, A.R, (2006) *Descartes error: Emotion Reason and the Human Brain*, Vintage.

De Bondt, W.F.M, (1991) *What do economists know about the stock market,* The Journal of Portfolio Management, 18, 84Ð91.

De Bondt, W F.M. and Thaler, R., (1995) *Financial Decision Making in Markets and Firms: a behavioural perspective:* In *Handbook of Finance.* Edited by R. Jarrow, V Maksimovic, and W. T. Ziemba. Elsevier-North Holland:

De Bondt, W.F.M. & Thaler, R (1985), *Does the Stock Market Overreact?*; The Journal of Finance, Vol. 40, No. 3.

Department for Transport, Road Casualties Great Britain: 2007 - Annual Report, http://www.dft.gov.uk/pgr/statistics/datatablespublications/accidents/casualtiesgbar/roadcasualtiesgreatbritain20071 accessed 26/4/10

Dickman, S.J (1990) *Functional and dysfunctional impulsivity personality and cognitive correlates*; J of Personality and Social Psychology 58 95-102

Diener, E & Biswas-Diener, R; (2008) *Happiness: Unlocking the mysteries of psychological wealth*; Blackwell.

Einhorn, H. (1974) *Expert judgment: Some necessary conditions and an example.* Journal of Applied Psychology, 59, 562-571.

Ekman, P, Davidson, R.J,, Ricard, M; Wallace, B.A (2005) *Buddhist and psychological perspectives on emotions and well being*, Current directions in psychological science 14:2, 59-63

Emmons, R. A; (1999) *The Psychology of ultimate concerns: motivation and spirituality in personality*, Guilford Press.

England J and Chatterjee P, (2005), *Financial education: A review of existing provision in the UK,* DWP research summary, (http://www.dwp.gov.uk/asd/asd5/summ2005-2006/275summ.pdf)

Ferguson, N (2009) *The ascent of money: A financial history of the world,* Penguin.

Festinger, L. (1954). *A theory of social comparison processes.* Human Relations, 7(2) 117-140.

Feynman, R.P (1985) *QED: The strange story of light and matter,* Penguin

Fiske, A.P; (1992) *The four elementary forms of sociality: Framework for a unified theory of social relations;* Psychological Review, **99,** 689-723.

Fiske A.P (1991) *Structures of Social life, the four elementary forms of human relations,* New York, Free press.

Foley, S (2002) *Mind the yield gap, bulls insist equity markets are set to rebound.* http://www.independent.co.uk/news/business/analysis-and-features/mind-the-yield-gap-bulls-insist-equity-markets-are-set-to-rebound-746753.html

Frankl, V (2004) *Man's search for meaning,* Rider.

Frith, U; (1990) *Autism: Explaining the Enigma,* Wiley Blackwell.

FSA (2008) *Consumer responsibility* http://www.fsa.gov.uk/pubs/discussion/dp08_05.pdf

Furnham, A & Argyle, M; (1998) *The psychology of money;* Routledge.

Furnham, A (2005) *Just for the money: What really motivates us at work.* Marshall Cevendish business.

Furnham, A (2008) *The economic socialisation of young people,* The social affairs unit.

Gazzaniga, M.S; (2002) *The split brain revisited,* Special Editions, Scientific American.

Gigerenzer, G; (1996) *On narrow norms and vague heuristics: A reply to Kahneman and Tversky,* Psychological Review 103 pp 592-96

Gigerenzer, G; (2007) *Gut Feelings: The Intelligence of the Unconscious;* Allen Lane.

Gigerenzer, G; (2002) *Reckoning with risk: learning to live with uncertainty*; Penguin.

Gigernezer, G and Selten, R eds (2002) *Bounded rationality: The adaptive toolbox*, MIT Press.

Gigerenzer, G; Todd, P.M and the ABC research group; (1999) *Simple Heuristics that make us smart;* Oxford University Press.

Gigerenzer, G. & Hug, K. (1992). *Domain-specific reasoning: Social contracts, cheating, and perspective change.* Cognition, 43(2), 127-171.

Gladwell, M (2001) *Tipping point: how little things can make a bit difference.* Abacus.

Gladwell, M (2006) *Blink: The Power of Thinking Without Thinking*, Penguin

Gladwell, M (2008) *Outliers: the story of success*, Allen Lane

Gleick, J; (1997) *Chaos: Making a New Science;* Vintage.

Goldberg, H & Lewis, R.T; (1978) *Money Madness: The Psychology of Saving, Spending, Loving and Hating Money;* Springwood, London.

Goleman, D (2004) *Destructive emotions*, Bloomsbury Publishing

Goleman, D (2003) *Healing Emotions: Conversations with the Dalai Lama on Mindfulness, Emotions and Health*, Shambhala Publications

Goodman, B (2002) *Active Mismanagement: The Case for Index Funds*, http://www.thestreet.com/story/10036923/active-mismanagement-the-case-for-index-funds.html

Gribben, J; (2005) *Deep Simplicity: Chaos, Complexity and the Emergence of Life*; Penguin Books.

Groenewold, N & Fraser, P; (2001) *Violation of the IID-normal assumption: Effects on tests of asset-pricing models using Australian data*; Journal of Empirical Finance, Volume 8, Issue 4, September, 427-449

Gross, D.B & Souleles, N.S; (2002) *Do Liquidity Constraints and Interest Rates Matter for Consumer Behaviour? Evidence from Credit Card Data*; Quarterly Journal of Economics 117; 149-185.

Grove, W.M; Zald, D.H; Lebow, B.S; Snitz, B.E and Nelson, C; (2000) *Clinical versus mechanical prediction: A meta-analysis*. Psychological Assessment. Vol 12(1), Mar 2000, 19-30.

Haidt, J; (2006) *The happiness hypothesis*, Arrow books.

Harvey, D, (2005) *A brief history of Neo-liberalism*, OUP, Oxford

Henrich, J; Boyd, R, Bowles, S; Camerer, C, Fehr, E and Gintis, H eds. (2004) *Foundations of Human Sociality: Economic Experiments and Ethnographic Evidence from Fifteen Small-Scale Societies*. London: Oxford University Press.

Henrich, J; Boyd, R, Bowles, S; Camerer, C, Fehr, E and Gintis, H, (2001) *Cooperation, Reciprocity and Punishment in Fifteen Simple Societies*, www.umass.edu/preferen/Class%20Material/jgames.ppt accessed 16/5/10

Herzberg, F., Mausner, B. & Snyderman, B.B. 1993, *The Motivation to Work*. Transaction Publishers; New edition)

Hey, T & Walters, P; (2003) *The New Quantum Universe – Second Edition*; Cambridge University Press.

Hilpern, K (2008) *Stuck together*, Guardian
http://www.guardian.co.uk/lifeandstyle/2008/aug/27/relationships.divorce

Hogarth, R.M; (2006) *Is confidence in decisions related to feedback? Evidence from random samples of real-world behaviour*. In Fiedler, K and Juslin, P (Editors) *Information sampling and adaptive cognition*. Cambridge University Press

Harford, T (2007) *The undercover economist*, Abacus

Hölldobler, B & Wilson, E.O; (1990) *The Ants*; Springer.

Imberg M, (2007) *Credit Risk and Bad Debt Management in the UK Retail Lending Market*, Datamonitor.

Iyengar, S.S & Lepper, M.R (2000) *When Choice is Demotivating: Can One Desire Too Much of a Good Thing?* Journal of Personality and Social Psychology, Vol. 79, No. 6, 995-1006

James, O (2008) *The selfish Capitalist: Origins of Affluenza*, Vermillion, London

Janis, I.L; (1982) *Groupthink: 2nd Revised edition*; Houghton Mifflin (Academic).

Johnson, S; (2002) *Emergence: The Connected Lives of Ants, Brains, Cities and Software*; Penguin.

Kabat Zinn, J (2008) *Full catastrophe living*, Piatkus.

Kahneman, D, Slovic, P & Tversky, A (1982) *Judgment under uncertainty: Heuristics and biases*, Cambridge University Press.

Kahneman D and Tverky, A; (1973) *On the psychology of prediction.* Psychological Review 80, 237-251

Kahneman D and Tverky, A; (1979) *Prospect theory: an analysis of decision under risk;* Econometrica, 47,(2); 263- 291

Kahneman D and Tverky, A (1996) *On the reality of cognitive illusions*, Psychological Review 103 pp 582-591.

Kandola, B; (2009) *The Value of Difference: Eliminating Bias in Organisations*; Pearn Kandola.

Kasser, T (2002) *The high price of materialism*, MIT press, London.

Kasser, T & Ryan, R.M (1996), *Further examining the American dream; differential correlates of intrinsic and extrinsic goals*, Personality and social psychology bulletin 22, 3 280-287

Kay, J.A (2009) *The Long and the Short of it: A Guide to Finance and Investment for Normally Intelligent People Who Aren't in the Industry,* The Erasmus Press Ltd.

Kirton, M.J; (2003) *Adaption-Innovation in the context of diversity and change*; Routledge

Klein, G; (2003) *The Power of Intuition*, Random House.

Klein, G; (1999) *Sources of Power: How People Make Decisions* MIT Press.

Klein, G; Orasanu, J; Calderwood, R & Zsambok, C.E; (1993) *Decision making in action: Models and methods.* Ablex; Norwood, NJ.

Kringelbach, M.L, (2009) *The Pleasure Centre*, Oxford University Press, New York.

Krugman, P (2009) *How Did Economists Get It So Wrong?* New York Times

– 2/9/09 http://www.nytimes.com/2009/09/06/magazine/06Economic-t.html?sq=krugman&st=cse&scp=3&pagewanted=all;

Kunst-Wilson, W.R & Zajonc, R.B. (1980) *Affective discrimination of stimuli that cannot be recognised,* Science, Vol 207, Issue 4430, pp. 557-8

Langer, E quoted in Makridiakis, S; Hogarth, R & Gaba, A; (2009) *Dance with chance: Making luck work for you*; Oneworld.

Lareau, A (2003) *Unequal Childhoods: Class, Race and Family Life,* University of California Press

Lea, S.E.G, Tarpy, R.M and Webley, P (1987) *The individual in the economy*, Cambridge University Press.

Lepper, M.R & Greene, D (1978) *The hidden costs of reward*; Morristown NJ; Lawrence Earlbaum.

Lepper, M.R , Greene, D & Nisbett, R.E (1973) *Undermining children's intrinsic interest with extrinsic reward: A test of the overjustification hypothesis*; Journal of Personality and Social Psychology; 28, 129-137

Levitt, S.D & Dubner, S.J (2005) *Freakonomics*, Penguin

Linton H, (2006), *Personal Finance Education in Schools; a UK Benchmark Study,* Financial Services Authority, web only. (http://www.fsa.gov.uk/pubs/consumer-research/crpr50.pdf)

Livingstone S M and Lunt P K; (1992), *Predicting personal debt and debt repayment: Psychological, social and economic determinants*; Journal of Economic Psychology 13 (1992) II l-134

Locke, E.A & Latham, G.P (1984) *Goal Setting: A Motivational Technique That Works* Prentice Hall

Long, J. S. (2007). *Are you a wealthy type? A new study of type, gender, and money.* Paper presented at CS228 at APT-XVII, the Seventeenth Biennial International Conference of the Association for Psychological Type, Baltimore, MD.

Lunn, P; (2008) *Basic Instincts: Human nature and the new economics;* Marshall Cavendish.

Lynch, P & Rothchild, J (1993) *Beating the Street,* Simon & Schuster

REFERENCES

Lynch, P & Rothchild, J (2000) *One up on wall street: How to use what you already know to make money in the market.* Simon & Schuster Paperbacks.

Makridiakis, S; Hogarth, R & Gaba, A; (2009) *Dance with chance: Making luck work for you*; Oneworld.

Malkiel, B.G; (2005) *Reflections on the Efficient Market Hypothesis: 30 Years Later,* The Financial Review 40 (2005) 1—9

Malkiel, B.G; (1995) *Returns from investing in equity mutual funds 1971 -1991;* The Journal of Finance, 50 (2), 549-572

Mandelbrot, B & Hudson, R.L; (2008) *The (Mis)Behaviour of Markets: A Fractal View of Risk, Ruin and Reward*; Profile Business

Mann, J (1992) *Nurturance or Negligence: Maternal Psychology and Behavioural Preference Among Preterm Twins* in Barkow, J.H, Cosmides, L and Tooby, J, editors; (1992) *The Adapted Mind*, Oxford University Press.

Matthews, A.M; (1991) *If I Think About Money So Much, Why Can't I Figure It Out?: Understanding and Overcoming Your Money Complex*; Summit Books.

McAdams, D.P (2001) *The Psychology of Life Stories,* Review of general psychology, Vol 5, 100-122

Meehl, P; (1954) *Clinical versus statistical prediction: a theoretical analysis and a review of the evidence.* The University of Minnesota Press.

Miller, W.R & Rollnick,S (2002) *Motivational Interviewing: Preparing People for Change,* Guildford Press

Mischel, H.N & Mischel, W (1983) *The Development of Children's Knowledge of Self-Control Strategies*, Child Development, Vol. 54, No. 3, pp. 603-619

Mollon, J.D; (2000) *Cherries among the leaves: the evolutionary origins of color vision;* in Davis, S ed; (2000) *Color Perception: Philosophical, Psychological, Artistic and Computational Perspectives;* Oxford University Press, New York.

Moloney, M.J (1951) *Facts from Figures*, Penguin.

Nagel, K and Paczuski, M (1994) *Emergent Traffic Jams,* Physical review 51 (4) 2909–2918

Neenan, M & Dryden, W; (2002) *Life coaching a cognitive-behavioural approach*; Routledge.

Nettle, D, Coall, D & Dickins, (2009) *Birthweight and Paternal Involvement Predict Early Reproduction in British Women: Evidence from the National Child Development Study,* American Journal of Human Biology, http://www.staff.ncl.ac.uk/daniel.nettle/ajhb.pdf accessed 24/5/10

Niederle, M & Vesterlund, L (2007) *Do Women Shy Away from Competition? Do Men Compete Too Much?* The quarterly journal of economics, August 2007, Vol. 122, No. 3, Pages 1067-1101

Norman, D.A (1988) *The Psychology of Everyday Things*, Basic Books

Northcraft, G.B. and Neale, M.A. (1987) *Experts, amateurs, and real estate: An anchoring-and-adjustment perspective on property pricing decisions*, Organizational Behaviour and Human Decision Processes Volume 39, Issue 1, February, Pages 84-97

OFT scams report
http://www.oft.gov.uk/shared_oft/reports/consumer_protection/oft 1070.pdf

Odean, T (1998) *Volume, Volatility, Price, and Profit When All Traders Are above Average*, The Journal of Finance, Vol. 53, No. 6 (Dec., 1998), pp. 1887-1934

Odean, T (1999) Do investors trade too much, *The American Economic Review*, Vol. 89, No. 5, pp. 1279-1298

Offer, A (2006) *The challenge of Affluence: Self-control and Well-being in the United States and Britain Since 1950*, OUP, Oxford

Olsen, R.A (2002) *Professional Investors as Naturalistic Decision Makers: Evidence and Market Implications,* The Journal of Psychology and Financial Markets, Vol. 3, No. 3, 161–167

Oxford Dictionary of economics, http://www.enotes.com/econ-encyclopedia/reverse-yield-gap, viewed, 30/6/10

Parsons, R (2005) *The Money Secret*, Hodder & Stoughton.

Payne, J.W, Bettman, James, R & Johnson, E.J (1993) *The adaptive decision maker*, Cambridge University Press.

Payne, J.W, Bettman, James, R & Johnson, E.J (1990) *The adaptive decision maker: effort and accuracy in choice,* in Hogarth, R, editor (1990) *A tribute to Hillel J Einhorn, University of Chicago Press.*

Peltier, B (2001) *The psychology of executive coaching: Theory and application,* Routledge.

Pinker, Steven; (1994) *The Language Instinct*, Penguin

Pinker, Steven; (1997) *How the Mind Works.* Penguin.

Pinker, Steven; (2000) *Words and rules*, Perennial

Pinker, Steven; (2002) *The Blank Slate: The Modern Denial of Human Nature*; Allen Lane.

Pinker, Susan; (2008) *The sexual paradox: troubled boys, gifted girls and the real difference between the sexes*; Atlantic Books.

Prelec, D & Simester, D (2001) *Always Leave Home Without It: A Further Investigation of the Credit-Card Effect on Willingness to Pay,* Marketing Letters 12:1, 5±12,.

Prochaska J.O & Diclemente C.C. (1994) *The transtheoretical approach: crossing the traditional boundaries of therapy.* Malabar FLA: Kreiger Publishing Company.

Prochaska, J.O; Norcross, J.C & DiClemente, C.C; (1994) *Changing for good*; Quill.

Profet, M; (1992) *Pregnancy sickness as Adaptation: A deterrent to Maternal Ingestion of Teratogens;* In Barkow, J.H, Cosmides, L and Tooby, J, editors; (1992) *The Adapted Mind*, Oxford University Press.

Reid, P.R. (1952) *The Latter Days at Colditz*, Coronet books.

Ricard, M (2007) *Happiness: A guide to developing life's most important skill*, Atlantic Books, London

Rollnick,S; Miller, W.R & Butler, C.C (2008) *Motivational Interviewing in Health Care: Helping Patients Change Behavior (Applications of Motivational Interviewing)* Guildford Press.

Rosenthal, J.S; (2005), *Struck by lightning*; Granta Books.

Sanfey A G., Rilling, J.K., Aronson, J.A., Nystrom, L.E. & Cohen· J.D (2003) *The neural basis of economic decision making in the ultimatum game*, Science Vol. 300. no. 5626, pp. 1755 - 1758

Sapolsky, R (1994) *Why zebras don't get ulcers*, W.H. Freeman & Co, New York.

Schleifer, A (2000) *Inefficient Markets: An Introduction to Behavioural Finance*, Oxford Univ. Press, Oxford.

Seligman, M (2003) *Authentic happiness: Using the new positive psychology to realise your potential for deep fulfilment*, Nicholas Brealey Publishing

Seligman, M (2006) Learned *Optimism: How to change your mind and your life*, Vintage.

Senge, P.M; (1990/2006) *The fifth discipline: The art & practice of the learning organisation*; Random House.

Shafir E and Tversky A, (1995) *Decision making* in Osherson, D.N, Smith, E.E & Gleitman, L.R, editors *An Invitation to Cognitive Science: Thinking*, Cambridge, Mass.: MIT Press

Shafir, E., Diamond, P and Tversky A. (1997). *Money Illusion*. The Quarterly Journal of Economics, Vol 112, 2, In Memory of Amos Tversky (1937-1996), 341-374

Sheldon, K M & Kasser, T (2008) *Psychological threat and extrinsic goal striving*, Motivation and Emotion 32 (1) 37–45

Silverman, I & Eales, M; (1992) *Sex differences in Spatial Abilities: Evolutionary Theory and Data*; In Barkow, J.H, Cosmides, L and Tooby, J, editors; (1992) *The Adapted Mind*, Oxford University Press.

Sky News (2009) *Secret Debts: Do You Lie To Your Partner?* http://beta.news.sky.com/skynews/Home/UK-News/Hidden-Debts-Britons-Keep-Money-Secret-From-Parnter-Credit-Report-Reveals/Article/200902415229933?chooseNews=UK_News

Slovic, P; (1969) *Analyzing the expert judge: A descriptive study of a stockbroker's decision processes*. Journal of Applied Psychology, 53, 255-263.

REFERENCES

Smithers, R (2010) *Secret debt: one in three consumers hides financial problems from family. http://www.guardian.co.uk/money/2010/apr/22/hidden-debt*

Soon, C.S., Brass, M., Heinze, H., Haynes, J. (2008). *Unconscious determinants of free decisions in the human brain.* Nature Neuroscience

Stewart, I (1997) *Does God Play Dice? The New Mathematics of Chaos.* Penguin

Surowiecki J; (2004) *The wisdom of crowds: Why the many are smarter than the few;* Abacus, London

Taleb, N.N; (2007) *The Black Swan: The Impact of the Highly Improbable;* Penguin.

Taleb, N.N; (2007) *Fooled by Randomness: The Hidden Role of Chance in Life and in the Markets;* Penguin.

Tasler, N (2009) *The Impulse Factor: Why Some of Us Play it Safe and Others Risk it All,* Simon & Schuster.

Thaler, R (1992) The *Winner's Curse: Paradoxes and Anomalies of Economic Life*; Princeton University Press.

Thaler, R., (1980) *Toward a positive theory of consumer choice*, Journal of Economic Behavior and Organization, Vol 1, 1, 39-60

Thaler, R.H & Sunstein, C.R (2008) *Nudge, Improving decisions about health, wealth and happiness*; Yale University Press, New Haven and London

Tiger, L & Shepher; (1975) *Women in the Kibbutz*; Harcourt Brace Jovanovich, New York.

Törngren G and Montgomery H. (2004) *Worse than Chance? Performance and Confidence Among Professionals and Laypeople In the Stock Market,* The Journal of Behavioral Finance, Vol. 5, No. 3, 246–251

Trivers, R.L; (1972) *Parental Investment and Sexual Selection*; in Campbell, B, editor; (1972) *Sexual Selection and the Descent of Man 1871-1971;* Chicago, Aldine.

Tversky, A and Kahneman, D (1981) *The framing of decisions and the psychology of choice*, Science, Vol 211, 4481, 453-458

Tversky A and Shafir E, (1992) *Choice under conflict: the dynamics of deferred decision*, Psychological science 3, 6, 358 -361

Van Boven, L; Gilovich, T (2003) *To Do or to Have? That Is the Question.* Journal of Personality and Social Psychology, Vol 85(6), 1193-1202.:

Velle, W; (1987) *Sex differences in sensory functions;* Perspective in Biology and Medicine, **30**, 490 -523

Webley, P & Nyhus, E (2006) *Parents' influence on children's future orientation and savings*, Journal of Economic Psychology, 27, 140-164.

Weber, E.U & Johnson, E.J (2009) *Mindful Judgment and Decision Making,* Annual Review of Psychology, Vol. 60: 53-85

Williams, M, Teasdale, J, Segal, Z and Kabat-Zinn, J (2007) *The Mindful Way through Depression: Freeing Yourself from Chronic Unhappiness*, Guilford Press

Whitmore, J (1996) *Coaching for Performance*, Nicholas Brealey Publishing

Wiseman, R (2004) *The Luck Factor*, Arrow books.